PELICAN BOOKS
A 391
THE MUSIC MASTERS
VOLUME FOUR

The Music Masters

VOLUME ONE
FROM THE SIXTEENTH CENTURY
TO THE TIME OF BEETHOVEN

VOLUME TWO
AFTER BEETHOVEN TO WAGNER

VOLUME THREE
THE ROMANTIC AGE

VOLUME FOUR
THE TWENTIETH CENTURY

★

EDITED BY

A. L. BACHARACH

EDITOR OF
The Musical Companion
British Music of Our Time
ETC.

PENGUIN BOOKS

The Music Masters

VOLUME FOUR

THE TWENTIETH CENTURY

BY

W. R. ANDERSON
MARTIN COOPER
A. E. F. DICKINSON
HUBERT FOSS
RICHARD GORER
CHRISTOPHER GRIER
DYNELEY HUSSEY
ARTHUR HUTCHINGS
EDWARD LOCKSPEISER
COLIN MASON
DONALD MITCHELL
M. MONTAGU-NATHAN
ROLLO H. MYERS
HENRY RAYNOR
LIONEL SALTER
H. G. SEAR
NILS L. WALLIN
CHRISTOPHER WHELEN
D. MAXWELL WHITE
ERIC WALTER WHITE
RALPH W. WOOD

PENGUIN BOOKS

Penguin Books Ltd, Harmondsworth, Middlesex
U.S.A.: Penguin Books Inc., 3300 Clipper Mill Road, Baltimore 11, Md
AUSTRALIA: Penguin Books Pty Ltd, 762 Whitehorse Road,
Mitcham, Victoria

—

First published by Cassell 1954
Published in Pelican Books 1957

Made and printed in Great Britain
by The Whitefriars Press Ltd
London and Tonbridge

CONTENTS

Preface to Volume Four ... 7

1	BARBER	W. R. Anderson	11
2	BARTÓK	Colin Mason	17
3	BAX	Christopher Whelen	25
4	BERG	Martin Cooper	35
5	BLOCH	W. R. Anderson	42
6	BRITTEN	Eric Walter White	48
7	BUSONI	Dyneley Hussey	55
8	CASELLA	D. Maxwell White	65
9	COLERIDGE-TAYLOR	Hubert Foss	71
10	COPLAND	W. R. Anderson	78
11	DOHNÁNYI	Ralph W. Wood	84
12	DUKAS	Edward Lockspeiser	89
13	FALLA	Ralph W. Wood	94
14	GLAZUNOV	M. Montagu-Nathan	102
15	GRANADOS	Ralph W. Wood	109
16	GRECHANINOV	M. Montagu-Nathan	116
17	HARRIS	W. R. Anderson	122
18	HINDEMITH	H. G. Sear	128
19	HOLST	A. E. F. Dickinson	135
20	HONEGGER	Arthur Hutchings	147
21	IRELAND	Hubert Foss	155
22	JÄRNEFELT	Nils L. Wallin	162
23	KHACHATURIAN	M. Montagu-Nathan	168
24	KODÁLY	Ralph W. Wood	176
25	LEKEU	Hubert Foss	186
26	MALIPIERO	D. Maxwell White	193
27	MARTINŮ	Donald Mitchell	200
28	MILHAUD	Rollo H. Myers	206
29	NIELSEN	Nils L. Wallin	212
30	PALMGREN	Nils L. Wallin	217
31	PFITZNER	Donald Mitchell	221
32	PIJPER	Ralph W. Wood	226
33	PIZZETTI	D. Maxwell White	233
34	POULENC	Rollo H. Myers	240
35	PROKOFIEV	W. R. Anderson	247
36	RAKHMANINOV	W. R. Anderson	255
37	RAVEL	Martin Cooper	263

CONTENTS

38	REGER	*Donald Mitchell*	273
39	RESPIGHI	*D. Maxwell White*	283
40	ROUSSEL	*Rollo H. Myers*	289
41	SCHÖNBERG	*Ralph W. Wood*	296
42	SCHUMAN	*W. R. Anderson*	304
43	SHAPORIN	*M. Montagu-Nathan*	310
44	SHOSTAKOVICH	*M. Montagu-Nathan*	316
45	SIBELIUS	*Christopher Grier*	324
46	SKRYABIN	*Martin Cooper*	336
47	STRAUSS, Richard	*Colin Mason*	346
48	STRAVINSKY	*W. R. Anderson*	355
49	SUK	*Richard Gorer*	363
50	SZYMANOWSKI	*Lionel Salter*	368
51	TURINA	*Henry Raynor*	374
52	VAUGHAN WILLIAMS	*A. E. F. Dickinson*	380
53	VILLA-LOBOS	*Henry Raynor*	397
54	WALTON	*Dyneley Hussey*	404

Appendix – Chronological Index   413

PREFACE TO VOLUME FOUR

The Music Masters, of which this is the fourth and last volume, was planned with certain objects in view. Whether or not the plan has succeeded, as indeed whether it was worth undertaking, must be a matter of opinion, but no fair opinion can be formed without knowledge of what the plan was. I have already indicated its nature in the Prefaces to earlier volumes, and also in the Preface to the original (1935) and subsequent editions of *Lives of the Great Composers* (of which all twenty-nine are incorporated in Volumes I to III of *The Music Masters*). Nevertheless, I may perhaps say once more what we have tried to do.

The Preface to the twenty-nine *Lives* – and the same applies to the 165 chapters of *The Music Masters* – laid down that they were meant to be about 'the lives of composers, not about their compositions – a ridiculous division of the indivisible, you may well observe'. It went on 'we have attempted to show the man, explained, if you will, by his creative work, where that has been necessary and possible, rather than the work explained by the man'. In a further attempt there to make our object clear, I also wrote, with apologies to the late E. C. Bentley,

> The art of Biography
> Is different from Musicography:
> Musicography is about Cellos
> But Biography is about Fellows.

In fact we set out then, as we have again set out here, to answer the question of the ordinary listener who, having heard some work on the air, on a record or in the concert hall, says, 'I wonder what sort of a chap so-and-so was, whose composition I have just heard'. Judging by the sales of the *Lives* and of the first three volumes of this series, the number of people seeking this kind of information is sufficient to justify the labour of having collected and written about it in the way the authors of *The Music Masters* have done.

With this book, then, there ends the project forecast in the Preface to Volume I. Like all human projects – even the best, among which its contributors' valuable work would incline, but editorial modesty forbids, me to include it – it has turned out somewhat differently from what was planned. True, the projected four volumes have all appeared, but over a much greater interval of time than originally intended. Perhaps the reader may be consoled by remembering that the difference between twelve and fifty months is, after all, small compared with the 400 years of music-making covered by the four volumes – itself, a small fraction in time of Man's history.

However that may be, enforced omissions have been just more than set off by some stop-press additions, so that the four volumes include 165 chapters instead of the 163 originally planned and promised: during our attempts to execute the plan and fulfil the promise the difficulties mentioned in the first Preface continued to recur, unexpectedly on occasion. They included the absence of sufficient biographical material, for various reasons, among other obstacles to finding a suitable chronicler and have lengthened the list of composers whose lives had, for one reason or another, to be excluded. The curious reader may want to know their names: these he can find for himself by a little deductive exercise, but even then he will not know the reason why any particular one has got left out, and it might be indiscreet of me to tell him – at any rate about contemporary composers! Of these some seem to have lived in an impenetrable cloud of modest un-notoriety.

The appendix gives chronologically the years of birth and death of the world's leading composers over 427 years. Since *The Music Masters* was planned, the ranks of these composers have been sadly depleted by the deaths of Bartók, Bax, Casella, Medtner, Pijper, Prokoviev, and Strauss: who can say what accessions to the Music Masters have during the same time been recorded in the world's birth registers? Nor can we begin to guess who even to-day will step into the musicographical shoes of F. Bonavia, Hubert Foss, Ralph Hill, W. McNaught, and E. H. W. Meyerstein, whose deaths since 1948 are a public loss as well as a sad personal one to the editor of these four books.

It was difficult, partly for the reasons mentioned in the Prefaces, to give a logical explanation for the particular assembly of names to be found in each of the first three volumes of *The Music Masters*: it is just as difficult with Volume IV, if not more so. The nearer we get to our own times, the more do apparently irrelevant factors come to bear on our aesthetic judgements, and in no branch of art more than in music. Even allowing for the unavoidable omissions already noted, many will doubtless question some of the editorial commissions, for these are clearly deliberate. Indeed, there are fifty-four of them, half as many again as in any of the first three volumes. So I must insist that, apart from the few enforced omissions, the choice of composers for Volume IV, as for Volumes I, II, and III, is the responsibility of the editor and of no one else.

All the same, the four books are the work of many hands – there have in fact been in all forty-five contributors. Each has been asked, nay encouraged, to make his individual approach to his subject, within the general remit that I have tried above to restate, and to write in his own individual way. Thus the treatments, and even more the styles, of the various contributors differ widely. Nothing else is to be expected unless either such a book as this is written by one man or the editor superimposes an artificial uniformity both of style and of treatment on his team of contributors. The former alternative has serious limitations as well as its obvious advantages: the latter would hardly be acceptable to readers and would certainly be resisted by contributors.

The lack of uniformity inherent in a book of this kind is believed – by me, at any rate – to be a virtue. The important thing about a collective book surely is that all the contributors shall enjoy writing for it – never mind what problems this may incidentally present to the editor. These problems can only be reduced to a minimum if every contributor is given as much latitude to write from his own angle and in his own idiom as is consistent with a single general plan. It is my belief that the contributors to these four volumes have suffered no unnecessary miseries at the hands of the editor. I trust that their adaptability and good humour, as well as their enthusiasm and erudition, may commend them all to a widening circle of readers.

A. L. BACHARACH

London NW3
December 1953

NOTE

Some slight additions to the biographies by the late Hubert Foss are the work of W. R. Anderson.

SAMUEL BARBER

B. 1910

W. R. ANDERSON

Art's Melting Pot

An acute observer of the American scene, Nathan Broder, wrote in the *Musical Quarterly* in 1948: 'To those who are familiar with the work of American composers produced during the last fifteen years or so, one of the most fascinating aspects is its variety. Every type of idiom that has made a place for itself in the world of serious music in this century, and some that are still struggling to do so, has its adherents among our creative musicians.' He goes on to deprecate the too easy tendency to pigeon-hole artists. This inevitably being done, Samuel Barber has been put into the 'Neo-Romantic' category. That designation, says Broder, 'while helpful in describing his earlier works, disregards significant elements in his later and more important products'. After about 1939, traditional procedures 'begin to be mingled with, and replaced by, methods that can only have arisen in the musical climate of our time'. That growth, 'perhaps not yet fully consummated', shows itself in all the chief elements of Barber's compositions.

America is still the Melting Pot, wherein many bright talents have lost what seemed a promising individuality. Barber is one of comparatively few men who have neither relied overmuch on folk-music or popular styles, such as those of the jazzmen, nor been too deeply deflected by the earthquakes of the 1920s.

A Native-Trained Artist

This composer, who is one of the two from America now probably best known in the capitals of Europe (the other being Copland), was born on 9 March 1910, the son of Dr S. LeRoy Barber, of Westchester, Pennsylvania. He thus missed the immediate stirs of the twenties, though he was composing even before then – as a boy of seven. He had the unusual advantage of being taught to sing by his aunt, the famous contralto, Louise Homer, well remembered at Covent Garden at the turn of the centuries as a Wagnerian artist, who won high reputation also on the concert platform and in oratorio.

It was natural for a Pennsylvanian to study at the then recently founded (1924) Curtis Institute in the State capital, Philadelphia. This, backed by private munificence, was intended to offer to Americans the type of musical education available at the Paris Conservatoire. Here Barber studied singing under Emilio Edoardo de Gorgoza, the exceptionally widely educated baritone: born in America, he was trained in Spain, France, England, and the States. The pianoforte was studied under Isabelle Vengerova and conducting under Fritz Reiner. It was quickly seen that work at composition would most highly repay concentration, and the young man underwent the necessary discipline under Rosario Scalero, who (Broder remarks) 'laid more emphasis upon counterpoint than any other element, and prescribed innumerable part-writing exercises in various styles, insisting upon vital and meaningful inner voices. The beneficial results of this intensive training are apparent throughout Barber's output. His music is seldom static, and even where the harmonies are ambiguous, the contrapuntal texture is alive. He seldom employs the old polyphonic principles, such as those of the passacaglia and fugue, that have been enthusiastically revived by many of his colleagues; but when he does, it is to good effect.'

Prizes, Foreign Recognition

Barber graduated from the Institute in 1932, with his *Overture* to *The School for Scandal*. His alma mater in 1945 honoured him with the degree of Mus.D., the year in which also he received one of the Guggenheim Awards made to mature artists for creative work or research. This was the culmination of a number of prize-winning adventures. At eighteen he won the Bearns Prize of Columbia University for composition, and in 1935 and 1936 he twice enjoyed the travelling scholarship known as the Pulitzer Prize (the first time such a double event had been brought off by a musician). In 1935 he had secured also the Prix de Rome award offered by the American Academy in that city. The candidate, as in the comparable Prix of the Paris Académie des Beaux Arts, resided in Rome. (In 1942 residence was discontinued, prizes of a thousand dollars being given instead.)

In 1937 his *Symphony* in one movement was the first American work to be played at the Salzburg Festival. He was then obviously influenced by some Russian trends – one recollects Shostakovitch's manner – but there was clear individuality in his nervy music, conveying (at least to the foreigner) aspects of American ways – the eagerness, perhaps impatience, the tendency to overdo things, to overpress excitement: something lusty, even swaggering, in the pre-war spirit: strong feelings, if not often heart-on-sleeve emotion. Even then Barber wrote an excellent slow movement – the most difficult in which to convince, persuade, and move on. He is, as Broder remarks, a lyric poet; one naturally thinks of his early training as a singer and its probable beneficial effect.

From Romance to Tone-Rows

Barber was first hailed as a conservative neo-romantic. He has changed, in part, but, in Broder's words, this is chiefly a 'natural technical enrichment, the first evidence of which appears in the Violin Concerto', where, as in several later works, he is seen as seeking 'to fuse an essentially lyric spirit with an awakened awareness of the restlessness and discordance of our times'. As ever, the artist's problem is to master and mould these factors, turning them to power in some form or other of beauty.

Barber has not despised the twelve-note-rows made so fashionable through Schönberg's usage. Here key, with its pillar-notes such as tonic and dominant, is abolished. The twelve notes of the chromatic scale form an equalitarian democracy. One of Barber's late works, the *Pianoforte Sonata*, Op. 26, of 1951, described by a critic as 'a virtuoso's paradise', may be reckoned the culmination of his treatment of this style: not by any means necessarily his last experiment, for he was then little over forty. In this work, not seeking sharp innovations in structure, and even maintaining some key-centre feeling, he employs a twelve-note-row, adding to his chords notes from other rows. For form his respect has always been high: he has, as Pitts Sanborn remarked, a respect for brevity, 'which is the soul of more than wit. When he has said his say, he has the good sense to stop.' We are sometimes reminded, in this matter, of Sibelius's mind and habit. One of Barber's most successful essays, especially from the point of view of form, is the *Symphony* in one movement, which he describes as a 'synthetic treatment of the four-movement classical symphony'.

Of the earlier works few are familiar to British audiences. The best known is the *Adagio for Strings*, taken up, played and recorded by Toscanini in 1938. This, one of the first American pieces that Toscanini performed with the new National Broadcasting Company's Symphony Orchestra, holds the warm romanticism of Barber's youth. It was originally the slow movement of a *String Quartet*, Op. 11 (1936), dedicated to his aunt and uncle, Louise and Sidney Homer: an apt connexion with a great singer, for the music flows in broad cantabile.

The composer's development through romanticism to his mid-century style has occupied more than half of his composing life. The strongest signs of change in the larger works may perhaps be found in *Knoxville: Summer of 1915*, a work for soprano and orchestra to a poem by James Agee, and in the second *Symphony*. The former work, like many written up to, broadly, the immediate post-war period, contains suggestions of what has been well called a 'homespun' feeling, much cherished, in one form or another, by American writers: and, indeed, a quality to be enjoyed by every nation, after its own nature and genius.

Wartime Service

Before this there was a succession of not-too-quickly produced works, through the popular *Essays* of 1937 and 1942, to the *Violoncello Concerto* of 1945, which had been preceded six years earlier by the *Violin Concerto*. During the war, like most American composers, Barber made his contribution to patriotism, with a *Commando March* for military bands, and took his part in active field-work as a corporal in the Army Air Corps, being stationed at Fort Worth, Texas, and engaging in many flights. As a result of these experiences, we are told, he brought into the slow movement of his second symphony, which he dedicated to his Corps, a 'tone generator' simulating the sound of a radio beam used as a directional code in night or blind flying. This was in 1944; in revising the work in 1947 he removed this instrument.

Like most of his colleagues, Barber has been attracted by ballet. In 1946 he wrote music for one entitled *Serpent Heart*, on the subject of Medea. This was danced by America's best known artist in that kind, Martha Graham. The action covers both ancient and modern times, the characters over the ages taking on the nature of Medea, Jason, or other figures in the tragic myth, with much powerful dissonance attending the story's unfolding. This ballet was produced in New

York just before the composer sailed for an extensive tour of Europe, in most of the chief cities of which he has conducted his works. In London he was welcomed by the B.B.C., conducting for its programmes several items, the chief novelty being his *Capricorn Concerto*, a work written in 1944, when the composer was home on leave from the Air Arm. The name is that of his house, a modern bungalow type at suburban Mount Kisco, in Westchester County. Flute, oboe, trumpet, and strings, in something of the old concerto grosso style, give expression to the sense of freedom and delight that the composer felt during his home leave from the soldier's life. In comparison with, say, the more familiar, and earlier, *Adagio*, this music sounds rather desiccated: it is clear that Barber had not escaped the influence of Stravinsky; but most composers have paid some tribute to this revolutionary leader. With Barber such influences never stifle ingenuity, individuality, and imagination.

Poetry and Choralism

An aspect of Barber's work little known in Britain is demonstrated in a number of striking choral pieces, several of which belong to the period just before the war and mark the range of his poetic interests. There are works for women's voices (*The Virgin Martyrs*, text after Sigebert of Gembloux, the medieval monk, chronicler, and controversialist), and for male choir (*A Stop Watch and an Ordnance Map*, a setting of a poem by Stephen Spender, accompanied by three kettle-drums: a poignant reflection, in march style, upon a war death). There are also mixed-voice pieces, the poems drawn from native sources (Emily Dickinson, for instance, in *Reincarnation*).

Barber has set some of James Joyce's poems, and (movingly written for solo voice and string quartet) Matthew Arnold's *Dover Beach*.

The composer has taken his fitting place as a member of several professional societies, including the American Society of Composers, Authors and Publishers (ASCAP), and has been elected to the National Institute of Arts and Letters. One typically American form of recognition, unlikely to be paralleled in Britain, is that yearly shown to the composer most highly thought of by the New York music critics' society. Barber was their choice in 1946.

His life, save for the war's disturbance, has been quiet – that of a bachelor happily pursuing his work amid widespread approval both at home and abroad. His friendly spirit has enabled him to share his 'Capricorn' home with another composer, Gian Carlo Menotti, whose operas brought him into prominence of late years. It would seem rash in a leading American critic to find Barber's 'métier and style rigidly settled' in 1949. He has been exploring since then; and as he should have many years to come, we may expect, on his record, that he will remain in the forefront of American composers who are not anti-romantics, and perhaps stand out, when the century ends, as one of the two or three biggest men who have triumphed as masters over that wild and inauspicious art-era in the United States of America, the Twaddling Twenties.

Indeed, as time goes on he seems to be regarded by the most inseeing appreciators as the strongest creator in the now very extensive American list. Though he has turned increasingly to the use of dissonance, he has never let that element get out of hand. Most of his largest works of recent years have been for choirs. One of them is the impressive cantata *Prayers of Kierkegaard*, for which Barber selected prayers interpolated among the theologian's writings and sermons, and set them variously for male chorus, soprano solo, mixed choir, soloists with chorus, triple chorus, and finally as a chorale. His friendship with Menotti instigated an opera, *Vanessa*, for which his fellow-composer wrote the libretto. This, the first American opera for some years, was scheduled for production at the Metropolitan in 1958.

As to American opera in general, it may be said that outside the work of Menotti, showing the first successful post-Puccinian dramatic use of elements long so popular, and apart from the perennial *Porgy and Bess*, there is no clear proof of the evolution of any strong native style in the U.S.A. *Porgy*, based on jazz elements and a particularly appealing type of sentiment, has been enjoyed by audiences in a great many countries. It may, indeed, outlive the work of men like Harris and Barber. A recent book upon contemporary problems in the art concludes that jazz is the only order of music that appeals (or, we are perhaps to gather, that ever will appeal) to the wide American public. That, as the saying goes, is anybody's guess.

BÉLA BARTÓK

1881–1945

COLIN MASON

Early Changes

Bartók was born on 25 March 1881, in the village of Nagyszentmiklós, then part of Hungary, but now Rumanian territory and called Sannicolaul Mare. Both his parents were keen amateur musicians: his mother played the piano, and his father, by profession Director of an agricultural college, played in a local orchestra and even tried his hand at small compositions. Bartók, according to his mother, displayed an early interest in sounds and rhythms, and learned almost before he could walk how to pick out tunes with one finger on the piano. He began to have his first systematic lessons, from his mother, when he reached his fifth birthday.

The reasonably favourable material circumstances and comfortable atmosphere of his home life changed abruptly when he was eight years old. His father died, and his mother was compelled to take up her old profession of teacher. During subsequent years she was transferred, with her family, from place to place until in 1894 she was able to settle with an adequate permanent post in Pozsony (now Bratislava). In the intervening years Bartók had made good progress with the piano and had given his first public concert as early as 1891 in Nagyszöllös, since absorbed by Russia, playing the first movement of Beethoven's *Waldstein Sonata* and a patriotic symphonic poem of his own for piano, called *The Danube*.

First Serious Opportunities

Pozsony was the first sizable town his mother had been sent to, and it was only now that she was able to find her son a well-equipped teacher, in the person of László Erkel, son of Ferenc Erkel, one of the most celebrated of nineteenth-century Hungarian composers. Bartók now began to hear much more music than he had ever had an opportunity to do before. He became familiar with the standard classical symphonic and operatic works, frequently took part in performances of chamber music, and met many musicians, including Dohnányi, his senior by four years, who was already making a name for himself as a virtuoso pianist and composer. At this time Bartók much admired and was greatly influenced by Dohnányi, upon whose advice he decided a few years later to continue his studies of music at the Hungarian Royal Academy of Music in Budapest, instead of at the Vienna conservatoire, where he was offered a scholarship. Later, radical differences in their outlook, both musical and political, led to a cooling off. Bartók deplored Dohnányi's falling in with the conservative official policy, with which he was himself always in disagreement and often in open conflict. Throughout their careers Dohnányi occupied the influential administrative posts, virtually ruling Hungary's musical destinies at one time, while Bartók was never entrusted with anything more than his piano professorship at the Academy until very late in life, when he was allowed to devote himself entirely to preparing for publication his vast collection of folk-music material, as a State-paid official.

When Bartók entered the Budapest Academy as a student in 1899, he was already composing, under the influence of Brahms and Dohnányi. His teachers now were István Thomán for piano and Hans Koessler for composition. His studies there for the first two years were frequently interrupted by serious illness, but with treatment abroad his health improved. In 1891 he won the Liszt Scholarship and soon began to make rapid headway as a pianist, being acclaimed after one public performance at a students' concert as 'a second Dohnányi'. As a composer he made no impression, owing to an inner confusion and indecision that prevented him from composing. He had transferred his allegiance from Brahms to Liszt and Wagner, whose scores he studied seriously, but in which he did not find the necessary stimulus for composing himself. Only when Richard Strauss's *Also Sprach Zarathustra* was performed in Budapest early in 1902 was the creative spring released. He devoured every Strauss score he could find and became so enthusiastic that he learned *Ein Heldenleben* as a piano solo and played it first in Budapest and a month later, in January 1903 at a Tonkünstlerverein concert in Vienna.

Youthful Compositions

The first fruit of this new enthusiasm was Bartók's first major orchestral work, the unpublished symphonic poem *Kossuth*, in which the technique of *Ein Heldenleben* is applied to the history of the great national hero of the nineteenth-century revolutionary movement for an independent Hungary, which ended so disastrously. It includes a caricature of the Austrian national hymn, which caused a scandal among the Budapest orchestral players, many of whom were Austrian. The performance went through, however, on 13 January 1904, and Bartók, who came on to the platform afterwards in Hungarian national costume, was acclaimed – more perhaps for political than for musical reasons. It was his first great public success in Hungary, the first of few enough. His first introduction to England was with the same work, when Hans Richter gave it in Manchester a month later. Within a few years Bartók became dissatisfied with it, as with all his works of this period except the *Rhapsody* for piano and orchestra (Op. 1). This was written in 1904 and was originally called *Konzertstück*. Bartók entered it for the Rubinstein prize in Paris in 1905, but lost the prize by one vote to Brugnoli. The competition was apparently conducted most inefficiently, and he was disgusted with the whole business. The *Rhapsody* is no very distinguished piece, but Bartók occasionally played it in later years, even after the first *Piano Concerto* was written.

Friendship with Kodály

As an ardent nationalist, Bartók had long taken an interest in Hungarian music, but it was not until 1905 that he began to realize that what was generally accepted as Hungarian folk-music bore only a superficial resemblance to the real music of the peasants. He began to try to seek out the genuine folk-music in the villages and in this way came into contact with Kodály, one year his junior, who was already doing the same thing. This was perhaps the most important meeting in Bartók's life. Each found in the other a lifelong friend and champion. Sharply contrasted as personalities, with utterly different aims as composers, they were united by a passionate interest in folk-music. Each could provide what the other needed, above all encouragement in the face of constant hostility from other musicians at home. In this respect Bartók was particularly reliant on Kodály, the extent of whose influence on him is difficult to calculate. Kodály had the broader educational and more comfortable material background, the more serene temperament, and in a sense the wider interests. Although

Bartók had visited France in 1905, it was not until Kodály drew his attention to it in 1907 that he became familiar with Debussy's music.

Their first joint endeavour was a collection of twenty *Hungarian Folk-songs*, published with piano harmonizations in 1906. It met with moderate success. From that time onwards Bartók made many folk-song arrangements, and elements deriving indirectly from folk-music are to be found in nearly all his original works after the *Second Suite* for orchestra. Until the war made it impossible, he constantly widened his field of folk-music research, going as far abroad as Biskra in 1913 to investigate Arab music. He was fascinated by the overlapping of Hungarian, Slovakian, and Rumanian folk-music, and his first published book, printed in Bucharest in 1913, was on Rumanian folk-song. Most of this research had to be financed out of his own pocket, which was by no means well lined. He had been given a piano professorship at the Academy in 1907, and he made numerous appearances as a concert pianist. But he now had a wife to support (he married a pupil in 1909), and he could ill afford such luxuries. His compositions were bringing him nothing. In 1909 Busoni invited him to conduct his orchestral *Scherzo* in Berlin, but at home conductors and orchestras were hostile or apathetic. An attempt by Bartók, Kodály, and several other young composers in 1911 to form a New Hungarian Musical Society with an independent orchestra was a failure, because no adequate subvention could be obtained. A certain sum of money was contributed by a Budapest publishing firm, and several small recitals and chamber concerts were given. The new music and its composers, however, immediately became the butt of both critics and cartoonists, and the venture soon collapsed for lack of support. Bartók also submitted his recently completed one-act opera *Duke Bluebeard's Castle* to the opera committee, but it was rejected.

Works for the Stage, Politics Again

Bartók was bitterly affected by these setbacks, and Kodály has suggested that they were in part responsible for the aggressiveness of some of his later music. He withdrew entirely from the general musical life, seeking an outlet for his creative impulse in the many folk-music arrangements that date from this period. In 1914, however, Béla Balázs, who had written the libretto of Bartók's opera, aroused the enthusiasm of the director of the opera for a ballet, *The Wooden Prince*, for which he had written the scenario. He persuaded him to let

Bartók write the music, which was completed in 1916. After certain difficulties and disputes, the ballet was staged at the Royal Opera House in Budapest on 12 May 1917. It was a success, which Bartók attributed greatly to the conscientious musical direction of Egisto Tango, who was also entrusted with the preparation of *Duke Bluebeard's Castle* for the following year.

The favourable reception of these two works would probably have meant the beginning of greater popularity for Bartók, but his chances were now spoilt by politics. After the overthrow of Béla Kun's short-lived Communist government in 1919, his active supporters were imprisoned or hounded out of the country. Balázs was amongst them, and any performance of a work to which he had contributed was out of the question. Bartók himself, whom the Communists had placed on the list of 'protected persons', on account of his association with Balázs, was half-suspect as a fellow-traveller, but, perhaps fortunately for him, although there had been talk of making him director of the opera during the Communist period, he had had no official appointment, and his political sympathies were not taken too seriously. Nevertheless he made no secret of his opposition to some of the political tendencies of the new régime, and although he, like Dohnányi and Kodály, was invited to write a work (the *Dance Suite*) to commemorate the fiftieth anniversary of the union of Buda and Pest, he undoubtedly lost much thereby in the way of official and public recognition. The two stage works were revived (with Balázs's name suppressed) only in 1935, several earlier attempts having failed. On this point, however, it is known that Bartók himself was not very satisfied with the musical form of *The Wooden Prince*, and probably did not press the matter as much as he might have done.

The post-war works did nothing to help him. Just after the war he had written another ballet, *The Miraculous Mandarin*, but this stood as little chance of reaching the stage as the others, not for political but for moral and musical reasons. The score is the most 'barbaric' Bartók ever wrote, and the action deals with a prostitute who entices passing men into the hands of a gang of bullies to be beaten and robbed. Cologne risked a performance in 1926 and Prague in 1927, but both were immediately banned. It was only in 1945 that it was staged in Hungary, again rather as a political demonstration than out of artistic conviction.

Folk-Music Publications

The next few years were a period of indecision for Bartók. He composed comparatively little, and even when he had written the two *Violin Sonatas* he could not make up his mind about them. It was not until 1926 that a new creative outburst began. Meanwhile he worked at his folk-music collection, devising his elaborate system of classification and comparison, and saw to the publication of his two most important works on folk-song, one in Germany, the other in Hungary. Even this activity brought him into conflict at home, and when publishing works on Rumanian music in Germany he was accused of cultural treason by offering ethnographical support for the Rumanian case in Transylvania.

In Western Europe, however, his reputation was steadily growing. His music, now published outside Hungary, was circulating widely, and he began to tour again as a concert pianist, introducing some of his own compositions. He even toured Russia in 1929. In 1927 he made his first visit to America, and in the following year he won the Philadelphia Chamber Music Prize with his third *String Quartet* – to the shamed astonishment of his compatriots. After the stream of compositions of the last few years of the twenties, culminating in the *Cantata Profana*, which there is reason to believe he at one time considered setting as a work for the stage, and the second *Piano Concerto*, he devoted himself once more to folk-song, orchestrating a number of his own early piano arrangements and completing the arrangement of a new set of *Twenty Hungarian Folk-songs*, the most advanced in treatment that he ever published. During these years he also visited Egypt and Turkey on folk-song missions. In 1934 he was released from his piano professorship for work on folk-song, and in the same year, with the fifth *String Quartet*, began a series of masterpieces, considered by some to be the greatest works he ever wrote, that ended with the sixth *String Quartet* in 1939 – the last work he wrote in Europe. Even at this period Hungary still offered little but discouragement.

Emigration

As political tension throughout Europe increased, and the Hungarian régime made ever greater compromises with Hitler, Bartók became increasingly opposed to it and was torn between the desire to stay in Hungary, where he still had so much work to do, and to get away from the atmosphere of political oppression that hung over Europe. Even when war broke out, he could not make up his mind to leave all that he valued, his vast work on folk-song uncompleted. After months of indecision, when it became clear that any real liberty of thought and action was anyhow at an end, he left for America with his wife in autumn 1940, their younger son following some time later.

Of his life in America there is still much to be learned. That he was unhappy there is clear, but there is nothing in his published letters to suggest that he regretted his choice. Probably he would have been happier if he had had more financial security. But America, though blameworthy, is possibly not alone in that. He lived precariously, keeping above water financially, it seems, only with the help of ASCAP, the society of American composers, which provided him with money in excess of the royalties due to him at the time. Soon after his arrival he was given an honorary doctorate at Columbia University and an appointment there to work on folk-song. After 1942 the appointment was not renewed. When he was invited in the following year to lecture at Harvard, he was so worn out with trying to make ends meet that the three lectures completely exhausted him. Even concert engagements became infrequent when the novelty of what one American cartoonist called 'the mild-mannered revolutionist' had worn off.

Aid too Late

It was probably a combination of overwork, worry, and the difficulty of getting used to an entirely new way of life that crushed the creative impulse in Bartók during this period. When he finally produced the *Concerto for Orchestra* in 1943, the music revealed, more clearly than any letter, the deepest cause of his unhappiness. Every bar of it cries out with homesickness for Hungary. It was dedicated to the Kussevitzky Music Foundation, in memory of Natalie Kussevitzky, and was first performed in 1944. Various commissions followed. Yehudi Menuhin, struck with admiration for the *Violin Concerto*, had already commissioned the *Sonata* for solo violin, which dates from 1944. William Primrose commissioned a *Viola Concerto*, Ralph Hawkes a new *String Quartet*, and Nathaniel Shilkret a movement for his composite work *Genesis*. But these were all too late. Only a preliminary draft of the *Viola Concerto* and a few sketchy bars of the seventh *String Quartet* were completed. Bartók had been ill for some time, and in 1945 his health declined rapidly. The strain of the past five years had been too much for him, and finally he had to enter a New York hospital, working till the last moment to complete the third *Piano Concerto* for his wife. A few days later, on 26 September 1945, he died from leukaemia. In a few weeks he was to have embarked for Hungary, having already received from the Provisional Government an invitation to return. Perhaps, in view of the disillusionment he might have suffered, it was just as well that he never went back.

ARNOLD EDWARD TREVOR BAX

1883–1953

CHRISTOPHER WHELEN

Early Days

A 'brazen romantic' by his own description, Arnold Bax was born at Streatham on 8 November 1883. Thus his historical position is on the continent that of a generation between Sibelius and Hindemith and in England between Vaughan Williams and Walton. His companions in this intermediary generation include the Italians, Casella and Malipiero, the Hungarian Kodály, the Jewish-American Bloch, and Falla from Spain, besides Bartók and Stravinsky.

Various episodes from his early life can be glimpsed in *Farewell, My Youth*, a small volume of autobiography produced during World War II. His father was fond of choral music, but being a good Victorian was quick to warn both Arnold and his younger brother Clifford that art was, and should remain, a luxury. His mother, more broadminded as were so many women of that period, must have been a remarkable woman; the composer recalls that she constantly examined all types of religion, and the story goes that when present at Bax's reception of an honorary degree of D.Mus. at Durham, she was more concerned with the quality of the salmon he was to eat afterwards than with the presentation of the degree itself.

In the atmosphere of the late-Victorian suburb of Golders Green the young Bax, a brilliant sight-reader, began to devour yellowing editions of Beethoven symphonies and to generate his own first ideas. At about the same time (1890) came his first conscious apprehension of beauty. He was taken to Arundel Park at sunset, and in his own words 'as we stood there an unimaginable glow of flame developed in the west, so that all the wooded heights seemed on fire ... to my childish perception this sight was all-conquering splendour and majesty, untroubled by the transitoriness of all lovely things.'

Sixty years later it seems that this experience may well have prompted a solemn vow in the six-year-old boy to pursue beauty as a burning ideal. Certainly he has been loyal to such an ideal, and it has helped to give his work a clear sense of direction, without the more restless experimental twists that characterize the music of his great contemporaries Bartók and Stravinsky.

Precocious Talent

Soon Bax began to attend the Sunday concerts at the Crystal Palace, where he could watch his uncle, E. Belfort Bax, and a Mr G. Bernard Shaw, both representing London papers, sitting together. In 1896 he began taking violin lessons from an Italian bandmaster. Later that year the Bax family moved to Hampstead, and here he and his brother Clifford were able to indulge freely in their favourite pastime of cricket, while Wagner scores began to pile up on top of the drawing-room piano. Then Arnold joined Cecil Sharp's Hampstead Conservatoire, taking piano, theory, and composition lessons. Haunted by the aroma of *Tristan* and *The Ring*, the young musician became accompanist to his father's private choral society. In 1900, his seventeenth year, he entered the Royal Academy of Music. Tobias Matthay was entrusted with his piano tuition, and a period of serious composition began, Debussy and Richard Strauss being his favourite models. *Don Quixote* in particular pleased him because he felt the sheep sounded so anxious! He astonished his teachers by being able to read any full score at sight on the piano and developed a solid but discriminating view of the classics; he still classes Schubert's *String Quintet in C* as 'one of the loveliest works ever written' and the orchestration in Brahms' two *Piano Concertos* as being 'too full of beer and pudding'. Again, the semiquaver theme in the first movement of Schumann's *Second Symphony* was once referred to by him as 'sounding like fleas hopping about in a circus!' Meanwhile, aged twenty, Bax was reading everything: *Epipsychidion* on the bus and French novels during A.B.C. lunches. In the summer he was still playing cricket.

Celtic and Russian Influences

In 1904 he wrote *A Celtic Song Cycle*, which was performed at an R.A.M. chamber concert. As a result of reading Yeats for the first time in 1902, he was becoming immersed in Celtic atmosphere. Later in the same year he went to Ireland in a state of considerable spiritual excitement; he visited Aranmore immediately after Synge's *Aran Islands* had been published, learnt to speak Gaelic, studied folk-lore and legends and began to explore the more remote corners of Connemara and Donegal. Soon he was writing short stories and poems under the pseudonym of Dermot O'Byrne and having them accepted by Dublin publishers. In this way he became known in Ireland as a writer and in England as a composer, and under this new influence his music began to loosen its Straussian handcuffs and to acquire curves that were distinctly Irish.

In 1906 came a visit to Germany. This was the year of *Salomé*, and Bax also heard symphonies of Mahler and Bruckner, neither of whom seemed to register strongly with him. Far more important was a purifying visit to Russia, which he undertook in 1910, hot on the trail of a young beauty called Loubya. This visit lasted for about a year and took in the Ukraine besides Moscow and St Petersburg. Many critics have discussed the Russian influence on Bax in relation solely to such piano pieces as *May Night in the Ukraine* and *In a Vodka Shop*, pieces indeed written immediately after his return to England. In fact the Russian influence is firm and decided throughout his work, particularly in the symphonies and larger orchestral works. Both in spirit and in technique Bax the musician gained immeasurably from his visit. He composed a good deal, drank Georgian red wine in the Ukraine, and saw *Prince Igor* in Moscow, never losing his haunting desire for the north, in whose chaffing air he felt free and completely at ease.

Dublin and Glencolumcille

By 1911 he was married and living in Dublin. Here he found a good friend in the old Celtic poet-philosopher George Russell (AE), with whom he once had a strange experience. They were together in a summer house in the dripping Breagly Woods one day; AE was painting at his easel while Bax sat reading at the window. They had not exchanged a word for a quarter of an hour when suddenly there were sounds that both men heard clearly and that neither had heard before. Bax described them as 'a kind of rippling water and tiny bells tinkled', adding, 'yet I could have written it all down in ordinary musical notation.' The slow movement of his *Third Symphony* contains an enchanting passage for finely divided strings, celeste, harp, and solo horn, which may well be this experience recollected in tranquillity. Many more poems and short stories followed from the pen of Dermot O'Byrne, and back in London Arnold Bax composed a torrent of music, most of which he later destroyed. Few in Dublin knew of his music, fewer in London of his writings.

About this time he met Harriet Cohen, then a student at the R.A.M., and in doing so he met one of the staunchest allies he was ever to have, a vital and courageous woman who has done more for his (and other British) pianoforte music than any other pianist of her generation. There can be little doubt that her infectious enthusiasm spurred Bax on over many hurdles and on occasions both great and small gave extra life and positive belief to the creation of his very personal world. It was during these years that Bax discovered Glencolumcille, a small horse-shoe shaped village on the west coast of Donegal. In the future this sea-splashed cluster of grey rocks and houses was to become one of his homes. There is nothing between Glencolumcille and America but the great expanse of dove-grey sea, which cringes behind breakers that often thunder on to the heather and stones of the small valley. It was here later, in 1931, that Bax worked out the first movement of his *Fourth Symphony*; music that sprang from the sea as the composer readily acknowledges, from the place that is, for him, 'the most beloved place in Ireland'. His constant returning to this place stamps Bax an arch-mystic of nature, and for many years he went regularly to the tiny village where he knew everybody from the local weaver to the fantastic publican who sang folk-songs from morning till night. He would play 'twenty-five' in the inn kitchen, talk ghosts and legends with the locals and watch the dramatic meteorological effects of the sky in vivid colours of red and gold. Was it the proximity of Glencolumcille to the Polar Ice that drew Bax here year after year, seeking always a northern air for his work, an air transparent and cool?

No sooner had he begun to spend a good deal of his time in Ireland than he became associated in many minds with the so-called Celtic Twilight. Such a Twilight in fact never existed. It was invented by English journalists, who in their turn derived it from the spurious Ossian and the title of an early book by Yeats. Supposing such a melancholy state of twilight to be the natural legacy of the Pre-Raphaelites they were ignorant of the fact, or had forgotten, that primitive Celtic colours are bright and jewelled. In this way the Celtic quality in Bax's work, even in much of the early music, is of an earthy kind: the product of a man who spent years exploring the most remote parts of Western Ireland (and later Scotland), walking and climbing and designing musical tapestries often as tough as the bald stones on the road.

In 1913 came a tour in Spain; in the company of Holst, Balfour Gardiner, and his brother Clifford, Bax went to Catalonia and the Balearic Islands, thus satisfying his constant desire to travel by visiting the south as well as the north that he knew so well.

Return to London

Armistice Day 1918 found him seated at the piano in Hampstead working on his *Symphonic Variations*, a concerto for piano and orchestra; at one point in the score there is the mark: '11 a.m. At this moment the guns are firing.' Yet Bax has cared little for contemporary events, and nothing at all for politics. In 1919 *Tintagel*, probably the most frequently performed of all Bax's orchestral works, received its première at Bournemouth, where, the composer recalls, there was the customary back-chat between the trombone players and the indefatigable Sir Dan Godfrey. It was also about this time that Bax aroused the deep interest of Edwin Evans, a leading critical writer of his day. Evans began to champion the young composer's work, as did Henry Wood, who had previously performed *In the Faery Hills* (written in the hills and valleys of Co. Kerry) at a 1910 Promenade Concert. Both men became intimate friends of Bax, and in 1920 Wood produced the *Symphonic Variations* with Harriet Cohen as soloist. That year was one of fresh fields in every direction for Bax. He went to live in two music-littered rooms in Hampstead and joined Barrie in the production of a ballet *The Truth about the Russian Dancers*. Private means enabled him to be free from the usual routine jobs, and by 1921 he had produced two important works, the tragic and economically written *Sonata for Viola and Piano* and *Mater ora Filium*.

The Symphonies

By the end of 1922 the *First Symphony* was ready. The dedication to John Ireland is significant. Ireland and Bax had been friends for many years, and living in neighbouring villages they often exchanged acrid and humorous comments on the so-called anti-romantic age in which we live. The symphony burst like a bombshell upon Queen's Hall on 2 December 1922. Even now after thirty years its impact and rhythmical power remain fresh and startling. Yet the conflict, which is typically ironed out into a firm march in the Epilogue, was not of the past war. There is no Ypres or Flanders in this music. The demoniac force is a personal one, and through it once or twice can be glimpsed, like a sudden shaft of sunlight, the beauty the composer was later to reach. The *First Symphony* was half seriously nicknamed 'Adventures on the Edge of a Precipice' by an amateur friend of the composer, who also coined the phrase 'Centuries in the Abyss' for the *Second Symphony* that followed a couple of years later. Part of this most difficult and tense of all the symphonies was written at Geneva, where Bax wintered during 1924–5.

Performances, Scotland

Still living in Hampstead, though always in Ireland for some months of the year, he was never in these days far from pen and manuscript paper. But he was always restless, and in 1926 journeyed in Yugoslavia with Balfour Gardiner. Late in that year he visited Delius in Italy at Rapallo, where the Bradford-born composer was then living in Max Beerbohm's house. In 1928 the beautiful and highly original *Sonata for Viola and Harp* appeared, and Bax went for the first time to Arisaig on the west coast of Scotland, taking with him the rough sketches of the *Third Symphony*. Here, opposite the islands Rum, Eigg, and Muck ('Three Scotch Cocktails', says Bax), he was able to fashion the peace for the processional last bars of the symphony. At the first performance, under Henry Wood, to whom it was dedicated, the work was an instantaneous success, and the composer felt that he was in touch with the public on their own ground for the first time. Again his friend was not slow to propose a third appropriate motto: this time it was 'A Successful Rockclimb'. In a later *Piano Concerto* Vaughan Williams was to quote the descending wood-wind theme from the Epilogue, and Wood was soon playing the symphony in Zurich. In Rome, although hissed by the general public, it made a deep impression on Respighi, Sinigaglia, and Casella.

From 1929 on, Bax generally spent the winter at Morar and Arisaig. This jagged part of the Inverness-shire coast, close to the place where Prince Charles landed in 1745, provided the setting for final touching up and orchestration, as symphony duly succeeded symphony. Staying at the local inn at Morar, which lies at the head of the deepest loch in Scotland, Bax could read, take long walks, and work.

ALBAN BERG

1888–1935

MARTIN COOPER

Youth, Studies with Schönberg, Early Works

Alban Berg was born in Vienna, the youngest of the four children of Conrad Berg, an export merchant of Bavarian stock, and Johanna Braun, a Viennese by birth. The first twelve years of his life, until his father's death in 1900, were spent in a happy and carefree atmosphere mostly in Vienna, though the family moved every summer to a house in Carinthia. The death of his father almost coincided with the first signs of awakening musical consciousness in the boy and also with a severe attack of bronchial asthma from which he was never afterwards completely free. His education could only be completed thanks to the financial assistance of an aunt, and there was as yet no question of regular musical studies, though he was composing on his own and his interests were entirely musical and literary. His favourite author at fourteen was Ibsen and at fifteen he was sufficiently precocious to be suffering from an unhappy love affair and boy enough to have failed in an examination and to attempt suicide as a way out of both troubles.

The family were certainly left badly off by the death of Conrad Berg. When an elder brother answered an advertisement by Arnold Schönberg, offering musical instruction to private pupils, and showed him the young Alban's compositions, the first two of the six years' apprenticeship (1904–10) were given free of any charge by Schönberg, for he had divined an unusual talent whose development he was anxious to further at any cost to himself. Berg threw himself into his musical studies with a feverish energy. He spent days in a small bungalow belonging to the family in the suburb of Hitzing, working at his exercises for Schönberg and composing on his own account, with all the windows shut and consuming endless tea. The great events in his life were the performance of his master's works – the D minor *String Quartet*, the *Kammersymphonie* and *Verklärte Nacht* – and besides these, Strauss's *Elektra* and Mahler's *Sixth Symphony*. It would be difficult to imagine a more unhealthy musical diet, or indeed a more unhealthy mode of life, for a young man – hardly more than a boy – who had already shown such marked signs of nervous instability.

Decadence in Vienna

Vienna in the opening years of the present century was pervaded with a decadence as extreme as, though quite different from, the more famous fin-de-siècle movements in Paris and London. The last years of the obviously disintegrating Austrian Empire were not illumined by any of the mystical and apocalyptic fervour that was characteristic of the same years in Russia and found expression in the music of Skryabin. Vienna itself was an anomaly whose only *raison d'être* lay in the Court and the Empire, both doomed and both obscurely conscious of the precariousness of their existence.

The world in which Berg came to maturity was the world from which Sigmund Freud filled his case-books and from which he was generalizing when he laid down the principles of his psychology. As in Russia, so in Vienna a fury of materialism was offset by a hothouse spirituality cultivated by a minority: only in Russia the spirituality was mystical, often theosophical, whereas in Vienna the emotional world of Wagner lived on, its temperature raised still further, technical complexities increased, and emotions deliberately harrowed to breaking-point, until reaction inevitably set in.

Schönberg and Mahler

Arnold Schönberg and Gustav Mahler were the chief musical representatives of this world and twin gods of the young Berg. The overwhelming emotionalism and the Messianic pessimism that marked the music of both these composers found a frustrated expression in technical complexity, in sheer size, and emotional chaos (as in Schönberg's *Gurrelieder* and Mahler's *Eighth Symphony*). When Berg was studying with Schönberg, the basic sterility of this form of expression was becoming obvious to the composer, and he was concentrating on technical experiments that finally issued in the conscious abandoning of tonality and the substitution of 'atonality' and later of the 'twelve note system'. Berg's early works are therefore situated, as it were, on the extreme edge of the tonal system. His first public performance was in 1907 – a *Double Fugue* for string quintet and pianoforte. In the next year he completed his Op. 1, a *Piano Sonata*, and in November his

Twelve Variations on an Original Theme, also for piano, were performed in Vienna. Opposition to the works of Schönberg and his pupils was intense, and concerts were frequently the scenes of violent protest, even of free fights between enthusiasts of both sides. One critic summed up his impressions of Berg's latest work in the single *mot* – 'no theme and twelve Variations on it'.

Formative Friendships *and* Wozzeck

Berg's friends were among the vanguard in all the arts, men who achieved an intense local fame, even though their names never achieved European importance and were scarcely known outside Vienna in some instances – Oscar Kokoschka, Peter Altenberg, Karl Kraus, Adolf Loos. It was the era of small, bitterly hostile cliques in Vienna as well as in Paris – with this difference, that the Parisian cliques contained men of universal European interest, whereas those of Vienna were little more than local lights, so far had she sunk in cultural importance in the hundred years since Haydn, Mozart, Beethoven, and Schubert had made her name synonymous for a time with music itself. In the four years (1910–14) between the end of his study with Schönberg and the European War, Berg wrote a *String Quartet* (Op. 3), his *Five Orchestral Songs* to picture-postcard texts by Peter Altenberg (performed with great scandal in 1913), and *Four Pieces for Clarinet* (Op. 5). In 1911 he married Hélène Nahowski, and in the May of 1914 he saw a performance of Georg Büchner's *Woyzeck*, which immediately gave him the idea of the opera for which he was later to become world-famous.

During the war Berg worked in the Austrian War Ministry, having been declared unfit for active service, and by 1917 he had completed the text of his opera. The music was completed in short score by 1920, the orchestration in the following year, and in 1922 the pianoforte score was printed, with the financial assistance of Mahler's widow, to whom the work was dedicated, and sent round to various opera houses. The first performance of extracts from *Wozzeck* was given by Hermann Scherchen at Frankfurt and the first performance of the complete work by Erich Kleiber in Berlin, on 14 December 1925. The whole genesis of the work thus falls into a time of the most bitter disillusion and privation – the actual years of the war and the terrible aftermath of inflation and starvation that followed immediately upon the peace. Berg had grown up in the atmosphere of a minority that was unpopular and yet at the same time conscious of great gifts. The intensity of the bond that united Schönberg with his disciples – of whom Berg and Webern were the chief – was inevitably increased by what they felt to be persecution and wilful misunderstanding. These eventually bred in the group a kind of superiority complex, a dogmatic and intolerant gospel rejecting popularity and seeing salvation only in the acceptance of the theories and the music of Schönberg and those, like Křenek, who sympathized with him.

Wozzeck is a closely-knit musical structure, a deliberate symphonic whole, in which each scene of the three acts corresponds to a purely musical design. The five scenes of Act 1 are five *Charakterstücke* (*Suite, Rhapsody, Military March and Lullaby, Passacaglia, and Rondo*). Act 2 is a symphony in five movements, Act 3 a series of six Inventions (on a Theme, a Note, a Rhythm, a Chord, a Scale, and a Continuous Quaver Rhythm). That the audience is unaware of this is of little importance; the problem of form, which was the major preoccupation of any composer who jettisoned tonality completely, is solved at least on paper. Berg made use of the hybrid *Sprechgesang* – half sung, half spoken dialogue – which Schönberg had used in his *Pierrot Lunaire* (1912), and this gave an added eeriness, rather than greater naturalness, to the already macabre story. The impression of the work as a whole is one of unquestionable dramatic power and immense musical ingenuity and skill and these combine in certain moments to create a real, if morbid, beauty. But the music moves in a closed, desperately airless world (one thinks of the bungalow at Hitzing with all the windows shut), and the brutal 'realism' of the story is rather the apparent realism of a Kafka story, or a hideously real nightmare, than an expression of human feelings. Humanity seems quite as far away as in the dream world of Maeterlinck's *Pelléas*. No breath of fresh air ever enters this shuttered and permanently darkened world.

After Wozzeck

In the years after the composition of *Wozzeck* Berg turned from the theatre and composed his *Kammerkonzert* and the *Lyric Suite* for string quartet, played by the Kolisch Quartet in January 1927 in Vienna. The gradual success of *Wozzeck* was bringing him fame outside German-speaking countries and even slightly more money. In 1928 he visited Gerhardt Hauptmann at Rapallo to discuss the possibilities of using his *Und Pippa tanzt* for an opera, but he eventually abandoned this idea in favour of *Lulu*, a story taken from Wedekind's *Erdgeist*. A concert aria, *Der Wein*, based on a text from Baudelaire, was composed in 1929 and performed the next year at Königsberg, and at the same time Berg was made a Member of the Prussian Academy of Arts and offered a post at the Berlin Musikhochschule, which he refused. In 1932 he was able to buy a small house on the Wörthersee in Carinthia and a Ford car, and he spent as much time as possible in the country, working on the music of *Lulu*, which was finished in short score in 1934. The orchestration was interrupted by the request of the violinist, Louis Krasner, for a new violin work, the *Violin Concerto*, which Berg conceived and wrote in an amazingly short space of time, partly inspired by the sudden death of the daughter of his friend Alma Mahler. The concerto and the orchestration of *Lulu* finished, Berg went in the autumn to Prague for a meeting of the International Musical Society. He had apparently recovered from an abscess caused by an insect bite in September, but when he returned to Vienna from Prague he was obviously ill. He condition grew rapidly worse in December and developed into general blood poisoning, from which he died on 24 December 1935.

'*Atonality*' and Berg's Music

In his last works, from the *Lyric Suite* onwards, Berg accepted the new formal principles embodied in Schönberg's twelve note system. The basis of this is the chromatic (i.e. twelve-note) scale. By arranging these twelve notes (or a portion of them) into a basic pattern, by inverting this pattern, horizontally reversing either the original or its inversion and transposing any or all of these patterns to any degree of the scale, the composer arrives at a musical 'datum' on which he can work. Working horizontally – with the consecutive notes in one part or distributed – furnished the line, and working vertically the texture of the music. The obvious difficulty lies in making this intellectual scheme a vehicle of musical expression in any way comparable with the old system of tonality. It is perfectly possible to construct algebraical formulae and patterns of the acrostic type with sounds in place of letters: but is it possible to substitute this algebraical schematism for the key system and achieve the same richness and variation, the same alternation of rest and tension, ebb and flow, that has characterized Western European music since the sixteenth century? Berg was absolutely convinced that it was possible, and he saw in Schönberg a musical figure comparable with that of J. S. Bach, not only in stature but also in character and circumstance. In his *Credo* published in *Die Musik* (January 1930) he quotes word for word Riemann's words on Bach and applies them to Schönberg, only substituting the necessary changes to suit the different centuries. Schönberg's music he regarded as the end of the harmonic style associated with our major and minor scales, just as that of Bach ended the polyphonic period based on the ecclesiastical modes. To compose tonally in the third decade of the twentieth century seemed as pointless to him as to compose modally 200 years earlier. Only time can show whether he was right, but it is possible to distinguish between the characteristics of the two ages, those of Bach and of Schönberg. Tonality grew organically, and largely by empirical practice, from modality: whereas atonality was a laboratory experiment, a conscious and deliberate 'system', satisfactory to the eye (that is, on paper) and to the intellect, like the solution of an algebraic problem. The ear is violated, certainly to begin with, but this may be of less importance than it seems, as the ear has been permanently protesting against novelties and yet has hitherto shown itself almost infinitely adaptable. What is certain is that atonality is a complete break with the past, not merely a point in the evolution of music.

Atonality stands in the same relation to previous music as Communism stands to the political tradition of Western Europe, and it was a perfectly healthy instinct that dubbed the music of Schönberg and his pupils *Kulturbolschewistisch*. But since all revolutionaries must have been born and grown up, their characters and personalities formed, in the tradition against which they eventually revolt, it is inevitable that they perpetuate their own personal reactions and experiences under the old régime in the 'new world' they create. Unfortunately in the vast majority of instances these experiences are bitter. No order is content to disappear without a fight, and thus Lenin and Trotsky, growing up in the last days of the old Russia of the Tsars, were well acquainted by experience with Tsarist police methods, which they, perhaps unconsciously, perpetuated in their new order. Schönberg and his disciples, growing up in the last days of the Austrian Empire, imbibed the atmosphere of shiftlessness and hopelessness inseparable from social, political, and artistic bankruptcy. The new music sprang, therefore, from the world of over-heated emotionalism, morbid and hysterical – the same world as produced Strauss's *Salomé* and *Elektra* and the romantic pessimism of Mahler's symphonies. Inevitably it bore the mark of its origins deeply ingrained and the combination of this pathological nature with the intense Jewish analytical intellectuality of Schönberg has been the distinguishing mark of atonality hitherto. The music of Berg is as distinctly mid-European as the music of Falla is Spanish and, like all art that is consciously 'modern' at the time of its production, it has aged quickly. After a second European War almost anything seems preferable to the music that was the outcome of the first and so profoundly symptomatic of the years between the two. No one listening to *Wozzeck*, the *Lyric Suite*, or the *Violin Concerto* could doubt that here was a giant musical talent, something approaching genius in its tireless inventiveness and subtlety. It is impossible as yet to foresee whether the purely musical quality of Berg's works will in the future outweigh the narrowness and airlessness of its emotional atmosphere. Skryabin, a comparable figure, has suffered an almost complete eclipse; Berg's more exclusively musical quality may prevent this happening to him.

ERNEST BLOCH

B. 1880

W. R. ANDERSON

The Man in the Music

Not always does a composer, as a person, measure up to his music. We probably expect too much; having been moved, perhaps even inspired, by his art, we think how much we should like to meet the man. When we do, we are apt to be disappointed; the voice may be thin, the aspect slight: here is little of the fire or fervour, vivacity or devilment, that the music showed forth. Similarly, if after hearing the music we read something the composer has said or written, we are likely to feel disappointment even more keenly; but we should not expect him to express himself equally well upon both ruled and unruled paper. His music is his message; very rarely has he much else of significance to say.

To these conceptions Ernest Bloch is the most outstanding exception I remember. A first hearing of his music (it happened to be the astonishing *String Quartet*) was almost bewildering. It lasted sixty-one minutes; heard in an excellent little resonant chamber, a crypt in Westminster, it produced more than one kind of strong effect. Who can really listen to a new and fairly 'advanced' work for a solid hour with fit attention? So, there was strain, and some labour was needed to withstand it; but, for all that, the music immediately bespoke a *big* man: one imagined in him something of the prophet, something liberal, broad, humane – this despite certain asperities in the music that were more startling thirty years ago than they are now. When one came to meet Bloch and to read something he had written about art and life, these impressions of breadth, of a spirit distinguished, sincere, generous, and humane, were fully sustained. He has at one time gone clean-shaven, at another worn a beard; with it, his likeness to what one imagines as the Old Testament prophet is keen. There are the powerful eyes, which can shine with goodwill: there is the strong upper lip, the broad forehead; one would say, a thinker, not only in music but in humanity; and that sense is borne out by his writing. This has not been extensive, but Bloch has composed sufficient to give a satisfying glow to anyone who can still believe in mankind's brotherhood.

Hard Beginnings

First, a few facts about his early years. They were dark enough, from the worldly point of view, for his father, a Jewish dealer in clocks in Geneva, did not consider composition a likely career for his son; there appears to have been no decided hereditary musical skill on either parent's side. But Ernest, born in 1880, began to compose very early. On his way to school, Mary Chiesa has told us, he pondered the music for an opera *Roland and Roncesvalles*, a work never to go very far; but he had the pleasure of using one of its early themes in *Macbeth*, which was produced in Paris in 1910. He had the usual small delights of the musical child whose parents can be expected to indulge him in a simple instrument or two, if not to acquiesce in a design that had already behind it the force of a very strong will; for he is said to have written out a vow that he would devote himself to composition, and to have made a solemn rite of burning the written vow upon a pyre of stones, probably under the influence of the ritual of his religion.

His mother had bought him a cheap flute before he was six; soon after he was learning the violin and writing themes for it. The burning of the vow took place when he was eleven. At fourteen, like so many children, he left school, expecting only to follow his father's or some other commercial occupation, though still determined to fulfil what he felt was his certain destiny; how, or when, he could not tell. He had the advantage of some superior tuition in his native city from Émile Jaques-Dalcroze, later to become famous as the founder of the system of Eurhythmics always associated with his name. This teacher had returned to the Geneva Conservatoire in 1892 as professor of harmony. With him young Bloch worked, and with Louis Rey, the violinist.

Adolescent Fruits

When he was fourteen he was already showing traits of the future composer of music influenced by Jewish oriental traditions. He wrote an *Oriental Symphony* in three movements, with the titles *Prayer*,

Desert Caravan, Oasis, Funeral Rite, using therein some of the Hebrew themes his father had sung to him. About the age of sixteen he succeeded in obtaining, for a couple of years, tuition at the Brussels Conservatoire, where the famous Ysaÿe developed his violin playing, and he worked at composition under François Rasse, himself also a violin pupil of Ysaÿe's and a late starter in music, for he was twenty before he began it. Rasse took the Prix de Rome in 1899, and was later well known as orchestral conductor and composer.

Seeking further experience, Bloch worked from 1899 to 1901 with the Russian teacher of composition, Ivan Knorr, at the Hoch Conservatorium in Frankfurt. It is characteristic of his individualistic, almost wilful spirit that, though he played the violin so well, he did not enjoy the prospect of specializing in it; especially was he distrustful of what he called the 'prima donna' element in the soloist. At Brussels he had written a fair amount of music for the voice, as well as chamber music, including a *Cello Sonata*, an *Orientale* for orchestra, and a *Violin Concerto* (not the one that is now among the most enjoyed of all his works).

He was naturally attracted by the best French music, particularly by Debussy's songs, some qualities of which his own reflected; but there are few composers in even whose early work one can less surely point to 'influences', at least of any broad or obvious kind. He felt at Brussels the effect of the love for Franck, a native of Belgium (whose quartet was not understood in Geneva, for Bloch recalled that the audience left the hall when it was being performed).

About a year was spent with Ludwig Thuille, who at Munich had become distinguished for his guidance of brilliant youths, in what was widely known as his Tonschule.

Small Rewards

In 1900–1 he had written a symphonic poem, *Vivre-Aimer*; needless to say, this side of his writing was somewhat under the influence of the all-powerful Richard Strauss, who, beginning in 1889 with *Don Juan*, had by this time written all his best tone poems.

In 1901, Bloch, trying to earn a living by composition and performance, went to Monaco, where he wrote a *Symphony* that was rather harshly received when done (in part only) at a festival of Swiss and German music. His way of life had so far been poorly rewarded, but he had no intention of giving it up. A period in Paris followed, and it was then that he first saw any music of his in print, in 1903 – some songs to words by Camille Mauclair. Here also he conceived the first of a two-part symphonic poem called *Winter-Spring*, one of the most readily enjoyable of his earlier works: perhaps as good as any for a first taste of Bloch. But it was impossible to live by composition, as many another artist has found; and Bloch was never a sycophant or time-server. The family business needed his attention, and Ernest took it over, travelling as a commercial agent, acting as salesman, but doggedly pursuing, in his spare time, the career for which he was created.

In 1909 he secured some engagements as conductor in Lausanne and Neuchâtel; with the enthusiastic help of Madame Lucienne Bréval, one of the stars at the Paris Opera (who had in her early years been a pianoforte student at Geneva), he obtained a production in Paris of his opera *Macbeth*, a drama upon which he had been working for a good many years; in this he shows something of the same power, at its best, as did Musorgsky. After fifteen performances, amid strongly divided opinions, the work lay unheard for twenty-eight years, until a production at Naples in 1939 made an immense impression upon a new generation of listeners. Bloch has since completely revised the work, which is described as a 'lyric drama in seven tableaux'.

Interpreting the Jewish Spirit

From about 1911 Bloch deepened the aspect of his musical thought that has made him best known to laymen, the Jewish penetration. Though he is by no means narrowly Hebraic – much of his music could have been written by a Gentile, albeit by no common one – yet for some years there was an intensity of interest in the ancient Biblical Hebrew spirit, 'the complex, glowing, agitated' Jewish soul, as he called it: 'the freshness and naïvety of the patriarchs; the violence of the prophetic Books; the Jew's savage love of justice; the despair of Ecclesiastes; the sorrow and immensity of Job; the sensuality of the Song of Songs. . . . It is all this that I endeavour to hear in myself, and transcribe into music: the sacred emotion of the race that slumbers far down in our soul.'

Few emotions appeal more vividly than those in his *Three Jewish Poems*, dedicated to his father's memory, or the rhapsody *Schelomo* (Solomon); in the *Israel Symphony*, with a choral section. Oriental colouring and intervals are marked; and few composers can better

Bloch in a burst of barbaric eloquence. For *Schelomo*, largely inspired by Ecclesiastes, Bloch first thought of the solo voice: then, hearing the cellist Barjansky, he decided to use the greater scope of his instrument for a prophetic exposition of *Vanitas vanitatum, et omnia vanitas*. That text does not by any means sum up Bloch's attitude. A man of real penetration, he has thought deeply upon the world's woes and knows that hate is no solvent; only love can avail: but how, and when, shall it prevail? So, in much of his music, we feel his depth of probing, outcries, and questionings.

Down to Earth

After a short period as professor of composition and musical aesthetics at Geneva Conservatoire, he had to take advantage of a business opportunity: to conduct in America for the dancer, Maud Allan. He had many fears as to his inexperience of metropolitan life; he asked a fee that his employers doubled, by cable, though it dwindled fast when it came to payment. The whole family went to America; the tour was unsuccessful, and soon Bloch had to seek fresh work. Fortunately some interest was aroused in his music through the activities of a few friends, but it was not then lasting. His first *Quartet* was written about this time – part of it at sea. It was during the war years, and the music holds some sensibility of their harrying effect, as well as other impressions of the nostalgic wanderer.

The Academic Administrator

In 1920 he was made Director of the Cleveland Institute of Music (one remembers Dvořák, earlier, in New York). Some rest from that arduous work was found in brief holidays among the Indians of New Mexico. America is apt to disabuse an artist's mind of some hopes and induce realism rather than the glamour of a mirage. A writer in the *New Yorker* thought that 'the ardour of the prophets had turned to satire, and yet there tingles somehow in his bitterness a lusty joy. ... The man's music is wrung from him as the ultimate cry of life, so perhaps, unconsciously, he makes of his life a crescendo of tangled adventures – that the result be music.'

In 1925 Bloch went to the San Francisco Conservatoire, and in 1930 returned to Switzerland, living quietly at Ticino. It was in these years that he composed the *Sacred Service*, which has been heard not only in synagogues but in the concert room and the Anglican cathedral – for this Jewish music is felt to have a wider significance than any rite can bestow.

A Glorious Testament

There is a full orchestra, the baritone cantor, and a mixed choir for this philosophical, contemplative music, written in 1932–4 near Lake Lugano. Its composition was facilitated by the generosity of a group of Americans of Bloch's own faith, who provided a subsidy. Its simplicity seems to conceal inner clashes: of hope and faith, with anxiety such as every man of goodwill feels as he ponders upon the earthly scene. Bloch evokes tender thoughts of what the world might be if man willed it. Religion, to him, is not ritual outside life; it is a 'a kind of sublimation of simple, common things. ...' A *Sinfonia Breve*, on a germ theme, was, as the title shows, upon a concise scale. It was not, like some of his Jewish music, of which a few more orchestral examples had appeared the year before, at all oratorical; rather its chief impression was that of the quietness – perhaps also the sadness – of old age.

Bloch has remained enviably free from most of the commercial or social stresses increasingly apt to influence composers who obtain the ear of any one of the numerous publics (diverse, and often opposed) into which the devotees of music divide themselves. In an age that, despite the enormous increase of the means of communication, has lamentably witnessed the progressive diminution of the public eager for 'contemporary' music, Bloch has earned yet more of our grateful admiration by producing several long-gestated string quartets which seem to me to be among the richest intimations of musical philosophy offered to us since Beethoven set pen to paper for his last quartet.

In 1929 the Accademia di Santa Cecilia, Rome, made Bloch an honorary member. At the end of 1938 he made his home in the U.S.A., finally settling at Portland, Oregon, and going to California for summer teaching sessions at the State University.

In 1956 he composed his fifth String Quartet, which was introduced to the U.S.A. by the Grille Quartet in January 1957.

BENJAMIN BRITTEN

B. 1913

ERIC WALTER WHITE

Early Years and Training

Benjamin Britten was born on St Cecilia's Day, 22 November 1913, at Lowestoft, Suffolk. His affection for East Anglia has always been strong. When he was made a freeman of Lowestoft in 1951, in reply to the honour that had been done him he went out of his way to pay a tribute to the corner of England where he had been born and where he was to spend so many years of his life. 'Suffolk, the birthplace and inspiration of Constable and Gainsborough, the loveliest of English painters; the home of Crabbe, that most English of poets; Suffolk, with its rolling, intimate countryside; its heavenly Gothic churches, big and small; its marshes, with those wild sea-birds; its grand ports and its little fishing villages. I am firmly rooted in this glorious county.'

The early years at Lowestoft were passed quietly in the family circle and were marked by the young boy's precocious musical abilities. He learnt to play the piano and viola and began to compose at the age of five. His earliest compositions were elaborate, but extremely brief, tone poems inspired by events in his home life, such as the departure of his father for London, the appearance of a new girl friend, or a wreck at sea. A little later he began to write sonatas, quartets, symphonies, and songs; excerpts from some of these juvenile works were later used as the basis of his *Simple Symphony* (1934). While still at Gresham's School, Holt, he received from Frank Bridge special private tuition in harmony and counterpoint during his school holidays; on leaving school he won a scholarship to the Royal College of Music, where he studied composition under John Ireland and piano under Arthur Benjamin.

At the age of eighteen he set about earning his living by composition; the need for him to become independent was stressed by his father's death in the next year. His earliest works include a *Sinfonietta*

(Op. 1) for chamber orchestra, a *Phantasy Quartet* for oboe, violin, viola, and cello and an extended set of choral variations for unaccompanied mixed voices, entitled *A Boy was Born*. All these received performances within a year or two of composition, but it was clear that he would have to look elsewhere for his bread and butter.

An introduction to the cinema led him to work for the G.P.O. Film Unit. This Unit concentrated mainly on documentary films; at least twenty of those made between 1933 and 1939 had music of some sort specially written for them by Britten. His contribution ranged from title music only to full and important scores, as in *Coal Face*. On the whole, he found the discipline of the cinema bracing, especially since the company he was working for could not afford to hire large and expensive orchestras; he thus had to exercise considerable ingenuity to obtain the maximum effect with a limited number of instrumentalists. Later, when writing his operas, he was to turn to good effect the experience he had gained in this medium.

As soon as it was realized that he had a flair for occasional and incidental music, commissions for other types of work followed. He was asked to write incidental music for plays, feature broadcasts, and puppet shows. In this respect, he proved himself a reliable man of business, who could work expeditiously and satisfactorily to order; these qualities have always stood him in good stead. In addition, he has the advantage of being able to complete the greater part of the composition of a new work in his head, so that the act of committing it to paper becomes an almost mechanical process and can be carried out at high speed.

Two Friendships

Through his work for the G.P.O. Film Unit, Britten met the poet, W. H. Auden; their collaboration on such films as *Coal Face* and *Night Mail* soon led to a close friendship and collaboration outside the cinema. Even at that comparatively early period, only five years after the publication of his first book of poems, Auden was recognized as being the leading English poet of his generation. Britten set a number of his lyrics, including a set of five songs entitled *On this Island*; and Auden devised a libretto for *Our Hunting Fathers*, a symphonic cycle for high voice and orchestra, commissioned for the 1936 Norwich and Norfolk Triennial Festival. Auden undoubtedly did much to familiarize Britten with the treasuries of English poetry and the subtleties of English prosody and to strengthen his literary taste and judgement. His influence was stronger and deeper than is usual in an artistic collaboration, for by 1939, when he had decided to break away from England and Europe and to seek the full realization of his genius in the United States, Britten decided to follow suit.

With him went his friend, Peter Pears, who during the last two or three years had been a member of the B.B.C. Singers. This friendship was destined to have an even more enduring effect than Auden's. Pears was not only a fine singer, but also a sensitive and imaginative musician. In the course of the last fifteen years he has become unrivalled interpreter of Britten's music – having created the title parts in *Peter Grimes* and *Albert Herring* – and Britten has returned the compliment by writing many songs, song-cycles, canticles, and other vocal works specially for him, particularly the *Serenade* for tenor, horn, and strings and the two sonnet sequences from Michelangelo and Donne.

American Visit

The American visit was not an unqualified success. Britten at first, like Auden, intended to become a citizen of the United States; but as he stayed on, his doubts grew. It was not that the Americans were inhospitable. Quite the contrary. They received him gladly. His compositions were performed; various commissions came his way. His work was hardly interrupted by the outbreak of the war in Europe, and among other new compositions he managed to finish the *Violin Concerto*, *Les Illuminations* for high voice and orchestra, the *Sinfonia da Requiem* in memory of his parents, and *Paul Bunyan*, an operetta to a libretto by Auden. But as time went on he found himself more and more anxious to return to England. The War had reached a sombre phase. The pattern of victory had not yet been revealed. He knew that if he went back, his conscience would not allow him to fight; but he felt there must be ways in which his non-combatant services might be used. The decision to return was confirmed by a strange incident that occurred to him one day in California. Picking up an old copy of *The Listener*, he found in it an article by E. M. Forster on Crabbe that began 'To think of Crabbe is to think of England'. Reading this gave Britten such a feeling of nostalgia for Suffolk that he made up his mind. He would return home.

But by this time (Spring 1942) it was not easy to cross the Atlantic. While he and Peter Pears were waiting on the eastern seaboard for a passage, he had an opportunity of visiting Boston, where he met Serge Kussevitsky, who suggested that he should write a full-scale opera and arranged for the Kussevitsky Music Foundation to put up a 1,000 dollar commission for this purpose. Britten accepted. In his mind he had already decided that Crabbe's story of Peter Grimes, the Aldeburgh fisherman, should form the subject; as soon as he was back in England he set about finding a librettist.

The Opera Composer

On their return Britten and Pears both secured exemption from military service. They appeared together at various concerts throughout the country: in fact it is from this period that their custom of giving song recitals dates – with programmes including English songs (particularly Purcell), German *Lieder*, English and French folk-songs and Britten's own compositions – and these have spread their fame as executants not only throughout Great Britain, but also in Europe and North America.

Apart from this concert work, the whole of Britten's efforts during the last year and a half of the War were devoted to the composition of *Peter Grimes*. Montagu Slater had written the libretto. Joan Cross, the war-time director of the Sadler's Wells Opera Company, was interested in the new work. Peter Pears had already joined the Company. And so it came about that *Peter Grimes* was produced at Sadler's Wells on the night the Theatre re-opened after its war-time closure (7 June 1945). Eric Crozier produced; scenery and costumes were by Kenneth Green; Reginald Goodall conducted. The opera had an immediate success, the repercussions of which were felt far outside Great Britain; in the course of the next five years it had twenty-three productions in fifteen different countries. The composer was praised for the subtlety with which he had rendered in musical terms the psychological cross-currents of the action, particularly the psychopathic character of Grimes; his idiom was welcomed as being simple, bold, and memorable.

But the path of the opera composer is not a smooth one, particularly in this country, and it was not easy for Britten to see how this success could be followed up. Clearly Sadler's Wells had only a limited power of absorbing new English works into its repertory. As for the Royal Opera House, Covent Garden, this was re-opened in 1946 with the Sadler's Wells Ballet in residence and the promise of a new permanent opera company. But it would take time for this company to be built up; here, too, the possibilities for a new English opera composer seemed very limited. At this point, Britten hit on a bold solution. Making a virtue of necessity, he decided to plan his next opera on a much smaller scale – without a chorus on the stage or a large orchestra in the pit – and a new opera company should be formed to present it. In this way the Glyndebourne English Opera Company, later the English Opera Group, came into existence.

The venture was launched at Glyndebourne in the summer of 1946 with *The Rape of Lucretia*, a chamber opera for eight solo singers and twelve solo instrumentalists, which Britten wrote to a libretto adapted by Ronald Duncan from André Obey's *Le Viol de Lucrèce*. This remote classical subject formed a strong contrast to the romantic element in *Peter Grimes*; in his score the composer displayed an even greater command of his musical material. The producer was Eric Crozier; scenery and costumes were by John Piper; Ernest Ansermet conducted. The following year Britten wrote *Albert Herring* for the English Opera Group as a pendant to *The Rape of Lucretia*. This was a through-composed comic opera to a libretto by Eric Crozier based on a story by Guy de Maupassant. The setting was transferred from France to East Anglia. Frederick Ashton produced; scenery and costumes were by John Piper; Britten himself conducted the first performance at Glyndebourne.

It had never been the purpose of the English Opera Group to produce only the works of Britten. Already during the first Glyndebourne season an announcement had been made of their intention to revive Purcell's *Dido and Aeneas*. In the event this had to wait until the Group's season at the Lyric Theatre, Hammersmith, during the Festival of Britain, 1951. But for 1948 Britten prepared a new version of *The Beggar's Opera* realized from the original airs. The link with Glyndebourne having been broken, this was produced at the Arts Theatre, Cambridge, by Tyrone Guthrie, with scenery and costumes by Tanya Moiseiwitch; like the Group's preceding chamber operas, it was subsequently seen in London and on tour.

The Aldeburgh Festival

The English Opera Group did not confine its operations to Great Britain. There were tours abroad – to Holland and Switzerland in

1947, to Holland again in 1948, to Norway and Denmark in 1949, and to Germany in 1951 and 1953. In the course of the visit to the 1947 Lucerne Festival Peter Pears made a suggestion that was to bear almost immediate fruit. 'Why not,' he said, 'make our own festival at home?' He and Britten had just moved to Aldeburgh; the local people were enthusiastic when consulted, and so the idea of the Aldeburgh Festival was born.

The first Aldeburgh Festival was held in June 1948, and lasted just over a week. Its success was immediate, and thereafter it became an annual event. Despite the restricted accommodation available in this comparatively small seaside town, the programme generally managed to include opera, concerts, lectures, and exhibitions. Britten himself, who with Peter Pears and Eric Crozier was one of the original founders of the Festival, appeared not only as composer, but also as conductor, pianist, and host.

Let's Make an Opera! was specially written for the 1949 Aldeburgh Festival. This entertainment for children, devised by Eric Crozier, included a one-act opera by Britten, *The Little Sweep*, with spoken dialogue. It was written for solo singers (both adults and children), string quartet, piano (four hands), and percussion. This was presented by the English Opera Group and subsequently performed in London and on tour. It proved to be the most popular of all the Group's productions, reaching its 200th performance on 24 June 1951.

Later Operas and other Compositions

In a lecture at the first Aldeburgh Festival, E. M. Forster had speculated on what *Peter Grimes* might have become, had he himself written the libretto. When Britten was commissioned to write a full-scale opera for the Festival of Britain 1951, and found his imagination kindled by Hermann Melville's *Billy Budd*, he instinctively turned to Forster as a collaborator. The libretto was in fact written jointly by Forster and Eric Crozier. The opera, which was first performed at Covent Garden on 1 December 1951, has certain unique features: the whole of the action takes place at sea, and only men are involved. The production was by Basil Coleman, and the setting and costumes by John Piper. Britten himself conducted.

Early the following year Queen Elizabeth II gave her permission for Elizabeth I and Essex to be chosen by Britten as the subject for an opera to be given at Covent Garden on the occasion of the Coronation. *Gloriana*, written to a libretto by William Plomer, was accordingly performed at the Royal Opera House on 8 June 1953, in the presence of the Queen and other members of the Royal Family. The same month Britten was created a Companion of Honour.

Possibly *Gloriana* suffered slightly in comparison with his other operas because of the episodic way in which the historical material was presented. But, if that was so, the defect was fully remedied in his next opera, *The Turn of the Screw*, where Myfanwy Piper's skilful adaptation of the Henry James story gave him an opportunity to show that by use of the variation form a mosaic of sixteen short scenes could be integrated into as strictly disciplined and dramatically effective a score as Berg's *Wozzeck*. This chamber opera for half a dozen singers and thirteen instruments was specially commissioned by the Biennale of Venice and was given its first performance by the English Opera Group at the Teatro la Fenice on 14 September 1954.

Britten is undoubtedly a master of the operatic medium. He understands the prime importance of the vocal element, and everything is subordinated to it. Although he appreciates the fact that syllables are the raw material of his vocal structure, he sees also the words behind the syllables, the ideas beyond the words, and the implications of the ideas. His understanding of the psychological factors involved is particularly shrewd; and he has an extraordinary knack of being able to express such subtleties in musical terms. His fundamental harmonic language is simple and readily understood; but he often combines streams of different musical elements, and this technique demands strongly developed powers of analysis and synthesis in the auditor. From the resulting tension and friction, some of his most powerful and original effects have been derived.

The greater part of his output after his return from America was directed to opera, but he by no means neglected other fields of composition. Of special importance were his *String Quartet No. 2* (1945), *The Young Person's Guide to the Orchestra* (1946), and the *Spring Symphony* (1949) for three soloists, mixed chorus, boys' choir, and orchestra. Several of his existing works have been adapted as ballet music, particularly *The Young Person's Guide* and the *Variations on a Theme of Frank Bridge* for string orchestra, which was originally played by the Boyd Neel Orchestra at the 1937 Salzburg Festival. *The Prince of the Pagodas* (1957) was his first specially composed ballet score.

FERRUCCIO BUSONI

1866–1924

DYNELEY HUSSEY

Parents and Godparents

Ferruccio Dante Michelangiolo Benvenuto – Ferdinando Busoni, with a fond father's faith in the extraordinary character of his infant son, fairly piled Pelion upon Ossa in the matter of distinguished Christian names. All the grandest geniuses of Renaissance Tuscany were to act as sponsors at the baptism, and, perhaps, they did respond to the invitation and endow the child – Alighieri with something of his poetic sensibility, Buonarroti with his grandeur of design, Cellini with his fine craftsmanship, but not his lack of principles. Ferdinando may, indeed, have included Benvenuto to avoid any unfortunate incident such as befell the Princess Aurora in Perrault's tale, owing to the negligence of her parents over inviting the Fairy Carabosse to the christening.

Ferdinando, who was born in 1834 and survived until 1909, was a virtuoso clarinettist from Empoli, a small town between Florence and Pisa. On one of his tours he had met and married in Trieste Anna Weiss, a pianist of considerable distinction, who thereafter toured with her husband under the name of Anna Weiss-Busoni. Her father, Josef Weiss, was of Bavarian origin. He was born at Laibach (Ljubljana) in what is now Yugoslavia, and had settled early in life at Trieste, the Adriatic port of the Austrian Empire, as an employee in a firm of grain merchants. Weiss soon assimilated himself to the predominantly Italian culture of Trieste, and Italian, or rather the Venetian dialect of it, was the native language of his children. He married an Italian lady of good family and he was by no means pleased when Anna fell in love with the handsome young clarinettist, whom he perceived to be a lover of applause rather than of hard work and a man who would be ready to exploit his wife's talent for his own advantage. But Anna was infatuated and the marriage took place in 1865.

Ferdinando continued his concert-tours with his wife as pianist, and next March they played in Rome before an audience that included the Abbé Liszt. Anna's condition by now was such that an interruption of her musical engagements became imperative, and Ferdinando hurried her back to his native Empoli, where, in a house occupied by his sisters, Anna gave birth to a son on 1 April 1866. So soon as the mother was fit to travel again, the infant Ferruccio was dispatched with a nurse to his grandfather Weiss in Trieste, while his parents resumed their concert-giving.

Childhood in Trieste

Ferruccio remained for a while under the care of his grandfather and his aunt, who had two young daughters. These cousins became his devoted and lifelong friends, and their companionship lightened a childhood that had little fun in it. At two years old the boy was back with his parents on a tour that brought them to Paris, where they enjoyed a considerable success. They remained in Paris until rumours of war put an end to this profitable state of affairs early in 1870. The family returned to Trieste, where grandfather Weiss, now a widower, was in the unhappy condition of Dr Bartolo – under the thumb of his housekeeper, who showed all possible ill-will to Ferdinando and his son. So for a while Ferdinando departed on a tour by himself, leaving his wife and son with her father, as an economy in housekeeping. Anna was miserable and was not made more happy by her father's frequent pointing of the moral. She devoted herself to the education of her son and made a little money by giving pianoforte lessons. Then suddenly and without warning, early in 1873, Ferdinando turned up again. They met him in the street, leading a poodle on a chain.

Ferdinando removed his family to lodgings and began to undertake the supervision of Ferruccio's musical education. He was less accomplished than his wife as a teacher of pianoforte, and his sense of rhythm was extremely inaccurate. Yet at the end of his life Busoni expressed his indebtedness to his father for having 'kept me strictly to the study of Bach ... and that at a time when the master was rated little higher than a Carl Czerny'. It is, indeed, remarkable that this poorly educated Italian, whose own repertory on the clarinet consisted mainly of operatic fantasies, one on *Il Trovatore* being his special 'war-horse', should have schooled his son in the works of the German composer who represented the very opposite of all the music he himself performed. There must have been more virtue in Ferdinando than his feckless character and unstable conduct suggest. His son never failed in devotion to him, even though he was often distracted and hampered in his own career by his father's lack of principle and lazy reliance upon other people to pay his debts.

In January 1875 Ferruccio made his first public appearance as a pianist and in May played Mozart's *C minor Concerto*, his father conducting. Ferdinando perceived possibilities in the boy and, like Leopold Mozart and Anton von Weber before him, sought to exploit them. Writing of this time his son later recorded:

> He considered me mature and marvellous enough to take to Vienna as a pianist, composer and improviser, shielded under the sonorous name of Ferruccio Benvenuto Weiss-Busoni; not forgetting to bring his clarinet, but otherwise provided with hardly means enough to make his way and without knowing a single word of German.

Travels Abroad

Notwithstanding, they stayed at the most expensive hotel, where they were fortunate to find Anton Rubinstein, whom the importunate Ferdinando persuaded to give the boy a hearing, without any practical result, though the great pianist later wrote a testimonial rather in the nature of an injunction to work hard than a certificate of achievement. More fortunate still, Ferruccio became acquainted with the family of Theodor Gomperz, the philosopher, whose sisters took an interest in him and for some years supplied him with money to enable him to continue his studies. He entered the Vienna Conservatoire with little profit to his education. The important experiences of this visit were the opportunities of hearing Beethoven's *Mass in D* and performances by Brahms and Liszt of their own music. He exercised himself in composition, and Hanslick, who had the usual German contempt for any Italian composer, had his complacency shaken by the seriousness of the boy's outlook.

Illness necessitated a move from Vienna, and at the age of fourteen Ferruccio found himself at Graz, where he had the good fortune to become the pupil of Wilhelm Mayer. Mayer was a great teacher, with a liberal view of his responsibilities. He understood that a narrow specialization led to pedantry and that the true artist needed the widest possible culture. He inspired his pupil with a love of Mozart and increased his understanding of Bach. He also put before him as orchestral models the works of Berlioz. Under his guidance Ferruccio developed a musical personality of his own.

At the end of this period of study, in March 1881, the boy gave a farewell concert at Graz, playing Schumann's *Pianoforte Concerto*, Beethoven's last *Sonata in C minor* and a *Prelude and Fugue* by himself. Already he was tackling the most exacting music of Beethoven, of which he was to become in maturity one of the greatest interpreters.

The family returned to Trieste and Ferdinando once more departed on a tour of his own. Ferruccio occupied himself meanwhile with composing a *Requiem Mass*, modelled, sometimes by contrary suggestion, upon Verdi and Berlioz. A concert tour of Italy with his parents included a visit to Bologna, where Ferruccio, like Mozart and Rossini before him, received the diploma of the Accademia Filarmonica, as a mere child. The climax of the tour was reached in March 1883, when at Arezzo a performance of a *Cantata* by Ferruccio was conducted by Mancinelli and brought him to the favourable notice of Boito, the composer of *Mefistofele* and Verdi's librettist for *Otello* and *Falstaff*.

In Vienna and Leipzig

The boy, now in his seventeenth year, returned to Trieste as something of a celebrity. Vienna, however, remained unimpressed. An attempt to get Richter to perform an orchestral *Suite* was met by evasion and procrastination. The conductor was willing, but the orchestra did not wish to play it and so on. Perhaps Ferruccio, modelling his conduct too closely upon his father's, was too importunate. He called on Richter every day; and Richter was more and more 'not at home'. The allowance from the Gomperz sisters also arrived less regularly. The 'duodecimo edition' of Liszt with his mop of golden brown hair was finding that the power of his juvenile charm was waning.

He escaped to Leipzig, at that time the centre of the musical world, whither every serious musician sooner or later gravitated. An introduction from Brahms opened doors, and, though Leipzig had no better opinion of Italian musicians than had other German towns, he soon aroused, on that very account, surprise and admiration by his powers as a pianist. He became friendly with the Dutch leader of the Gewandhaus Orchestra and of a string quartet, Henri Petri, whose son, Egon, became in after years Busoni's most distinguished pupil and interpreter. He met also Grieg and Delius and Gustav Mahler.

Finland and Marriage

Apart from occasional concert tours, which took him to Trieste where his mother, always possessive, found him 'greatly changed', Busoni remained at Leipzig till 1888. In April of that year he was offered the post of teacher of pianoforte at the Conservatoire of Helsingfors. In spite of his mother's horror at the idea of his going so far away – she could never reconcile herself to the fact that he had grown up – he could not induce her to accompany him. She suggested that his father should join him – the last thing that, despite his real affection for the old man, Ferruccio wanted. He sailed for Finland alone and there spent a year of dreary routine in a musically uncultivated community – Sibelius was an unknown young man of twenty-three – teaching his pupils, mostly girls, whom he called 'the performing geese', to play Cramer and Clementi.

But he also found there his happiness. For he met and fell in love with Gerda Sjöstrand, the daughter of a Swedish sculptor, who had studied in Italy. During one of the vacations, he induced his parents to visit him in Weimar where, after some tactful preparation, he broke to them the news of his engagement and was relieved to find that they accepted the *fait accompli*. Ferdinando returned to Empoli, and Ferruccio took his mother, still suspicious and antagonistic, to meet his bride. She did her best to wreck the marriage, and in the end, on 27 September 1890, the young couple were hurriedly married, with the connivance of the bride's father, by a Protestant pastor in Moscow, where Ferruccio had been appointed to the Conservatoire.

He remained but a short while in Moscow, which he cordially disliked, and gratefully accepted the escape afforded by an offer of a teaching post with a much higher salary in Boston. Despite the presence there of Nikisch, the great conductor, New England proved quite as backward as Helsingfors. After a year, during which a son (Benvenuto) was born, Busoni could endure the soul-destroying work of teaching 'performing geese' no longer and resigned. He moved to New York, and for the next few years he became a travelling virtuoso with little time to devote to composition.

He had not yet developed that monumental and intellectualized conception of musical performance that those who heard him play in his last years will never forget. He was still at the stage of great technical brilliance, and, even at a time when great pianists were not rare, he came quickly to the fore as a virtuoso. He was to become much more than that. His father had set before him the ambition to become a great creative musician – and one can be creative in interpretation as well as in composition. Basing his artistic creed upon Mayer's dictum that an artist needs the widest and most varied cultural experience as the basis of his work, Busoni did not allow himself to become a specialist, a mere (if one can apply the adjective without any derogatory sense) pianist. He sought to be a whole man, capable of composing and conducting as well as performing, and in his own compositions he worked towards the creation of a *Gesamtwerk*, an all-embracing work. He even exercised himself in drawing, for which he had some gift – a gift inherited by his two sons, who became painters.

A Home in Berlin

This mature development took place in the twenty years between 1894 and 1914, when he made Berlin his headquarters, while he toured the world. Already in 1895 Safonov, the great Russian pianist and conductor, greeted him when he played in Moscow with: 'Your playing is a revelation – you left us a young man; you have returned a great artist.' By the end of the century he was at the very height of his powers as a pianist. His enormous vitality and exuberance was controlled by a severely intellectual approach to the music he played. He was not immune from criticism. His playing of Beethoven was by some condemned as extravagantly violent; others complained that his Chopin lacked sensibility. The fact was that he would not make concessions to the conventionally sentimental view of Chopin. He defended himself against the charge of 'modernizing' Beethoven by pointing out that his music was in its own day revolutionary and extremely impassioned. 'I built up for myself', he continued, 'an ideal (of Beethoven) which has wrongly been called "modern" and which is really no more than "live".'

Similarly in the editions and transcriptions of music by J. S. Bach, to which he devoted much of his time, he sought not so much to translate literally into the technique of the grand pianoforte music designed originally for the older keyboard instruments and the organ, as to recreate the music in the new medium. Transcription, of which Liszt was the greatest exponent, was the nineteenth-century equivalent of improvisation, which was, until Beethoven's day, an indispensable part of the virtuoso pianist's equipment. From his practice in this art Busoni proceeded to those compositions upon themes of Bach, of which the outstanding examples are the *Fantasia* dedicated to the memory of his father and the great *Fantasia Contrapuntistica*, which is in the nature of an enormous improvisation controlled by a massive intellectual grasp of musical form. As Professor Dent has well said, these are commentaries on Bach written not in words but in music.

In 1902 Busoni turned his attention to conducting and in a series of concerts given in Berlin, produced there for the first time a number of important works by his contemporaries and by himself. Among these novelties were the Prelude and Angel's Farewell from Elgar's *Gerontius*, Debussy's *Prélude, L'Aprés-midi d'un Faune* and two of the *Nocturnes*, Sibelius's *Second Symphony*, Delius's *Paris*, D'Indy's *Symphonie sur un Chant Montagnard*, and a work by Béla Bartók. His own compositions included a *Comedy Overture*, a *Violin Concerto* and the vast *Concerto* for *Pianoforte, Orchestra and Male Chorus*, which was his first major essay in the direction of a *Gesamtwerk*. The Berlin public, never receptive of new or foreign ideas, were duly ungrateful and the critics abusive.

Tales of Hoffmann

During this Berlin period, which lasted until the outbreak of war in 1914, Busoni continued his concert tours abroad, but his mind turned more and more towards composition, and especially towards opera. Only in the opera-house could he realize his idea of a *Gesamtwerk* embracing all the arts. In 1902 he was already considering the possibility of setting *Aladdin* by Oelenschlager 'not as an opera, but as a combination of drama, music, dance and magic – if possible compressed into one evening'. Witness the *Pianoforte Concerto*, in which he used verses from *Aladdin* in the choral finale; Busoni was not unaffected by the fashion for magnitude, for the *kolossal* prevalent in Imperial Germany. And he had a liking for the fantastic and for magical effects. His first completed opera, *Die Brautwahl*, produced in Hamburg in 1912, was based on one of E. T. A. Hoffmann's tales. He wrote the libretto himself, as he did also for his later operas.

Die Brautwahl was a comedy with magical and fantastic episodes, but none more Hoffmannesque than one that really happened to Busoni when on tour with Ysaÿe. At Birmingham the famous violinist serenaded Busoni with a performance of Bach's *Chaconne* on a pochette or dancing-master's fiddle, which produced such queer, ghostly squeaks, that the sensitive Busoni began to think he was going mad. When he opened his door, Ysaÿe had disappeared down the hotel corridor round a corner, whence the macabre bat-like sounds once more proceeded. So it went on until the now terrified Busoni at last came upon the grotesque sight of the enormously fat Ysaÿe scraping away at his tiny fiddle. He was too frightened to laugh and it was a long time before his nerves recovered from the fright.

Die Brautwahl was about six years in the making, and, even allowing for the inevitable interruptions caused by his concert tours, it suffered probably from being over-elaborated. Busoni took Verdi's *Falstaff* as his model, and, as we know, even that masterpiece suffers from the extraordinary swiftness of its movement and the subtlety and wealth of the ideas packed into it. Moreover, like most composers who are also the interpreters of other men's music, Busoni could hardly distinguish between what was his own thought and what was reminiscence. His music tended to be eclectic and derivative, though his intellectual greatness, which always makes itself felt, commands respect. *Die Brautwahl* had a *succès d'estime*, but never won a permanent place in the repertory.

'Turandot' and 'Faust'

For his next opera Busoni adapted Carlo Gozzi's *Turandot*, a subject already treated by Weber and yet to be used by Puccini. Before thinking of it as an opera, he had composed an orchestral Suite, which was played at one of his Berlin concerts in 1905. In 1913, while in London, he saw Carl Volmoeller's spectacular production of the play with his own music supplemented by pieces by Rimsky-Korsakov and Saint-Saëns and badly played by an inadequate orchestra. He fled after two acts, but the performance gave him the idea of setting the whole play as an opera. This project was not realized till 1917, when it was completed and produced at Zürich, with a one-act 'theatrical capriccio', *Arlecchino*, another essay in the manner of the *commedia dell'arte*. *Turandot* is probably Busoni's most successful stage-work. It does not make the mistake of removing the tale from the plane of fantasy to the world of real emotions, in which it becomes revolting and indecent. Busoni does not wring the audience's heart with a pathetic, self-sacrificing Liu, but maintains the integrity of Gozzi's gruesome fairy-tale.

This puppet-like conception of opera was developed a stage further in *Doktor Faust*, the most important and ambitious of Busoni's operas. This has no connexion with Goethe's philosophic drama, but is the outcome of Busoni's study of the old German puppet-plays on the subject. In one sense it is closer to Marlowe's tragedy than to Goethe. But Busoni overlaid the grotesque and fantastic and magical incidents with his own philosophical ideas, so that in the end he produced a work of the most austerely intellectual character, which will always win the respect of musicians, though it is never likely to gain a general popularity or to receive more than an occasional performance on account of the large resources, both musical and scenic, that it demands.

Doktor Faust occupied Busoni for nearly fifteen years. It is first mentioned in 1910, and it was not quite finished when he died. The final scene was completed from his sketches by Philipp Jarnach, one of his pupils, and the opera was produced at Dresden in 1925. In a lengthy preface to the score Busoni proclaimed his aesthetic faith, whose chief article is that an opera must be a complete and self-sufficient musical composition, not dependent upon its libretto, but using words and action as the basis or scaffolding of its musical form.

Bologna and Zürich

In 1913 Busoni accepted an invitation to become director of the Liceo Musicale at Bologna. He hoped to develop the teaching at this great institution on the advanced lines that he practised in his own work and to restore it to the position of importance it had occupied in the days of Padre Martini. But he soon found that his ideals conflicted with the practical requirements of academic studies. He was not gifted with patience to suffer fools gladly, and he was not a teacher for the ordinary musician, however stimulating he might be to young men of exceptional intellectual capacity in sympathy with his own ideas. He was no more successful at Bologna than he had been with the 'performing geese' at Helsingfors or the Meisterklasse at Vienna, where he had taught for some years, carrying on the while a guerilla warfare with the pundits of the conservatoire. After a year he left Bologna and returned to Berlin.

Then came the war, with Italy on one side and Germany on the other. Busoni's mind was of that idealistic cast that saw in war only horror, futility, and waste; and this conflict cleft his soul in twain – the true Italian that he was in sentiment and instinct sheared off from the

German that he was in intellectual outlook and musical affinity. He retired to Switzerland, where he settled in Zürich, refusing to play in any of the belligerent countries. He was able to devote more of his time to composition, and there *Arlecchino* and *Turandot* were produced and much of *Doktor Faust* was written.

The Last Years

After the war he returned to Berlin, which he had left a despised Latin foreigner at a time of Teutonic frenzy, and found a new public more ready to accept him as a leader. He resumed his concert-giving and early in 1921 there were three orchestral concerts devoted to his works, at which he played his *Concerto*. He visited London, too, once more, and those who heard him play remarked that, while the massive intellectual grasp of the music remained, something of the fire had died out of his performances. The great lion's mane – he still wore his hair in the abundant style of the nineteenth century virtuoso – had become grizzled.

For many years Busoni had suffered from minor illnesses of which he took no account. If he had a professional engagement to keep, he kept it, whatever his temperature. His will sufficed to ensure that he would surmount any physical disability and keep his performance up to his own standard. But neglect and the gruelling life of a travelling virtuoso, which too often meant rushing from concert to railway station for a long uncomfortable journey without proper meals or sleep, had told on his constitution. By 1923, at the age of fifty-seven, he was a sick man suffering from a disease of the kidneys. It was of this that he died in Berlin on 27 July 1924.

At the time there were malicious rumours that excessive drinking had contributed to his fatal illness. As these rumours were even given the more permanent currency of print, it may be well to state that in his biography[*] of Busoni, Professor Dent, who was one of his intimate friends and staunch admirers, produced conclusive evidence of the complete untruth of these statements. They had as their foundation Busoni's natural cheerfulness in company, his rumbustious sense of humour, and the fact that, like all Italians – and, indeed, all civilized men of good sense, he regarded wine as the normal beverage of man and not as some excitant drug to be indulged in (with a sense of guilt) on special occasions or to be abhorred as a moral poison.

[*] To this masterly study of Busoni's character and career, published by the Oxford University Press, this chapter is greatly indebted.

ALFREDO CASELLA

1883–1947

D. MAXWELL WHITE

The Reaction

In the nineteenth century music in Italy was curiously one-sided. Whereas in the time of Vivaldi and the Scarlattis keyboard and instrumental music, opera, oratorio, and the chamber cantata flourished, in 1900 Italian composers seemed interested in writing only veristic music drama. During the intervening 200 years opera, often conceived merely as a medium for vocal display, had gradually overshadowed other kinds of music and in the Risorgimento it became Italy's characteristic musical activity – a superb activity, which produced *Otello*, but a restricting one; church music was neglected and the tradition of instrumental music lost. Sooner or later a reaction was inevitable. In the second half of the century a few composers attempted to free Italian music from the pervasive influence of *bel canto*. Their efforts served to clear the ground. But as the century drew to a close opera reached new heights of popularity, and there was no decisive break with melodramatic writing until a musician appeared who wanted to revive Italian 'absolute music' by profiting from his awareness of contemporary musical developments in Europe. This composer was Alfredo Casella.

Paris 1896–1914

Casella is outstanding among twentieth-century musicians for his versatility. Besides being a composer of great virtuosity he was a concert pianist, conductor, theorist and critic, and the devoted champion of modern music. From his earliest years he seemed destined for a musical career. He was born at Turin on 25 July 1883 into a family of 'austere and noble musical culture'. His father was a brilliant violoncellist and taught at the Liceo Musicale. His mother, who was a most important influence throughout his life, was an excellent pianist. When Alfredo was four she began to teach him the piano.

Under her guidance he made such rapid progress that he could soon play Bach's *Forty-Eight Preludes and Fugues*; when he was ten he gave his first concert. But music was not Casella's only interest. He was fond of chemistry and for a time thought of being a scientist, until the composer Giuseppe Martucci advised him to take up music seriously. Casella began to study harmony at Turin with an admirably conscientious teacher called Cravero, but after the death of his father his mother decided to take him to Paris to complete his musical education (1896). Here, after passing with distinction a practical entrance examination, Casella entered the Conservatoire. He studied the piano with Louis Diémer and harmony with Xavier Leroux, and in the winter of 1900–1 he attended as a listener, with Charles Koechlin and Maurice Ravel, the composition class of Gabriel Fauré. During these years Casella was also influenced considerably by his friend, the Rumanian violinist and composer, George Enesco.

His studies finished (1902), after six years of harmony, counterpoint, and fugue, Casella travelled all over Europe as a pianist. He was successful, for within a few years he had given over 200 concerts. Besides performing, he frequently conducted the Concerts Colonne and many of the best European orchestras. In Paris he directed a number of the Concerts Populaires at the Trocadéro (1911), taught the piano at the Conservatoire as a deputy for Cortot and became music critic of Clemenceau's daily *L'homme Libre*. But all the time he was busy composing.

In the course of his life Casella wrote music of almost every kind. Born at a time when music was stagnant in Italy, he engaged in a lifelong search for a new musical language. And, though his work falls into several clearly defined periods, his aim was consistent – to create 'a modern Italian style'. Casella's early affection had been for the German classical composers, but during his travels he became enthusiastic over modern music. He met many of the greatest European musicians and made a profound study of their works. Strauss, Ravel, Debussy, Stravinsky, Schönberg, and his friend Gustav Mahler all became his idols in turn. At first Casella's music was largely derivative from this wealth of new impressions. But it always has a distinctive solidity, plasticity, and rhythmic vigour. In these early years Casella wrote a number of works including two symphonies, the rhapsody *Italia*, and a 'pure ballet', *Il Convento Veneziano* (1911). This was a choreographic comedy inspired by Diaghilev's Russian Ballet, a whimsical work set with a background of shimmering canals in eighteenth-century Venice.

War Years

For nineteen years Casella had lived in voluntary exile, but when World War I came he left Paris and went to Rome 'rich with every European experience'. He continued to write for several French and American journals and was soon appointed to teach the piano at the Royal Liceo Musicale di Santa Cecilia – a post he held for the rest of his life. But after the stimulating years in Paris, Casella found the Italian musical scene for the most part depressing. He introduced to Italy the work of Debussy, Stravinsky, and Ravel, though his enthusiasm for contemporary music was not really shared by the Italians. However, with a small following of young composers he was not long in finding his métier – he would counter mediocrity and provincialism and awaken in Italy an awareness of modern music. And with this end in view, in 1917, Casella founded the Società Nazionale di Musica Moderna and the propaganda magazine *Ars Nova*. In 1923 this Society was refounded at a meeting with Malipiero at D'Annunzio's villa in Rome and incorporated as the Italian Section of the International Society for Contemporary Music.

During these war years Casella attained to stylistic individuality as a composer. Since 1911 he had been feeling his way towards a new conception of tonality. He rejected polyphony because it made his music sound like Richard Strauss's and developed a very discordant idiom of horizontally moving chords. This 'second style' was established with *Notte di Maggio* (1913), a polytonal work for voice and orchestra completely free from romantic rhetoric. But 'modern' as Casella was, he never became an extremist. He was influenced to some extent by atonalism and at one period he expressed his admiration for jazz, but he kept notably aloof from the futurist experiments in music for 'noise instruments' of his compatriots Marinetti and Russolo. The war inspired several of Casella's compositions. The *Pagine di Guerra* are a set of symphonic sketches portraying war scenes – the passing of German heavy artillery and the ruins of Rheims cathedral. There is also an *Elegia Eroica* which Casella composed as an orchestral tribute to the allies. This is a sombre work, but it produced a riot of protest when it was performed in 1917 at the Augusteo in Rome. Other compositions of this period are the grotesque marionette pieces

Pupazzetti and the ironic *Sonatina*, about which Debussy said, 'My dear fellow, I am really very fond of you, and I sincerely hope you will compose many more works of that sort, since you are made that way. But I confess to not understanding how such music can have come into anyone's mind.'

'L'Evoluzione della Musica'

When Casella was in Paris he had become friendly with Debussy. He admired him immensely for the stylistic perfection of his works and for liberating music 'from all sorts of dogma'. He played his pieces at concerts sympathetically and with great variety of tone, but he privately thought that Debussy was far too concerned with gaining pleasing harmonic effects. Casella's music of the 'second period' was also harmonic – but it was anti-impressionistic. He wrote it according to theories, which he carefully formulated in a treatise with the imposing title *L'Evoluzione della Musica a traverso la Storia della Cadenza Perfetta* (1919). This is a selection of 100 perfect cadences illustrating the development of polyphony into chromaticism and an essay on the nature of modern music. Casella had come to consider that melody was 'the most elementary artifice of mankind' and that tone-colour and harmony were the true foundation of modern music. He looked forward to a time when 'a "simultaneity" of sound and colour' would arouse the same emotions as a whole musical fragment does to-day.

Neo-Classicism

After the war Casella wrote no music for two years. He then began a series of compositions that evidence a marked change of manner. In 1924 he composed a *Concerto for String Quartet*, about which he wrote in a programme note, 'This concerto belongs to my third style. I consider it to be the first work in which I have truly achieved what for fifteen years has been the goal of all my studies.' Always in tune with the times, Casella had renounced the harmonic theory of music in *L'Evoluzione della Musica*, looked into Italy's past and, inspired by the music of the seventeenth and eighteenth centuries, begun a relentless pursuit of a new music that should embody 'Italian classicism within an extended tonal framework'. Casella's compositions became fresher and gayer, simpler and more incisive. In six weeks he wrote a rollicking ballet, *La Giara*, set among Sicilian peasants at the time of the olive harvest. The work was based on a short story by Luigi Pirandello. Casella now affirmed his 'neo-classicism' in a series of pieces, the well-known *Partita*, the 'divertissement' *Scarlattiana*, and the *Serenade for Five Instruments*, which makes use of classical dance forms. Many of these compositions were first performed in America, where Casella frequently went on tour as pianist, composer, and conductor.

Opera

Casella had always disliked the melodramatic conventions of nineteenth-century music drama, but he eventually came to realize that opera was a vital form of musical expression. Nevertheless he was convinced that opera should not be veristic and that the music ought not to be constrained by the libretto. In 1931, at Olevano Romano, he completed *La Donna Serpente* – a work in the style of the eighteenth-century *Commedia dell'arte*. Casella himself conducted the first performance in Rome. It was not very successful. The fantasy did not come off and the audience thought the unnaturalistic parts a joke. *La Donna Serpente* was followed by *La Favola di Orfeo* and then by a 'mystery in one act', which Casella declared to be his best work, *Il Deserto Tentato* (1937). This is a 'lay oratorio' with a libretto by the poet Corrado Pavolini. In it poet and musician combine to idealize the Ethiopian war. According to Casella it is 'a poetic exaltation of the civilizing mission of a great nation which takes possession, thanks to a group of aviators, of an absolutely deserted and infertile land and brings to it the civilization and history which it has awaited since the beginning of time'. The work was performed at the Florence May Festival on the eve of the first anniversary of the Italian Empire. It was dedicated to Mussolini.

Last Years

Though an energetic teacher and composer, Casella devoted much of his time to writing and editing. He published revised editions of the works of Beethoven, Bach, and Chopin; in addition to *L'Evoluzione della Musica* he wrote critical articles, a profile of Stravinsky, treatises on the pianoforte and instrumentation, and two autobiographical works. In *21 + 26* (1931) he surveyed his musical development and attempted to justify his position as a neo-classical composer. *I Segreti della Giara* (1941) is a fuller autobiography and is especially important as a document of the society in which he and his contemporaries were formed. During World War II Casella went on composing. He wrote several large-scale works, including a majestic *Missa pro Pacis* (1946). But in his last years he suffered from a protracted illness and was practically confined to his bed. With tireless devotion however he still went three times a week to Santa Cecilia for his piano class. Casella died on the morning of 5 March 1947, aged sixty-three.

Casella exhibits to a remarkable degree the plight of the twentieth-century composer. His music has an unappeased quality and suffers at times from being too intellectually conceived. He rarely expresses deeply felt emotion, but even in parody he is sincere. Casella was searching for a contemporary musical language. He broke with the nineteenth-century melodramatic conventions, explored a whole range of musical styles, and directed Italian music towards fresher horizons.

SAMUEL COLERIDGE-TAYLOR

1875–1912

HUBERT FOSS

A Calm Life

Only those who have had to read the complacent and detailed reminiscences of Cathedral organists, singers, and other moderately successful performers can know how dull the working life of an English musician may be. Of this Coleridge-Taylor is an example. A less eventful life has fallen to the lot of few composers. It was suburban and commonplace in the extreme. Reading the record of its happenings is like reading a discarded engagement calendar, which may have significance as material for social history but very little that is personal or psychological. It is no exaggeration to say that, outside his own imaginative creation, only two dramatic incidents occurred to Coleridge-Taylor once he had passed through the enlightenment of adolescence – the sudden youthful success of *Hiawatha's Wedding Feast* and his no less sudden and unexpected death at the untimely age of thirty-seven. All that came between was the familiar round of the working composer – marriage, adjudicating, commissions for works, conducting some good, some bad orchestras, teaching mostly bad pupils, eternal travelling in trains – and never a penny piece to spare (though he did not much care!)

Yet drab though it may externally appear, there were certain points about this life that give off fresh and interesting rays of light, catching the eye still after forty years; these, too, quite apart from the music itself. There is the poignant mixture of success and failure, of worldwide fame won early, followed by an astonishing neglect, of the splitting of the musical world into two parties, those pundits who first encouraged him falling away after the first years. The very success was contributory to the failure, for all through we are aware of a tragic persistence of the necessity to write more and more music, some of it to have but a short span of life and the rest of it to last, through its sheer melodic charm, long after he could be aware of its vitality. There is the same fantastic disproportion that has assailed so many composers, between the quantity of labour given and the quantity of reward received, the toil never stinted in a willing and optimistic struggle to extract a bare living out of the social musical machine. Most extraordinary of all is the fact that the man who was hailed by his own people as 'the musical prophet of Africa' should come not from Africa (he did not even visit it) or from the Americas, but from a working-class neighbourhood in a large Surrey town near London. The problem of his colour, which he himself accepted with a natural simplicity, was never allowed to remain quiescent, but recurred in various forms throughout his life: gradually, it became an absorbing interest to Coleridge-Taylor, and great hopes blossomed in him for the future of the African races, only to be crushed by failures, like the one that attended his *Symphonic Variations on an African Air* (Op. 63), and a few years later by his early death.

A Doubtful Start

The town of Croydon, Surrey, in 1875 was perhaps even a less promising seeding-ground for a composer of partly African blood than the village of Nelahozeves on the Moldau was thirty-four years before for the Bohemian Dvořák. The town gave no glimmer of light on the dark world of English music in the mid-nineteenth century, though more than one famous composer was born there. There was little musical activity in the restricted social life of Croydon, and indeed there was a similar lack of musical intention in the mind of Daniel Hughes Taylor when, soon after Samuel Coleridge's birth, he left Red Lion Square, off Holborn, to take up a post in Croydon. Daniel Hughes Taylor was a West African negro educated at Freetown, Sierra Leone, and subsequently at Taunton College and University College, London. He studied medicine with some success, early becoming M.R.C.S. and L.R.C.P., and seems to have done well as assistant to a Croydon doctor. But on taking over the full practice he failed to keep it up and, faced by ruin, returned to West Africa and passed out of his son's life completely. Henceforth the English mother (Alice Hare) and her dark baby were dependent upon a farrier named Holman and his wife, who, out of fondness, gave the child a half-size violin at the age of five.

Chance and the kindliness of human nature played a very large part in Samuel's life at this next stage. Joseph Beckwith, then conductor of the Croydon Theatre (and father of Arthur Beckwith, later a famous violinist who led orchestras for Coleridge-Taylor), overheard the youngster playing and took him up, putting him in for soirées, 'at homes', and the like at a tender age. John Drage, headmaster of the elementary school that the boy attended, put him into touch with Colonel Walters (then Mr), the honorary choirmaster of St George's Presbyterian Church, Croydon. A narrow alley-way was opened, but it showed light at the end: the boy both sang and played. Eventually Walters paid the way for his entrance into the Royal College of Music, out of a purse that he has himself said was not wealthy.

The Royal College

Coleridge-Taylor (the hyphen was his own, for he was christened after the poet, by inversion) studied piano with Algernon Ashton (that most indurated writer of letters to the newspapers) and violin, working also with Charles Wood and Walter Parratt, who could not speak well of him. He wrote for violin, too, and eventually took composition, under Stanford, as his first study. He leapt at the composition fence and published anthems, keeping up his piano-playing as well. Stanford, to a point, took to him, but there were racial elements alien to the Irishman, which later became stronger. Yet we have to thank Stanford for the chance given to *Hiawatha's Wedding Feast* and for introducing the *Clarinet Quintet* to Joachim, who played it in Berlin. *Quartets*, a *Quintet*, a *Nonet* appear among the early works, and also a *Symphony*, which caused some dissent between Stanford and the pupil, the latter by this time becoming known in the world outside the college precincts. Home conditions were simple, and a scholarship helped him but did not make life, even in those cheaper days, very comfortable.

I remember as a boy meeting my fellow-townsman, Coleridge-Taylor; he was a short, dark man, with charming manners and correct dress, and a dreamy look in his eyes as if he could see Hy-Brasil. With a baton in his hand he was concerned only with how the music sounded, not with the personal traits of players; yet at the same time he had the curious radiant sympathy that can absorb all the oddities of the music-makers under him. There was an unusual combination of shyness and domination, quite removed from what has later been called an 'inferiority complex'. His colour must have caused difficulties in his school and student days, but it is possible, and indeed likely, that it was brought to his attention by the very kindness and sense of democracy of his fellow-students rather than by the actual hue of his complexion.

Professional Life

Launched from the nest on his own wings, Coleridge-Taylor, always devoted to composing and reading, and complaining later in life of his desire to read and contemplate, which the necessity to compose killed – a laziness he liked to dream about but never came remotely near to possessing – began teaching the violin at the Croydon Conservatoire of Music, a worthy but unimportant institution. A little later he began to take the string orchestra. There were recitals, of which the most important were those with Paul Laurence Dunbar, a coloured poet, himself of short life, who had already discovered the unknown negroid composer of Croydon.

A dramatic moment next arrived in this period of musical discovery. Edward Elgar refused an invitation to write a piece for Herbert Brewer's 1898 Three Choirs Festival at Gloucester and recommended Coleridge-Taylor as one who 'still wants recognition' and is 'far and away the cleverest fellow going amongst the young men'. Elgar here acted for Coleridge-Taylor in exactly the way Brahms did for Dvořák. The parallel is extremely close. The *Ballade in A minor* was the result, and the composer went to Gloucester to conduct it. The work was repeated at the Crystal Palace in November. He was now standing on his own feet as both composer and conductor.

Then came *Hiawatha's Wedding Feast*, that astonishing work for a man of twenty-three, of which the sheer originality of invention and the novelty of scoring have never failed (for one person at least) to strike an unfamiliar note on each performance heard again. A performance at the Royal College of Music, and publication (on no very generous terms), led to success unreached by any English composer then living. One thinks (as he did) of the early Mendelssohn, who, however, was brought up in sedate drawing rooms, not parlours, and of their not dissimilar ends through overwork.

After Fame has Arrived

Thereafter we find his life assailed with a series of distractions and commissions as regular and persistent as the perforations on a sheet of postage stamps. To detail them all would be to annotate a bibliography with personal details. On the whole it is a depressing list of works commissioned by depressing people, all of them demanding pieces of an over-tired period and an outworn fashion of music-making that at its best was never very good in itself. From 1898 to 1912 was a fruitful period for English music: English musicians, save for a few, did not discover this until a good twenty-four years later. Coleridge-Taylor, grinding like a slave at his daily jobs, had no time to find out about its existence. His mind was properly more attuned to his native continent and to the American offshoots of it.

There was conducting to be done at Croydon, at the Westmorland Festival, at Rochester, at the Handel Society; adjudicating at Welsh Eisteddfodau and many other Festivals, teaching of private pupils and as a Professor at Trinity College and the Guildhall School of Music (where he had to direct Gilbert and Sullivan); all this interspersed with public appearances as conductor in provincial and American performances of his own works, much of it resulting in small monetary reward and the debilitation of the composer. Great personal success came to Coleridge-Taylor, some of it despite and some of it because of his colour. He cannot but have enjoyed these recurrent acclamations, but he undoubtedly learnt early that they were over in a flash, and that next time – it might be to-morrow and could not be long delayed – he must win another success in order to live. Patronage came to him at the beginning, but it did not continue in the right way. For quiet contemplation, for sustained composition, there was too little time to fulfil too large a demand.

Dramatic Instincts

Near to the end of this long list of occasional works, which our fashions demanded should pretend to be of more lasting substance, occurs one that scored an echo of the popularity of *Hiawatha – A Tale of Old Japan*. Here can be found, in a more sclerotic form, some of that early picturesqueness that won instant response in the earlier work, but none of its humour, and a good deal more sentimentality. It is impossible not to notice the influence of Puccini on the musical style, though most likely it was unconscious. *A Tale of Old Japan* is theatrical and causes a wonder what this composer might have done in a country whose tradition was that of the opera house rather than of the choral society.

That Coleridge-Taylor took to the theatre is proved beyond doubt by the incidental music he wrote for Beerbohm Tree's productions of several of Stephen Phillips's blank-verse dramas and other stage pieces. He seems to have revelled in the theatre, and one legitimately feels that the cinema-set would have been no unfitting place for this vivid but well-schooled musical mind, which could course off into musical sketches at the sight of fields of flowering laurel.

Some Influences

The words of *Old Japan* were by Alfred Noyes, a poet who had attracted Coleridge-Taylor before. His literary taste seems to have been that of the uncritical but emotional appreciator. E. B. Browning's sonnets, the poems of Longfellow and Christina Rossetti, Allen Raine's *A Welsh Singer*, and works by even lesser authors appear as his special delights. They are representative of his personal life – blameless, even innocent, with no great cultural background but an instinctive eye and ear for beauty. His temperament had sweetness, his desires ranged (save in musical imagination) nowhere beyond the hearth. His humour was elementary but not elemental: it exactly fitted Longfellow's in being buoyant but not biting. At the same time the exotic called to his imagination; he might have justly quoted the later poet's words 'Chimborazo, Cotopaxi, stole my heart away', for he adored the odd-sounding names of Hiawatha's shadowy Redskins and Noyes's pasteboard Japanese. A deadly persistence of suburban environment starved this more ebullient side of his well-disciplined domesticity, and there is a depressing difference between Samuel Taylor Coleridge and Samuel Coleridge-Taylor in their visions of the stately pleasure dome in Xanadu.

The influence of Dvořák's music on Coleridge-Taylor's has been commonly noticed by critics; the pattern of their lives shows an equally curious similarity, especially in their humble origins, their successes in the choral world of England, and their respective visits to America. Dvořák took his native Bohemia with him on the boat when he crossed the Atlantic and re-established it there. To Coleridge-Taylor there was a strong racial call from the large population of his fellow-exiled Africans to compel him to go and almost to keep him there as a leader. His interest in the coloured races grew as his years increased, and he found an outlet for it among the coloured Americans who formed many Coleridge-Taylor Choirs to sing his music and who greeted him as an intellectual liberator of their kind. On this subject, the sincere but calmly-spoken composer could become passionate: we see it in a letter to a local newspaper of 1912, where his prose glows with the brilliant vividness of the *Wedding Feast* and an intensity of feeling seldom allowed by him to appear in his music. Without undue speculation – a profitless task, and indeed an unending one for any person interested in the biographies of the many composers who have died around their fortieth year – one may feel herein that the life of Coleridge-Taylor as we have it to-day was but the first chapter, the preparatory prelude, for a greater central act to come, when all his experience might have led a newly-found inspiration to a national music only so far hinted at in the extant works as a desire and an ideal. The past can show that neither London nor Vienna has taken enough trouble about her young men of genius, especially her composers. Coleridge-Taylor, worn out with ephemeral work in an unsympathetic climate at thirty-seven years of age, is but one more victim of an unthinking and undesigned system of life to add to the list.

AARON COPLAND

B. 1900

W. R. ANDERSON

Probing for Native Roots

Sometimes the effort to free themselves from 'classical' influences, or foreignly current ones, has brought distortion to the music of composers in the younger nations. Lacking traditions, a man may spend himself in reactions, including that against what he may deem 'reactionary trends'. Or, seeking to make the best of all worlds, he may lack the strength or scope for that, failing to fill his chequerwork with personality or piquant taste.

The American composer Roger Sessions thought that his brethren 'are dreaming of an entirely different music – a music that derives its power from forms beautiful and significant by virtue of inherent musical weight rather than intensity of utterance; a music whose personality and self-sufficiency preclude the exotic; which takes its impulses from the realities of a passionate logic; which in the freshness of its moods is the reverse of ironic, and in its very aloofness from the concrete preoccupations of life, strives to contribute from design a vision of colour and harmony.'

No one composer can safely speak for others; but in such musings as these we can pick out some qualities, both positive and negative, of a good deal of American writing in the last quarter century, since the older attractions of the Indian and Negro idioms ceased to have much potency. We are of course seeking the roots of music that is deliberately 'American' – nationalistic in some sense – rather than that which, deliberately or not, drew sustenance from Impressionism, from Stravinsky or Schönberg or Hindemith.

Many composers were caught (the best of them but momentarily) in the specious snare of jazz. Gershwin's success misled some, both abler and less able men. This influence touched but did not mar the career of Aaron Copland, a native of Brooklyn, who was born in the last year of the old century.

An Enterprising Immigrant

When the family, of Jewish race, came to America, its name was Kaplan. The authorities who received the immigrants wrongly took down the name as 'Copland', and thus it stayed. Aaron has always had a gift of words as well as of notes. In a book entitled *Our New Music* he has described himself as growing up in a not particularly musical family. He went to the ordinary elementary school, and then a Boys' High School. His sister was his first piano teacher, and he also had lessons from Leopold Wolfson, Victor Wittgenstein, and Clarence Adler. Starting the piano at thirteen, he soon wanted to compose. From about seventeen to twenty-one he worked under Rubin Goldmark (1872–1936), a well-known figure in American music, who had been a pupil of Dvořák. He was the nephew of that Karl Goldmark whose opera *The Queen of Sheba* had a good deal of European success.

Copland had the good fortune to be the first American to enter the music school at Fontainebleau, in 1921. He next studied with Nadia Boulanger, at Paris – a teacher who guided Roy Harris also and influenced other American composers. Before returning to the States in 1924 Copland worked at piano-playing for a time with Ricardo Viñes. This was during the time when French music, especially impressionism and the iconoclasms that followed, were clashing influences in Paris, that centre of artistic excitements. The spirit of Debussy was strong in America until a period after World War I, when the mounting European revolt of various mid-European 'extremists' begun to tell more keenly upon the constitution of American composers.

Finding the Focus

Copland, writing freely upon both ruled and unruled paper, began to explore and explain possibilities and to experiment in various styles. An early product of his return home was a *Symphony* for organ and orchestra, remodelled (discarding the organ) ten years later and played by Kussevitzky: a work scarcely standing for its composer's best thought and power, in either of its forms, though hailed by one critic as 'unquestionably pagan, undeniably exciting'.

Copland had for some time to support himself by various kinds of more or less hack work: one way was by playing at summer resorts. In 1925 he was granted one of the Guggenheim Memorial Fellowships, which enable artists to work without having, for a time at least, to worry about daily bread.

It was with works like *Music for the Theatre* and the *Piano Concerto*, in the mid-twenties, that dangerous time when so many young composers went to shipwreck, that Copland seemed to be finding a surer touch and a sharper focus of unity. His jazz period did not spoil him. Few composers have handled this pitchy material so ably.

The *Music for Theatre*, requested by the League of Composers, was begun at the famous MacDowell Colony, at Peterboro, New Hampshire* – the admirable practical memorial that, scattering log cabins through a wood, enables artistic workers to spend a summer in as much privacy as they wish.

Copland has shown an adaptable spirit in writing for various small forces. The *Theatre Music*, for example, can be played by a minimum of eighteen. This work represented the composer at the festival of the International Society for Contemporary Music, Frankfurt, 1927. The Society also chose a Copland work for its Amsterdam meeting of 1933 – the *Variations for Piano* – and another in 1938, this time the gay impression of a dance, *El Salon Mexico*. There has scarcely been anything so full of gusto since Chabrier's *España* days.

Besides a period of jazz rhythms, and besides his later astringent harmonies, there is in Copland a Hebraic element (notable in the *Vitebsk Trio*). Here is a lyricism, sometimes with the characteristic plaintive, even wailing, note that forms, for the foreigner, one of the attractive qualities in his art.

He may be said to have had several 'periods', from the three jazz years, 1925-8, to the more advanced modernism of the next six or seven years. The dates suggest what the British listener often notices: that fashions reach (or, at least, flourish in) the United States some time after their impact upon England's shores.

Exploring Many Avenues

During the last dozen years Copland has been extremely active in writing music that in one way or another may fairly be called popular: he has sought to make bridges between the man-in-the-street and the musician-in-the-ivory-tower. He has also been busy lecturing, doing occasional special teaching (as at Harvard and at the Berkshire Music Centre), taking a prominent part in running concerts and

* See MacDowell, *The Music Masters*, Vol. III.

festivals, in the League of Composers and in the American Composers' Alliance, a protective organization that he founded in 1937. He has written a couple of books, *What to Listen for in Music* and *Our New Music*, as well as many magazine articles.

He has explored *Music for Radio*, a piece with that title showing an agreeable blend of rhythmic piquancies with rather folky restfulness, diversified with more pretentious and less impressive passages. This was commissioned in 1936 by the Columbia Broadcasting System especially for performance on the air and is, as the composer put it, 'indicative of a desire on the part of so-called modern composers to bridge the gap between themselves and the public through a simplification of style'. Radio listeners were asked to suggest a title for the piece, and while none was entirely satisfactory, *Saga of the Prairie* was accepted. It emphasized, says Copland, a certain frontier atmosphere in the work. This quality has become one of the sought-after sentiments in much American music.

Copland had just before this written an opera for High School performance, *The Second Hurricane*. He shows, we notice, the practical spirit that Hindemith pleaded for when he asked that more *Gebrauchsmusik* should be written – music for workaday use. There is probably, too, something of the familiar Jewish adaptability and (if the term be understood in no pejorative sense) business capacity in Copland's willingness to turn his hand to the admittedly beneficent work of trying to bring more of the intelligent public into closer touch with contemporary composition. To this end has been directed much of his writing and lecturing, the latter activity having taken him into the New School for Social Research; for he has shown an interest in proletarian ideas: he became a vice-president of the Workers' Music Association of England.

Valuable 'Popularizing'

Perhaps his best known piece in this country is his *Outdoor Overture*, the result of a plea by a school Principal for something for his students' orchestra, a piece 'rather optimistic in tone, which would have a definite appeal to adolescent youth'.

His quick response to outward stimuli is a characteristic element in Copland. Such moving forces are apt, in the U.S.A., to be more frequent, and perhaps more potent, than they are here. His *Lincoln Portrait* was written in 1942 at the suggestion of the conductor

Kostelanetz, who wished for music glorifying the American past and present. The piece, which incorporated two ballads of Lincoln's time (one is *Camptown Races*), suggests in its three sections the sense of fatality around the President and the spirit of his times; and in the last part an orator enters, reading extracts from Lincoln's own words.

Such commissions, and prize contests, have often stimulated composers during the present century in America. As far back as 1932 the National Broadcasting Company offered 10,000 dollars in prizes, when 573 works were submitted. Then there have been commissions either to write brief pieces for gramophone production (as Roy Harris has done) or longer ones for broadcasting. Besides Copland, composers who have written for this last-named purpose have included Still, Bennett, and Gruenberg. The opportunity of hearing new works in performance, in these ways, has been of great benefit to many an American composer. In 1944 Copland won a Pulitzer prize for the ballet *Appalachian Spring*, commissioned for the dancer Martha Graham by the Elizabeth Sprague Coolidge Foundation. This, which some think the most poetic and mature of the works produced by Copland during a quarter century of high activity, paints the scene that Martha Graham's programme note describes thus: 'Part and parcel of our lives is that moment of the Pennsylvania Spring when there was "a garden eastward in Eden". Spring was celebrated by a man and a woman building a house with joy and love and prayer; by a revivalist and his followers in their shouts of exaltation; by a pioneering woman with her dreams of the Promised Land.'

In the interpretation of the strong roots of American life are interwoven these elements of religion, more or less primitive, of the horizon-stretching land, of the diverse toils and amusements of pioneers and of the meaning of modern sophistication – if that can at all be interpreted in art.

Speaking for the Time-Spirit

The critic David Hall has expressed the idea that *Appalachian Spring* synthesizes a number of elements in Copland's idiom, putting his feeling thus: 'The superb opening and closing pages, evocative of the American landscape and limitless open spaces, are Copland the tone-poet of *Quiet City* and the slow passages of *Music for the Theatre* and the *Lincoln Portrait*. The jagged figure of the first allegro and the restless rhythms of the bride's dance recall the more severe and abstract aspects of the composer's music, in the *Short Symphony* and the piano *Variations*. The wonderful square-dance sequence for the revivalist and the beautiful variations on the Shaker tune, *The Gift to be Simple*, bring us the Copland who has endeared himself most to the American public at large – the Copland of the cowboy ballets *Billy the Kid* and *Rodeo*, and of the *Outdoor Overture*.'

In 1944 he received yet another commission, to write a symphony for the Kussevitzky Foundation, founded by the famous conductor in memory of his wife. Copland earlier wrote a forty-minute score for the cinema showing of Steinbeck's *Mice and Men*. *Quiet City*, referred to above, was written for oboe, trumpet, and strings, to illustrate a scene in a play by Irwin Shaw, 'a realistic fantasy concerning the night thoughts of many different kinds of people in a quiet city' (1941). Through another connexion with men of the theatre he was commissioned by the playwright Clifford Odets to write a three-movement *Piano Sonata*. Then there is music for a documentary film *The City* and for *North Star*. Thus runs the prolific muse of a man who in his first twenty-five years of composing (1920–45) produced nearly sixty works and seemed likely to continue thus in his lively sympathy with the flow of events. Yet there appears to have been some loss in the later work of this highly prolific 'Dean of American Composers': not everyone feels that his diversity of styles wears well. There had been in his *Third Symphony* and in the opera *The Tender Land*, a sense of a rather dogged stretching of the attractive Semitic sensibility; but the former seems to be regarded by many judges as perhaps the best of Copland's extended works. The opera, commissioned by Rodgers and Hammerstein, is of a folky nature – about the lives of an isolated rural family in the West. It seems to have lacked the vital sense of the stage, but was well received by the press. It may be that Copland, like nearly all the composers who were rightly encouraged in early experiments during a not very critical or settled period of art-history, tended to live too much in his individual and often very attractive world of mannerism and fancy. Yet, in mid-century there is still time for further fresh developments, for which Copland has so far been notable.

ERNST VON DOHNÁNYI

B. 1877

RALPH W. WOOD

Place – on Map, in Life

The category of musicians in which E. von Dohnányi is to be placed, of which indeed he will be a very perfect and clear-cut specimen, is one that astounds us, if we give any thought to the matter, by its simultaneous ordinariness and mystery.

He was born on 27 July 1877. His birthplace, in those days of the Empire, you would have called Pressburg or Poszony according as you were a native of Austria or of Hungary, the two countries on whose frontier it lay. It became, when the creation of Czechoslovakia took a bite out of that vicinity in 1918, Bratislava. Through his infancy and boyhood, while he was a student and on until the time when, after he was an established figure in the musical world, Hungarian nationalism also had been brought to the fore in that world (by the efforts, above all, of such men as Bartók and Kodály), to the Hungarian patronymic of Dohnányi were liable to be added, in at any rate most parts of that world, the German labels 'Ernst von'. Increasingly, however, after the said renaissance his 'Ernst' has tended to be replaced by 'Ernö'. To anyone casting an eye back over the career of this musician who emerged from a second World War on the threshold of seventy, those variables of nomenclature denote a material situation, an environment (shall we put it?) in time as well as in place, and of course mental as well as physical, that – that can, at least, not be ignored. ... In August 1914 Dohnányi was a piano professor in the Berlin Hochschule; in 1916 he took up a similar post in Budapest, which he retained in 1919. Artists were, to anticipate our own term, 'in a reserved occupation'. In 1940 Dohnányi (aet. 63) was Director of the Budapest Hochschule (Royal Academy of Music), President and conductor of the Budapest Philharmonic Society, Music Director of the Hungarian Broadcasting Service, and so on and so on; 1945, and the liberation, found him 'over the border', the fugitive that so notorious a collaborationist, as he had proved himself, was bound to be.... These, however, are not matters of the blended ordinariness and mystery referred to above.

Training

'Ordinary', for one who later on was to qualify for space in musical encyclopedias, his beginnings must with emphasis be called. His father, Friedrich von Dohnányi, was a professor of mathematics at the Pressburg Gymnasium (loosely, the equivalent of an English secondary school) and an amateur cellist. His own general education was received at the Pressburg Gymnasium, whilst, having already been given some musical tuition by his father, he went from the age of eight for piano lessons to Carl Forstner (the then organist of the cathedral at Pressburg). Under Forstner, too, he presently studied harmony. To complete the picture, to ensure future historians their grounds for declaring his career both ordinary and mystifying, he during this period composed profusely – a *String Sextet*, three *String Quartets*, *Piano Sonatas*, songs, and other works. When one says 'during this period', one means until his departure from Pressburg in 1894 for Budapest and a more intensive musical training.

He was at the Budapest Royal Academy of Music (as it then was) for three years, a pupil of Stephan Thomán for piano and Hans Koessler for composition. (Koessler, it will be remembered, also taught Bartók and Kodály.) This brought him to the verge of twenty. The July and August of 1897 found him taking a few lessons, having graduated from the Academy, with the celebrated pianist, Eugen d'Albert. In that year had been performed a *Symphony in F*, which together with an overture, *Zrinyi* (Op. 2), had in 1896 won him the King's prize, a substantial cash award. The *Piano Quintet* in C minor (Op. 1), reckoned nowadays to be one of his best works, dates from 1893!

The Great Pianist

Unlike Rachmaninov, in some ways a similar figure though – paradoxically, in this connexion – perhaps a slightly more noteworthy one as a composer, Dohnányi early in life gave up being an 'international celebrity' as a virtuoso pianist. For many folk of even only one generation after his it must be enlightening, almost startling, to read about him in, say, *Grove's Dictionary* – where the inevitable danger, 'tween editions and even despite supplementary volumes, of out-of-date-ness when dealing with someone still above ground involves, in this instance, a conceivably compensating freshness of reaction to a phenomenon contemporary at the time of writing, though now so far from being so, and of such superficial or else unrecognized results, that it can be close to oblivion. *Grove* tells us that he was already a 'pianist of high attainment' when he took that brief finishing course with d'Albert. It relates that upon his début, at Berlin in October the same year, he was an immediate and tremendous success; that both there and at Vienna (spring 1898, towards the end of a tour that had included Cologne, Dresden, Frankfurt) he won very great prestige. It informs us, in a telling present indicative, that his technical prowess as a pianist is indeed formidable; it speaks in addition of 'breadth of phrasing' and of 'command of tone-gradation' and 'exquisite beauty of tone', which apparently are 'such as to satisfy the most exacting lover of classical and modern music', and 'in both', it states, 'an intensely poetical nature is revealed'. This is a vividness of impression that no after-the-event reconstruction, and no historical review, however it might have been seasoned with a sense of perspective, could quite have achieved. One can only compare to it the remarks of a fellow-Hungarian who grew up within the orbit of his pianism's spell. 'Everyone', this younger pianist recently said, ' – Everyone went to him. He was the master of us all.' If there can be such a thing as a natural, a born pianist – Dohnányi was that thing. Apparently he even to some extent neglected, or gave the impression of neglecting, practice; he didn't bother; and in a sense he doesn't seem to have needed to bother, so instinctive and complete were both his physical and his mental aptitudes. From the very first he played only Mozart, Beethoven, Schubert, and Brahms (nothing so far from the apostolic succession of classicism as, say, Chopin). And his readings were magistral. Hearing them one knew that what one heard was absolutely right.

So here we have the vision of the triumphant young maestro, with already every compartment of his portfolio crammed with compositions, bringing all Europe to his feet by his apparently quite outstanding piano-playing, England as well as the Continent (début at a Richter concert at the Queen's Hall, London, 24 October 1898 – Beethoven's G major concerto) – not to speak of the New World (frequent and successful tours there; first in 1899, second 1900–1).

Whether or not such a vision of his virtuosoship is exaggerated, certainly the memory of it has very much dispersed in the succeeding fifty years. Perhaps it is simply because he did choose to bring that part of his career to so early an end. Following the example of Busoni, he became a member of a teaching staff, at – in his instance – the Berlin Hochschule. But he did not, like Busoni, break out during or after that phase into any resumption of his virtuoso-wanderings. On the contrary, in 1916, after ten years of teaching (seven of them as Professor) at the Berlin Hochschule, he returned to Budapest to take up a professorship at the Hochschule there. In 1919 he became Director, head of the staff in the place where twenty-two years before he had made so magnificent an end of his pupilage.

Worldly Success

However, he only held that directorship for a short period in those extremely troublous times, losing it to Hubay in a matter of months. But in fact the political upheavals and civil strife of the day did not prove disastrous to him, any more than did – up to its dénouement – the cataclysm of twenty years later. And it must be said that Hubay, choice of the reactionaries to supplant the representative of briefly ascendant youth, behaved very well indeed. With really a minimum of interruption Dohnányi's period of piano teaching merged into the one of administrative appointments and high official recognitions. Also into the one of conducting. For in 1919–20 began his permanent conductorship of the Budapest Philharmonic orchestra, and presidency of the Society. His *The Tower of Voivod*, an opera that, although not really 'nationalistic' in the actual style of its music, paid so much homage to the growing fashion of the period as to be based on a Hungarian folk-ballad, was produced with success in Budapest on 18 March 1922. His standing was such that in 1927 on his fiftieth birthday he was awarded a grant from the State of 50,000 pengoes – in those days a splendidly substantial gift. Already, in 1924, he had received from an appreciative government the title of Superior Councillor of State. As for globe-trotting, resume that activity he at length did – but no longer as a pianist. He toured as a guest-conductor with many orchestras in both Europe and America (in 1925, for instance, he directed concerts of the State Symphony Orchestra in New York).

The 50,000 pengoes grant for his fiftieth birthday was paralleled by a like sum that he received in consideration of a *Mass* for the inauguration of the cathedral at Szeged, where he was created a Mus. Doc. honoris causa, 1930. Another honoris causa doctorate had been that of philosophy at the University of Kolozsvár, in 1922. From 1931 onwards he held the directorship at the Hungarian Broadcasting Service, and after Hubay's retirement in 1934 he for a second time became head of the Academy of Music.

Compositions

But this man has composed. His Op. 1 was admired, and admired strongly, by Brahms – who was not given much to admiration. It had been played at Vienna in 1893 and appeared in 1895 at Budapest. All his early reputation as a composer really rested on chamber and piano works, although a *Piano Concerto* (Op. 5) in 1899 won the Bösendorfer prize. But later came other concertos, the *Suite in F sharp minor* for orchestra (Op. 19), the *Variations on a Nursery Song* for piano and orchestra (Op. 25). *The Veil of Pierrette*, a 'pantomime' in three scenes to a text by Schnitzler and a one-act comic opera, entitled *Tante Simona*, were produced in Dresden, in 1910 and 1912 respectively. A comic opera, *The Tenor* (with a virtuoso part for that voice), came after *The Tower of Voivod*. There were fairly well-known *Sonatas* for violin and piano and cello and piano, more chamber music – including another *Piano Quintet* (Op. 26) – and of course a good deal for piano solo (e.g. the *Four Rhapsodies*, Op. 11, *Five Humoreskes*, Op. 17, and *Ruralia Hungarica*, Op. 32).

The list, though not a long one as such lists go, is largely made up of substantial scores. So far as the consumption of his time and energies is concerned it is essential to remark that, as well as being pianist, teacher, holder of exalted positions, and conductor, he has composed. This, of course, is where the matter of mystery arises. It is simply the mystery of barrenness unaware of itself; and of futile talent and fertile genius almost indistinguishable in their early prognostics. It is a mystery so often re-embodied as to be itself a commonplace, just like every one of its products.

Perhaps the oddest, conceivably even the most important, fact to be chronicled of Dohnányi is that Béla Bartók, about to do the conventional thing and go to the Vienna conservatoire to be trained, went instead to the conservatoire at Budapest – a momentous step indeed – by his, Dohnányi's, persuasion.

PAUL DUKAS

1865–1933

EDWARD LOCKSPEISER

Integrity and Devotion

Dukas's career is one of the least spectacular among those of the composers of his period. His evolution was slow, his works were few. By nature he was retiring, and of that philosophical turn of mind intent less upon action than upon pondering an aesthetic problem in its infinity of aspects; thus, inevitably, he approached creation with diffidence. Moreover, Dukas was a critic and a remarkable teacher as well as a composer, and many of his finest efforts were devoted to the encouragement of his talented pupils, among them the contemporary French composers Elsa Barraine and Olivier Messiaen.

The available biographical facts of Dukas's career show his exemplary integrity. Born of a Jewish family in Paris on 1 October 1865, he entered the Paris Conservatoire at an early age and there studied composition in the class of Ernest Guiraud. At this time he became intimately associated with his fellow-student Debussy. Among his distinctions were a first prize for counterpoint and a second Prix de Rome, which he won in 1888 with his cantata *Valléda*. Dukas then withdrew from a conventional scholastic career and over several years devoted himself to a study of the masterpieces of Bach, Beethoven, and Mozart. Two early works were the overtures *King Lear* and *Goetz von Berlichingen*. They were not performed publicly and were later suppressed. In 1892 a third overture, *Polyeucte*, on the tragedy of Corneille, was performed in Paris by Charles Lamoureux. A Wagnerian influence is noticeable in this work, as in so many French works of this period, yet the solid and convincing construction show also a mind bent on the classical ideal. In 1896 his *Symphony in C major*, dedicated to Paul Vidal, was given at the Concerts de l'Opéra conducted by Vidal, and in 1897 the first performance was given at the Société Nationale in Paris of his famous *Scherzo for Orchestra*, inspired by Goethe's ballad *The Sorcerer's Apprentice*. Two important works for piano appeared during the following decade – the *Sonata* in 1901, dedicated to Saint-Saëns, and the *Variations on a Theme of Rameau* in 1903. They were first played in Paris by a famous pianist of those days. Édouard Risler. In May 1907 five years after the production of Debussy's *Pelléas et Mélisande*, Dukas's only opera *Ariane et Barbe-Bleue*, based on another play of Maeterlinck, was produced at the Paris Opéra Comique. Thereafter he produced only one important work, the choreographic poem *La Péri* written on a scenario by himself and produced by the Russian dancer Trouhanova in 1913. Dukas died in Paris from a heart attack on 18 May 1935, the very date of the first performance of *L'Apprenti Sorcier* forty-two years earlier.

Music and Humanity

It is always a moving experience to see the admiration and respect of the more discerning minds among the musical public for an artist who has not quite fulfilled his mission. Perhaps it is the knowledge that the values of success, or for that matter of failure, can never be finite; that fulfilment for the creative artist on the rare occasions when it is nearly complete – it can never be entirely complete – must leave a fearful void, hardly less agonizing than the frustration of the imaginative though unproductive artist; perhaps it is these purely human aspects of a composer's work that will all the more endear his achievement to his fellow musicians. One is grateful that a composer of music is after all human. And should his entire achievement turn out in the end to be relatively small and incomplete, how high-minded is such a musician to renounce success for the untiring pursuit of an ideal, even though it remains undefined at the time of his death.

Such reflections are prompted by a perusal of the handsome memorial tribute to Paul Dukas published by *La Revue Musicale* shortly after his death in 1935. For the last twenty years of his life Dukas's severe self-criticism as a composer had condemned him to silence and to seek a reflection of his ideals in the efforts of his many talented pupils. As we have seen, even during his more fertile years his completed works had been few. Yet the distinguished men of letters and musicians from many countries who paid homage to Dukas in this memorial volume were unanimous in declaring his art to have been a vital and original contribution. The young Olivier Messiaen considered the philosophical symbolism of *Ariane et Barbe-Bleue* to have been inspired by the example of John the Baptist. Sir Thomas Beecham held *Ariane* to be one of the finest lyrical dramas of our time and proposed to produce it without delay (which he did, in the pre-war years at Covent Garden, with memorable success). Paul Valéry recognized the nobility and integrity of a rare philosophical spirit in music, who owed as much to Descartes and Schopenhauer as to Rameau, Beethoven, and Wagner. The virtuosity of Dukas, he observed, *'n'était point le fruit d'une quantité d'exercices tant que la récompense d'une méditation perpétuelle des moyens de la musique avec son objet.'*

A Way of his Own

Objet in this sense apparently means aim, and it was precisely the aim of creative activity that was always likely to be in doubt in Dukas's mind. As a youth he was a fellow-student of Debussy, his senior by three years, in the class of Ernest Guiraud at the Paris Conservatoire. But although during this period of his development he was closely associated with Debussy in a personal way, sharing his attractions to the Symbolist poets, and in particular to Maeterlinck, he remained unaffected by either the spell of the new Debussyan art or the lyrical grace (deriving from Massenet) of his master Ernest Guiraud. He was to find a way of his own. The early symphonic poems of Richard Strauss made the first important impact, the result of which was *L'Apprenti Sorcier* of 1897. Thereafter, the principal influence, often disguised or absorbed in an individual manner, seems to have been Beethoven – the Beethoven of the late sonatas and the *Diabelli Variations*.

Beethoven and Variations

The eternal problems of form and content are now his main concern and it is significant that the principal works of Dukas show some remarkable examples of the variation form. The variations in Act 2 of *Ariane et Barbe-Bleue*, prophetic of the variation form used for dramatic purposes by Alban Berg and Benjamin Britten, the vast Beethovenian *Variations sur un Thème de Rameau*, not to speak of the more tentative use of the variation form in *L'Apprenti Sorcier* – these provide an interesting clue to the Dukas complex mind, which could never accept the obvious and must surely have been attracted to the variation form precisely because it is the form best calculated to display an imaginative infinity of possibilities. This form is perhaps the simplest of musical structures in the scholastic sense though, paradoxically speaking, it can also be the most complex. Certain it is that, in the hands of a Dukas, a Delius, or a Mahler, it is the philosophical structure *par excellence*. Even in the symphonic poem of oriental character *La Péri*, which might have been modelled on the Venusberg music from *Tannhäuser*, a variation structure was probably at the source of the composer's inspiration.

There is another clue to Dukas's personality, to which I have already alluded, but it may be defined more precisely. With the performance of *L'Apprenti Sorcier* in 1897 Dukas was at once established in public favour. The public success of a work of Strauss himself had never been more striking. The composer, recognizing the success for what it was worth, resolved not to exploit it for reasons of personal vanity, but on the contrary to flee from it in search of ... well, in search of what? Beethoven probably, Beethoven as he was interpreted to the French mind by César Franck, the middle-period Beethoven as he is reflected in the huge and somewhat recondite E flat minor *Piano Sonata*, the work that immediately follows *L'Apprenti Sorcier*. The first movement of this seldom heard work is solidly built out of two contrasted themes. The andante owes much of its serenity to discreet re-iterations of the initial theme in the form of variations, and the impetuous Beethovenian scherzo has a bridge passage in which Dukas shows himself to be a master of the fugue. In the immense finale, forming more than a third of the entire work, Beethoven seems to have joined hands with Franck and Liszt.

More developed and assured are the monumental *Rameau Variations* in which Dukas infuses the conventional form with a new and powerful spirit, while the opera *Ariane et Barbe-Bleue* shows a masterly architectural sense and a brilliant use of the orchestra. Wagner was again a powerful influence here, as in his other orchestral or dramatic works, yet looking at Dukas's art as a whole, one is left with the impression that his main inspiration came from Beethoven. Probably his music is interesting to us to-day chiefly because it shows the hidden though binding chain between the musical civilizations of France and Germany. We have seen this chain before – in Berlioz, in Franck, in the music criticism of Romain Rolland of course, but it seems especially apparent in Dukas. It appears, too, that ultimately the art of Dukas displays the assimilation of Beethoven in French musical thought in much the same way as the art of Debussy, extending over a much wider sphere, illustrates the assimilation of Wagner. These are matters, however, on which one cannot be dogmatic; they cannot be more than the seeds of an aesthetic conception that, with time, may grow or wither. But Dukas may well have had some such conception himself. '*Il faut savoir beaucoup; et faire de la musique avec ce qu'on ne sait pas*', this philosopher among musicians once confessed. And, almost echoing thoughts of Beethoven himself, '*La véritable force de l'originalité est dans l'inconscience*'.

MANUEL DE FALLA

1876–1946

RALPH W. WOOD

Childhood and Training

In the year 1785 Haydn was asked by the Chapter of the cathedral at Cadiz for a piece of instrumental music suitable to be performed on Good Friday. He responded with *The Seven Words of our Saviour on the Cross*, a work for orchestra, though he later arranged it for two violins, viola, and bass, and later still for solo voices, chorus, and orchestra. Performances of *The Seven Words* became traditional annual ceremonies at Cadiz, but in 1888 it was done there in an arrangement hardly envisaged by the composer, a transcription for piano duet, in which form it was played by a Señora Falla and her eleven-year-old son.

Manuel María de Falla y Matheu, who when he died in November 1946 had long been the revered doyen of Spanish composers, was born almost exactly seventy years earlier (23 November 1876) in Cadiz. Both his parents were natives of that city, though the origin of the father's family was in the south of Spain, Andalusia, and of the mother's in the north-east, Catalonia. His first musical training was given to him by his mother, who was very well equipped for the task; she had herself received a thorough, all-round musical education, was a pianist of talent and had very wide knowledge and sympathies, covering both the classics and the modern schools. Other early teachers were Enrique Broca, well-known bandmaster, and Alejandro Odero, with both of whom the boy studied harmony. The duet presentation of *The Seven Words* seems to have been his first appearance in public.

He was still under fourteen when he got a first prize for piano playing at the Madrid Royal Conservatoire of Music. Only when he was seventeen did he for the first time hear a symphony orchestra. A little later still he encountered Wagner's music, a matter with him as with so many of an acquaintanceship developed at once into a passionate friendship that did not, however, prove undying.* At about the same time as that, he began a period of piano study at the Madrid Conservatoire under José Tragó. As late as 1905 it was that he won another piano-playing trophy, the 'Ortiz y Cusso' prize – a success, in a competition open to all Spanish pianists, that we are told was contrary to his own expectations.

Early Compositions

During those fourteen important years he was, of course, composing. In fact even earlier he had produced some small piano pieces. At the home of a Cadiz amateur named Viniegra he received opportunities both to hear and perform chamber music and, as time went on, to try over chamber works of his own. Apparently he was enabled in this circle to become familiar with much of the best of the chamber-music repertoire. Also, significantly enough, his interests began during this period to follow the northward trend by now characteristic of advanced Spanish musicians, to France. From Paris, by the early 1900s certainly, perhaps before, he was receiving the latest French compositions, which he was among the pioneers to make known, as a pianist, in Spain. Chiefly, too, owing to the lure of Paris, one gathers, it was that he presently expanded the field of his composing from piano pieces and chamber music to theatrical works. In what was perhaps a typical example of a clash between artistic preoccupations and the technique of mob success, precipitated as usual by financial needs, he tried to make money by turning out 'zarzuelas' (light operettas of the type peculiar to, and abundantly popular on, the Spanish stage). His first one was *Los Amores de la Inés*, which was produced in 1902 and was a complete failure. Another, *La Casa de Tócame Roque*, was never even produced (though Chueca – an eminent practitioner in the 'zarzuela' line – expressed much admiration for it). In fact, he raised no funds by this means for turning into a reality his dream of visiting Paris.

So by the end of 1904 Falla, aged twenty-eight, had behind him an

* In later life he was to declare: 'Of "Spanish" symphonic music very little can be said. It has been written in the German style and is a flat failure. "Der Fall Wagner" was the same in Spain as in other countries; a case of infatuation and frightful error, that might have been excusable in a land less endowed with musical wealth than Spain, but with us has been the cause of an all-too-manifest lethargy of our musical sense.'

era of solid musical activity – of piano playing, both solo and in chamber ensembles, and of composing. It is interesting to note that he ever afterwards declined to discuss, or even to acknowledge, not only the operettas that at the close of that era he wrote ostensibly in defiance of his own taste, but all the other music he had produced up to that point. Further light, too, must be considered to be thrown on the question of the operettas themselves by recorded remarks of his from a later date, besides light on Falla's mature personality as a musical historian, critic, theorist and idealist, roles that, as an enthusiast for nationalism and folk-music, he was not backward in assuming. After a typical contrasting of the folk-originated real Spanish characteristics in music with the methods of earlier Spanish composers, and the inevitable references to 'the ancient modes, those of the Liturgy and the Orient', he goes on: 'Our musicians ignored these sources ... and treated Spanish music in the Italian or German manner, being most successful in the Italian style because of the kinship of race and region. The sore point was, that they took over what was worst in Italy – the fearful, lamentable decadence of her music. From Monteverdi and his contemporaries they learned nothing, while enthusiastically aping Bellini and Donizetti. 'Twixt sheep and goat they chose the goat. The period of the "grand zarzuela" was an imitation of the Italian opera, often its superior, but after all only an imitation ... Chueca,' (1846–1908) 'whose style is the purest and most Spanish of any of our old musicians, pursued another path; he adapted foreign rhythms to Spanish music by "nationalizing" them so successfully ... that we moderns have been censured as "foreignized" because we avoid a rhythm whose origin is none the less wholly foreign. ...'

A Turning-Point

It was an era, too, as we have seen, of characteristically developing tastes and interests. Likewise an era of training. So far as that is concerned, the most important item has yet to be mentioned. For about three years, beginning in 1902, Falla took private lessons in composition with Felipe Pedrell. Those lessons, concurrent as they were with his futile attempts to make money by writing 'zarzuelas', must be reckoned to form the turning-point in his entire career. For it was certainly Pedrell who set Falla's eyes towards the ideal of truly Spanish music, based on folk-idioms (but avoiding direct quotation of folk-tunes), from which they never afterwards turned. It must be added that Falla proved himself an outstanding, indeed perhaps the only quite thorough and exact exponent of Pedrell's principles. Also, he imitated Pedrell in his actual study of Spanish folk-music, a subject upon which Falla came to be considered the greatest living authority.

In 1904 the Madrid Real Academia de Bellas Artes announced an open competition for a 'national opera'. And when the following year brought the declaration of the prize-winner it turned out to be *La Vida Breve*, by Manuel de Falla. This 'lyric drama' in two acts, with libretto by Carlos Fernandez-Shaw, is the earliest composition that Falla subsequently consented to recognize as his. It is clearly an outcome of his tuition by Pedrell; and, whatever its absolute value as music or as drama, it is generally accepted as embodying very strikingly the new, Pedrellian theories of Spanish national art.

After that success Falla was in Madrid for another two years, teaching the piano. And then he did go to France. One day in 1907 he took a week's excursion ticket to Paris. He only came back in 1914.

Paris

In Paris he was at once befriended by such men as Dukas, Debussy and Ravel. He was poor, making a scanty living for several years as a music-teacher, and combined devotion to a small circle of familiars with an otherwise retired existence. He was unceasingly alert and curious in all that concerned his art and was working, already with a characteristic slowness and self-criticalness, on compositions of whose existence his friends might chance to hear hints but of whose ultimate appearance they came to despair, so innumerable were the delays and rejections and restarts and shelvings caused by his difficulty in ever satisfying himself. He had brought with him one manuscript, dating from 1906, and through the good offices of Dukas and Debussy a Parisian publisher was at length found brave enough to accept it. Thus the *Quatre Pièces Espagnoles* appeared in 1909, the year of the death of Isaac Albéniz, to whom they were dedicated. They had been performed in public for the first time in 1908, by the well-known Spanish pianist Ricardo Viñes, friend of Granados and of Ravel, at a concert of the Société Nationale de Musique. And in 1909 Falla composed the *Trois Mélodies* (words by Théophile Gautier) that were issued in 1910. On just those two publications his standing as a composer had to be based up to the end of 1913. It seems to have been in

1909 that he began work on three pieces for piano and orchestra that gave him enormous trouble, three *Nocturnes* that in time became 'legendary' in his Paris circle by the inability of the composer to get any version of them through the sieve of his own fastidiousness.

As a concert pianist Falla only made his Paris début in October 1910, when in the first programme of modern Spanish music ever given in France (promoted by G. Jean-Aubry, as a memorial to Albéniz) he accompanied songs of his and played the *Pièces Espagnoles*. Seven months later, when Franz Liebich gave a concert of Spanish music, old and new, in London, Falla appeared there too, at the instance of Jean-Aubry, with the four piano pieces. It was at the conclusion of a concert-lecture given in Paris by Joaquin Nin and Jean-Aubry that the latter, who was to become so stout a friend and champion, first met Falla. He has left lively records of his first visual impressions of the composer – 'a small man, dark, full of nervous energy, with piercing eyes regarding one keenly from under an imposing forehead . . .'; and of Falla's conversation – 'while his brief, rare words gave me, from the start, the impression of a man at once passionate and meditative. . . . His talk would always breathe the same spirit, the same impassioned conviction, the same thirst for truth and the same sensibility. . . .'

Ironically enough, while he was in France Falla received a 'tempting offer from one of the most influential operatic concerns in Europe', by which he was to write Spanish operas of the accepted, conventional style, using libretti given to him. He refused. He also said 'no' to a suggestion that he should become a naturalized Frenchman, a step that was reckoned likely to make performances of his works in France come more readily.

La Vida Breve should, according to the terms of the Academy of Fine Arts competition, have been staged at the time of its winning that contest, but it was not. Its première took place at Nice, the Municipal Casino, in April 1913, with Lilian Grenville as Salud. It was a great success. Eight months later Marguerite Carré sang the same role at the Opéra Comique in Paris.

Return to Spain

We are now into 1914, a year doubly notable in Falla's career. First, it is the year of perhaps his most widely known and successful composition, the *Sept Chansons Populaires Espagnoles* for voice and piano. Secondly, a world war broke out, and he had to return to Spain.

So peculiarly bound up with the land of his birth, and with his almost unbroken residence within its frontiers, was his subsequent career that one is put to it to imagine on what lines that career would have developed had not the outside and, so far as he was concerned, fortuitous factor of the war caused his transfer at that point from Paris to Madrid.

His return in 1914 certainly had much to do with the birth at Madrid of the 'Sociedad Nacional de Musica'. For some time he travelled a good deal about the peninsula. In 1921 he settled down in Granada, where he so cherished his beautiful home and garden, in most romantic surroundings near the Alhambra, that only a second world war sufficed to uproot him.

The years 1914–18 were themselves for him years of much activity and of a rapidly expanding fame. *La Vida Breve* at last reached the stage of the country in whose national music it was, in a sense, such a landmark; it was produced at the Teatro de la Zarzuela, Madrid, in November 1915. Seven months before that, the Lara Theatre in Madrid had housed a performance of the opera, as it then was (with libretto by no less a man than Gregorio Martinez Sierra), *El Amor Brujo*. It was a failure. Subsequently Falla cut out almost all the words, enlarged the orchestration, and made a 'symphonic suite' of the thing. More or less in that form it was, and has since from time to time been, staged as a ballet. It was early on utilized by the famous Spanish gypsy dancer, Pastora Imperio. Of his other ballet, *El Sombrero de Tres Picos*, an early version was performed in Madrid in 1917, under the title of *El Corregidor y la Molinera*. For this too the 'book' was by Sierra, based on a 'novel' by Alarcon (early nineteenth century) taken from various earlier sources. (It is, in fact, the same story as that used by Hugo Wolf in his opera *Der Corregidor*.) This work was commissioned by Diaghilev, by whose company it was produced in its final form for the first time at the Alhambra Theatre, London, in July 1919.

Meanwhile, in 1915 Falla had actually finished those three pieces for piano and orchestra on which he had been toiling intermittently ever since 1909. They were now entitled *Noches en los Jardines de España* and received their première in 1916, in Madrid. Before very long they had reached Cadiz, Granada, San Sebastian, Barcelona, Paris, London, and

Geneva. London heard them for the first time in 1921, when the composer was at the piano.

From 1919 dates the *Fantasia Bética* for piano solo (dedicated to Artur Rubinstein). 'Bética' is the ancient name for 'Andalusian'. The year 1918-19 covered the writing of *Fuego Fatuo*, a comic opera based on music of Chopin – an oddity neither published nor performed. Further, in 1919 Falla began work on the puppet-opera, based on an episode in *Don Quixote*, *El Retablo de Maese Pedro*. In 1920 he wrote *Homenaje*, a piece '*pour le tombeau de Claude Debussy*', for guitar – an instrument for which he had immense respect and affection and that is here, in a work of deep emotional intent, treated *au grand sérieux*.

Final Phase

In Granada in 1922 he organized a folk-song festival; and it must have been soon afterwards that he founded the Orquesta Bética de Camera, which was conducted by his pupil Halffter. *El Retablo* received a première, in concert form, at Seville in March 1923, and first appeared on a stage the following July at Paris in the private theatre of the Princess Polignac. It quickly progressed to Bristol (five performances in 1924), New York (December 1925) and Zürich (1926). It reached the boards of the Paris Opéra-Comique in 1928. Concert performances had been given in southern Spain by the Orquesta Bética de Camera in 1925. This work, together with the *Concerto* composed between 1923 and 1926, illustrates a special interest that Falla conceived in the harpsichord. In 1924 *Psyché*, a poem by Jean-Aubry set for voice and small orchestra, made its escape into the world from that place from which escape was never easy for a piece of manuscript music, this composer's study. In 1927 emerged *A Córdoba*, a sonnet by Góngora set for voice and harp. The death of Falla's benefactor of old caused the appearance of the *Andante, pour le Tombeau de Paul Dukas*, for piano, in 1935. Begun in 1928, and still only 'virtually completed' more than ten years later, was a huge composition for solo, chorus, and orchestra, for which Falla himself wrote the text, based on M. Jacinto Verdaguer's Catalan poem *La Atlantida*. The work deals with Christopher Columbus's discovery of America. Just before World War II he was engaged also upon a suite for piano, *Pedrelliana*, an act of homage to the teacher whose decisive influence on his orientation as a creative artist he has avowed.

He officiated as conductor at a festival of his own works in the Salle Pleyel, Paris, in May 1930. There were also visits to London and Mallorca. But, especially after 1934, he was away from home very little indeed. The Civil War did not cause him to budge. In May 1938 he was made President of the Instituto de España that had been created under the Franco régime. He was unable, for health reasons, to go to Burgos for the inauguration, and so the Secretary of Education came to Granada to administer to him at home his oath of office. In October 1939, however, budge he did, and with a vengeance. He went to Alta Gracia, in Argentina, where he passed with his sister the remaining seven years of his life. His migration was marked by an appearance, that autumn of 1939, in Buenos Aires as conductor.

Falla never married and was to a large extent a solitary, but his life included notable friendships. At no time was he a regular teacher of composition, though he had various private pupils, among them not only Ernesto and Rodolfo Halffter, but also Joaquin Nin-Culmell and Adolf Salazar. With his pronounced Catholicism and his passion for folk-music, he blended scholarship and mysticism (both, perhaps, could be termed rather narrow) – as, indeed, the compositions on which he bestowed such pains, which he re-cast and shelved and reconsidered and polished so often and relinquished into public view with so much reluctance, well demonstrate.

ALEXANDER KONSTANTINOVICH GLAZUNOV

1865–1936

M. MONTAGU-NATHAN

A Waning Influence

It is extremely difficult to determine the present position of Glazunov in relation to the world's music, but much easier to decide the extent of the benefits he bestowed upon the music of Russia.

A composer whose symphonies number only one less than those of Beethoven might be expected to have made an important contribution to musical literature, and, one by one, as they made their appearance, they were heralded as such. But, like Hans Breitmann's 'barty' and Mr Wegg's perusal of Gibbon's *'Decline and Fall-off'* they have not 'very lately' been accorded much performance – orchestras having, as was intimated to Mr Boffin, been 'otherways employed'.

The symphonies have suffered at the hands of the recording companies a neglect that at first sight seems curious. This circumstance should not, however, be over-stressed, since the making of reasonably faithful records did not begin until Glazunov's symphonic labours were virtually at an end. He may be said to have missed, through an accident of date, this particular bus – a vehicle that so eminent a personage could hardly be expected to hail and pursue. His absence from this vehicle has had two results. These works do not now greatly interest such orchestral bodies as are engaged in recording and, in consequence, their music is not at the disposal of the vast public that derives a considerable measure of its musical pabulum from the gramophone. So much for Glazunov's influence on the musical world as a whole.

The 'Little Glinka'

His most important contribution to the music of Russia may be said to be that of having got born at the right moment (29 July 1865) into the most appropriate possible family. The date upon which, to quote his biographer, 'God blessed the union of his parents with a first-born destined to bring world-wide lustre to the family name' was particularly propitious, for Russian music was at that time much in need of someone whose training would fit him to apply the process of perfecting the experimental. This event occurred when the Kuchkists were campaigning for the Russification of native music in general and for the reform of opera in particular. Four members of this body, as is now familiar, were amateurs under the trained leadership of Balakirev. When their emancipation was reached, their wings were not sufficiently matured to support them in flight. They knew what they wanted to say, but lacked the faculty of full expression. What Russian music most needed was a composer who had been trained from the outset in the fullest measure – someone really qualified to assume the function of consolidation.

It has been said of Pushkin that he appeared just in time to make use of an instrument (his native language) that had been constructed by a succession of grammarians. The role enacted by Glazunov proved eventually to be that of a grammarian attempting to formalize the expressive medium of musical poets whose vocabulary had hitherto been decidedly deficient. He did not long adhere to the nationalistic theories of his friends of the Kuchka. The fact that his earliest creative efforts earned for him the soubriquet of 'the little Glinka' is merely proof that if the term 'wishful thinking' was not in those days current the phenomenon it describes certainly did exist.

Appraisals

It was imperative that a man destined to play such a part should be by nature as well as by tradition a conservative. And herein lies the excellence of Glazunov's choice of a family in which to be born. His father owned a controlling interest in an old-established firm of booksellers and publishers. His mother came of merchant stock. The Glazunovs were prosperous, and only ambitious to the extent of desiring to maintain that standard of material comfort to which the family had for generations been accustomed. They were, as one might expect, thoroughly cultured folk, who took an interest in, and delighted to associate themselves with, the artistic life of the capital.

The general effect of this environment on Glazunov's attitude towards life as a whole was pointedly described by his principal biographer when the composer was forty-two years of age. 'From the very date of his birth,' wrote Ossovsky, 'Glazunov has lived, and will, it is to be supposed, continue to live not merely in the same building but in the very flat in which he first saw the light. He sleeps in the bed on which his birth took place. His father, too, had been born there. His visits abroad have been comparatively rare and brief. Whilst other composers have needed change and a wide experience of life to inspire them, Glazunov has always drawn inspiration from within.'

This was assumed by such writers as the one quoted to be a remarkable instance of the simultaneous advent of the hour and the man. Later contributors to the literature relating to the composer have maintained with some stoutness that his work may be regarded as of permanent value. In an article published in 1929, Sabaneev, the well-known Russian musicologist, whose views on the permanence of Skryabin's output are to-day somewhat discounted, informed us that Glazunov's music had been 'canonized' and was assured of a definite place in Russian musical history, and he of a niche in its Pantheon. In commenting on these verdicts we have their deliverers at a disadvantage, since we are able to profit by the passage of time, which, in determining the value of works of art is, by general agreement, in the essence of the contract. Our verdict is that if Glazunov occupies space in the Russian musical Valhalla it is by virtue of his great influence as a teacher. It is strange that Tchaikovsky, whose judgement of the music of others was usually a little unfortunate, should have been prompted to express certain doubts as to the real value of Glazunov's creative output – misgivings that proved subsequently to be well-founded – in a letter couched in the kindliest of terms. On the other hand it is interesting to observe that so superb a technician as Taneev should, in Glazunov's maturer years, have been ready to take the latter's advice upon matters affecting creative technique.

And so, if we are ready to accept the gradual decline in popularity of his works as undeniable, we are bound to agree not only that his creative methods once had a distinctly steadying influence upon his contemporaries, but also that, as a result of his years of professorial and directorial period of office at the conservatoire, a number of first-rate composers emerged from that institution. A great deal of significance has been attached to an episode occurring during his term of office. In the middle of the performance of one of Prokofiev's early works the Director expressed his strong disapproval of the student's 'futuristic' tendencies by leaving the hall. Of this it may with safety be said that Glazunov erred in numerous company, some of whom did not profess, as he did, a deliberate conservatism.

There is one more circumstance that seems to have been arranged by the fates to benefit the development of Russian music and to encourage the native composer. It was the performance of Glazunov's youthful *First Symphony*, in 1882, that led to Belyaev's eventual determination to establish a non-commercial publishing company, which bore his name and exerted so immense an influence upon the progress and quality of native composition of every class. It may therefore safely be declared that if Glazunov's monument is not constituted by his own music, one has only to look around and to note the liveliness of present-day activity in the land of his birth. By this he is worthily celebrated.

Early Successes

Glazunov's career as a musician began in the most favourable circumstances it is possible to imagine. His mother, who was personally acquainted with Balakirev, heard from him of a teacher who would, he believed, be willing to give her a general musical instruction. That was in 1878. The individual in question was none other than the future composer of *Sheherazade* and fifteen operas. About two years later Mme Glazunova decided that her son, then receiving lessons from the well-known pianist Elenkovsky, should, like herself, become a pupil of Rimsky-Korsakov. The boy's progress was exceedingly rapid under his new master, who quickly came to regard him as a 'show' pupil. Balakirev held, so to speak, a 'watching brief' and was equally delighted at the success of his introduction; he resolved to signalize his gratification by undertaking to conduct the first performance of the youngster's initial essay in symphonic form at a Free School concert. A little later Rimsky-Korsakov himself repeated the *Symphony* at a concert in connexion with a Pan-Russian Exhibition in Moscow. This was the young composer's first acquaintance with Belyaev. The latter had heard the work at its first performance and had made the journey to Moscow with the express purpose of hearing it again. He introduced himself to Rimsky-Korsakov, who had known him only by sight, at the first rehearsal and sought permission to attend them all. This was the beginning of an enduring friendship between Glazunov and Belyaev, which lasted until the latter's death in 1903, when the composer found himself entrusted, together with Rimsky-Korsakov and Lyadov, with the control of the great publishing concern whose formation his own music had inspired.

Liszt's Patronage

Glazunov now began a rapid advance in both professional and public esteem. His friendship with the Kuchka brought him to the notice of Liszt (through Borodin's agency), who put forth vigorous efforts to make known the youthful *First Symphony*, which the Hungarian master himself conducted at Weimar in 1884. An important widening of his reputation occurred five years later, when, as the result of Belyaev's enterprise, a series of Russian concerts were held during the Paris Exhibition. At these the *Second Symphony* and *Stenka Razin* were introduced. Meanwhile he had attracted the attention of a number of prominent figures, among whom was Hans von Bülow, and his reputation in Western Europe was becoming firmly established. It was no doubt through Liszt's influence that he became interested in Wagner, for soon after the performance of the *First Symphony* at Weimar, having journeyed to Spain and Africa in company with Belyaev, he went on to Bayreuth for the purpose of acquainting himself with *Parsifal*. The influence of Wagner's music was deepened when Neumann's opera company visited St Petersburg in 1889 to give performances of the *Ring*. This influence, outwardly indicated by his dedication of *The Sea* (Op. 28) to Wagner, is reflected sharply in other works of the period. By 1892 Glazunov's reputation had spread to the United States, and he received a commission to compose a triumphal march for performance at an International Exhibition at Chicago in celebration of Columbus. Then, in 1896, came a visit to England, where his works had achieved a remarkable popularity. In 1902 he was again in London and was elected an honorary member of its ancient Philharmonic Society. A year later he received the honorary Cambridge degree of Doctor of Music. The present writer well remembers the unconcealed excitement of a musical amateur who had met the great composer on the stairs one evening at the late Edwin Evans's home in Bedford Park. In the same year Glazunov made appearances in France and Belgium.

Expanding Output

Glazunov had now reached middle age and had composed over eighty works, among which were the eight *Symphonies*, *The Forest* – an orchestral fantasia inspired by contemplation of Slavonic mythology – the *Oriental Rhapsody*, and the *Middle Ages* suite, also seven contributions to the repertoire of the string quartet, in addition to which were the collaborative works in which he joined forces with Lyadov, Rimsky-Korsakov, and other members of the Belyaev circle in paying tribute to its benevolent leader. Subsequently came two *Concertos* for piano and one for violin – the latter being for a time frequently performed by leading players.

Although he attempted no work in operatic form, he did not altogether neglect the dramatic. Among his essays in ballet, by which he was greatly attracted, *Raymonda* has, perhaps, been the most popular, but the *Ruses d'Amour* has enjoyed considerable favour, and the one-act ballet *The Seasons* was rendered famous by its association with Pavlova, in whose repertoire the brilliant *Bacchanale* scene figured prominently. His music to the Grand-Duke Constantine's libretto for the Passion play *The King of the Jews* deserves mention among the dramatic works.

Glazunov wrote a group of choral compositions including a *Cantata* for tenor solo, chorus, and orchestra, in collaboration with Lyadov, the *Triumphal March*, already mentioned, and a *Hymn* for women's voices in memory of the poet Pushkin. His few songs do not rise above the level of ordinary.

The Soviet Dispensation

After the Revolution of 1917 Glazunov's output was slight. It need hardly be said how little he was in sympathy with that world-shaking change of dispensation. In a recent utterance attention was drawn to the dilemma upon which Glazunov then found himself impaled. The composer, it was stated, was conservative enough to evince a strong distaste for this New Order, but too conservative to summon up the energy required to remove himself from its influence. Eventually he left Russia for France (1926), but it is greatly to his credit that in the nine interim years he stuck to his post as director of Leningrad conservatoire and did valuable work in organizing musical instruction under the Soviet régime – thus maintaining the flow of Russian composition that might otherwise have suffered a serious interruption. He died in Paris in 1936.

Someone has provided him with a flippant epitaph, which describes him as 'a Russian composer of music rather than a composer of Russian music'. But the fetish of nationalism in the arts is no longer worshipped as once it was, so that it may perhaps be considered that of the two qualifications the first is the worthier!

PANTALÉON ENRIQUE GRANADOS Y CAMPIÑA

1867–1916

RALPH W. WOOD

Personality

'I only knew Granados when he had reached the forties, at an epoch of his life when he was often enough ill, when he had to take great precautions and discipline himself to prolonged rests, but I shall never forget the fire that carried him away and that, when he was chatting lazily stretched on a divan, would suddenly jerk him upright, gesticulating and laughing like a youngster. Nothing would have been able to make him grow old, he carried in him the same inextinguishable youth that we had known ... in Albéniz. The same perpetual impromptu had guided his life: alternately he remained at Barcelona or departed abruptly on a concert tour across Spain or abroad, and in the midst of that chopped-up existence he composed piano pieces, songs, even operas. ... You could not see him, speak a moment to him, without being struck by the charm of his personality, by the passionate languor that permeated all his actions.' He and G. Jean-Aubry, who wrote the foregoing, spent two evenings together in Paris discussing 'what we all expected from the young Spanish school'. The second evening they were dining at the house of the pianist Joaquin Nin and Falla was present. 'After dinner, Granados, who had been ill for some time, had not the strength to go to the piano; but, half-lolling, had been evoking for us pleasant or tender memories; the last evening ... I can still hear his musical voice when we shook hands at the carriage door. This was before the war. ... There was in his nature such a feminine tenderness that this characteristic will always adorn his image when my mind evokes it. ...'

'Granados confided to us that his ideal interpreter was precisely M. Joaquin Nin', says the same chronicler, speaking no doubt of the music; but let us hear that very Nin on the man. 'I met Granados', runs Nin's obituary article, 'towards 1898, at Barcelona, in the *salon* of Narcisa Freixas. ... Granados was living then gripped in the tenacious claws of teaching; he was living modestly, with an heroic resignation. ... We were neighbours; we lived not far from each other in the outskirts of Barcelona, at San Gervasio. And I was fascinated by his exuberant imagination, his delicious "howlers", his disconcerting faculty for the unexpected, his distinction, his tragi-comic outbursts, his great eyes always ready to weep, to laugh, to admire or to be astonished at everything, the fantastic recitals of his extraordinary adventures, his chequered medley of irony and candour, of activity and contemplation, of refinement and earthiness, of humour and gravity, of elegance and unbuttonedness, of disquietude and serenity. ...'

Another biographer, Henri Collet, declares that Granados in maturity was possessed by a 'pessimisme goyesque'. Collet also asserts that: 'His indifference to the political farce was simply one aspect of his general indifference to vulgar things.' He speaks of Granados's 'incurable romanticism, which made him sob when hearing *Tristan*'.

Granados had long, sleek, drooping hair – black, of course – and a huge moustache; his eyes were large, dark, rather bulging.

This, then, was the composer of *The Belle and the Nightingale* (*Quejas o la Maja y el Ruiseñor*, No. 3 of the *Goyescas* for piano). There really seems a remarkable, and rare enough, correspondence between the traits of the man and of at any rate that, possibly his finest and certainly his best-loved, creation.

Youth

His full name was Pantaléon Enrique Granados y Campiña; he was the son of Calixto Granados, a Cuban born in Havana, and Enriquetta-Elvira Campiña, a Galician from Santander. The date of his birth was 27 July 1867; the place Lerída, in Catalonia. He showed in infancy a precocious taste for music. His father was an officer in the Spanish army, and so he received early lessons in the elements of solfeggio and of piano technique from a bandmaster, a Captain José Junceda.

It was in Barcelona, where the family shortly settled down, that Granados was brought up. His studies were continued at what Collet calls 'L'Escolanie de la Mercé'. First he worked at the piano with Professor Francisco X. Jurnet and finally with J. B. Pujol.

Also, during the last three years of that initial Barcelona period of his, he was studying composition under Pedrell. It ended in 1887 when, having graduated as a pianist in Barcelona, he set out to do likewise at the Conservatoire in Paris. Patronage enabled him to go to the French capital in September 1887, but he was prevented by an attack of typhoid from taking the Conservatoire's entrance examination. By the time he had recovered from this far from negligible spell of illness he had passed the age-limit for entry. So the instruction that, for a year, he did obtain – from Charles de Bériot – was unofficial, in a private capacity, and somewhat below his original hopes.

In Paris he lived in the little Hôtel de Cologne et d'Espagne, 10–12 rue de Trévise, in company with Ricardo Viñes – a companionship recalling, it is said, the famous earlier one, at Brussels, of Albéniz and Arbos. We hear of the two young Spaniards' musical ardour; of the fascination for them of the music of France; of their bohemian *blagues* and of Granados's *crise de 'montmartrisme'* and passion for painting.

Granados returned to Barcelona in 1889, though the reputation that he proceeded to establish as a pianist was obtained by playing not only there but all over Spain and also back in Paris. He gave his first Barcelona concert – a lively success – on 20 April 1890, playing a programme of romantic music and including his own *Spanish Serenade*, *Arabesque*, and certain *Spanish Dances*. Of the latter, particularly, he had begun the composition when a youth, and significantly enough among the eminent musicians, all foreigners, who first showed interest in, and even enthusiasm for, the *Dances* were Massenet, Saint-Saëns, de Bériot, and Gigout. Others were Edvard Grieg and César Cui. In the collection of twelve *Dances* that the four published volumes comprise, No. 7 is dedicated to Cui, No. 1 to the composer's future wife. At another concert in Barcelona, 10 April 1892, he appeared with the orchestra of Pérez Cabrero, which accompanied him in Grieg's concerto and played three of the *Spanish Dances*. The following July saw great success of the *Dances* in a concert of the Orfeó Catalá.

Husband

That same year he married. His wife is referred to as *l'exquise* Señorita Amparo Gal. He went, as a matter of fact, into something like retirement, for no less than three years. His first-born, Eduardo

Granados, saw the light on 7 July 1894, at Barcelona. In all there were five other children of the marriage – Soledad, Enrique, Victor, Natalia, and Francisco. Perhaps it is appropriate to number too among the fruits of the union the two *Spanish Dances*, the 'Andalusian' and 'Valencian', and likewise the *Poetic Waltzes*, which were composed in 1893. Also dating from 1893 is the music for the stage-work *Miel de la Alcarria* (Feliú y Codina) – of which, however, the *Jota* had been written long before in Paris, complete with a dedication to Ricardo Viñes.

Renown

Granados reappeared in public at the end of October 1895, in concerts given by the Catalan Concert Society. On November 14 of that year Albéniz organized a concert at the Lyric Theatre for the 'Gracia reservists', and Granados played there Albéniz's *Spanish Rhapsody* and his own *Poetic Waltzes*. This occasion was something of a triumph for him. He also gave some performances in Madrid, besides making several provincial tours.

About this time the Catalan Concert Society was dissolved, whereupon Crickboom, the Belgian violinist, founded the Barcelona Philharmonic Society. Granados was among the first soloists to appear at the concerts given by the new body. It was with Crickboom that he gave sonata recitals at the end of 1896, and in 1897 he took part in chamber concerts with the Crickboom Quartet. (His *Piano Quintet* in G minor dates from 1895.)

We are brought now to 1898, important as the year of the production, in Madrid, of his opera *María del Carmen*. Performances soon followed in other Spanish cities, including Barcelona and Valencia. The Barcelona production came just before a notable two-piano recital given in that city by Granados with Joaquin Malats, an affair that was reckoned to have 'greatly increased his reputation'. After the première of *María del Carmen* the thirty-one-year-old composer received from the hands of Maria Christina the cross that accompanies a knighthood of the Order of Carlos III.

In 1900 Granados himself founded a concert society in Barcelona, the short-lived Sociedad de Conciertos Clásicos, and directed its performances. One programme was actually provided by three pianists, Granados, Malats and Vidiella. The piano-school that also he founded in Barcelona, in 1901, the Academia Granados, was sturdier. He remained personally at its head for the ensuing fifteen years.

During those same years his life as a concert star continued to be a busy one. Joining forces with the choir of the Orfeó Catalá in May 1902, the following year giving sonata recitals with Crickboom *au foyer du Liceo et à la Philharmonique*, appearing for the Wagnerian Association, the Orfeó, the Philharmonic (with Ysaye), the Musical Union, not to speak of at his own Academy, in 1904 – to Paris in 1905, where he brought out seven hitherto unknown *Sonatas* by Domenico Scarlatti, and where his Chopin playing so affected the pianist Risler (thus is the matter presented to us) that Risler made approaches that had as their sequel a two-piano recital by Granados and him the next year, in Barcelona; another two-piano concert in October 1907, with his first partner in such deeds, Malats; and another in 1908, with Saint-Saëns at the Liceo under the auspices of the Barcelona Musical Association; in 1909 and 1910 memorable recitals with Thibaud; officiating as a member of the jury for the *prix Diémer*; and in 1911. ... But at 1911 it is appropriate to pause.

The Goyescas *Suite*

It was probably in the very earliest of the years thus rapidly reviewed, in 1902, that Granados began to transform into music the impressions made upon him, keen amateur of pictorial art that he was, by the Goya paintings in the Prado. *Goyescas*, the suite of piano pieces 'named after scenes from the paintings and tapestries of Goya and episodes from the Goyesque period in Madrid', is said to have been completed, to have advanced from those initial fragments of 1902 or so into its final state, in 1909; but the date of the suite's first performance suggests that its completion was not so early even as that. Meanwhile, 1901 had seen the production at Barcelona of *Picarol*, a *zarzuela* with libretto by Apeles Mestres. Granados turned out at intervals no fewer than five other stage settings of the same poet: *Foletto* (incomplete), *Gaziel*, *Liliana*, *Petrarca* and *Ovillejos*. There was also the suite *Elisenda*, for piano and small orchestra (dedicated to Casals and first performed 7 July 1912), which was based on a poem by Mestres; not to speak of numerous Mestres song-settings that Granados made.

The première of the *Goyescas* suite was on 11 March 1911, at the Catalan Music Palace. The *Song of the Stars* – for chorus, organ, and piano – was first heard on the same occasion, and also a piano piece, *Azulejos*, left unfinished by Albéniz (d. 1909) and completed by

Granados. In the following month Granados organized a programme of his works in chronological order, when the *Goyescas* were again performed.

Climax and War

The climax to his theatre activities now remains to be spoken of. It has been conjectured that Granados may almost from the beginning of his Goya musings have had some idea of an opera at the back of his mind. At any rate, after the piano suite had been brought out, Fernando Periquet was approached to fit, as it were, words to the score – a task that one scarcely needs to be told he only accomplished with much difficulty. The opera *Goyescas* was nearing readiness for performance by 1914 and was accepted for production in Paris. On 4 April that year, in the Salle Pleyel, Granados was fairly fêted by the S.M.I. The *Serenata* for two violins and piano was played on this occasion, and the *Tonadillas* were sung for the first time. The whole affair was a huge success. The applause was tremendous; numerous encores were insisted upon and were played with the entire audience standing. Just before August 1914, Granados, already Officier de l'Instruction Publique, was made Chevalier de la Légion d'Honneur. The outbreak of war found him in Switzerland, where the pianist Ernest Schelling (dedicatee of Granados's *Paisaje* for piano, Op. 35) had invited him to spend the summer at his (Schelling's) *seigneuriale* residence while finishing work on the opera.

The war changed things. The Paris production of the opera was cancelled. Granados retrieved his score and offered it to New York. He went to America in 1915. His two symphonic poems, *La Nit del Mort* and *Dante*, were given their American premières by the Chicago Symphony Orchestra, 5 and 6 November 1915. He himself figured as a pianist in New York. He was invited by President Wilson to play at the White House. He told U.S.A. reporters that America knew nothing about Spanish music and that Bizet's *Carmen*, for example, was not in any sense Spanish.

The concurrent roles Granados was playing just then, of pianist and composer, were entirely characteristic. That dualism had existed all his life – to a greater extent, it is perhaps right to emphasize, than in the many other composer-executants whose names spring readily to mind. It has often been declared that he was in fact a pianist first and foremost. He possessed a superb technique and used it as a means to admirable artistic ends. He was, indeed, reckoned to belong among the greatest virtuosos of his era. Jean-Aubry calls him an 'interprète incomparable', adding – be it said – that his interpretations tended to vary with his mood and thus to have the air of improvisations. ... He was an effective teacher, founder of an Academy where he worked assiduously and with system. He wrote a text-book on the use of the pedals. Studies are included among his compositions. (He also, on the one hand, arranged for the modern piano twenty-six unpublished *Sonatas* by Scarlatti and, on the other, rescored Chopin's *F minor Concerto*.)

The production of the stage *Goyescas* took place in New York at the Metropolitan Opera House on 26 January 1916. Afterwards Granados told his friend Amadeo Vives: 'At last I have seen my dream made real. It is true that I have a head full of white hairs, and that I am hardly at the beginning of my task, but I am confident and work with enthusiasm. ... All my actual happiness is rather for what must be to come than for what I have done so far. I dream of Paris and I cherish a world of projects.' ... He set forth to return to Spain, by way of Liverpool and the English Channel; and so it happened that he was on board the *Sussex* on 24 March 1916 when, between Folkestone and Dieppe, she was torpedoed by a German submarine and went down. The chronicles have it that Granados was seen to throw himself out of the raft on which he was, to rescue his wife, who was struggling in the water; he was only just able to reach her and they perished in each other's arms.

ALEXANDER TIKHONOVICH GRECHANINOV

1864 - 1956

M. MONTAGU-NATHAN

Nationalism as Expedient

Much has been written on the subject of nationalism in music; even after the most attentive perusal of this abundant material it is still puzzling to determine whether nationalism in the Arts is a quality or a defect. On the whole one is inclined to conclude that the only moment at which its introduction should be fully sanctioned is when a nation is in sore need of *amour-propre*. It is possible that a people may succeed in reviving its feelings of patriotism either by a display of bunting or by the incorporation of folk tunes, or other of the paraphernalia of artistic nationalism, into its operas. Once this end has been attained there seems no further purpose in continuing the process.

When reviewing the early career of Grechaninov as a creative artist it becomes tolerably clear that he is to be ranked as a disciple of the pioneer nationalists. The heroes who fell before Thebes were seven in number. Grechaninov is to be placed among the epigoni of the famous 'Five'. His attempts at nationalism were not sanctioned by vital necessity; they were, rather, in the nature of interesting experiments. He had no real need to emulate '1860 and All That'. A biographer and compatriot has further classified him as one of few Russian composers who had a humble origin. This, in view of what he has achieved as an artist, does not appear to have proved a handicap, and, judging from the latest portraits available, in which his countenance appears to be somewhat more aristocratic than those of some of his better-known precursors and contemporaries, he has nothing to complain of on that score. But the story of his early days (he was born on 30 October 1864) reveals that Alexander Tikhonovich suffered from discouragements that would hardly be likely to have assailed him had he found himself during boyhood in the more cultivated environment enjoyed by most of his compatriots who have earned musical distinction.

Parlour Piano

His father, Tikhon Gerasimovich, was a semi-literate shop-keeper in Moscow, who, like some of our own north-countrymen of the mercantile persuasion, held the belief that 'where there's muck there's brass'. It would probably be an injustice to declare that in his view music and 'muck' were synonymous, but he did believe that the former could not be expected to yield an adequate increment to those who adopted the art as a profession. We are further assured of a contention that the place of musicians in the social economy was well below 'the salt' and, presumably, the shop-keeper.

Young Grechaninov's mother possessed a greater measure of enlightenment despite the fact that until after marriage she was unable to read or write. She was not, however, lacking in the power to express her views, and one occasion on which she exercised the prerogative of her sex by claiming the 'last word' was when she insisted that her daughter should be provided with a piano. That was a momentous victory, for it was the presence of this instrument in the Grechaninov's parlour that inspired our subject to try conclusions upon it with his index finger. Having succeeded in multiplying this humble medium by five, and having in due course reached ambidexterity, he became satisfied that he had something to express, and presently he fell among some musical friends who readily endorsed that view. Meanwhile, a friend of his father, whose opinion was valued by that obstinate individual, prevailed upon him to abandon his ambition that his son should succeed him in the family business and to give him a reasonable general education.

In one way his attendance at a Gymnasium had a favourable consequence. That institution held occasional evenings of chamber music, and there its new alumnus first listened to a string quartet. In another particular, however, he suffered a certain discomfort. That the 'mugging-up' of irregular verbs and grammatical 'exceptions' proved distasteful to him anyone having even a nodding acquaintance with Grechaninov's mother-tongue will readily understand. At the age of seventeen he began to feel old enough to make his own plans. He drove a bargain that if allowed to enter the Moscow conservatoire he would supplement his studies there with a process of self-education.

The circumstance that the first teachers selected for him were Kashkin and Safonov made it clear that his talent was already manifest. It is stated that his attendance at the class of Laroche was irregular, and this may indeed have been due to that critic's conservatism of outlook. Whatever the cause, the pupil contrived to get himself transferred to the more congenial Hubert. It is interesting to observe that Arensky, with whom he had been placed for the study of harmony and form, exhibited his characteristic lack of discernment and denied that Grechaninov possessed any marked degree of creative talent.

Change of Conservatoire

Having graduated from Safonov's piano course he left the conservatoire, and after a period of private instruction from Taneev also left his native city to enter the rival institution in St Petersburg. It is worthy of mention that these interim lessons were greatly appreciated, and the dedication of his early *Piano Trio* testifies to the esteem in which his temporary master was held. He appears to have escaped the musical influence of Tchaikovsky, but he vouchsafed a youthful opinion that the composer of the *'Pathetic' Symphony* and the author of *The Kreutzer Sonata* were the greatest of contemporary spirits.

For three years he studied under Rimsky-Korsakov. At the end of that time he left the conservatoire, but continued to live in the northern capital. During this period two significant compositions emerged, namely, a 'diploma work', a Cantata entitled *Samson*, for solo voices, chorus, and orchestra, and the *String Quartet in G*, which gained him both the Belyaev prize and its public performance in December 1894. A year later his *B minor Symphony*, Op. 6, dedicated to Rimsky-Korsakov, was performed at a Russian Musical Society concert. The statement that Grechaninov's association with the composer of *The Snow-Maiden* and Kuchkism had no influence upon him should be accepted with reserve. There can be no doubt that in his early operatic venture, *Dobrinya Nikitich*, he tried to embody some of the nationalistic features of which he had heard from their advocates.

Back to Moscow

In order to support himself after leaving the conservatoire he gave music lessons, but, despite a large number of pupils, he found it necessary for material reasons to return to Moscow in 1896. It was at this point that he entered his second creative phase. While in St Petersburg his interest in Church choral music had been aroused. He had been in contact with a distinguished body of choral singers and with the famous baritone, Melnikov, and was inspired by this experience to compose a series of works in the region of sacred music. While thus engaged he had the good fortune to become acquainted with Smolensky, the honoured director of the Synodal School, who secured for him the performance of a number of compositions of a devotional character. He had now become a recognized authority on the principles of ecclesiastic song.

Despite this entry into what eventually proved to be his appropriate creative sphere, Grechaninov was still to some extent under the spell of his nationalist friends in St Petersburg. Having provided testimony to the possession of a dual personality by furnishing incidental music for the newly-founded Moscow Art Theatre's production of Ostrovsky's *Snow-Maiden*, he was encouraged by Stasov to resume work on his opera, *Dobrinya Nikitich*, begun in 1895. The work was eventually produced at the Moscow Grand Theatre in October 1903. It was given twelve performances, but such popular success as it achieved was attributed to the presence of Fedor Shalyapin, then in his zenith, in the cast. It is a curious mixture, in that its ingredients of operatic nationalism, rendered familiar by a number of experiments, beginning with Dargomizhsky's *Stone Guest* – a series that may be said to have concluded with Rakhmaninov's little-known *Niggardly Knight* – are applied in a manner more or less photographic. The composer did not contrive, as did Rimsky-Korsakov, to absorb his native folk-song into his musical system. Again, he retained the conventional operatic forms.

It should be mentioned that Grechaninov was himself personally interested in folk-song research and was for a time associated with the Musico-Ethnographic Commission – hence the collection of Mussulman melodies, a volume of the Songs of Great Russia, and another devoted to twenty melodies from the land of Burns.

Baudelaire and Maeterlinck

He was now approaching a third, and somewhat unexpected, phase. His essays in musical 'impressionism' evoked pained surprise and some opprobrium on the part of contemporary critics afflicted with a pronounced conservative tendency. There is a hint of things to come in the *Autumn Sketches*, Op. 43, for voice and piano, more particularly in *October*, which is apparently the spring-time of his new style. By the time he had reached the setting of Vyacheslav Ivanov's Tryptich he had become a true disciple of the *fin-de-siècle* French movement, and with the adoption of Baudelaire's *Fleurs du Mal* as textual material he had set up a significant signpost. A final tribute had been paid to his St Petersburg friends by the adoption, in his second opera, *Sister Beatrice* (Maeterlinck), of the declamatory method in the duet between the Holy Virgin and Allette. This work was begun in 1909.

The *String Quartet*, Op. 70, shows him persisting in his new style. When first performed, in manuscript, in 1915, it was described by a Russian critic as containing 'the débris of modernism', and allusion was made to 'fashionable spices', which were pronounced unbecoming. This utterance was mitigated by praise of the slow movement, but in the summing-up the composer was accused of having abandoned 'neo-nationalism' for 'pseudo-impressionism'.

France and America

With the establishment of the Revolution Grechaninov was one of those who failed to see eye-to-eye with the new dispensation. On leaving his native country he spent some time in France. He was doubtless beginning to realize that, in the land of its origin, 'impressionism' was no longer regarded as 'modernistic' and also that his true métier was the composition of the sacred music that many years earlier had attracted so much attention from those competent to judge of its merits. It has been seen that he had no fear of the unorthodox. In some of his earlier Church music he had even dared to introduce an instrumental accompaniment – a step that, to put it mildly, rendered him in the eyes of the Tsarist ecclesiastical authorities a *persona non grata*. While he was in France the Religious Congress of 1937 awarded him a prize for a *Missa Festiva* and six *Motets*. After proceeding to the United States, where he lived until his death in 1956, he confined himself almost exclusively to this field of composition. In addition to composing a *Missa Oecumenica*, intended for Catholic devotion, he dedicated two *Psalms* (Nos. 92 and 97), Op. 164, to the purposes of Hebrew worship; these have a vernacular text.

There seems every likelihood, from what has been written about these works, that when his more recent compositions become available in this country there will be a revival of interest in a composer whose output has always commanded the respect of those acquainted with it.

ROY HARRIS

B. 1898

W. R. ANDERSON

The Farmer's Boy

Two generations before Roy Harris was born, Oklahoma was Indian territory. In 1889 a large tract was opened for settlement by whites on the principle of 'first come, first served'. An hour was fixed; at the stroke, 20,000 settlers raced forward to stake out homes. Many will remember the book and film *Cimarron* dealing with this homestead rush.

It was on a farm built on one of these plots that, nine years later, Roy Harris was born, in Lincoln County, on Lincoln's birthday, 12 February 1898. He had five generations of Scots-Irish ancestry as backing; for prospect, the hard life of a farmer's son, whose parents had no use for music as a son's career.

After five years in this Oklahoma log-farm, the Harrises removed to a ranch in the San Gabriel valley, California. Here work amid Nature pervaded Roy's mind, as we may feel it in his music. He has said: 'The barbarism or ruggedness of my progenitors undoubtedly placed asymmetry in my blood, but the Sierra Madre mountains, the fertile San Gabriel valley, with its constant evolution of eternal life, its regeneration from within itself, had its definite effect on the development of my acceptance and belief in life. Here, for twenty years, I saw the sun rise and set in the same spot, and its reiteration of a purpose developed a pantheistic worship in the very roots of my being.'

He ascribes to his maternal grandmother most of his share of hereditary musical quality: she, unusually for a woman, was an able player of the organ. He had very little instruction in music until he was twenty-five. At eighteen he was farming in his own right and playing the piano and the clarinet for his own pleasure. He served in the first World War and went back to work at its close.

A Late Decision

It was only after a period at the University of California in 1921 that he decided to devote himself to music. He drove a van by day and worked at music by night, during two years with Arthur Farwell. Modeste Altschuler started him upon orchestration.

He hitch-hiked to New York in order to hear his first orchestral composition played by the city's Philharmonic Orchestra. He was twice awarded a Guggenheim Fellowship, which allows artists to devote a period, often abroad, to intensified study. Thus he was able to go to Europe and spend four years in Paris, where he studied with Nadia Boulanger and other teachers. It was only when nearing his thirties that he began the works that were to put him in the front rank of American composers.

In Paris he sustained an injury to his back and, thus temporarily crippled, returned to New York. One result was what he called his emancipation from chordal writing and the tyranny of the piano. Lying on his back for months, and so having to compose away from the piano, he found himself emphasizing melodic line rather than harmony. Much of his work contains complexity of counterpoint.

In that period, too, he made intensive studies of the music of the past. Gregorian music, in particular, had long attracted him; he found the asymmetry of its design akin to that of Nature: its proportions being 'regulated by its growth from within, in adjustment to its environment'.

Upon his study years followed others (1930–2) under the auspices of the Creative Fellowship of the Pasadena Music and Arts Association. Immediately thereafter he was teaching at the summer school of the great Juilliard Foundation in New York; from 1934 to 1938 he was professor of composition at the Westminster Choir School at Princeton, and in 1940 he was made head of that faculty. He then became 'composer in residence' at Cornell University, and in 1946 held that title at Colorado State College.

Vitality and Gusto

His *Second String Quartet* was chosen to represent contemporary music at the Chicago's World Fair of 1933; the *Third String Quartet* similarly figured in an International Conference of Musicologists concert in New York in 1939. In various broadcast polls he received, in 1935–7, the highest vote for an American composer. At least fifteen of his works have been recorded for the gramophone (but few, notably the *Third Symphony*, have appeared thus in England). He has celebrated not only great figures such as Walt Whitman, but the common man: on the one hand, in his *Folk-Song Symphony* for choir of young people and orchestra (usually performed by massed High School choruses and large city orchestras) – a work in which American airs, some of them of English origin, are used; and on the other hand, in his *Ode to American-Soviet Friendship*, played in Moscow in 1945 at a commemoration of America's Independence Day.

Sometimes he seems to strain the medium: the *Piano Quintet*, it has been argued, being more effective as a piano concerto, with strings. His muscular-mental vigour is more notable than (as yet, at any rate) his lyrical power: spontaneity, curves, persuasion are not so striking as vitality, and a deep interest in such forms as the passacaglia and the fugue.

His output has been large: up to 1938 alone he had produced over forty sizable works, for orchestra, choir, and chamber combinations. Besides several *Symphonies* there are the *Farewell to Pioneers*, a *Passacaglia, Cadenza, and Fugue* for piano quintet, the *Song for Occupations* (Whitman), a *Symphony for Unaccompanied Voices*, and some works based on American folk-songs or ditties brought from England. He shows a power that one might compare to Bunyan's. There is rough speech, at times, and intensity, with an abruptness akin to that of Sibelius – whose influence is to be expected in almost every composer of Harris's generation. He re-uses his melodic material less than does Sibelius, though.

Harris grew up, artistically, in the turbulent, troubled years of boom and slump in the United States between the wars. There are obvious comparisons between his growth and that of other ripe American characters besides Lincoln – Whitman, for example, whose thought he has found congenial and whose poetry he has more than once paralleled in music.

Some Bases of Belief

Self-confident, he induced others to believe in him. He has been lucky in getting his music performed and recorded (but 'the lucky cat watches').

He has written notes about his music, and also about 'The Growth of a Composer' – the latter in the *Musical Quarterly* of U.S.A. It is clear that he is no dogmatist, for he realizes that the creative impulse – 'the desire to capture and communicate feeling' – can pass under many names – 'romantic fervour ... a longing for truth ... the atavistic burgeonings from the depths of the race-soul'. He speaks of 'race-expression', using the word 'race', presumably, without the too close connotation that has brought it into disrepute: for surely, of all peoples, those of the U.S.A. are the most diversely rooted. Harris feels the creative impulse as 'a lonesome hunger'; the creator must ever be an individualist, one set apart, however closely he may mix (as, we have seen, Harris has mixed) with the earthy life of his fellows. The artist has to interpret the spirit of his own time; to that adventure he comes 'with fear and trepidation'; there are so many pitfalls: he may merely say what has been better said before; may 'translate something unworthy' or be unintelligible. And if he be so fine in spirit as to excel in 'sensitiveness, initiative, moral courage, power of co-ordination' – why, that may be dangerous 'in a democratic society in which all men are held to be created equal'. The masses may look with suspicion upon him. His fellows, both those who interpret his music and those who hear it, are cautious and timid about novelty; they may fail 'morally to stand behind the music'.

A Philosophy of the Folk

The composer's gospel is one of hard work. He realizes that imaginative impulses can only convince the hearer if they are clear, intelligible, onward-marching, unfaltering. Learning must be fertilized by contact with the people, until music provides an 'acting philosophy of positive values'. He must learn to feel and think simultaneously, analyse and criticize his own work. And thus, as he grows, he 'no longer goes through the torture of trying to pull something out of himself. And, ironically enough, he discovers that his best impulses come without being sought.' A decade of apprenticeship may bring him to a balance between 'a strong sense of social responsibility and a sense of humour about himself and even his generation and his people'. One feels a link with Bloch's spirit, in the mention of 'social responsibility'.

So the composer seeks adjustments that will assure placidity; he must radiate confidence and attract the best elements of men and movements to sustain him and afford him means of expanding his spirit; only in such balance and such confidence – which must be won by self-activity, by the sublimation of every experience, happy or trying – can the composer create music 'that will be true to his race, to his time, to himself.'

It is not difficult, in such of Harris's works as we have heard in this country, to enjoy his interest in what we take it he means by 'race'. He has ample faith in Americans, as well as in 'a new classicism'. A note about his *Fifth Symphony*, first performed in 1943, perhaps expresses, as well as any short writing of his, the intention behind the work. 'I hoped,' he wrote, 'to express qualities of our people which our popular dance music, because of its very nature, cannot reveal. Our people are more than pleasure loving. We also have qualities of heroic strength, determination, will to struggle, faith in our destiny. We are possessed of a fierce driving power – optimistic, young, rough and ready. And I am convinced that our mechanistic age has not destroyed an appreciation of the more tender moods. It is right that these gentler moods should live in us. Otherwise, our strength and vitality might degenerate into a ruthless brutality. ... As the work unfolded it seemed to assume the character of our times. It became more martial, more savage, more ominously brooding and intense than I had imagined it in the beginning. The symphony seemed to possess an independent life of its own which I had to accept and translate.'

The Epitome of Native Style

We read into these remarks a reflection of the spirit of Lincoln; and in their close we remember what many novelists have said about their characters taking control and altering the course of a book. In Harris's outlook, then, appears something of that 'tough, atavistic wisdom' that in another magazine article he said he felt 'stubbornly sifting and weighing' American life, with its 'spendthrift energies and giddy enthusiasms': a life that for many observers and participators is a 'sullen, colossal thing', though millions have never accepted the machine as valid for living.

Asked to write a piece that would fill two sides of a gramophone record, he sought a synthesis of native qualities: 'A noisy ribaldry, a sadness, a groping earnestness which amounts to suppliance towards those dearest spiritual yearnings within ourselves, and finally a fierce struggle of the will for power, sheer power in itself; there is little grace or mellowness in our midst.' He took for treatment *When Johnny Comes Marching Home*, because it was one of his father's favourites, whistled jauntily as they went out to work and pensively as they came back.

That emphasis upon human companionship, upon man's life and work as fit bases for artistic creation, are again revealed in a piece of writing that Harris produced for a three-part book upon such bases, the work of creators in literature, in art and in music (Rutgers University Press, 1942). After the first satisfaction of physical needs, man explored his consciousness and environment, creating in his own image, whether with joy or disappointment at the results. The hypnotic effects of sound created for him a new world, in which 'he could contemplate his past, his present, his future'. Repetition of these emotional states allowed him to control with increasing surety his 'generative, active self', his 'emotive power-house'. Harris proves in this essay that he can employ words as evocatively as orchestral colours. He finds music to-day meet for contemplation of man's inner being, in its highest emotions; it can unite humanity; it is 'a time-space language', abstract, but not divorced from the heart. The composer 'must be able to live and grow in an acutely focussed, *subjective* world arising out of an intense emotional field of activity'. Harris sees the folly of trying to overthrow tradition, as well as of allowing it to fossilize a spirit. The emotional experiences of the ages flow through a man; he translates, intensifies, reaffirms and releases them 'into serviceable idioms of culture. Innately of the past, reflecting the present, they in turn modify the future'. Reflecting the present; in that view, we can watch Roy Harris growing, as part of the great 'living affirmation of man's faith in himself'. It is a privilege that assures us excitement and satisfaction.

His *Seventh Symphony*, played by the Boston Orchestra, does not appear to have aroused as much enthusiasm as some of the earlier ones, especially the *Third*, generally regarded as one of the best of American works in this kind. This seventh, composed in 1952, is a dance-symphony, using twelve-note melodic resources and polytonal harmonic textures. Among other recent works are listed the 1946 *Celebration*, variations on a theme by Howard Hanson, a contemporary of Harris's (born in 1896); a *Cumberland Concerto*, *Piano Concerto*, *Symphony* for Band, *Fantasy* for Piano and Orchestra, an orchestral *Epigram* and a Cantata, *Abraham Lincoln Walks at Midnight*.

PAUL HINDEMITH

B. 1895

H. G. SEAR

Early Opposition

Of Hindemith it must be said at the outset that the work is the man. He resolutely refuses to vouchsafe biographical details, referring the enquirer to Riemann's *Lexikon* and relying on his publisher to make the necessary additions.

The bare facts of his external life can be stated in a few paragraphs. Born at Hanau, near Frankfurt-am-Main, on 16 November 1895, Paul Hindemith began his practical musical studies before he entered his teens; he showed far more than a proficiency for both violin and viola, and an expert knowledge of a dozen orchestral instruments was added. His parents opposed his following music as a profession, but his perseverance and passion were not to be restrained. Rather than abandon his vocation he left home, supporting himself for a time by playing in café and theatre orchestras.

The breach cannot have been wide, for he was able to pursue his studies at Hoch's Conservatorium in Frankfurt, where his masters were Arnold Mendelssohn, a composer of late-romantic tendencies, and Bernard Sekles, whose works have a more forward character. At twenty Hindemith was leading the orchestra of the Frankfurt Opera; he became chief conductor in 1923.

For a number of years he played viola in the Amar String Quartet, which took its name from the first violinist, Licco Amar, a Turk; Rudolf Hindemith, his brother, was cellist. This combination soon became acknowledged as forming an apostleship of modern chamber music, making signal appearances at the yearly Donaueschingen Chamber Music Festivals (founded, mainly at the instigation of Hindemith, in 1921). There much of his music in this field was heard for the first time.

Hindemith has always been an industrious composer. By 1930 he had an imposing list of works to his credit, but not a great following.

Most of his compositions were performed, and even repeated, and many were published. If this implies that his music was difficult or forbidding, it becomes plain that some assessment of the influences that worked upon this sincere but reserved artist must be attempted.

When the first world war ended he was twenty-three. Thus, while his art was still in the formative stage, his mother-country was plunged into political and economic chaos. The means by which culture was promulgated were straitened; it was a period in which material re-creation proceeded piecemeal, by makeshift methods requiring ingenuity rather than inspiration. The younger artists of Germany threw off the dreams of romanticism and pondered stark reality. That they were constrained to use the simplest of materials, often with a harsh bareness, is visible in the architecture, stage design, and painting of the period, as well as in the music.

Revolt against Romanticism

Hindemith is to be regarded as one of the pioneers of the period. The fact brought him into conflict with musical pundits and political authorities. The first retarded his appeal, the second caused major crises in his external life. But it is perfectly clear that the seeds of the movement he represented were already germinating before Hindemith acquired what measure of notoriety was his. The desire, at least, to rebel against the overblown romanticism of the past can be traced to Reger, and more commandingly to Busoni. Their return was to Bach rather than to the polyphonic school as a whole, and so their music was never entirely purged of subjectivism. Hindemith's vision was at once wider and more self-effacing, and he desired to be objective. During this phase so-called experts were themselves remarkably hazy about the looming innovations; each, according to his bias, dubbed the new music atonal, polytonal, duodecimal. The truth is that it was all these, but Hindemith's own development has, in the main, left such things behind. Linear his music remains, though he is now definitely concerned with tonalism.

The historical cleavage can be seen in the Donaueschingen festivals that absorbed so much of Hindemith's energies. The move to this comparatively isolated town was made because it was felt by the vanguard that to play the new music, the chamber works of Hindemith, Schönberg, and the rest, alongside the marked tonality of Beethoven, or even of Strauss, was to do it a disservice. Yet it is significant that at the initial festival in 1921, composers of the rank (and styles) of Strauss, Pfitzner, and von Haussegger, all committeemen, professed active interest in the proceedings. The following year their sympathy, if it ever existed, was withheld. It is also significant that Busoni and Schönberg maintained a warm feeling for the festivals.

So far the chief label that attached itself to Hindemith was one of neoclassicism. When, in 1924, he became a member of the Selection Committee, he added his influence to that of Heinrich Burkard, with the result that a directive for the 1925 festival was issued calling for the creation of new music couched in the neglected 'expression-forms', the chamber chorus for instance, compositions for the generally accepted open-air combinations and, what is maybe more startling, for mechanical instruments.

The ever-practical Hindemith made experiments in the composition of music for the piano-player and mechanical organ. He believed that a musician should be prepared to compose for any occasion and for any medium. He saw that the piano-player, as opposed to the pianist, postulated a different texture. The limitations of ten fingers, of the keyboard itself, would disappear. And because, at that time, the possibility of endless reproduction and circulation appeared enormous, he was quick to realize that for an audience many times multiplied, unintelligible complications must be avoided. It is an attitude of mind that has never ceased to be his.

Utility Music and Experiments

This branch of music the composer himself called *Gebrauchsmusik* (variously translated as utility, workaday, functional music), but the label has stuck to it, obscuring the vision of those who hold that music is anything but a mundane task. The fact remains that his *Sonatas* for solo violin, viola, or cello, the fruits of these years, are equally *Gebrauchsmusik*, being intended for use in the privacy of the study and not in the limelight of publicity.

Hindemith's appointment as professor of composition, in 1927, to the Berlin State Conservatorium cut down the time he could spare for the festivals and probably caused him to leave the Amar Quartet in 1929. By this time the list of his works shows with what seriousness and initiative he had devoted himself to composition. He had produced four *String Quartets*, a *Quintet for Clarinet and Strings* (Op. 30), a

String Trio (Op. 34), and a *Trio for Viola, Heckelphone, and Cello* (Op. 47). With three groups of *Sonatas* bearing the opus numbers 11, 25 and 31, for violin, viola, cello, viola d'amore with or without piano, and the canonic *Sonatina for Two Flutes*, this makes an imposing catalogue for an artist of thirty-four, much of whose time was spent in touring as a virtuoso.

Plenty of the music is patently experimental, not all of it decisive – not nearly so decisive, indeed, as his critics. The *F minor Quartet* (Op. 10) is linear and displays a consequent melodic angularity still present in his work; its innovations are those of external form. The *Cello Sonata in A minor* (Op. 11) uses the twelve-tone scale without allegiance to the harmonic background. The *Third Quartet* (Op. 22) is decidedly atonal, decidedly horizontal, and independent in its parts. Op. 23, a cycle of six songs, *Die junge Magd*, for contralto, flute, clarinet, and string quartet, makes the vocal part declamatory and independent in the main. Yet, hard on the ear though so much of this music is, the composer's undeniable sense of humour was even then discernible. If it is true that, a competent master of several instruments, Hindemith forged a line that was the outcome of executant promptings, it is also true that early experiences in the art of life infuse his work. He boasts that he had tried his hands at everything from opera to jazz, from café to cinema; and it was suggested by the late Edwin Evans, that as 'he took to every phase of activity the same resilient spirit, extracting from each whatever exhilaration his ingenuity could devise' he became a master of parody.

Nevertheless parody was kept in place. The best examples would be found in compositions that Hindemith never intended for publication. Some of them are occasionally brought out for the delectation of private gatherings. The more legitimate employment of this brand of humour was reserved for stage works. His earliest operas, *Mörder, Hoffnung der Frauen* and *Das Nuschi-Nuschi*, both one-act works, appeared at Stuttgart in 1921, followed the next year, by *Sancta Susanna*, also in a single act. The subject-matter of all three has a somewhat unsavoury character; the music is described as brilliantly modernistic and vividly dramatic. The fact that none of them has been revived outside Germany (with the exception of performances at the German Opera in Prague, 1923) is perhaps their own fair comment.

But with *Cardillac* (1926), to a text adapted from E. T. A. Hoffmann's *Das Fräulein von Scuderi*, Hindemith steps into the front rank of operatic composers. The very connexion with Hoffmann implies that Hindemith was not, even then, devoid of Romanticism; but the work reveals less a departure from a style he had made for himself than a bias, not fully to be withstood, towards humanistic expression. At the first production in Dresden, critics who thought it important to label it an atonal opera, to point out that Hindemith, like the hero, pursued art for art's sake, critics who went to scoff, remained to admire. *Cardillac* follows the old tradition of separate numbers; the singers and the orchestra are independent of each other, the latter contriving a series of fugues and other set forms, the former rarely luxuriating in occasional voluptuous flights.

The music critic of *The Times*, who heard it in Prague in 1927, remarked that the orchestral design 'sounded like Bach played on a nightmare organ, all the pipes of which had been mixed up by some devilish joker'; but he was obliged to add that he found 'great beauty in the alternation of ominous reiterated chords with the perpetual weaving of contrapuntal patterns.' And, significantly, he came to the conclusion that in this work Hindemith expressed something that could not have been said in any other way.

Next, in company with Milhaud's *Rape of Europa*, Toch's *Princess and the Pea* and Kurt Weill's *Mahogany*, came *Hin und Zurück*, a 'satirical sketch' with music, staged at the Baden-Baden festival (1927). In keeping with the action, the second half of which reverses the first half, the music does the same, an intellectual effort that, brittle as it is, scored a success there and then.

In *Neues vom Tag* (*News of the Day*, 1929) jazz and fugue rub shoulders. Though the topicality of this opera has shortened its life (it is more a series of press-cuttings than a connected drama), it must be regarded as important to Hindemith's own story. Besides a chorus of stenographers singing to the accompaniment of clattering typewriters, it contains a bathroom scene. This episode incurred the marked displeasure of that eminent moralist, Dr Goebbels, and may well have caused him to examine the composer's personal background more closely.

Mathis der Mahler

The episode brings us to a work that has done more to add to Hindemith's audience than any, before or since. *Mathis der Mahler* had its première outside Germany, at Zurich, in 1938. The opera, inspired by Grünewald's Isenheim altarpiece, was composed to Hindemith's own text. It was to have been given in Berlin under the conductorship of Furtwängler, but already in 1933 hints that Hindemith was a Jew were made current. This was not the fact, though he had committed the unforgiveable sin of marrying a Jewish wife. His talents were admitted, but he was publicly accused of living, working, and feeling with Jews. When Furtwängler made the mistake of undertaking that first performance of *Mathis* in Berlin, there was a violent scene with the authorities back stage. In publishing a brave defence of Hindemith the conductor joined the composer in 'error'; he dared to proclaim that the accused artist was one of the few creative musicians living, a pioneer of the return to simplicity and the reaction against pseudo-romanticism.

Exile

Interestingly enough his works gained in popularity from this conflict. Music that had been received coldly was brought out and applauded. But Nazism had no room for Hindemith; in 1935 he went to Turkey, there to reorganize the musical life of the country, an appointment doubtless advanced by his one-time colleague Amar.

Mathis the Painter, which the Nazis hated because the libretto dealt with the defeat of German liberalism in the Peasants' War, has suffered in Britain by presentation in concert form; it is true that the symphonic suite prepared by Hindemith himself won adherents here, but stage performance is the only proper vehicle for its genuine dramatic power. The composer has gone behind Grünewald's paintings, realizing them in terms of a music that will not conform to the aesthetic of a Verdi or a Wagner. It is as far from them as was Grünewald from the canons accepted in his time. While its static moments are admitted, Hindemith's creativeness is rarely in doubt, or his humour, or even a relaxation from his more extreme personal disciplines. 'It would not be too much to say that *Mathis* is the noblest work of art that has come out of Germany for years.'

In 1937, at the invitation of Elizabeth Sprague Coolidge, Hindemith toured the United States as soloist and as conductor of his own works. Eventually he settled there as composer and teacher of composition at the Berkshire Music Centre, then at Yale University, proceeding to Harvard in 1949.

America and Definitive Theory

Since then America has claimed him as her own. There, he has been absorbed in his academic duties, and most of all in creative work. Important theoretical treatises have come from his hand, his *Groundwork of Musical Composition*, for instance, a lucid exposition of his method, which is based entirely upon the laws of sound. The chromatic scale is his fundamental, the relative values between any two notes producing a fresh series of intervals. The end result is a 'system of chords built on intervals that subsist from their own individual merit and are not the result of an arbitrary system. ... No chord is forbidden, provided its use seems essential to the composer.' Hindemith regards atonality as a cheap excuse for mental laziness.

These theories are best explored in the *Ludus Tonalis* for piano, described by Hindemith as studies in counterpoint, tonal organization, and piano playing. His consistency is such that they can be equally well discerned in his most moving works, such as the poignant *Requiem, For our Loved Ones*, to Whitman's *When Lilacs in the Dooryard Bloom'd*, or in the incomparably brilliant orchestral variations *Metamorphosis of Themes by Weber* or in the (relatively) euphonious ballet-overture *Cupid and Psyche*. The utilitarian aspect of his music should be seen in relation not only to works composed for mechanical instruments, or the *Music for Amateurs*, but in such things as the children's play *Let's Make a Town* or the *Mourning Music*, composed for the B.B.C. in two or three hours, for the death of George V.

There are contradictions in his work that belong as much to the times as to the man. Deploring the gap that has indubitably widened between composers and their public, Hindemith essayed to write music of simplicity to bridge it. It may be that his mind is too essentially logical to attract wide favour. But it may also be that national education as a system, or educators themselves indeed, have failed to keep abreast. Whatever the verdict, one thing seems beyond doubt and that is his unswerving musical genius, which mellows in Hindemith the man and in us according to the measure of our understanding.

GUSTAV HOLST

1874–1934

A. E. F. DICKINSON

> 'Most people are overcome by mountain air at first...
> the remedy is to have more and more and more.'

Tradition and London

Gustav Holst was the elder brother of the fourth generation of a Swedish family of professional musicians, which left Baltic Russia in 1807 and settled in Cheltenham. His father was an accomplished pianist, gave orchestral concerts at the Rotunda, and taught many piano pupils, one of whom, Clara Lediard, he married. She died in 1882. Later he married another pupil, a theosophist. Meanwhile, Gustav, not overburdened with attention or understanding, with a weak sight and a weak chest, both neglected – he was 'miserable and scared' – learnt piano and violin and fell for Grieg. He went to Cheltenham Grammar School. An early perusal of Berlioz's *Instrumentation* led by devious routes to student life at the Royal College of Music, in 1893.

After a term or two of the needed groundwork, Stanford accepted Holst as a composition pupil. Stanford's froward and uncompromising retention of certain personal habits of style may be questioned, but his thoroughness and insistence on the proper absorption of technique were what Holst wanted. Another pupil, Fritz Hart, became a good companion; in two vivid articles he has left an admirable account of Holst the young man, musically ignorant by London standards but tremendously in earnest about what he knew and observed. The two joined forces, Hart with the words, in several operettas: *Ianthe*, *The Idea*, *The Revoke* (Stanford rehearsed this Op. 1 and would have put it on as a curtain-raiser to *Shamus*, if the latter's run had not come to an end too soon) and *The Magic Mirror* (destroyed as too Wagnerian). These sharpened Holst's sense of the theatrical and untheatrical, and enabled him to let certain raw impulses out of his system.

Two of Professor Hart's pictures especially deserve preserving. One of Holst, bicycling to Cheltenham and back, 'looking one of the weirdest figures imaginable ... his trombone slung over his shoulders,' dismounting at night on some lonely hill in the Cotswolds and blowing soul-satisfying blasts, to the consternation of a neighbouring farmer. The other, dragging Hart to Barnes Common to see the sun rise, after returning on foot from a performance by the choral class at Buckingham Palace, in glad rags, the epitome of the morning after.

From Keyboard to Trombone

At College Holst 'learnt the piano' with Herbert Sharpe; but neuritis was now so pronounced that he had to accept the inevitable and give up all idea of becoming a pianist of any eminence. He took up the trombone, which might at least exercise his lungs. In 1894 he at last obtained a composition scholarship, supplementing this with playing trombone on Brighton Pier, or in Wurm's White Viennese Band, where he once gave an astonishing performance of what proved to be the piccolo part. It was a big dip from the Busoni level, but accepted.

Social Contacts

In 1895 Holst met Vaughan Williams. They became mentors to each other for life, and the best of friends. It is odd that Ireland did not come into the circle at the time. An interest in Fabian Socialism introduced Shaw into Holst's life; he was also influenced by William Morris, to whose memory he paid tribute in the *Elegy* of the *Cotswold Symphony*. Whitman was an early affection that found a title for an overture in 1899 and remained a constant creative stimulus. Holst conducted the Socialist Choir (in Morley, Purcell, and Wagner). One of the sopranos was the lovely, sunny-haired Isabel Harrison, with whom he fell at once in love. They were married in 1901, living first in lodgings, as he was on tour. In 1898 he regretfully left the College to be first trombone and répétiteur to the Carl Rosa Company, and later trombone in the Scottish Orchestra.

'The Bhagavad Gîtâ'

In 1899 Holst developed first an interest in Sanskrit literature and then a determination to learn it well enough to be able to make his own translations. It is apparent that the unworldly philosophy of the

Bhagavad Gîtâ touched deep springs in Holst's mind. His first considerable work, however, was the so-called *Cotswold Symphony*, performed at Bournemouth under Dan Godfrey in 1902.

School Appointments

In 1903 Holst became music master at the James Allen School for Girls, East Dulwich. Thus began his major career on the teaching side. Considered 'eccentric' at first, he soon won the admiration of the headmistress, and some of his concerts are long remembered. He stayed on until 1919, when other work called him.

In 1905 Holst conducted the Scena, *The Mystic Trumpeter* (Whitman), at a Patron's Fund Concert at the Queen's Hall. In this year began his historic connexion with St Paul's Girls' School, London, at that time full of healthy conservatism about music classes. An early pupil writes: 'The "Beaver" was an untidy young man, who used to run his hands through his hair in moments of excitement. His shining spectacles and his questing nose always seemed to be egging him on – and his enthusiasm knew no bounds. ... We all thought his echo choirs etc. quite mad. ... Do mention the Masque, *The Vision of Dame Christian*, performed every six years. It is beautiful.' Certainly Holst was fortunate in having the co-operation both of the High Mistress and of other mistresses on the spot to cope with the bald and pertinent details of school organization and adjustment. In time the musical life of the school grew to something like abundance on the performing side, with enthusiasts eagerly and competently devouring Vittoria, Morley, Bach *et hoc genus omne*. For Holst the composer, the impersonal urge of all this voluntary counterpoint gave him a lasting and entire satisfaction, about which he sometimes had misgivings later, as an other-worldly style that might dominate unwisely his appeal to a wider world.

He did not believe in 'musical appreciation'. To him it meant theorizing instead of doing. He was seemingly unaware of what had long been done for listeners elsewhere and how well the ground could be prepared at school for active listening to *The Planets*, for example. On the other hand, he certainly did believe in influencing the taste of the young, for it took some Paulinas years after school to enjoy the 'sentimental' Schubert or Verdi. Which sounds uncommonly like theorizing instead of listening.

Folk-Song

In 1905, noticeably late, Holst became aware of the revival of English folk-song and of its virtually fresh qualities. Undoubtedly his sympathies lay with the popularists. His folk-song studies reflect the communal, infectious side, rather than the inward stress.

Happy Events

In 1906 the Holsts acquired a house in Richmond, Surrey, and also a two-roomed cottage on the island of Sheppey in Kent. (A few years later they moved into a house at Barnes, overlooking the Thames.) Imogen was born in the spring of 1907. In other ways that year was eventful: Sanskrit bore fruit in the opera *Sita* and some of the *Rig Veda* settings for solo-voice or chorus (Edith Clegg sang some of the solo-hymns, with *The Heart Worships*); and Holst was put in charge of the music at the Morley College for Working Men and Women. At the Morley classes, used to vague enjoyment of recreational melody, the new director's artistic seriousness at first caused dismay and resignations, but a new and more responsive group appeared, or were found, just in time. One singer described the College as 'a sort of heaven we go to on Mondays and Wednesdays,' and soon the general enthusiasm was tremendous. Byrd motets, a Bach cantata, and a Haydn symphony became annual events, and at the crest of the wave, *The Fairy Queen*, parts of the *B minor Mass* and *Die Meistersinger*, and the Vaughan Williams *Mass*.

Unhappy Events and The Planets

In 1908 *Sita* was submitted for the Ricordi opera prize (£500 and promise of performance and publication). By three votes to one the judges (Stanford, Ricordi, Joseph Bennett, and Percy Pitt) chose E. W. Naylor's *The Angelus*, which was performed at Covent Garden in 1909 and revived in 1921. *Sita* had taken the composer (and copyists) seven years; but since the opera remains to this day in manuscript, the judges cannot be blamed who hesitated to back (for publication and production) a grandiose Indian opera in a far from matured, indeed rather derivative, modern style, barely capable of absorbing a plot so thrilling that it might easily become a riot. However, the blow fell on top of acute neuritis, and the doctor ordered Holst to a warm spot, which (with friendly aid) materialized as Algeria, with a bicycle. This contact reverberated later in the distinctive *Beni Mora* suite (1910). In the autumn Holst wrote the opera *Savitri*, another Indian work. But no performance came in sight. In 1910 followed *The Cloud Messenger*, an ode founded on a poem of the dramatist, Kalidasa (fifth century A.D.), and the third group of choral hymns from the *Rig Veda*.

In 1912 a new patron appeared in Balfour Gardiner, at whose orchestral concerts were given the *Beni Mora* suite and, in 1913, *The Cloud Messenger*. The latter did not go well, and only the piano score is printed. To cheer the composer up, Gardiner invited him to Spain with Clifford and Arnold Bax. Clifford Bax has described the holiday in *Inland Far*.

Holst returned to find in the new music wing, just opened at St Paul's, a sound-proof room for his own work, centrally heated. Miss Holst (six at the time) generously testifies that this was what he had always wanted. Here he could be on Sundays and school holidays in absolute quiet. He wrote the cheerful *St Paul's Suite* for strings there almost at once, partly by transcribing for the finale the Dargason movement (*cum Greensleeves*) from the second military band *Suite* – a strange economy.

So far, on the large scale, Indian culture had been made vocal in the melodic lines of English vernacular, illuminated by orchestral motives and contrasts. Inevitably, perhaps, the orchestra had been less cultivated for its own sake. In 1914 astrological hobbies, and horoscope reading in particular, somehow suggested the proposition of an orchestral suite that should mirror in turn the guiding-forces of our destiny, under the names of the planets. *Mars* was thus sketched in full with a powerful, unromantic verisimilitude that now seems prophetic of the overwhelming and ruthless struggle for world dominance since. When Great Britain had declared war on Germany, Holst tried to join up, but apart from his neuritis and short-sightedness he was counted out on the name that an ancestor had taken to himself. At this time, as it happened, he extended his enthusiasm for the English madrigal composers. (I once heard him introduce to a Whitsun gathering 'a madrigal by one of my favourite composers: Thomas Tomkins'.)

The situation evoked *Dirge for Two Veterans* (male voices, brass, and drums). *Venus* and *Jupiter* followed, in 1915 *Saturn*, *Uranus*, and *Neptune* and in 1917 *Mercury* and the completion of this tremendous and unparalleled suite.

Whitsun Singing and the Hymn of Jesus

Holst was now living in an old cottage on the top of a hill at Thaxted in Essex, and for the first time, it seems, became aware of the grim vicissitudes of rural life, as well as of its kindly compensations to a disinterested observer. The spacious and well-lit church seemed to call for a richer music than the unaccompanied plain-song of the parish choir. Could not he unite past and present pupils from Morley and St Paul's in Bach and Palestrina and Purcell? The vicar, Conrad Noel, consented. Thus in 1916 the first of the Whitsun week-ends of music took place. The wider scope and purpose of these meetings have been indicated in the opening quotation of this essay.* Holst also made this pertinent comment: 'As far as it went it was heaven. Just as the average amateur's way of using music as a seductive or stimulant is purgatory, and the professional's way of using music as a topic of conversation or as a means of getting money is hell.' Heaven included *Turn back, O man*, and *A Festival Chime* (*St Denio*).

In 1916 *Savitri* was at last produced at the London School of Opera under Hermann Grünebaum, with a re-arrangement of the choral parts for women's voices, which became permanent. It was notably revived in 1921 at the Lyric Theatre, Hammersmith, and in 1923 at Covent Garden.

After the completion in 1917 of *The Planets*, which no conductor was prepared to venture upon then, Holst sat down to a rendering of the *Hymn of Jesus* from the Apocryphal Gospels, in his own free translation from the Greek (as learnt from Jane Joseph, a Paulina). Plain-song tunes, ecstatic periods in quintuple metre, and strange sequences of choral antiphony and multiple harmony, blend in a supremely infectious devotional recital. Neither orthodox nor universal, it was bound in the end to confirm the faithful and to rouse the non-committal to a realization of its genius. The *Four Songs for Voice and Violin* followed.

Service in the Near East

In 1918 Holst had the 'von' taken from his name. He then joined the music section of the Y.M.C.A. universities committee, of which Percy Scholes was principal, and was appointed music organizer at

---

* From Imogen Holst's *Gustav Holst*, to which I am indebted for many facts about her father's movements.

Salonica. As a farewell, Gardiner gave him the services of Queen's Hall and Adrian Boult with the London Symphony Orchestra for a private performance of *The Planets*. Earlier in 1918 Vaughan Williams's *London Symphony*, revised, had been given under similar auspices before the composer left for active service in the R.G.A.

Holst was on his way out when the Armistice was signed. At Salonica the teaching was continuous though completely at random; but he managed to arrange a concert of British works in the teeth of demobilization. It was a stab both for British music and for the concern of soldiers for vital music; a slight rejoinder to the peasant ploughing the battlefield, 'the greatest sight on earth'. After a revealing leave spent at Athens, Whitsun found Holst at Constantinople, organizing a music competition with concerts by massed choirs and orchestras every night. Part of the Byrd three-part *Mass* thus found its way into strange surroundings (an audacious choice). The *Festival Chime* became *A Chime for Homecoming*. Holst missed the saturation of former Whitsuntides, but was satisfied.

The Composer's Return

In 1919 Holst resumed most of the old threads. He gave up Dulwich for new work. At the R.C.M., H. P. Allen had succeeded Parry, leaving vacant the charge of music in what was then University College, Reading. Holst filled the post for four years. He also joined the R.C.M. staff as 'professor' of composition. Meanwhile, he had set Whitman's *Ode to Death* for chorus and orchestra. The work was dedicated to Cecil Coles (the composer) 'and the others', including doubtless Edward Mason, and remains one of the composer's deepest utterances. It was introduced at the Leeds Festival, 1922, and in London in 1923 by the Bach Choir under Vaughan Williams. In 1919 the *Hymn of Jesus* was published by the Carnegie Trust. It was first presented by the Philharmonic Choir newly formed by C. Kennedy Scott, the composer 'conducting' (with fives almost sixes). Myra Hess, Percy Scholes, and others tried in the interval to secure a repetition, but there was no further room in the programme. The Oxford Bach Choir gave an enthusiastic performance under Allen, as a prelude to – *Gerontius*!

World Success

Meanwhile *The Planets*, played to an enthusiastic invitation audience under Boult in 1919, repeated in part in 1920 with sundry old codgers in the orchestra applauding the composer quite wildly at the end, and later performed entire under Albert Coates, was becoming assured of a *succès d'estime*. It came to New York and Chicago (competing for the American première) and then to Berlin under Goossens. Typewritten slips had to be provided for autograph-hunters and other nuisances. Holst also refused all invitations to become vice-president and all honorary degrees or titles. For that, an extra trumpet must have sounded for him later. But the distractions were becoming real.

More Opera

Early in 1923 Holst took a false step on a platform during a rehearsal and suffered slight concussion. The after-effects were serious, but he was able to accept an invitation to conduct at Ann Arbor for the University of Michigan, refusing the offer of a Chair there during his visit. Meanwhile, the British National Opera Company under Goossens had produced the brief and amusing *The Perfect Fool* at the opening of the Covent Garden season. Its simple humour proved disturbing, and the whole thing too much of a mix-up to strike home, but the ballet music was soon picked out for orchestral concerts. A new *Fugal Concerto* for flute, oboe, and strings was produced with *The Planets* at Queen's Hall, twice in one week, to a full house, with a 'tremendous reception' of the suite at the second performance.

However, Holst was nearing a breakdown. After seeing *The Perfect Fool*, an anonymous man of wealth gave him a large sum to encourage composition. He stopped most of his teaching for three months. In spite of a new symphony, it did no good. Working lightly and resting slightly were a strain on his nerves, and sleeplessness added to the burden of living, 'sinking lower and lower into a grey region where thought and feeling had ceased to exist'. Under medical advice Holst retired to Thaxted for a year, living now in a 'square, solid, comfortable house' in the middle of the town, with an ex-batman from an officers' mess in attendance. Before long he was feeling better, and stronger spectacles secured him a sight he had not known for years. Meanwhile the new symphony grew up, as he remarked, alongside the flowers and vegetables. It was to be the First Choral Symphony, with words taken from his favourite poet, Keats. It was a strange favour, that he thus wished the *Ode on a Grecian Urn* and lighter stuff to achieve symphony, not in Mallarmé's metaphorical sense, but in the transformed medium of choral-orchestral recital, in the four conventional divisions. However, the first draft was finished.

The next work was the short Falstaff opera, *At the Boar's Head* (dictated). It arose, again rather oddly, from the chance perception that one of the many country dance tunes lying about the house could be 'fitted' to some words of Shakespeare. A 'fascinating task' (Holst)? Shakespeare did not write his lines to be carried off their feet by a folk-dance enthusiast.* However, the folky tunes carried the composer along, as they had carried Byrd and Farnaby and, for racier doctrine, Bach.

Friendship and Honour

On Holst's fiftieth birthday he received from Jane Joseph, on behalf of friends and pupils, a cheque for £350, to enable him to have a foreign holiday. 'They were the names of real friends. They would have agreed with the one who told him, "You have long ago created a terrifically high standard of being companionable, and you are always surpassing it".' Elsewhere Miss Holst states that comradeship was the chief article of her father's conscious belief.

A few days later came a letter from Yale University offering the Howland Memorial Prize, awarded for distinction in literature or art, not without some 'idealistic element'. Holst had no hesitation in deciding to make this exception to his rule, considering it a real and undeniable honour.

In 1925 Holst returned to London. The B.N.O.C. were rehearsing *At the Boar's Head*, which they gave in Manchester and Golders Green, London, under Malcolm Sargent. It was generally thought to show too much contrapuntal craftsmanship – an odd judgement in the land often without opera but never without fugue. It was rather that mere fugal enthusiasm cannot integrate material meant to be itself. The composer lay low and produced a *Terzetto* for flute, oboe, and viola in triple tonality. It was one of the things that had to grow even on him. After being lost for many years, it was published around 1944. A setting of seven songs for women's voices and strings, to words by Bridges, made a contrast.

Keats in Symphony

The symphony made a striking appearance at the Leeds Festival under Coates, and then in London at a concert held by the Royal

* In her second book Miss Holst seems to have come round to this estimate

Philharmonic Society to mark the centenary of their first performance of the Ninth Symphony. Holst considered this honour overwhelming, as well he might, if only because the great classic celebrated Communion and comradeship and saturation and all that he stood for. Coates secured the symphony a rousing performance, so that it held its ground in the context of classical revival usual at such assemblies of choral and orchestral works. Unhappily the London performance was spoilt by having to take its chance after a night journey and a heavy day of recording. Adrian Boult achieved the right spirit and an astonishing finish in the performance in 1934, just within the composer's hearing. The critics' initial reservations did not daunt Holst, who had said what he meant, and meant what he said; but Vaughan Williams's candid confession of 'cold enthusiasm' (probably a wide impression to-day) was more disturbing.

In 1926 this confirmed anti-appreciationist gave a lecture-course at Liverpool University, and the Cramb Lectures at Glasgow; the latter on orchestration! The Holsts now moved to Brook End, a house near Thaxted, with a 'perfect' music-room. But Holst only appeared for an occasional week-end. He always had a strong wanderlust. The General Strike left him distressed both at his own ignorance and at the unconcern that had made it possible; he was a confessed 'half-hogger', but determined to cleave to his own path in life, without ulterior motive, according to his fundamentals.

At Home and Abroad

In 1927 citizens of Cheltenham decided to recognize publicly Holst's 'genius, combined with hard work and self-denial', chiefly in the form of a programme of his works given by the Birmingham Orchestra after three full rehearsals. The main work was *The Planets*. Holst conducted, with Boult manfully in readiness in case of strain. In the same year he was asked to be conductor of the Bach Choir (London). He accepted, but the doctor forbade it. He would particularly have liked to build up a rendering of the *B minor Mass*, culminating in the *Sanctus*, whose rare air had from the first (Worcester, 1895) given him the sensation of 'floating through time and space'.

In this year he wrote *Egdon Heath*. Heard in London shortly after Hardy's death, it became a tribute to his art. Its severe texture, 'like man, slighted and enduring', was extraordinarily characteristic of Holst's latest development. It remained his favourite work; and possibly the forbidding title and associate Hardy quotation have prevented some listeners from perceiving the passion that left the ground to lose itself in this slow, quiet piece, compressed to the barest essentials. (In Paris it was fiercely hissed.)

In 1929, while on holiday in Italy, Holst heard of the death of Jane Joseph; an irreparable loss of guidance in the art of clear thinking, exact statement, and patient study, as well as of personal co-operation. He proceeded to fulfil an invitation to New York. On returning, he settled down to work (with periods of numbness) with twelve Humbert Wolfe settings (including *Betelgeuse*), a two violin *Concerto* in two-keys-in-one for the Aranyis, a *Choral Fantasia* (Bridges's *Man born of Desire*), *Hammersmith* for the B.B.C. Military Band, and *Tale of the Wandering Scholar*, a chamber opera (Clifford Bax).

America again

The year 1931 was desultory. A film job wore him out and then came to nothing. The Whitsun Singers gave the Vaughan Williams *Mass* at Chichester on August Bank Holiday, in a full cathedral. The *Fantasia*, 'a sadly neglected masterpiece' according to Gerald Abraham, appeared unconvincingly at Gloucester. But now Harvard asked him to be lecturer for six months, and the Boston Symphony Orchestra invited him to conduct three concerts of his own works. Invitations to conduct at Washington and Ann Arbor followed (along with sundry offers of degrees). Besides *The Planets* and *The Perfect Fool* there were, later, the *Fantasia* and *Dirge*. In the middle of it all he was taken ill and had to have a blood transfusion. He rallied after one bad night, during which he felt a deep gratitude for three things: 'music, the Cotswolds, and Ralph Vaughan Williams.' On returning to England, he wrote some *Canons* in three keys (three, at least, to the eye) and resumed work at St Paul's.

Last Works

Just after Christmas he was again taken ill. In and out of a nursing home, he was able to write the *Lyric Movement* for Lionel Tertis and orchestra, which he heard broadcast later, and *Brook Green*, a second St Paul's Suite; also music for a film and a pageant, both abortive. In 1934, after a test period of rigid diet, he had to choose between a major operation and a minor operation with a restricted life. The major operation was decided upon.

He heard the broadcast of the *Choral Symphony* and finished scoring *Scherzo* (of a symphony) begun in 1933. A second choral symphony (1926) had gone no further than the choice of some Meredith poems and a number of fragments.* Finally he sent his greetings to the Whitsun Singers.

After a 'successful' operation his heart gave out on 25 May. His ashes were buried in Chichester Cathedral, at which the Whitsun Singers sang his *This Have I Done for my True Love*. Boult's tribute at the B.B.C. that week included the *Dirge*, *Egdon Heath*, and *Ode to Death*. In 1937 the sound-proof Holst Room was opened in Morley College as a memorial from his friends.

The Holst Tradition

That peculiar unity of Holst and his friends in the Whitsun and other gatherings filled in most gaps between one creative effort and another. It comes to later generations as a historical model of what music-in-itself can mean to all sorts of people in the simplest circumstances, if the spirit is right. His creative efforts and strivings will not so simply be ours. But they remain a striking encouragement to all to pursue their stars without fear or compromise, from the native worth of Swansea Town and Brook Green and Egdon to the no-man's-land of Neptune and Betelgeuse, and from the quiet austerities of *Savitri* and the *Ode to a Grecian Urn* to the unbridled ecstasies of the *Hymn of Jesus*. There is still plenty to hear and consider, almost as a novelty; and more than one neglected masterpiece.

* See Miss Holst's autograph quotations in her second book.

ARTHUR HONEGGER

b. 1892

ARTHUR HUTCHINGS

'Les Six' in the Twenties

The history of music in this century has been that of many isolated artistic movements, guided by conflicting principles. So far there is little to suggest a common direction of progress, unless we take as wide a view as did Constant Lambert in *Music Ho!* and are blessed with his critical acumen.

One of the movements that achieved notoriety in the twenties was centred round the group of French composers styled 'Les Six', after the manner of the Russian Five of the preceding century. Their activities were much publicized and still find a prominent place in accounts of twentieth-century music, in which they are honoured as leading the reaction against impressionism and advocating the return to 'down-to-earth everyday music'. Paris became, as before in history, the stage for discussion of a stylistic change. After three decades and another world war, the enthusiasm and antagonism engendered by the sensational exploits of this group seem excessive, and the passage of time has dimmed the reputation of most of their number. Of the original six, Auric, Durey, Honegger, Milhaud, Poulenc, and Tailleferre, three only can lay claim to international recognition; of these we accept Poulenc as a writer of exquisite wit for the piano and sometimes of poignant sentiment for voice with piano. Arthur Honegger and Darius Milhaud hold our interest both by their achievements and by their promise of further development, for both have retained their pleasure in exploration. Unlike Poulenc, in whom the invention of new toys, so to speak, is a merit and not, as say those who would relegate all but 'noble' music to commercial composers, a defect, Honegger and Milhaud have succeeded in throwing off their childish delight in novelty. Novelty is germane to Poulenc's muse; in theirs, its piquancy soon went stale and merely reminded us of their vocbulary during the twenties.

Early Influences

Of 'Les Six', Arthur Honegger was the least addicted to this toying with fashion; from the outset he showed a more earnest bent. This we may perhaps attribute to his ancestry, which is German-Swiss; he did not acquire the Gallic wit that was the common language of all his five associates. He was born on 10 March 1892 in Le Havre, where his father was engaged in the import business. As often happens in tracing musical influences, we must look to the composer's mother for his chief artistic inheritance; she passed on to her son her own love and understanding of the classical composers – a rare endowment in a town where musical events were few. Arthur was taught the violin and soon began to compose, though he also found time for athletic pursuits, later to find expression in music. His first composition teacher was an organist, Robert-Charles Martin, and an equally valuable influence was his first acquaintance with Bach, through the good work of André Caplet.

Though it was intended that he should enter the family business, his parents were persuaded to a recognition of his true vocation, and he spent two years at the Zürich Conservatoire. On his return to France, he continued his studies at the Paris Conservatoire, where his teachers included Gédalge for counterpoint, Widor for orchestration, and d'Indy for conducting. His most valuable lessons were the opportunities given in d'Indy's class to hear his own works and the discipline and advice that Gédalge administered to his pupils. In view of Honegger's later works we may ask whether in fact he accepted Gédalge's insistence on the absoluteness of music – 'neither literature nor painting'. One of his first friends at the Conservatoire was Darius Milhaud, his exact contemporary, though already a prolific composer. Honegger spent far more of his time in studying the great composers than did most of his fellow-students and so matured later in the field of composition. At the same time he preserved along with his musical devotion the early interest in sport. His delight in machinery seems curiously at variance with the normal concept of an artist and was possibly the result of his parentage. As with Tonio Kröger in Thomas Mann's story, the father's preoccupation with business affairs and the mother's artistic appreciation produced an unusual synthesis, '*ein in die Kunst verirrter Bürger*'.

First Compositions

After a year's service in the Swiss Army, Honegger settled down to composition. His first works, dating from 1914 onwards, are songs showing the influence of both Debussy and Wagner and a few piano pieces in which the pianism has affinities with Ravel's 'piano scoring'. One of the first piano works, *Toccata and Variations* (1916), was performed by a young pianist, Andrée Vaurabourg, whom Honegger had met at the Conservatoire. Her help in producing his first works was valuable, and the friendship matured during the next few years to culminate in marriage. Another early work, which has received occasional performance in this country, is the *Rhapsody for Two Flutes, Clarinet, and Piano* of 1917; it is wholly undistinguished, apart from a vague tribute to Debussy, and serves to show us the starting-point from which Honegger has developed.

The first work of any significance is the *String Quartet* of 1916–17. The passionately chromatic first movement shows in its vigorous polyphonic treatment a clear break from Debussy: the parts pursue their own course in a contrapuntal web in which harmonies are incidental. The slow movement is similarly complex, though here the harmony can be more directly traced back to romantic predecessors. A feature that was to become common practice with Honegger is the presentation of the thematic material in reverse order on its restatement. Also completed in 1917 was Honegger's first notable orchestral work, *Le Chant de Nigamon*, written for performance at d'Indy's orchestration class. Apart from its assured handling of the orchestra, the work is interesting in its macabre underlying programme, taken from *Le Souriquet* by Gustave Aimard, an account of Indian tribal warfare in North America and a description of the torture of captured warriors, who are scalped and burned by their opponents. In the midst of the flames they sing their death-song, falling silent to listen to Nigamon, their chieftain, who sings on rapturously to his death. Honegger's predilection for such themes is seen in his later works *La Danse Macabre*, *La Danse des Morts*, and *Jeanne d'Arc au Bûcher*. Strict adherence to the programme is forfeited in the cause of musical design; Wagnerisms persist still, though Nigamon's song is primitive and quasi-mixolydian, and again there is great contrapuntal ingenuity. The barbarous subject calls for angular motives and percussive rhythms, and Honegger is deficient in neither.

In the following year, Honegger was commissioned to write incidental music for a masque or mystery-play by Paul Méral, *Le Dit des Jeux du Monde*. There are ten dances, two interludes, and an epilogue, each dance accompanying the appearance on the stage of a pair of characters in a representation of man's relation to the elements of nature and his eventual eclipse by them. Another musical influence appears in this work, that of Stravinsky, detected both in the rhythms (two movements are for percussion instruments only) and in the colourful use of the orchestra – a small group of strings, flute, trumpet, and percussion. Yet the old influences still show through, and the dance in which 'Man and Woman' are paired inevitably recalls that apotheosis of erotic emotion, *Tristan*. Thus, although this work was Honegger's most satisfactory achievement to that date, confirming and crystallizing his skill as a contrapuntist, orchestrator, and musical architect, it suffers from too wide a variety of style. This has continued to be a defect of his works in the eyes of many critics, though others acclaim him on just this score. On its first performance in Paris, where it was produced by Jane Bathori, a loyal patron and helper of young artists, *Le Dit des Jeux du Monde* was badly received; but this was to be expected in a city still under the spell of the more placid Debussy.

Not only Honegger had felt the need to steer French music from the pervading influence of the Impressionists. In a manifesto published in 1918, Jean Cocteau had called for a school of composers with new models of brevity, line, and precision, such as he found in Couperin, Erik Satie and jazz. Of these three widely different sources Satie had the most immediate influence on the school that came into being in 1920, to receive its name, 'Les Six', in an article by Henri Collet. The six composers had but little in common beyond their situation of relative obscurity and their desire to create a new, more virile French music. None had as yet made a reputation as a composer, and so they were bound by friendship, not by a common aesthetic programme or musical style.

At the time of this establishment of the group Honegger was engaged on a set of sonatas. They show no advance in his personal style, but would serve as introductions to his work if they were played more often in this country. The *Sonata for Two Violins* is particularly attractive and ingenious, while the *Cello Sonata* is the most profound. The clarinet *Sonatina* secures occasional performances over here and has been recorded: it uses jazz rhythms without descending to the mere cleverness often found in such *jeux d'esprit*. Another work of this time is the orchestral *Pastorale d'Été* (1920), a lyrical essay with diatonic or modal themes (the opening horn theme is mixolydian), though contrapuntal devices crop up even here.

A friend of Honegger, who was associated in the production of *Le Dit des Jeux du Monde*, Guy-Pierre Fauconnet, was responsible for the next important work, *Horace Victorieux* (1921), a dramatization of the story from Titus Livius. Fauconnet's death ensured that the original version was not completed, but Honegger used his music for a 'mimed symphony'. In this portrayal of a barbaric scene, the composer again appears at his best. Though Gédalge preached against 'painting' in music, there is plenty of it here, and as incidental music to what is seen it is admirable. As the two parties of three soldiers from Rome and Alba Longa prepare for the battle, fanfares ring out from three trombones and then three trumpets. The clash of the swords is depicted, and a fugue represents the flight of the surviving Roman. The structure is highly organized and shows a technique in which leading themes are transformed resourcefully on each re-appearance. Although Honegger considered it to be his best work, the stylistic inconsistencies already noted are more prominent than ever.

King David *and* Pacific 231

But in the same year Honegger wrote music that overrides these inconsistencies by its unquestionable sincerity and force. *King David*, produced in its original dramatic form in 1921 and in a concert version with full orchestra in 1923, has become Honegger's best-known work. He was engaged to write the music for the biblical drama by René Morax (on the recommendation of Ernest Ansermet, who had conducted *Horace* on its first performance) only after Stravinsky had been approached and had declined. Honegger began on 25 February 1921, and the rehearsals were due to begin in March; the choruses were written first and the entire work completed by 28 April. It is in three main sections and twenty-seven short episodes, a factor that helped its rapid composition, for there is only one extended movement in the work. The nobility of the subject and Honegger's sincerity in its treatment (his first biblical setting) carry us through this long procession of scenes, for which he provides apt and often simple music. Many of the choruses are in only two parts and predominantly diatonic. Atmosphere is evoked in a few bars, as in the opening (the barbaric march of the victorious army), David's psalm-singing while Saul hurls the javelin, and the loneliness of David in the wilderness. After David's coronation and the Israelite victory there is a long dance of jubilation, which makes a fitting centrepiece, propelled by an impulsive 12–8 rhythm. In the final section David sings two penitential psalms (musically welded together by a common theme) after his sin against Uriah, and these are among the most moving parts of a work that is far more human than any other by Honegger; the only macabre element is the scene in which the plague strikes Jerusalem and cries of fear and pain are interupted by loud orchestral hammer-blows. *King David* placed Honegger in the front rank of modern composers and rapidly became popular in both France and Germany. In England it has been received well on its few performances, but has not become part of our musical life; where choral music is concerned our attitude is insular.

Almost equally well known is Honegger's next work for orchestra, the symphonic movement *Pacific 231* of 1923. This is his first musical expression of that interest in mechanical engineering already mentioned. The piece depicts in a long accelerando the journey of an express locomotive. Unfortunately, while such music would make (and has made) an excellent background for a film, not all critics agree that it constitutes a satisfying piece of orchestral music. In his verdict on this 'mechanical romanticism' Lambert says 'A little more thought might have told the composer that music which depends on varying degrees of stylized noise and speed for its expression is, on the face of it, the last medium in which to attempt an evocation of non-stylized noise and speed.' Although I agree with Lambert's point in general, I am among those satisfied by *Pacific 231* as a concert piece. In orchestration and structure (on a canto fermo) the work is admirable, and the contracting note-values of the accelerations are cleverly contrived. Honegger has written two more symphonic movements; the first, *Rugby* (1928), is less directly pictorial than its predecessor, while the third has no title.

The Tireless Experimenter

Other works of this period deserving more frequent performance in this country are the *Piano Concertino* of 1924 and the *Cello Concerto* of 1929. Both contain elements of jazz, though they do not disturb the flow, for Honegger's rhythms are always virile. A less popular successor to *King David* is the oratorio *Judith* (1925), also written for René Morax. It is not possible here to discuss fully either this work or his operas, though mention must be made of *Antigone*, a musical tragedy with a libretto translated by Cocteau.

Honegger's first essay in absolute orchestral music, excluding the concertos, was the *Symphony* written for the fiftieth anniversary of the Boston Symphony Orchestra in 1931. It is in three movements, each based on one main theme, though subsidiary themes appear and are combined with Honegger's usual contrapuntal skill. The resultant atonal polyphonic texture, which is characteristic of the composer, gives way in the rondo to a naïve diatonic refrain, appearing in endless variants. Though this is not a great symphony (nor can it compare with some of our English symphonies), its appearance suggested that Honegger had turned away from illustrative music. Later works disproved this, and the three movements of the *Symphonie Liturgique* (1943) bear programmatic titles – 'Dies Irae', 'De profundis clamavi' and 'Dona nobis pacem' – though the movements are musically self-sufficient. The first is polyphonic and ceaselessly rhythmic, the second shows a return to consonance interrupted by an anguished middle section, and the finale achieves the peace of its title only after a grotesque and percussive climax has drowned the serenity of the previous movement in an outburst of cacophony.

Other late works of Honegger that have been broadcast in this country are *La Danse des Morts* and *Jeanne d'Arc au Bûcher*. The former is a retrogression to his earlier macabre and vulgarly descriptive style, but the second has enjoyed a vogue almost rivalling that of *King David*. It was written in 1938 to a text by Paul Claudel, originally as incidental music to the stage production, but later in a concert version. Though Honegger's music is always apt, and probably enhances stage performances of the work, it does not strike deep enough to justify the isolation of the concert hall, for there is none of the spontaneity and true emotion of *King David* here. Honegger can give a very good imitation of pigs to ridicule Porcus, the President of the Court, but the effect of this intrusion into a serious and at times moving work is disturbing. Similarly the card-game played by Pride, Stupidity, Greed, and Lust may be excellent satire, but it has no place in the account of a human being's death, whether she be peasant-girl or saint.

Thus, in our time, Honegger provides a distinct and serious musical personality; like that of Franck (though of a very un-Franckian temperament) it shows a fusion of French and Teuton traditions. With many others, he had to forge his way through eclecticism, armed only with natural facility and not, as are far less clever men, such as Sibelius or Vaughan Williams, with the kind of artistry that soon finds a dogged and unique personal idiom. For a composer who is so much 'of his age' – an age of philosophic, social, and artistic flux – to achieve even two or three fine works is to justify a number of less successful experiments. Honegger remains a tireless experimenter.

JOHN IRELAND

B. 1879

HUBERT FOSS

The Edwardian Age

No lances need be broken here in the tournament of discussion about the importance or negligibility of personal experiences in a composer's finished music. Biographically John Ireland's years have been spent in the service of the art of music, almost wholly in the composition of music, though some time has had to be given to performing as a means of continuing to compose; in his music he has expressed his soul fully and to our satisfaction: we need enquire little farther. The outward musical circumstances of a composer's life are a different matter altogether – into what sort of musical world was he born? What were his chances, his steps to fame? And there are a hundred other little questions we might well explore.

At the turn of this century, John Ireland had reached his majority, already a trained and experienced musician. Fifty-odd years later his fame is so solidly established that a younger generation, perhaps, may find it hard to look on him, as he was looked on, not so long ago, as one of the 'white hopes' of the modern English renaissance, as a neglected and individual genius fighting against circumstances. So rapid have been the changes in our English musical status and polity that a few words about the Edwardian period may be illuminating of his achievement.

It was a rich ten years, which began with Elgar's *Enigma Variations* and *Dream of Gerontius*, produced most of the best of Delius, and discovered Vaughan Williams. One could extend the list by fifty living names of high musical value. Henry Wood was establishing a new tradition, both of popular performing and of English conducting; Thomas Beecham appeared over the horizon. Parry, Stanford, and Mackenzie, too, were powerful figures in the new movement. 'Almost without our being aware of it', writes Charles Kennedy Scott of 1912, 'a great ferment of musical activity had been taking place in our midst – great in quality as well as extent. We discovered, almost suddenly, that we had produced a veritable "school" of composers, though its elements were so diverse and individual.' The whole conception of English song had changed. The inane Victorian 'ballad', with its cheap words and catch-penny music, was not dead: 'professional singing was still going round in circles in its own back eddy, with oratorio and the "royalty" ballad taking their turns in the wash,' wrote Harry Plunket Greene, pioneer in the performance of good songs set to intelligible words. George Henschel was one reforming factor, according to Greene, Cambridge another, Cecil Sharp and his folk-song discoveries a third: 'imagination had come again into British music, Purcell's lone star was shining through the clouds again, and the Elizabethans were moving in their graves.' And, most important, English literature, with its ages of tradition in verse and scholarship, had once more joined hands with English music.

It need hardly be said that the English people themselves did not in the main believe all this, or even notice it; too few of them believe it now, unfortunately, for the Victorian legend that music always comes from somewhere else is obstinately vital. Ways and means of performance for new works by the unknown and up-coming composer were difficult. Few orchestras were available, none able to take financial risks. The chorus was the popular medium for 'festival' and other national expression. Wood gave clear outlet for new works at the Promenade Concerts, one or two rich patrons – Balfour Gardiner and Beecham among them – supported the new English music in performance, as Cobbett did in the chamber-music department. But music publishers were shy of new names; major works are costly to print and (it seemed to them) not even speculative, merely a dead loss! Various groups of musicians were formed – the League of English Music, the Society of British Musicians, and so on. Heroic struggles were being made on all sides, to give not only scope for the new-born native art – showing, in Kennedy Scott's words, 'an indubitably English approach freed from Continental fetters, by which perfectly sincere emotions could be expressed in an original way; a liberation not only of formal processes, but of the imagination itself' – to give scope not only for its life and growth, but for its performance and publication. At a time of so much ebullience of the musical spirit, the most difficult and irksome task was perhaps that of knocking loud enough on the public's front door.

First Influences

Into such a musical world, equally full of hope and obstacles, John Ireland was born on 13 August 1879 in Bowdon, Cheshire. His father was a literary man; by profession the Editor of the *Manchester Examiner & Times*, he was of bookish tastes and interests, consorted with friends of like mind, and generally created in his family life a literary and cultivated atmosphere. The boy showed musical talents by the age of six, and by the age of fourteen he had made up his mind that music was to be the occupation of his grown-up life – an early resolution, but one firmly kept. Some little money was available under his mother's will for early studies; he entered the Royal College of Music in 1893. In 1894, however, his father died, and after that he had to look, for his continuance of study and support, mainly to scholarships and his own efforts. While he was at the R.C.M., he became a pupil of Stanford. 'Our world is peopled by his pupils', Stanford's biographer has written, and indeed the broad creative and salutary influence of Stanford's teaching is keenly felt in the larger part of modern English music.

Ireland first entered the profession of music with his appointment, at the age of seventeen, as sub-organist at Holy Trinity Church, Sloane Street, London, SW1, under Sir Walter Alcock, and also played at St Jude's Church, Upper Chelsea, from 1897. There was work to be found in teaching and examining, and in 1904, he became organist at St Luke's, the Parish Church of Chelsea, a post he retained until 1926.

Two important early influences in Ireland's life may here be recapitulated. In his home he learned to appreciate poetry and other literature; the use of words, the making of books, were as much a part of the household as the furniture. Then came Chelsea, that never-stale joke for 'the practical man who sticks to facts': Chelsea had much to offer the young man, for it is in many places beautiful to the eye, and it is one of the homes of pictorial art. A great part of his music shows Ireland to have been much affected by the visual objects around him; he had the perceptive awareness of eye and ear that characterized Schubert, and he was perhaps more influenced than the latter by the poetical atmosphere enveloping the physical sights. We meet the quality in his orchestral *Mai Dun*, written about the ancient earthworks outside Dorchester, in the piano pieces *Soho Forenoons* and

Amberley Wild Brooks and *Chelsea Reach*, more consciously poetical in *The Darkened Valley*, most picturesquely expressed in *A London Overture*. As a song writer Ireland showed a critical but eclectic taste in the choice of words at a time when English music and poetry were still too widely separated.

Tutelage under Stanford lasted until the composer was twenty-one, after which he poured out music in some spate (it is the best way to learn how to compose); but a growing critical sense led him to destroy most of his work written before he was twenty-six.

Chamber Music and Teaching

At this period the amateur violinist, W. W. Cobbett, was spending time and money on the revival of chamber music, amongst other ways by offering prizes (with the Worshipful Company of Musicians) for works in what he called 'phantasy' form – a re-creation in modern times of a musical structure familiar to the Elizabethan and Jacobean composers. John Ireland's *Phantasy Trio* for piano and strings won a prize in 1908; it was his first public recognition as a composer, his co-winners in the class being Frank Bridge and James Friskin. In the following year, he entered again with his first *Sonata for Violin and Piano*, in D minor, which also won a Cobbett prize. There were songs and piano pieces being written during this 1905–15 period, *Sea Fever*, for example, now a world-famous song; accepted (despite its high quality) by the most hardened balladmonger, it was first rejected by several publishers before Willy Streker (a German, at that) issued it in 1915.

Decorations, a set of three piano pieces (1913), contains *The Island Spell* – a successful piece, of some biographical importance, for it is a direct record on the keyboard of impressions received by the composer during a holiday in Jersey. From the moment of its incidence, the Channel Islands have exercised a powerful influence on Ireland's imagination – their isolation, their contours, their light, their primitivism have enchanted him. His first orchestral piece, *The Forgotten Rite*, expressed this love in fuller scale, and the cycle of piano pieces *Sarnia: an Island Sequence*, perhaps the most important of his keyboard works, is a much later evocation of the same places.

Though written in 1913, *The Forgotten Rite* was not performed publicly until 1917, under Sir Henry Wood at a Promenade Concert. That year of 1917 was of importance in Ireland's public career as a musician, for then his second *Violin Sonata*, in A minor, was greeted with a resounding and unusual success on its performance at the Wigmore Hall, London, by Albert Sammons and William Murdoch: Ireland could say with Byron, 'I awoke one morning and found myself famous.'

The record of the composer's life after this point is almost entirely concerned with his works. The years 1917 to 1920 brought us well-loved pieces like *The Holy Boy*, *The Towing Path*, *Merry Andrew*, and the characteristically cockney *Ragamuffin*. Before continuing, we must consider Ireland in his capacity as a teacher of composition; he assumed the role in the 1920s and from 1923–39 was on the professorial staff of his own school, the Royal College of Music. Among his private pupils was E. J. Moeran (1894–1950); Alan Bush and the young Benjamin Britten are only two of the distinguished composers who worked with him. As a teacher Ireland had the gift of understanding the pupil's intentions and developing his talents; he was critical, especially in matters of texture and form; above all, as the names quoted above testify, he did not impress his own fingerprints on his pupils' style. Teaching was abandoned after 1939.

Mature Romanticism

The second orchestral work, *Mai Dun, a Symphonic Rhapsody*, appeared in 1921 and had some immediate success, though it hardly holds a place in the orchestral repertory. A major work of greater significance is the *Pianoforte Sonata* of 1920; there have been few piano sonatas in our English revival – that by the young Benjamin Dale and the four by Arnold Bax come to mind – and Ireland's ranks with the best, indeed with the best of its period from any country. Here he fully expressed for the first time his remarkable gift for the pianoforte, and here we find the mature romanticism of Ireland's mind. Equally big and equally romantic in conception is the *Violoncello Sonata* of 1923, a work at first overlooked but discovered, somehow, in Spain by the cellist Antoni Sala, who pronounced it 'the best cello sonata of modern times' and played it in London with the composer at the piano.

The music of Brahms hung like a sun-tinged golden cloud over the latter half of the nineteenth century; rootedly English as Ireland was, he did not escape wholly from its shadows. But the 'new paths' of the twentieth century offered immediate and attractive interest to his mind, and as he matured we find evidences of Stravinsky in his works – which, I hasten to add, were never and never will be theoretically conceived, or anything but spontaneous expressions of his feelings. A somewhat cynical phase seems to have followed the *Cello Sonata*, which is by its nature a work that ends rather than opens a period whose finest product was the succinct, acid, and entirely brilliant *Sonatina for Piano* (1927); the composer at this time was drawn to the poems of Thomas Hardy (in the *Three Songs* and *Five Songs*, 1925 and 1926), and we meet cynicism turned to near disillusionment in the deeply felt cycle (two songs and a piano piece), *We'll to the Woods no More* (to A. E. Housman's words, 1926).

Hope and the romantic spirit seemed to have awoken anew in the next large-scale work, the *Piano Concerto* of 1930, which combines in an entirely unreminiscent score the musical qualities of his previous work, and in the pert (but still nostalgic) *London Overture* of the same year (written for the British Broadcasting Corporation), which is an engaging summary of Ireland's observation of the cockney and his colourful surroundings. The curiously neglected *Legend* for piano and orchestra dates also from this period (1933), a nature-picture that takes us back to *Mai Dun* and its predecessor. In 1932 he received the honorary degree of Mus.D. from the University of Durham.

Late Works

The years 1936 and 1937 were largely occupied with the composing of an extended choral and orchestral piece to the commission of the B.B.C. – *These Things Shall Be*. The words of John Addington Symonds are expressive of the vague social hopefulness, the belief in the progress of mankind towards a glorious millennium, that coloured so much of Victorian philosophy. With his sensitive literary feeling and his years of choral experience, Ireland was able to surmount the technical difficulties before him. The backbone of the work is a big-hearted, somewhat Parry-like melody that, 'writ large', expresses the common touch often shown by the composer in his more popular pieces and songs. Something of the same all-embracing spirit prompted the composer when he later wrote his *Epic March*. It should be observed that Ireland has entered the field of brass and military bands (e.g. with *A Downland Suite*) and that in 1946 he wrote the music for the film, made in Australia, called *The Overlanders*. Ireland has not, as have some of his contemporaries, widely exploited the newer musical media, but besides his film score he created an evocative sequence for a broadcast performance of *Julius Caesar*.

In *Sarnia*, as we have seen, Ireland gave special play to his love of landscape; in the *Concertino Pastorale* his area of delight is wider and more vague. A charming lyrical work, it was written for the Boyd Neel String Orchestra in 1939 and subtly adapts the composer's idioms to a new delicate medium. *Satyricon*, on the other hand, is an ebullient overture based upon the satire of the same title written in prose and verse by Petronius (d. A.D. 65), arbiter of the pleasures at Nero's court. It may be called the only essay in pure orchestral writing that Ireland has yet made. Two new chamber-works have appeared during the composer's mature years – an experimental and thoroughly interesting *Sonata for Clarinet and Piano* and a third *Trio for Violin, Violoncello, and Piano:* the last, though based on earlier material conceived but withheld in 1915, is a ripe as well as a new composition.

Historically, Ireland stands in an important position in the English revival. He is a product of his time; indeed, nearly every composer of importance has been, but Ireland is essentially an individual, impressed by current events, though never carried away by movements or fashions or sudden demands. Formally, he had discarded nothing from traditional practices save those that had become useless fetters or meaningless labels; his straight-voiced speech he has not curbed but only controlled for proper presentation. There is (though a mere look at his scores may seem to contradict the statement) spareness in both his thought and its musical expression. He is no writer of rhetoric for its own sake, and his ideas when they come to us are not tricked out with arabesques or apologetic frills of any kind. On the other hand, Ireland has always been supremely interested in musical texture, in the sounds his written notes make, and the delight they may give to others. His harmony, mainly diatonic with a leaning towards the flattened seventh, is thus studied with aural care, and he delights to decorate a plain chord with a garland of extra notes, creating a kind of luminous mist around his triads. Underneath the musical technique, there are two things – poetic expression and a true Englishness of soul.

EDVARD ARMAS JÄRNEFELT

B. 1869

NILS L. WALLIN

The Family

The Järnefelts are an old Swedish-Finnish noble family that can be traced right back to the stormy age when Sweden, with Finland at her side, was counted among the Great Powers of Europe. During the Thirty Years War, there was entered on the rolls of the Swedish Army a German-born captain by the name of Keldunck, who in 1651 was raised to the nobility under the name of Järnefelt. According to the custom of this time the bearers of the name had traditionally to choose the military profession or that of a civil servant. This tradition was maintained in the Järnefelt family for generations, and it was not broken after the family had been introduced into Finnish nobility. Finland was at this time united with Russia; the ancient political bonds with Sweden were broken, but not those of culture. Most of the property-owning class still regarded the Swedish language as their mother tongue. There was, however, a strong movement at work trying to increase knowledge of the Finnish language and there was a wide desire for liberation from the Swedish influence.

Armas Järnefelt's father, the Lieutenant-General and Finnish senator Alexander Järnefelt, joined this movement. He had made his career as a geodesist of the Russian General Staff. According to a statement by Sibelius he was 'a very original character, who had, in spite of great difficulties, carved out a career for himself in the Russian empire, but who had all the time maintained a strong feeling for his native country and developed a very independent view of our domestic policy.' Armas Järnefelt's mother belonged to the artistically talented Baltic family Cloot von Jürgenburg. She has been described as 'lively, amiable, liberal-minded, having a real sympathy for the lower classes, and interested in literature and art'. Thus, in this family the feelings for things Finnish was fused with an inherited culture.

The parents no doubt had counted upon a future for their sons as civil servants in Finland. Armas Järnefelt's brother Arvid, who as an author was strongly influenced by the doctrines of Tolstoy, wrote in his book *The Story of my Parents* these words, which he places in his mother's mouth: 'They are Finnish boys, and I used to think of them as high officials with bright buttons in this out-of-the-way country; I used to think of them speaking this unintelligible, soft language.' But the sons were instead to devote themselves to art, one as an author, one as a painter, and one as a musician. Remarkably enough their father is said never to have tried to influence his sons in their choice of profession, in spite of any disappointment he may have felt. There was, however, a keen interest in art in this family. The General himself is said to have had an ear for music, and the mother was an able pianist. Thus Armas Järnefelt had a musical inheritance.

Studies and First Compositions

After matriculation at the Finnish high school of Kuopio, he studied law for some time at the University of Helsinki, but soon gave himself up to music and entered his name at the Academy of Music there.

The Academy had by then been in existence for six years. Among the students was Jean Sibelius, already the great hope of Finnish music, who was later on to become Armas Järnefelt's brother-in-law. The Director of the Academy was Martin Wegelius, a musician possessed of a good all-round education, who had after many difficulties succeeded in founding a Finnish Academy of Music of international status.

His greatest pupil, Sibelius, has given the following testimonial of his personal qualities: 'Martin Wegelius was, if anybody, the right man in the right place. He devoted himself passionately to his calling as a teacher. He lived only and solely for the Academy, and he knew how to inspire teachers and pupils with the joy he himself had in his work and the same burning enthusiasm.' Wegelius was a great admirer of Wagner and probably this meant much to his talented pupil Järnefelt, who was later on to show both Scandinavian and Wagnerian traits in his compositions.

The Academy also had another famous teacher, the great pianist Busoni, a brilliant man as well as a musical genius. It is natural that a man of his qualities should have inspired his pupils. Järnefelt and Sibelius soon became his personal friends, and he was often in their company outside the Academy. Their place of meeting was Ericson's café in Helsingfors, and if Busoni was in good spirits he would invite his young friends to a musical entertainment, when they extemporized on the piano. Armas Järnefelt's studies had as yet given no conspicuous results in the form of finished works, but they were to come within a short time.

Berlin and Paris

In 1890 Armas Järnefelt left Helsinki and went to Berlin to study composition under Albert Becker. Then followed a time full of influences, during which Järnefelt finished a great variety of compositions. The years from 1890 to 1903 may be said to have been his composing period; later he became more prominent as a conductor. The cause of this change is easy to understand. Järnefelt felt that he would forever have to stand as a composer in the shadow of Sibelius's genius. He himself states this in the following words: 'Sibelius has put an end to my work as a composer of symphonies. The greatness of his works has enraptured me and made me realize my own limitations. But to write songs – that has always had a great attraction for me.'

Already in 1890 Järnefelt had composed three major works: *Ouverture Lyrique*, the Finnish rhapsodie *Lapsuuden Ajoilta*, and *Suite for Violin and Piano*. In 1892 he moved to Paris and there pursued his studies of composition as a student at the Conservatoire and also often attended Massenet's lectures in composition. He seems to have derived most profit from Massenet's teaching of instrumentation. Järnefelt himself especially mentions Massenet's lectures on Wagner's *Die Meistersinger von Nürnberg*, when he used to play from the score and point out details of instrumentation. During this time Järnefelt composed his *Serenade for a String-band*. This work and two of those mentioned above were performed in Helsinki under Robert Kajanus, Finland's leading conductor.

After Järnefelt's stay in Paris there followed a short concert-tour in Finland, and he then returned to Berlin. His creative power did not yet show signs of exhaustion. On the contrary, it was just at this time that he wrote his *Korsholm*, which is still greatly admired. In this composition Järnefelt stands out as an exceedingly proficient master of orchestration, one who knows every instrument. The influence of Wagner is easy to trace, it is true, but at the same time the composition can be said to possess originality and great individual power. It was performed for the first time at the musical festival at Vasa, in 1894. This was, however, not the only work he composed at this time. The compositions include several large works, such as the *Symphonic Fantasia*, the symphonic poem *Heimatklang* to words by Lenau, two *Suites for Orchestra*, and the ballad for orchestra *Koskenloskijan Mossiamet*. Further, he wrote a number of works for choir, the most outstanding being *Laula Vouksella* for choir and orchestra. With this and other compositions Järnefelt had become one of the group of composers that have given Finland perhaps the finest collection of choral compositions of all the Scandinavian countries.

During these years of studies and composing Järnefelt was, however, also attracted by conducting, and in the years 1896–7 we find him assistant conductor at the opera houses of Magdeburg and Düsseldorf. Then, in 1898, he had an orchestra of his own at Viborg in Finland. Here he remained until 1903, when there began his great period as conductor of the Royal Opera at Stockholm.

Stockholm

At about the beginning of the new century Finnish music began to be known in Sweden, especially in Stockholm. The fame of the young Sibelius was by then rapidly spreading, and the first performance of a work of his in Stockholm took place in the year 1900, when Robert Kajanus with the city orchestra of Helsinki gave a concert there on his way to the Exhibition in Paris. Finnish male choirs were also touring Sweden, and now and then the name of Armas Järnefelt could be seen on the concert programmes. The first occasion is said to have been at a concert given by Mrs Leander-Flodin. Järnefelt himself came to Sweden in the spring of 1903 as accompanist to his wife at that time, the singer Maikki. In the autumn of the same year he returned as conductor, and he then performed, with the city orchestra of Stockholm, the *Second Symphony* of his brother-in-law Sibelius and his own composition *Korsholm*, both for the first time in Sweden. Earlier in the same year he had conducted the performance of some of Wagner's operas in Helsinki, and soon he had the opportunity of conducting *Tannhäuser* and *Die Walküre* in Stockholm. He had an enormous success, and the direction of the Royal Opera hastened to engage him as third conductor for the autumn season of 1905. The chief performances were, it is true, conducted by the first and second conductors of the Orchestra Royal, but we may note one brilliant performance of *Die Meistersinger von Nürnberg* conducted by Järnefelt.

At this time each year the Orchestra Royal usually gave a certain number of symphony concerts, and during the season 1905–6 Armas Järnefelt conducted two of them, each resulting in a considerable success for him. After the first concert, when the *Seventh* and *Eighth Symphonies* by Beethoven were on the programme, the severe critic Wilhelm Peterson-Berger wrote: 'The proof he has given by this performance of his skill as a conductor is the most important and decisive that from a musical point of view he has as yet had opportunity to give us, and after this concert we can with so much greater certainty than before emphasize that in Mr Järnefelt Stockholm has acquired an executant musical artist of a really high rank.' There was no doubt at all that as a conductor Järnefelt had conquered Stockholm.

Conductor of the Orchestra Royal

In the autumn of 1906 Järnefelt was back again in Finland, now as Direktor of the Academy of Music at Helsinki, where he had been a student so many years earlier. He did not, however, make a complete break with his work in Stockholm. The symphony concerts given by the Orchestra Royal during the season 1906–7 were all but one conducted by Järnefelt, the exception being the last concert, on Easter Day 1907, when the first conductor, the elderly Conrad Nordquist, performed Beethoven's *Ninth Symphony*. Later in the same year Järnefelt was back in Stockholm to direct the first performance of *Salome*. Järnefelt had by now acquired a firm position in the musical life of Sweden. In 1906 he had taken his seat in the Royal Academy of Music, and in 1911 he was appointed second conductor of the Orchestra Royal. During the following years he conducted a great number of Swedish operas, and in 1917 Wagner's *Parsifal*, the first performance in Sweden. During these years it became a custom at the Stockholm Opera for the *Der Ring des Nibelungen* to be performed only once a year and to give some of the individual operas separately. Järnefelt also initiated the custom that *Fidelio* was to be performed only once a year, and it has since become a tradition that this opera must be conducted by no one but the first conductor of the Orchestra Royal, a title bestowed upon Järnefelt in 1923. Järnefelt's work has, however, not been confined to the Royal Opera only. He has often appeared with the city orchestra of Stockholm, above all in the great symphonies of Bruckner and Mahler, Schönberg's *Gurrelieder*, and, of course, Sibelius's orchestral works. In 1932 Järnefelt left Sweden and was appointed artistic director at the Opera of Helsinki. In 1936 he returned to Sweden, appearing as star conductor at the Royal Opera, with the city orchestra, and at the Radiojänst (the Swedish B.B.C.). In 1940 the title, honour, and rank of Professor was bestowed upon him by Helsinki University.

Järnefelt's work as a composer will not be epoch-making in Scandinavian music, for there are two other dominating personalities with whom he cannot be compared. But he will be greatly admired as a fine interpreter of Scandinavian poetry and as a fanciful, albeit somewhat impersonal, composer of orchestral works. He has, however, acquired a fame as a conductor, and every one who has heard him lead the Swedish Royal Orchestra in Beethoven's *Leonora* overtures must place him among the great conductors of our time.

ARAM ILICH KHACHATURIAN

B. 1904

M. MONTAGU-NATHAN

Salute to British Culture

In a slender booklet, entitled *Armenian Popular Songs*, which was issued in 1852 from the Mekhitaristic Society's headquarters at the monastery of San Lazzaro in Venice, its author, Dr Leo Alishan, inserted a Preface to the address of the British Public, in which he expressed a fervent hope that this first appearance of these folk-songs in any European language 'might find favour with a People so enlightened'.

De-Russification

Between the moment at which this high compliment was paid to us and the October revolution of 1917 the Tsarist government was busily engaged in the 'russification' of Armenia, and the head of a distinguished noble family was entrusted by the government with the task of confiscating its ecclesiastical property, closing its schools, suppressing its language, and, in fact, launching a campaign directed at the extinction of Armenia's national life. Little wonder that this long-suffering people should have committed themselves to a declaration that 'The Turk kills the body, but the Russian destroys the soul.' Since the Revolution there has been a complete change of method. The Soviet authorities decided that the strength of the Russian nation would be increased by encouraging the perimital republics to take the utmost possible interest in their own national development. It was fairly simple to devise a suitable plan; they had only to reverse every method that had been adopted by Russia's former rulers.

And so Armenia, which boasts one of the oldest civilizations, has been encouraged not only to be proud of so glorious a heritage, but to be worthy of it. In no sphere of social life has this movement been more active than in music. It is not at all strange that, among a people in whom an appreciation of music has been described as a 'sixth sense', there should exist a vast wealth of folk-song of so varied a character as to provide a musical commentary for every occasion from cradle to grave. Its dissemination has been undertaken with immense industry. Research has been organized on a huge scale, and with the aid of both the lay and the professional folk-singer there has been amassed a store of folk-melody (some of it dating from pre-Christian times) that has furnished a tempting source for the native composer of art music.

Intensive Studies

Among the most celebrated of the younger Soviet composers is the Armenian Khachaturian, and he may be regarded as the foremost exponent of the art of embodying his native melodies in music of the more sophisticated kind. As a composer Aram Khachaturian is in a peculiar class. Glinka, his remote precursor, though in some respects a backward child, exhibited at a tender age a marked enthusiasm for music of one kind or another. Khachaturian, whilst apparently of normal mentality in all the usual respects, seems to have taken little interest in the musical art until reaching the comparatively advanced age of nineteen, at which many who have appeared as 'prodigies' have reckoned themselves to be approaching musical maturity. No record appears to be available as to the *fons et origo* of Khachaturian's suddenly manifested interest in music. 'It is difficult,' says his biographer, Georgi Ghubov, 'to trace to its source the creative inspiration of such artists as Khachaturian. His product seems to sparkle and scintillate in the light of a dazzling sun whose rays reflect upon it a veritable profusion of colours.' Of his childhood and youth we are afforded little information other than the facts that Aram Ilich Khachaturian was born at Tiflis in 1904, that his father earned a somewhat precarious livelihood as a bookbinder, and that in the autumn of 1923 Gnesin, the eminent pupil of Rimsky-Korsakov, heard a quite unexpected knock at the door of his music-school. His young visitor immediately plunged in *medias res*. He wanted to be a composer. He knew nothing of the musical art and was ignorant both of its theoretical basis and of its literature. What he did know was, to quote Khubov, 'that he felt an irresistible urge to labour in the realm of musical creativity.'

First Compositions

Fortunately Gnesin possessed sufficient discernment to grasp that the young man's convictions were to be taken seriously, and, as he must have been aware that his candidate came from a land in which everyone is endowed with a native talent for musical expression, he had good grounds for his attitude towards a matter distinctly unusual. Lessons were begun immediately and were carried on under intensive conditions. Before long the teacher was entirely convinced that his pupil was gifted with a marked creative talent, and after two years of study, pursued with unremitting application, Gnesin took him into his composition class. Young Khachaturian, who had now a considerable acquaintance with both classical and modern masters, does not appear to have exhibited any marked preferences. For him every flower in the musical garden into which he had so suddenly made his first entrance had an intensely attractive perfume. The rose called Bach, Ravel the carnation, Glinka the clematis, or Skryabin, the short-lived but exotically fragrant viburnum, were to him equally fascinating, and he revelled in the scent of each of these novel blooms. Work under Gnesin's guidance proceeded with rapidity, and before long Khachaturian found himself realizing his cherished ambition. In 1926, when he was twenty-two years old, he composed a *Dance* in B major for violin and piano, and a year later came a *Poem for Piano* in C sharp minor. Both works were accepted by the Armenian State publishing concern, and they have frequently been performed in public. They are not, we are informed, by any means representative of that maturity the composer was soon to reach, but are evidence of a nonage in which Khachaturian was flitting from one bloom to another, attracted by the superficial charm of its colour or perfume, without regard, as it were, to its contour or constitution. These pieces have an oriental character, but were written before the later-developed intention of drawing attention, in a full-scale symphonic work, to the individual style of a particular oriental type. Again to quote his biographer, who reminds us that oriental is a generic term covering a multifarious motley of styles, 'an essential task, when resorting to "orientalism" is to discern and recognize the special and peculiar characteristics of each of the numerous and highly varied musical cultures of the East.' Which to us means that what used to be termed 'Earl's Court Oriental' – the species associated with a succession of popular exhibitions held in temporary buildings constructed of papier mâché – will no longer do.

Folk Melody

The special type for Khachaturian was, of course, to be the folk-music of his native Armenia. Thanks to the already mentioned systematic official research, this source was ready to furnish a vast store ranging from agricultural or ceremonial songs and dances to the already considerable collection of soldiers' patriotic ditties in which the Red Army has so frequently been apostrophized and the enemy vocally 'strafed'. Even in these early days Khachaturian evinced a clearly-marked individuality of manner, whether the task in hand was an exploitation of melodies of his fatherland or an experimental emulation of the French expressionist school. There is, for instance, an early *Valse in Ninths*, not yet, I believe, published, which was apparently intended to pay homage to Ravel, but which, despite a derivative tendency, provided a strong hint that its composer would, before long, succeed in being entirely himself. The 'scrap-heap of tinsel ... acquired from Western European sources' was now to be swept aside. In 1929 Khachaturian entered the Moscow Conservatoire. Here he remained under the guidance of Gnesin, but was able to profit by the teaching of Myaskovsky, in whose composition class he was placed. The veteran Vasilenko took charge of his study of orchestration. (It seems worthy of mention, as an awful warning to the academically-minded, that one professor, named Litinsky, who evidently belonged to the hide-bound category of teachers among whom Arensky was so conspicuous a figure, 'completely failed to understand either the character or dimensions of Khachaturian's gift' and was therefore left to stew in the flavourless juice emanating from a one-track musical mind.)

Military Music

During the five years spent at the conservatoire, Khachaturian made important progress in two directions, moving astride two roads that were eventually to be joined. On the one he eagerly sought that technical perfection without which, he well knew, his ambition to compose major works could never be realized. On the other he searched the treasury of his native folk-song and lore, which, he instinctively felt, would be his most likely and fruitful inspirational source.

In his third year he wrote two chamber-works of distinction, a *Sonata for Violin and Piano* and the *Trio for Clarinet, Violin, and Piano*; and in his fourth he felt ready to attack the composition of the long-awaited major work. It was a *Dance Suite* for full orchestra. Before completing his formal education he had undertaken a variety of compositions, such as songs, military marches, and dances for the masses, which attracted a large measure of attention when performed at the Gorky Park of Culture. Meanwhile, in the sphere of military music further sources of inspiration were being made available by collectors, as is shown by the publication, in 1944, by Dolukhanian, of thirty-six Armenian soldiers' songs simply harmonized by a number of collaborators.

Symphonic Socialism

Khachaturian had for some time also been busily engaged in assisting administrative work in such institutions as the Moscow Cultural Centre for Soviet Armenia and in the Composers' Union. By 1934 he felt ready to undertake a symphonic work in which the dual manifestation of his artistic trend could be made clearly apparent. He now believed himself capable of translating folk-song into art music by passing it, so to speak, through the furnace of his own temperament, and he felt convinced that he had acquired sufficient power over the expressive media of his art to do both it and himself full justice.

In the above-mentioned year he completed the big three movement *Symphony*, which is considered to be a culmination of all his previous creative effort. When we are informed that he had abandoned his 'side-long glances in the direction of Western European music', and that this composition was nationalistic in form, we are able to follow the meaning of such an exposition of the composer's individuality. What is puzzling, however, to the musician of Western Europe is to hear that the music of this first symphony is 'socialistic in content'. The music we know to be of 1934, but we are left in ignorance as to the precise vintage of the socialism it is considered to contain. We ourselves remember that the conservatism of to-day contains quite a large measure of the socialism of the day before yesterday. Had Disraeli left us a symphony of the quality of *Coningsby* or *Tancred* we might still regard it as worthy music, but its ideological message, if it contained anything recognizable as such, would be hopelessly out of date, and probably meaningless. To us 'socialist realism' in terms of music must seem a figment of a particularly fertile political imagination.

It has often been, and it should here again be emphasized that to create a nationalistic atmosphere in his works a composer of the calibre of Khachaturian must regard the 'lifting' of folk-songs and their translation direct into concert or operatic music as being elementary. We know that Rimsky-Korsakov himself came to disdain this method, and that he succeeded, after steeping himself in folk-song and lore, in writing original melodies to which was paid the compliment of mistaking them for genuine folk-tunes. In the *Poem* for violin and piano, which was dedicated to the whole body of ashugs,* Khachaturian did in fact copy the essential feature of an improvisational manner. In the symphony, which was his diploma work, he strove for something approaching still nearer to the abstract, using in its opening movement a theme that has been described as recalling the improvisational style of Dzhivani (1846–1909), one of the most celebrated of the ashugs.

Prize Concerto

In the *Piano Concerto*, which followed the *Symphony* and is the work most familiar to the British music-lover, his striving after the abstract method is seen to bring a certain loss of spontaneity. The themes are obviously Armenian in character and bear a close stylistic resemblance to those quoted in Kocharian's collection. Yet there are moments when the spirit of Tchaikovsky hovers over the music. One can almost imagine the composer to be wishing that he had been born a few generations earlier, when a fuller expression of *cris de cœur* would have been more *à la mode*. But these derivative passages do not give the impression of coming, as they did with the earlier composer, straight from the heart. Again, the conventionally rollicking theme of the last movement does not seem to be quite in the picture, and here there is a distinct suggestion that its composer is throwing a sop to those who insist that the *Finale* of a piano concerto should induce in listeners a gradually worked-up excitement culminating in a climacteric condition. In the *Violin Concerto*, which won the 1940 Stalin Prize, Khachaturian is again using folk-style themes of a recognizably Armenian character; but he opens with material that will recall to its performers the elementary fiddle exercises written by the

* The ashug is a native Armenian minstrel or bard.

eighteenth-century violinist whom Beethoven immortalized through the dedication of the *Kreutzer Sonata*! In the pseudo-cadenza, however, the composer is seen revisiting his native heath. Curiously enough, in the third movement he relapses into an orientalism reminiscent of the Europeanized variety affected by such earlier composers as Borodin and Rimsky-Korsakov. One may declare with emphasis that the bravura of the concerto's conclusion is worthy of any violinist capable of executing its almost terrifyingly brilliant virtuoso passages.

Stalin Apostrophized

There are two other works well worthy of notice, the symphonic and choral *Poem to Stalin*, inspired by another famous ashug, Mirza Bairamov, a native of Azerbaidzhan, and also, of course, by the supreme head of the U.S.S.R., who, in the concluding chorus, is the subject of a somewhat banal glorification which, with an appropriate, though no doubt unconscious, plagiarism, of Voltaire, refers to the comrade-hero as being occupied in 'cultivating the garden' of his native land.

The ballet, *A Song of Happiness*, which is in three acts, divided into six scenes and an Epilogue, appears to be largely an affair of Armenian dance-tunes. It was written in six months and was first performed at Erivan in the Spendyarov Theatre. Khubov hails it as the 'first example of Soviet Armenian National Ballet.' The scenario was compiled by the esteemed native dramatist, Ovanesian, and its literary substance pays tribute to the happiness of the Armenian people and their love of the Socialist regime. Among the special numbers in the ballet is a *Dance of the Cranes* – a hint of the Armenians' love of birds, and their particular devotion to the winged harbinger of Armenia's notoriously brief but high-temperatured summer season.

Unending Quest

It has elsewhere been pointed out that the folk-song is by no means the sole item to be found on the palette of composers in search of nationalist colour. Apparently Khachaturian is ever engaged in the quest for the more elusive type of ingredients that, when fused into an artistic consommé, combine in recalling, through its bouquet and flavour, all those joys and sorrows with which his native land is associated. Even those who express a strong disbelief in the theory of aesthetic nationalism will agree that the search for its comprehensive expression is at least an interesting and absorbing pursuit. Khachaturian's enthusiasm and determination in the cause seems likely to render a signal service to the musical treasury both of his native country and of Russia as a whole.

ZOLTÁN KODÁLY

B. 1882

RALPH W. WOOD

The Man

If one is not indifferent to him, one has for the man Zoltán Kodály a respect, a reverence, an adoration amounting practically to love. And if one is indifferent to him it can only, one surmises, be because one is not acquainted with him or with his deeds. It is possible to make such statements, objectively, because the world that is yet manifestly Kodály's is still a small one; many are outside it, have for him the pure indifference inseparable from pure ignorance and – even if they cannot themselves well be taken to task over lack of respect, reverence, adoration, or love – are in a good position to observe and report the impact he makes, even if they may be a little less than adequately supplied when it comes to explaining what they observe.

A differentiation between the man and his compositions is important. The regions in which some at any rate of Kodály's output is known are far-flung and diverse. To a great many music-lovers, people here, there, and everywhere who listen to performances of music, he is a fairly familiar name, but apart from the music itself nothing whatever but a name. Moreover it is possible actively to dislike his music or just to be left cold by it. Those, indeed, seem to be possibilities even inside his personal world. ... But this is not to say that the man and his compositions have not some qualities in common, some of the links that, whether or not they are fruitful for the art of music, the student can usually expect to find.

As a man, Kodály is compact of intellectual power, breadth of knowledge and understanding, single-mindedness, modesty, simplicity – a collection of traits as endearing to spirits of however slight a predisposition to sympathy as they are disarming to spirits of however strong a natural aversion. (As with Holst, it is questionable whether all, or even any, of those traits can be clearly perceived in the music.) Both within and outside his personal sphere of influence, Kodály may have also, perhaps it is valid to hint, the special appeal of one who has been rather overshadowed, whether justly or unjustly, certainly through no fault of his own – except indeed so far as idealism, constancy, integrity, and humility have been contributing factors and can be called faults – by more successful colleagues. As we shall see, both Dohnányi and Bartók, though in very different ways, have at one time or another stood to him in something of a relationship to which the word 'colleague' can be applied.

Kecskemét, where in 1882 (one year after Bartók, five years after Dohnányi) Kodály was born, is a country town in Hungary, a substantial place, in a rich agricultural region noted for fruit. Devotees of apricot brandy have cause to be aware of its existence. Admirers of the *Psalmus Hungaricus* will perhaps remember seeing on the front page of that score the sub-title, 'A Hungarian paraphrase of the 55th Psalm by Michael Vég of Kecskemét (sixteenth century).' There is always rather more to be said for looking in a man's programme-music – above all in the texts he sets – for connexions between his personality and his art than for guessing at personality-interpretations and at messages, whether philosophical or emotional, in 'absolute' works such as sonatas or string quartets. One can hardly be astray in recalling that Kodály has written relatively little 'absolute' music, even in name, and that his whole career has advertised that for him at any rate choice of texts and creation of settings are as it were homologous processes, facets of one basic joint conception of art and life. 'When as King David sore was afflicted, By those he trusted basely deserted,' begins Edward J. Dent's translation of the Psalm, 'in his great anger bitterly grieving, Thus to Jehovah pray'd he within his heart.' And it ends, thirty-two stormy pages (piano reduction) later, with: 'These words King David wrote in his Psalter, Fifty and fifth of prayers and of praises, And for the faithful, bitterly grieving, As consolation I made from it this song.' There we have brought together the bents for the archaic and for the religious that a scrutiny of his list of works will show to have been dominant throughout. His musical technique itself is a different matter.

Early Years

Having been born, then, at Kecskemét, Kodály passed the first eighteen years of his existence in a rather nomadic style. His father was a State Railway official, and his family lived in a succession of small provincial towns, among them Galánta and Nagyszombat. At Nagyszombat (to-day Trnava, in Slovakia) he sang in the cathedral choir, which led him to compose a *Mass*, several *Ave Marias*, and other such music, and attended the Gymnasium.

He was still at the Gymnasium in 1897, when the students' orchestra there played an *Overture* by him. He had in fact been composing since childhood. Also he had studied the violin. His family environment was a musical one, and to the compositions already mentioned he now added chamber-works for performance in the home circle.

Nevertheless, when he ended his wanderings by going in 1900 to Budapest, the career still proposed for him was a scientific one. He did enter the Royal Academy of Music there, but he also entered the University. His two lines of study must perhaps be called not so much parallel as converging; in fact in 1906 he brought them neatly together by taking a degree in Philosophy, with a thesis on 'Strophic Construction in Hungarian Folk-Song', and by becoming a teacher of composition at the Academy.

Nationalism

His own tutor, at the Academy, had been Koessler, through whose hands also passed Dohnányi and Bartók. It must be mentioned that in those days Hungarian musical life was very much infected (things were bad enough for 'infected' to be the right word) by Teutonism. Weiner was applauded as the 'Hungarian Mendelssohn', Dohnányi as the 'Hungarian Brahms'. (Certainly the influence is still pervasive in an *Adagio* for violin (or viola or cello) and piano composed by Kodály in 1901, which became very familiar to Hungarian audiences and for some reason even found a soft spot later in its creator's heart and was among his first published works.) Affairs, however, were about to take a quick turn for what, in the circumstances, even the most resolute deprecator of nationalism must concede was the better. Bartók and Kodály had not been born within twenty-one months of each other for nothing.

In a very few years Kodály became immersed in a movement to promote a more self-respecting attitude towards music in Hungary. He began his folk-music studies, and 1906 found him collaborating with Bartók in the immense corpus of research that produced, among other things, Bartók's book on Hungarian Folk-music, Kodály's own several treatises on various aspects of the subject, the collection over some twenty years of between 3,000 and 4,000 folk melodies and their detailed classification – not to speak of numerous more or less direct transcriptions and various freer arrangements of folk-tunes made by both men and of the influence that their theories and their research exercised on their respective voices as composers. Neither his duties as a teacher at the Academy nor any other exigencies of earning a living were enough to prevent Kodály from undertaking those travels of his over the countryside armed with pencils and MS. paper and phonograph, getting into intimate enough contact with the common people of each region to be able to note down or else make records of the songs they sang and the airs to which they danced.

The Composer

In 1906, the year in which he both became a professor of composition and began his partnership with Bartók, Kodály also produced a rather long piece of orchestral music called *Summer Evening* – its première was at a students' concert in the Academy of Music. During 1906–7, moreover, he paid visits to Paris and Berlin. It can be called something of an epoch.

At this very period Bartók was attracting some attention as a composer, enough to be dubbed (it turned out to be one of the worst of gaffes) 'the Hungarian Richard Strauss'. Kodály's music did not get about until a little later. During 1907–9 Kodály wrote ten piano pieces, a *String Quartet*, two *Folk-Songs* for women's choir, some of a *Sonata for Cello and Piano* and the first movement of one for cello solo, and nineteen songs. That is to say, all those survived and eventually achieved print. For a composer so discriminatory and self-suspicious as Kodály has always been, it was something like profusion.

In 1910 came his first publications – the 1901 *Adagio*, the 1908 *String Quartet* (Op. 2) and *Nine Piano Pieces* (1909 – Op. 3). He also began to be performed, and not only in Hungary. The *Sonata for Cello and Piano*, finished in 1910, was played in several European capitals; the Op. 3 piano pieces were done, and taken notice of, in Paris; the *String Quartet* had a place in the Zürich festival of the Allgemeine Deutsche Musikverein and by 1915 – in the hands of the Kneisel Quartet – had reached America. Of the remainder of his first stretch of comparatively mature compositions (in 1910 itself all he seems to have produced are one piano piece and a movement of the *Sonata for Cello solo*) the songs were only published in 1921 and 1925, the two *Folk-Songs* for women's choir in 1923, and the other piano piece in 1925. The last-mentioned has a certain especial interest. It is the *Meditation on a Motif of Claude Debussy*, written in 1907. From Ch. Aladar von Tóth, a far from impartial but also far from uninformed critic, we have it that Kodály regarded Debussy as a medium for delivering Hungarian music from the yoke of Teutonic influences; in other words, that he deliberately gave his composing technique a drastic dose of Debussy as an antidote to the Brahms and Wagner (-Liszt) toxins. This is a suggestive, but not thoroughly realistic, notion. It is likely that the influence, however clearly its medicinal possibilities might soon have been realized and developed by him, pounced upon Kodály in the first place willy-nilly. To such a conclusion the nature of the *Meditation* (an apparently affectionate, even slightly hypnotized, rhapsody on a salient theme from Debussy's *String Quartet* and certainly in no sense a stylistic study) also helps to lead us. However obtained, the share of Debussy's technical apparatus in Kodály's idiom is certainly as prominent as it is undigested.

Tóth has also remarked on Kodály's passion for the music of J. S. Bach and a certain interest in classical subjects (for example, in several of the songs and a projected opera about Ulysses). He put forward a suggestion that Hungarian folk-music is for Kodály what plain-chant was for Bach, again a plausible but not entirely convincing thesis. It is indisputable that neither Kodály's absorption of folk-music nor his long-standing regard for Bach has enabled him to produce from his reservoir of material, if that is how we are to conceive of it, an integral idiom as Bach did. Perhaps it is because he is more self-conscious about the business than Bach was. Perhaps it is because his writing is hardly ever contrapuntal (the patches of canon and imitation, mostly automatic and ruthless, that we do encounter in the chamber and choral works are a very different thing from genuine, free part-writing). Indeed, whether a texture of free part-writing *can* be made on a strictly folk-melody basis is anyhow most problematical. But that is by the way. Kodály's folk-song research is exclusively concerned with melody, with single lines. The fact that instead of polyphony his technique has been an affair of adding harmonizations (in a strictly vertical sense) to those lines, and harmonizations that largely ignore the modal implications of those lines and sometimes seem even to ignore the lines themselves, may be crucial.

Marriage and World War I

Another event of 1910 was the composer's marriage to Emma Sándor. No composer's wife ever had a stronger claim to be mentioned in that composer's biography than she, who has been Kodály's helper, translator, amanuensis, and fellow-enthusiast. She also has compositions to her own name.

Kodály, with Bartók and others, tried in 1911 to start a New Hungarian Musical Society, but it failed to get going. In 1919 he became, for a brief period, deputy director of the Academy of Music. (Dohnányi, who had been teaching there since 1916, became director for a like brief period, and was succeeded by Hubay, but returned to the directorship when Hubay retired in 1935.) Between those dates lies a solid, if not exactly packed, record of composing – and World War I. In 1912 – three songs, two of them with orchestra; 1913 – three songs and a piece for choir; 1914 – *Duo for Violin and Cello*; 1915 – the final movement of the solo *Cello Sonata* and three songs; 1916 – four songs; 1917 – four piano pieces, one song, and a piece for choir; 1918 – one song, three piano pieces, and *String Quartet No. 2* (probably begun in 1916) completed: such was the list. Kodály was pursuing his destiny. For him the real battles were, in effect, the battles of styles and of emotions that shook the music he wrote.

The tensions of the outside world did, however, give a noticeable jerk to Kodály's existence when, in 1919, the brief Communist regime in Hungary was followed by the savage counter-revolution. For a year or two Kodály's teaching at the Academy of Music was interrupted. It was at this time, notably, that he worked as a critic and journalist, writing for leading Hungarian journals and also as correspondent for several foreign musical periodicals of eminence. All this amounted, and in more ways than one, to another epoch for him.

International Celebrity

In fact, the first half of the nineteen-twenties may be called the crisis of his whole career, at any rate as a composer. In 1920 itself he wrote a *Trio* for the little-used combination of two violins and viola (cf. a work for the same instruments in 1899, when he was seventeen). He called it a *Serenade*. In 1921 a whole batch of his music was published: *Sixteen Songs*, Op. 1; *Sonata for Cello solo*, Op. 8; *String*

Quartet No. 2, Op. 10; *Seven Piano Pieces*, Op. 11; *Valsette* for piano; and the new *Serenade*, which was Op. 12. The year after that something happened of considerable importance for all living composers; the inaugural gathering took place at Salzburg, on the initiative of Viennese musicians, of what was destined to be the International Society for Contemporary Music. And at that first festival one of the works lucky enough to secure performance was the *Serenade* for string trio, Op. 12, by Zoltán Kodály. The I.S.C.M. festival at once became an annual event, and so, for the time being, did the inclusion therein of a work by Kodály look like becoming. In 1923 the *Solo Cello Sonata* was thus honoured, and in 1924 the *Duo for Violin and Cello*. In this way Kodály became an international celebrity. But meanwhile something had happened at home that not only confirmed his eminence there but very soon solidified his reputation in musical circles all over the world. On 19 November 1923 occurred the fiftieth anniversary of the union of Buda and Pest, and for the occasion Kodály was invited to compose a piece of music. He responded with – the *Psalmus Hungaricus*, for tenor solo, chorus, and orchestra (printed 1924, Op. 13). Publications of his works had not ceased with the 1921 batch. And so by 1924 he was already a world name by virtue of his I.S.C.M. festival successes, his *chef-d'œuvre* had been written, on commission, and was before long to make that name a really esteemed one in every corner of the musical globe, and the *chef-d'œuvre* was in print, together with all his chamber music and, in fact, nearly all of the music he had so far produced. He was back in his professorship at the National Academy of Music (as it now was). He was on the very crest of the wave.

A 'Second Period'

It is a striking fact that during the next twenty-three years, from the hour of triumph that the production of the *Psalmus Hungaricus* may be said to have constituted, Kodály's output was rather sweepingly different in character from that of the previous twenty-three (which just takes us back to the eighteen-year-old's arrival in Budapest).

In terms of such externals as the media employed and the species of works written, we have to contrast a period giving one orchestral piece, a mere handful of short choral pieces, seven chamber works, and numerous piano pieces and songs, with a period giving a substantial religious choral work (*Budavári Te Deum*), numerous smaller choral works, either of folk-song or of religious inspiration, a musical play, a one-act 'lyrical scene', an *Ode to Franz Liszt* for mixed choir, some half-dozen large orchestral works, only three songs (Op. 14, published 1929 – possibly composed earlier) and no piano music or chamber music at all (if we except three *Chorale Preludes* of J. S. Bach made into pieces for cello and piano by Kodály in 1924). This summary omits the *Psalmus* itself, which stands on the boundary between the two phases, and it assigns to the former phase the orchestral *Summer Evening*, in virtue of its originally dating from 1906, although in fact it was after a couple of performances shelved for a quarter of a century and then revised, published, dedicated – with the quotation ' . . . Is etenim saepenumero me adhortatus est . . . ' – to Toscanini and given its première in the new version at New York by that conductor in 1930.

Whether there is between the two periods an equivalent contrast in nature, even in musical style, is not so easy to decide. Nevertheless we may be inclined to feel that there is some such contrast, when we consider on the one hand the tense, rather tortured, sometimes almost chaotic idiom of the early songs, piano pieces, and chamber works, and on the other the tremendous, even blatant, assurance of *Háry János*, the very quiet and beautiful assurance of the lyrical scene *The Spinning-room* (a work constructed almost entirely from folk-music) the positively light-hearted, and technically virtuoso-like, assurance of the *Marosszék* and *Galánta* dances. Both the latter works use folk-melodies. The *Galánta* set are based on an 1800 Viennese publication, *Hungarian Dances after several Gypsies from Galantha*. Descendants of those gypsy musicians still existed, a famous band, at Galánta (a small market-town on the railway between Budapest and Vienna) when Kodály was there for several years during his boyhood. The one consistent strand running through Kodály's entire output is his series of, mostly choral, folk-song settings and arrangements. Many of them are superb specimens of their kind.

Details of the latter half of Kodály's career are largely details of happenings abroad. Otherwise the record is simply one of quiet, sustained work as composer and teacher and folk-song pundit, the consolidation of a position as a unique fountainhead of spiritual and artistic strength.

The première of *Háry János* at the Budapest opera-house in October 1926 was followed by the première of the orchestral suite from it, in

December 1927, by the New York Philharmonic Orchestra under Mengelberg. The English première of the suite was under Wood at a Promenade Concert in August 1928. In 1928, too, the *Psalmus* was done at the Three Choirs Festival, Gloucester, conducted by the composer. It had already been given for the first time in England, by the Cambridge University Music Society under C. B. Rootham. Its first performance in Germany was in 1926. The world première of the 1930 *Marosszék Dances* was under Toscanini at New York. Kodály's activities as a conductor, chiefly of his own works, had begun in Budapest in 1927. To his other scholastic duties he added, in 1930, lecturing at the Budapest University. In 1933, the year when the *Galánta* dances were composed in readiness for the eightieth anniversary of the Budapest Philharmonic Society (1934), the *Psalmus* was performed with *éclat* at the Sheffield Festival. In 1937 Kodály was himself in England, again in fact at Gloucester, directing performances of the *Budavári (Citadel of Buda) Te Deum*, the unaccompanied motet *Jesus and the Traders*, and the *Galánta* dances. By 1938 the *Psalmus* had been translated into eight languages and performed over 200 times. The *Variations for Orchestra* were composed in 1940 and played on the Continent in 1945 and in England in 1946. A *Concerto for Orchestra* was composed for the jubilee, in 1941, of the Chicago Symphony Orchestra. Another product of the war years was the *Missa Brevis* for choir and organ. The spring of 1945 found Kodály writing some children's dances for piano, employing the black notes only.

Present Position

In the period of reaction after 1919 a very commendable part was played by Jenö Hubay, the veteran violinist, put into charge of the Academy of Music after Dohnányi's first so brief spell there as Director. Hubay combined tact with decency and artistic conscience and soon had both Dohnányi and Kodály taking their share again in Hungarian musical life. Dohnányi's official status became eventually a supreme one. . . .

It only remains to mention the condition of affairs in 1945, when fascism was at last prostrate and the liberation achieved. Bartók, become a pre-eminent world figure of a composer during his long exile, was on the very point of returning to his native land (on official invitation) when lamentably he died. Dohnányi was a fugitive, listed as a war-criminal by reason of his collaborationist record. Kodály emerged with unimpaired honour and redoubled prestige, the acknowledged leader of his country's music and in general a venerated and dominant figure of culture and humanity.

Among his recent offices are those of Director of the Academy of Music, Chairman of the Hungarian musicians' trade-union, President of the Hungarian Academy, and President of the Anglo-Hungarian Society. He led the Hungarian delegation to the 1946 festival, in London, of the I.S.C.M.

GUILLAUME LEKEU

1870–94

HUBERT FOSS

'Whom the Gods love ...?'

The composers who, dying before middle-life, yet made their indelible mark on musical history deserve much thought and study as a separate human group. They are strangely varied in time, place and circumstance. Some left behind them a corpus of music that to us groundlings would have seemed a Herculean labour had it occupied twice the number of years, and that aside from its genius. One remembers here one's ignorance of the complete works of Purcell (who died at thirty-six), Mozart (thirty-five), Schubert (thirty-one), Weber (thirty-nine), and Mendelssohn (thirty-eight). Wolf, whose working life lasted no more than thirty-seven years, was equally phenomenal. Our own Warlock (thirty-six) was prolific both in words and in music.

World War I cut off Butterworth at thirty-one and Gurney from active mental life at thirty-two. Hurlstone's death from illness at thirty was an incalculable loss, Walter Leigh's from war at thirty-seven another. Pergolesi, who died at twenty-six, is an exceptional figure, for he became a legend of such magnitude that dozens of works by other composers were falsely attributed to him. Two composers of very small output, each of whom lived only till twenty-four, stand alone: Julius Reubke (1834–58), with an organ sonata on Psalm xciv, which is an acknowledged masterpiece, and a less known piano sonata, and twenty-six years later Guillaume Lekeu, with a violin sonata and a pianoforte trio, two unfinished chamber works, and a handful of orchestral pieces.

A True Belgian

It is not easy to account for Lekeu's modest but undeniable niche among the masters of the nineteenth century. To say 'natural genius' and pass by in wonder is hardly enough. His slender product has indeed high quality, a quality, too, that is unique. Lekeu is not just another of the lesser composers of charm of whom the previous century was full. He speaks with an individual voice; but it is not the voice of a John Baptist crying in the wilderness; his was no stark, primitive, mountainous genius like Mussorgsky's. The work of a cultured man, his music is the outcome of high civilization; it speaks in the quiet, persuasive tones of the philosopher, not in the stentor voice of the agitator.

We must look for other contributory reasons, perhaps factitious, for his acceptance in the hierarchy of composers. The fact that Lekeu was born a Belgian is perhaps the most important. His small and so long undefined country made a fine contribution to musical history in the early years, with Dufay, Ockeghem, Josquin des Prés, Arcadelt, and Lassus. Then – there is a parallel in English musical history – there was a long silence; Belgium broke its own earlier than England did, with Grétry, Gossec, and Méhul. From the days of the last-named's influence, there has been considerable activity in music from Belgium. A great school of violin-playing sprang up, headed by Vieuxtemps, with Marsick and César Thomson in the middle, and brought down to our own times by Ysaÿe. Among Belgian composers we may single out that strange nationalist, half-intellectual and half-primitive, Peter Benoît (1834–1901) and the dominating figure of César Franck (1822–90). Franck, though Belgian born and eventually a naturalized Frenchman after many years' residence in Paris, was in fact of predominantly German lineage.

The Franck Influence

Another extraneous cause of Lekeu's continuing fame occurs through his connexion with Franck in the latter's last years, and that was no less than Lekeu's holding a position in French music of the second half of the nineteenth century. For Franck introduced him to the Parisian circle, and after Franck's death Vincent d'Indy took him up – indeed, finished his posthumous works for him. D'Indy was a powerful force in music, an aristocrat suited to Lekeu's cultural attitude to music, both master and pupil being primarily musicians. Lekeu knew the Franckist circle – Chausson and Castillon and Bordes and Duparc and the rest – and became one of them. He died just a little too early to meet Debussyism.

Revealing Letters

Guillaume Lekeu lived his short life in a gentle, sheltered atmosphere, warmed by a rare degree of family affection. Of outward incident there was hardly a ripple; he lived almost wholly in the mind, a full and rich thinking life, untroubled by financial anxieties. He was moved spiritually by love of his native soil and love of his family in equal degrees. The meeting with Franck and their brief subsequent friendship seem now to be part of his mind's natural growth, and perhaps the most startling event in his whole vital course was the death of Franck, which prostrated him. Of this narrow span of years there is an exceptionally detailed record, for, filial always and a born friend, Lekeu corresponded at length with his parents and one or two associates. Mendelssohn, we do not forget, was also a prolix letter-writer; but his mind was not only more developed than Lekeu's, it was far more objective. So revealing are Lekeu's letters that one could wish other composers had left similar personal annals.

Jean Joseph Nicolas Guillaume Lekeu was born on 21 January 1870, at Heusy, a pretty village near Verviers on the lower slopes of the Ardennes in the province of Liége. His mother was of Walloon stock and of limited literary education. The child was normal in development, with nothing of the prodigy about him, though musical instruction was given him, both in violin and piano, from the age of six. In March 1879 the family moved to Poitiers (Vienne), in France, where Guillaume attended the Lycée until 1888. Those nine years, often merely dull and formative, provide for Lekeu a period of unusual interest. He seems to have been a model pupil; his academic record is excellent—except for music, where he was considered passable! He continued his studies in piano and violin, made a beginning on the violoncello and (as will be seen) began to write music. In all other respects he was accounted diligent, tidy, and over-zealous; he read classics, including rhetoric and philosophy; he became deeply interested in poetry as well, even writing in the verse medium. This wide education in the humanities had marked effects on the young composer's mind; we find him quoting Pascal, for example, in support of his self-criticism as a beginner-composer. Sports and games held no attraction for him; his playground in youth was already the intellect: but we may observe him building a model theatre for his own delight.

Both sides of this rich young seeking mind are revealed in Lekeu's letters, the literary and the musical. Fascinating in themselves, they are even more remarkable as the product of a secondary schoolboy. The command of language is balanced by their naturalness of expression; they flow easily with full expression but classical restraint; they are introspective without a trace of morbidity – indeed, they are both hopeful and projective of their writer's own imagined development. Frequently the narrative is interrupted with the words '*Parlons un peu de musique*'; the subject uppermost in his mind gave an extra spurt to his pen but did not limit the philosophic thought; from early awakening through education, there was in truth no philosophy for Lekeu but music. Unconsciously or not, he followed Pater on this point.

Early Compositions

As early as 1885 we find him writing a *Trio* for two violins and cello; he also knew d'Indy's *Wallenstein* at that young age. In the same year he published (no doubt with his father's subsidy) his first piece, a *Tempo di Mazurka* dedicated to his mother. It is clearly revealed in the letters that it was Beethoven's string quartets that seriously attracted his whole intelligence to music. Performances at Poitiers (especially of the later quartets) must have been rare at that time; Lekeu tells us he knew the works from studying the pocket scores. For him '*l'aigle de Bonn*' is '*le dieu*' – so he continually refers to Beethoven in his letters. 'Never' (he writes in one) 'has this world seen a nobler artist; and never will.' And he goes on to specify the lesser giants over whom (in his opinion) Beethoven towers – not Bach, Mozart, Haydn, Wagner, Shakespeare, Corneille, Racine, or Berlioz is comparable.

Persistent though this love of Beethoven is throughout the letters, one finds many references to smaller composers who caught Lekeu's fancy – to Grieg, for example, to Bizet and to Max Bruch, to certain pieces in a violin album published by Breitkopf, especially one by the obscure eighteenth-century Musigny. Later, Lekeu found that after Beethoven he liked best the music of César Franck. Here we come across an exaggerated example of the personal emotionalism that illuminates with a living glow all the letters. Another example is the effect on him of Wagner – the score of *Die Walküre* he adjudged 'a pure masterpiece', and at a performance of *Tristan und Isolde* at Bayreuth the youth fainted during the Prelude. I advisedly wrote 'personal'; in truth, such intimate emotionalism was a musical characteristic of the 1880 period.

Lekeu was not only a slow starter in composition, he was a leisurely finisher. His letters continually give evidence of new ideas conceived, even begun in the process of composition, but of little that is finished, and some of the so-called finished work did not survive on reconsideration. He was a constant literary arguer about musical procedure. Thus at sixteen he found reasons and parallels in poetic or philosophical thoughts for the variation and development of musical ideas in their successive appearances. A year or two later he asked Franck for his views on programme music; Franck, no aesthetic enquirer but always the practical artist, replied equivocally that descriptive intention is of little importance, but that what mattered was for a composition to be musical, and emotional as well. This Lekeu duly recounted in a letter to his friend, the Belgian musical director, Kiéfer, with the comment: 'it seems to me that Franck the Master has not thought about the problem either very often or very deeply.'

Larger Works

It is in 1887 that we first meet the idea of a symphonic poem called *Hamlet et Ophélie*, and also of a *Méditation* for string quartet. A little *Mazurka* was quickly written in gratitude to Guisard, who helped him with the violin in the holidays. In the same year occur some *Morceaux Egoïstes* for piano, written (an introspective letter tells us) for himself alone. A *Cello Sonata* was produced, in some form or another, by April 1888.

The question of a career now arose, for Lekeu graduated *Bachelier ès lettres*. Father favoured commerce, mother the professions, the son music—and won his case! To prepare himself for the Paris Conservatoire he studied with Gaston Valin. The family went to Paris in June 1889; in July took place the visit to Bayreuth already mentioned, and there Lekeu soaked himself in Wagner.

The meeting with César Franck resulted from a chance introduction by a family friend, Charles Read, secretary of the French Society of Antiquaries. Franck, overpressed with pupils and other work at the time, refused to accept him; but, hearing at an interview that the young man had worked always on his own at music, consented to give him a theme four lines long to develop. The completed exercise so pleased the Master that he consented to take him 'at very high fees'; Lekeu himself attributed his change of mind to their first conversation's having turned to Beethoven, a subject deeply affecting to both. There is mention of finishing his studies in three-part counterpoint and progressing to five-part, also of Franck's demand for original works to criticize; and we know that at this time he wrote a study for a symphony (no doubt the *Hamlet* work in new form), which he sent to Kiéfer and actually heard rehearsed in Belgium in April 1890, much to his own satisfaction. Lekeu also worked at his *Piano Trio* this year and was encouraged by Franck to proceed with it.

The Last Four Years

The death of César Franck on 8 November 1890 came as a terrible shock to this passionate young man; he felt himself stranded, left high and dry, with insufficient faith in his own genius to continue. In 1891 Vincent d'Indy came to the rescue with loving sympathy and help, but could not fully take Franck's place in Lekeu's soul. Nevertheless, Lekeu rallied; he wrote an *Adagio* for orchestra and a *pièce d'occasion*, an *Epithalamium* for a friend. D'Indy insisted on his entering for the Prix de Rome; the youngest of the nine entrants, he came out second, but refused to accept the award, in the face of advice and although he thought *Andromède* his best work at that moment. Doubts about himself and his future in music creep into the letters with some frequency; yet in one of them he records that his health is always excellent and that he is working fourteen hours a day. A *Chant Lyrique* was played, parts of *Andromède* too, and early in 1892 there is the first mention of the *Violin Sonata*, along with three easy piano pieces.

By 1892 Lekeu was well known and well liked in the Franckist circle. He was taken up by the great Belgian player Eugène Ysaÿe, who performed his *Violin Sonata* on many occasions. A Nocturne was written in one night, and in 1893 he finished an orchestral *Fantaisie sur deux airs populaires angevins*; he heard the airs whistled casually at some family dinner party and made of them his best orchestral work, which delighted d'Indy and won from him high praise. At this time, the *Piano Quartet* was uppermost in the composer's mind. He worked at it intermittently yet persistently over a considerable period and wrote about it often.

This warm family portrait of a rich life, full of friendships and hopes and fine music, was ripped through by one paltry incident of tragic fortuitousness. A casual invitation caused Lekeu to dine with a party of friends and students at a restaurant; following the others' lead he ate an ice for his sweet course, though he himself preferred fruit. Ill effects followed; but instead of shaking them off, as the others did, Lekeu became worse; he struggled to get as far as Angers, where he was met by his father, and on 21 January 1894, the day after his twenty-fourth birthday, he died of typhoid fever.

GIAN FRANCESCO MALIPIERO

B. 1882

D. MAXWELL WHITE

Early Years

For 800 years the Malipieros have been distinguished citizens of Venice. The family is not of Venetian origin; it is said to have come from Altino or Bohemia, but as early as 1178 the city honoured one of them by electing him its Doge. In this position of high authority Orio Malipiero – or Magistrelli, as he was then called – encouraged commercial activity and helped the crusaders. Again in the fifteenth century a certain Pasquale received the same title. One Malipiero was an ambassador, another the mayor of Verona. Only in more recent times has the family lost its interest in politics and become prominent in art.

Gian Francesco Malipiero was brought up in a musical environment. His grandfather wrote operas and was considered in his day a second Verdi. His father, Luigi Malipiero, was a notable pianist. Luigi married the Venetian Countess Emma Balbi and soon after, on 18 March 1882, their eldest son Gian Francesco was born. At six he began to learn the violin. But as a child he was more interested in painting than music, and he wanted to become an artist. His father insisted, however, on training him as a musician. Malipiero's development was not without interruptions. When he was eleven a family catastrophe, which has remained a mystery, took him with his father and grandmother into voluntary exile. His regular musical studies were disorganized but, as a performer, he gained considerable experience by playing with his father in various small orchestras.

The family lived for a time in Berlin and later in Vienna. Here, in 1896, they met a Polish nobleman who took an interest in the boy and provided the means for him to continue a more regular musical education. As part of this he attended the harmony class of Professor Stocker at the conservatoire. But Malipiero now developed an intense dislike for Vienna. His grandmother died in distressing circumstances;

the tragedy weighed heavily on his mind, and in July 1899 he returned to live with his mother in Venice. Here, while continuing with piano and violin, he concentrated on studying composition under the stimulating direction of Marco Enrico Bossi at the Liceo Musicale. And now Malipiero had two experiences of fundamental importance in his musical development: he heard *Die Meistersinger*, and, rummaging in the Marciana Library, he discovered a wealth of seventeenth- and eighteenth-century music manuscripts. The Wagner revealed a musical idiom different from that of the all-too-familiar nineteenth-century Italian operatic tradition, which aimed, as he said, 'to sing for the sake of singing'. But the manuscripts were the more lasting revelation. He read and transcribed operas almost unknown to the rest of Europe, by Cavalli, Monteverdi, and Scarlatti, and instrumental music by Tartini – a labour of love that set him on the road to becoming a great authority on old Italian music and left a lasting imprint on the idiom of his own compositions.

New Horizons

At the Liceo Malipiero was devoted to Professor Bossi, and when the latter moved to Bologna he followed him there to complete his studies. Here it was in 1904, at the Liceo Musicale, that his first orchestral work, *Dai Sepolcri*, was given an enthusiastic reception. On the completion of his musical education Malipiero returned to Venice. In 1907 he began an opera but, always intensely critical of his compositions, he destroyed it, as well as several other early works. In 1910 Gian Francesco married the daughter of a Venetian painter. After this, in retirement, he devoted the whole of his energy to composition, but he was still dissatisfied. He was out of touch with contemporary music except for *L'après-midi d'un Faune* and the symphonic poems of Richard Strauss, though he knew *ad nauseam* the veristic operas of Leoncavallo, Mascagni, and Puccini. He felt the need for a breath of fresh air, so in 1913 he went to Paris. Here a new world opened up for him. He was welcomed into the hive of French musical activity by Alfredo Casella, the paragon of modernity, who introduced him to Fauré, Debussy, and Ravel. Malipiero was also present at the historic first performance of Stravinsky's *Le Sacre du Printemps*. The result was decisive. He realized that he had been too much under the influence of Wagner and Strauss and making too many concessions to conventional Italian taste. After this his own characteristic idiom began to develop quickly. This is a very free polyphony, in which startling dissonances produced by the interplay of lines are tempered by the free use of consonance. His melody is incisive and when vocal is moulded closely on the speech inflections of the human voice. His rhythms are varied and often have a primitive vigour. The instrumentation is sonorous. Since Malipiero's texts are often taken from old poetry, the music frequently has an archaic ring and this is increased by a perceptible influence of plainsong and free use of the ancient modes. His themes are very condensed, but, strangely, Malipiero has no interest at all in their formalistic development. This curious limitation – if limitation it is – has dictated the form of most of his music. The instrumental works tend to be suites and the operatic are conceived as a succession of short scenes.

Before coming to Paris, Malipiero had submitted several works to the National Music Competition of Rome under five assumed names. While still in Paris he learned that four of his compositions had won prizes. He hastened to Rome and wrote a letter of confession to the newspapers. The deception made him many enemies, however, and both *Arione* and an opera *Canossa* – prize-winning works – were received with open hostility. But Malipiero was not unduly worried that music in which he was no longer very interested should fail to captivate the ear of an Italian audience whose musical sensibility he considered corrupted by the sentimental lyricism of *Madame Butterfly*. Always shunning city life, he retired to the village of Asolo in the countryside near Venice. Here he wrote the first of his orchestral masterpieces, the second set of the *Impressioni dal Vero*.

During World War I Malipiero fell upon hard times. His health gave way and his creative powers were paralysed for a while. Never idle, he devoted himself to unearthing old music, transcribing it, and publishing it in scholarly editions. But even in Asolo he found no lasting peace. In October 1917 the village was overrun by the retreating Second Army, and Malipiero was forced to flee first to Venice and then to Rome, where he arrived so distraught that his friends feared for his reason.

The Ballet Pantea *and* Sette Canzoni

Malipiero had always been hyper-sensitive. The war and especially the flight from Asolo had been a nightmare to him, but he managed to objectify his psychopathic state and create a sombre work of art.

This was the symbolic ballet *Pantea*. Imprisoned in her chamber from which 'only the blue of the sky can be seen', Pantea is aroused from her dreams by singing outside. A captive, she hurls herself against her prison doors and in the agony of her despair is possessed by three hallucinations; she is climbing, falling on a mountain side; dancing on the green summit in the sun; fleeing from the blows of invisible hands in a forest of trees. She awakes and, in the twilight, compelled by the voice of a singer, she flings herself once more against her prison door. It gives. But there on the threshold lurks only the grim shadow of Death. She accepts her fate and dancing wildly falls lifeless on the floor.

After the war Malipiero returned to Asolo. His lugubrious vision of life seemed purged by *Pantea*, and he began a period of joyous creative activity. One of his main interests has been the music drama. His efforts have continually been directed towards the creation of a new kind of 'dramatic expression' that should be a sympathetic fusion of action, words, and music; modern and yet rooted in the finest Italian traditions. For him the key words of this are *Orfeo* and *L'Incoronazione di Poppea* by Claudio Monteverdi. On the other hand, he considered nineteenth-century opera decadent and an obstacle to the healthy rebirth of Italian music. He hated the kind of operatic expression that gave the voices only 'sustained notes, slurred notes, and brilliant passages', and resulted in 'false sentimentality'. Rigorously rejecting Wagnerian recitative and complicated plots, he looked back to the seventeenth and eighteenth centuries and steeped himself in Cavalli, Emilio de' Cavalieri, Monteverdi, the *Commedia dell'arte*, Gozzi, and the witty comedies of Carlo Goldoni.

The first of Malipiero's works negating the conventions of nineteenth-century opera was the *Sette Canzoni*. This is based on seven human episodes observed in his daily life, translated into short dramas for pantomimic actors. In a dark corner of a Venetian *calle* Malipiero used to see a small troop of street musicians – a lame violinist and a blind guitarist led by a woman. One day he noticed that the blind man was alone, sorrowfully plucking his guitar – his companions had run away together. This pathetic incident suggested his first song, the *Vagabonds*. When the curtain is raised actors, simply but colourfully clad, mime the seven scenes while hidden singers, supported by an orchestra, underline and intensify the drama by singing settings of poems by Lorenzo the Magnificent, Poliziano, and Jacopone da Todi.

In verse of this kind Malipiero detects the natural rhythms of Italian music.

Since World War I Malipiero has maintained a rich creativity. Besides operas, concertos, and large-scale symphonic works he has written oratorios of deeply religious conviction; a *Missa Pro Mortuis*, to mark the passing of his friend Gabriele d'Annunzio, chamber music, songs, and a notable collection of piano pieces. These works have all been regularly published, though at first there were numerous outcries against the innovations they contained. And in 1920 the first string quartet, *Rispetti e Strambotti*, was awarded the Coolidge prize of 1,000 dollars as the best chamber work performed at the Festival in Pittsfield (Mass.). In 1921 Malipiero was accorded academic recognition. He was appointed to teach composition at the Royal Conservatoire of Parma. Urban life did not suit his temperament, however, so he soon resigned and returned to Asolo, where, besides composing, he could give himself to his favourite recreation – entomology!

When the Fascists came to power Malipiero was acknowledged as one of Italy's most scholarly musicians. Yet he met with criticism on all sides. Admirers of *Pagliacci* disliked his unconventional attitude to opera; serious critics, except for G. M. Gatti, often disapproved of his instrumental music; and in general, as opinion became more nationalist, his compositions were condemned for not being 'purely Italian'. Malipiero was even decried as a futurist – an ironic judgement, for no composer could be more firmly rooted in the past. The futurists, needless to say, disclaimed him, and Marinetti and Maestro Giuntini in their Manifesto of Aeromusic denounced his 'artificial and monotonous primitivism'.

Operas

As the years passed Malipiero became increasingly interested in opera. He wrote several (with his own libretti), each of which has the same episodic structure as the *Sette Canzoni*, but the action is on the whole more unified. So far, however, he had been unable to produce one as dramatically acceptable to his public as to himself. But eventually he met the great Italian dramatist Luigi Pirandello, who asked him to set his enigmatic *Favola del Figlio Cambiato* to music – the perfect counterpart of Malipiero's own fantastically imaginative world. The *Favola* had a successful première at Brunswick in January 1933. In Rome the first act took seven curtains; the second was received in silence; after the performance Malipiero had to escape from the theatre to avoid being mauled. The Vatican declared that the theme contained a satire on royalty and on the following day the opera was banned by Mussolini 'on moral and political grounds'. Malipiero did not remain in political disfavour for long however. He chose an uncontroversial subject and wrote a choral work *La Passione*. Then, breaking away from his predilection for fanciful libretti, he turned to Shakespeare. First he arranged *Julius Caesar* and composed an opera that was completely in tune with the spirit of the times. This had a good reception at Genoa in 1936. The success was repeated with an opera based on *Antony and Cleopatra* at the May 1938 Festival in Florence. With unremitting energy Malipiero has since produced five operas, the ballet *Stradivario* (1948), five choral works (*Santa Eufrosina, Vergilii Aeneis, Li Sette Peccati Mortali, La Terra, La Festa de la Sensa*, 1942–50), String Quartet No. 7 (1950), and a wealth of orchestral music, including the *Sinfonia del Zodiaco* (1951).

Vivaldi and Monteverdi

In addition to composing, Malipiero leads an active musical life. As musicologist and teacher he is known and respected both by scholars and the younger generation of Italian composers. In 1933 he began to hold a senior composition class at the Liceo Benedetto Marcello in Venice, and in 1936 he was appointed Professor of Musical History at Padua University. He is now Director of the Venice Liceo, Director of the Library of the Istituto Editoriale of Milan, and Artistic Director of the newly founded Istituto Italiano Antonio Vivaldi. In this position he has been largely responsible for the present revival of interest in Vivaldi's music. But Malipiero finds public life distasteful and, except for occasional journeys abroad, lives at home as much as possible in the company of his second wife, who is English. Here he continues his lifelong study of old music, the most invaluable result of which has been a monumental edition, in sixteen volumes, of the complete works of Claudio Monteverdi. Malipiero's devotion to Monteverdi is symptomatic of his whole awareness of musical tradition. The profound study necessary for preparing the volumes has left a lasting mark on his own music, which, though highly original and contemporary in idiom, derives its strength from the most vital currents of Italian music and drama. 'We live in a century of noise, and noise is the negation of music,' he writes. 'If we mount towards the sources of antique musical art we shall be able to project ourselves with greater strength into the future, avoiding the abyss of the chaotic present.' Malipiero has avoided this abyss, making no concessions to popular taste or to 'modernism' and, like Casella and Pizzetti, he has played a leading part in the rebirth of Italian music.

BOHUSLAV MARTINŮ

B. 1890

DONALD MITCHELL

The Tower

Most artists, at one time or another, are accused of living in an ivory tower. If Martinů* was thus accused, he could nod his head in partial agreement – the walls of his tower were certainly not ivory, but he was born in one on 8 December 1890, and lived there for some years.

Martinů's father, Ferdinand, was a simple cobbler practising in the small Bohemian town of Polička: not only did he care for the boots and shoes of his fellow-citizens, but also for their place of worship – the Church of St Jacob, which stood on the Little Square. He tended the bells and kept watch for fires in the surrounding countryside. It was natural that the church tower should be a home for him and his family, and so it was that his youngest son came to be perched 100 feet above his contemporaries and had to descend 200 winding stairs to reach the outside world.

Bohuslav's mother was a severe woman, 'stern and domineering' is Šafránek's phrase for her, but his father was gentle and affectionate: what else could be expected of a man who cultivated great masses of flowers on the top of a tower?

In 1896 Martinů began to attend the local school and simultaneously to have violin lessons from Mr Černovský, the tailor. At school he was shy and reticent, 'weak in drawing and mathematics', but he was able to take note of the festive ceremonies of the peasantry and made extraordinary progress at his violin. In four years' time he wrote his first composition – a *String Quartet* – and from then on he never stopped composing. Two other important influences also made themselves felt during this period, books and the theatre. There is little doubt that this early enthusiasm for the stage later found expression in

---

* I must here gratefully acknowledge Miloš Šafránek's *Bohuslav Martinů* (Dennis Dobson, 1946), the only existing study of the composer of any length and substance.

the composition of the operas – eight in all – and the ballets. During his first years at the conservatoire, two ballets figured amongst his youthful productions.

Exit

Meanwhile the young Martinů's outstanding ability on the violin resulted in a group of prominent Polička citizens arranging for him to study at the Prague Conservatoire of Music when he reached the age of sixteen. This at least was a theoretical step out of the tower, and the practical exit occurred on his parents' moving house to the Polička Savings Bank.

Martinů entered the Prague Conservatoire, accompanied by a wooden trunk and feather bed, in 1906. His violin studies advanced, but it was more the external activities of Prague that turned out to be of significance – Wagner's operas at the New German Theatre, the concerts, the theatres, and books. He read the complete Dostoyevsky six times, besides being brought into contact with Turgenev, Tolstoy, and Strindberg.

But the academic discipline of the Conservatoire irritated him, and more and more he devoted his energy to the composition of symphonic poems, song cycles, and ballets. A transfer to another violin class failed to improve matters. He was expelled from the Conservatoire over some trifling indiscretion, returning on the intervention of influential friends only to be expelled again on some other charge. He then enrolled as a student at the Prague School for Organ, but here again he could not bring himself to observe the strict curriculum and did not succeed in passing his examinations – 'Can a composition start with a bare interval of a fourth?' asked an examiner, Martinů replying 'Yes'.

That monosyllabic reply meant no diploma. Another door was slammed in his face. Retreat to the tower was no longer possible – even if it were desired. He must go on.

Orchestra

However, another door opened. This time it was a stage door through which Martinů walked, in the company of his friend Stanislav Novák, to take up his position (eventually stabilized at the third desk of the second fiddles) with the Czech Philharmonic Orchestra.

Once again it was mainly the music he played in the orchestra, the visits by eminent conductors (Weingartner and Mahler amongst them) and the later foreign tours that proved to be so valuable. Martinů particularly admired Mahler's songs. World War I found him with his sympathies on the side of the Western powers and he managed to evade military conscription in the Austrian Army. (It must be remembered that Czechoslovakia was then part of the Austrian Empire.) He was not able to avoid a later romantic interlude, but that led merely to the composition of some songs to words by Baudelaire. Martinů remained in Polička (teaching music at a Junior High School) until 1920 and celebrated the conclusion of the War by writing in 1918 a joyous *Czech Rhapsody* for orchestra, organ, soloists, and mixed choir. In 1920 Martinů returned to the Czech Philharmonic, which now had Vaclav Talich as musical director. Already he was beginning to feel something of a creative conflict within him, but his discovery of the French School – Debussy, Ravel, Dukas, Roussel – and the compositions of Stravinsky helped him towards finding a solution.

In 1922 the ballet *Istar* was given at the Prague National Theatre, and Martinů also re-entered the Prague Conservatoire, this time at the suggestion and as a pupil of Josef Suk. He left it within a year – for all its improvements, Martinů still found the academic restrictions irksome.

One day in Prague the orchestra was playing Roussel's *Poème de la forêt* and '... he suddenly realized where his loyalties lay ... he knew that he must go to Paris.' This inner conviction, strengthened by his profound admiration for the new French music, he was able to put into effect – he was offered a State grant, sufficient for three months, and in September 1923 left for Paris.

Paris 1923–40

For a while Paris bewildered Martinů. It was some time before he settled down with any kind of permanence in Montmartre; and it was not long before he made further moves that culminated in the possession of a small room in the rue Delambre in Montparnasse. After he had wandered all over Paris at night (no doubt viewing the sleeping city from the steps of Sacré Coeur) and had ransacked the bookstalls on the banks of the Seine, he began to take lessons from Roussel and also earnestly to work – but his work consisted chiefly of reading scores and, above all, thinking of his personal relationship to his art.

He was little affected by the latest Parisian musical fashion-shows (the gymnastics of 'Les Six', for example), though in Stravinsky he discovered something of lasting value and worth. But even Stravinsky did not provide the necessary stimulus and during this period Martinů composed practically nothing.

These eighteen months of 'silent receptivity' were abruptly broken by the composition of an orchestral work *Half-Time*, written when Martinů was on his summer vacation in Polička in 1925. As the title suggests, the piece is directly inspired by a football match, and here Martinů shows himself to be as acute a musical journalist as Kurt Weill. *Half-Time* introduced Martinů's music to America, and two later works, *La Bagarre* and *La Rhapsodie*, helped to bring him wider fame. As late as 1945 Martinů produced a highly topical scherzo for orchestra on the American aeroplane *Thunderbolt P-47*. Kussevitsky, Paul Sacher, and Ansermet were among some of the important conductors who recognized early that Martinů had more to say than most of his French contemporaries and gave him practical assistance. Even so, poverty still dogged his footsteps, and he had by no means succeeded in formulating a personal style. There were still many echoes of Honegger and Stravinsky to be muffled – or assimilated.

Up to 1942 Martinů composed almost exclusively chamber music or music written for chamber orchestra. Such works as the *String Quintet*, the *String Sextet*, the *Piano Trio*, and the first two *Violin Sonatas* date from this period; and a notable event in his life occurred in 1931 when he married Charlotte Quennehen, a young dressmaker. His wife was not a robust person physically, and matters were not helped by Martinů's precarious financial position. She was taken seriously ill with pneumonia in 1932 and Martinů's relief when he heard that his *String Sextet* had won the Coolidge Prize in America for that year can hardly be imagined; it ensured that the hospital bills would be met.

Martinů's fame was spreading, but, in spite of his growing reputation and the fact that every new work received an encouraging and sometimes enthusiastic response from the public and critics, his domestic situation was not eased to any great extent. The year 1938 found him and his wife in two attic rooms in the Avenue du Parc Montsouris and it was here that he began work on the *Concerto Grosso*, which received its first performance in 1941 in Boston under Kussevitsky (always a loyal friend of Martinů). The *Concerto Grosso* led to the *Double Concerto*, but this was completed in Switzerland where Martinů had been invited in the autumn of 1938. Already the shadows of impending war were darkening the European scene. 'During this time,' wrote Martinů, 'I was at work on the *Double Concerto*: but all my thoughts and longings were constantly with my endangered country, where only a few months before I had been filled with such hope and joy...'. This mood of torment and anxiety is only too apparent in the music: within twelve months the shadows had become a terrible reality.

In the winter of 1940 Martinů wrote to Miloš Šafránek from Paris: '... I keep thinking of Prague and our countrymen and of how they must be feeling. It would be better if we did not have to think at all. I have no coal and cannot work...'. This spiritual numbness continued, although he was moved to write a *Field Mass* for the Czechoslovak Army. It was his one musical gesture to the military, apart from a *March* for an Army band, and eventually he was able to gather sufficient energy to compose the first *Sonata for Cello and Piano*.

On 10 June Martinů and his wife 'carrying only one small suitcase and leaving behind them irreplaceable scores and manuscripts' joined the chaotic queue of refugees fleeing from Paris. There followed months of dramatic anxiety and tension. Martinů was on the Nazi black-list and an attempt to escape across the French frontier failed miserably; at length he began to make his plans to reach America. There were frustrations, interminable delays, weeks of indecision, muddles over visas, appeals for financial aid, exchanges of urgent cables. It was not until 31 March 1941 that the distracted composer and his wife arrived in New York. It is a tribute to his courage that even during this troubled period he had succeeded in producing a *Fantasia and Rondo* for piano and the *Sinfonietta Giocosa* for piano and orchestra, the latter expressing some of the joy he felt on being granted a visa to America and freedom. Certainly the *Sinfonietta* is a child of our time.

America

The American period, from 1941 to date, has been one of unbroken creative activity. Martinů returned to the sphere of the orchestra. The first four *Symphonies*, the *Violin Concerto*, the *Concerto da Camera*, the *Cello Concerto*, the *Concerto for Two Pianos and Orchestra*, and much chamber music exist as proof that the United States provided

Martinů with the environment and peace of mind in which he could write his music. But the *Second Symphony* (dedicated to his compatriots who lived in Cleveland) and the *Memorial to Lidice* show that by no means had he forgotten his native land. There was always the longing to return, the recurrent spells of home-sickness and nostalgia.

It was in 1945 that the wheel turned full circle. The Prague Conservatoire – from which Martinů had been twice expelled as a young man – invited him to accept a professorship in the Master School of Composition. He could have gone back to a Czechoslovakia where the church tower at Polička was a Martinů Museum and where the Square was re-named 'Bohuslav Martinů Square'. It seems, however, that finally he felt unable to accept what must have been a peculiarly tempting offer, perhaps influenced by political considerations, or by recollections of the never very stable history of the country of his birth. Since 1945 he has, apart from a couple of visits to Europe, continued to live in America; there he teaches (he has taught at the Berkshire Music Festival and from 1948–9 was Guest Professor at Princeton University) and still composes prolifically. His exile, be it voluntary or enforced, at least does not appear to have hampered his creativity, and Bohuslav Martinů remains one of the most fertile of contemporary composers.

DARIUS MILHAUD

B. 1892

ROLLO H. MYERS

Precocity

Darius Milhaud was born at Aix-en-Provence on 4 September 1892. One day, when he was two years old, his mother heard someone in the next room slowly picking out a tune on the piano. Believing it to be her mother-in-law, who played the instrument, she called out to her wondering why she was playing so badly; but there was no reply. Entering the room a few minutes later she discovered Darius on the piano stool. Four years after that he began to learn the violin, and at the age of ten he gave his first concert in public. So began the career of one of the most remarkable musicians of our century, and one of the most prolific, too; for Milhaud's output includes some ten ballets, eight operas, seven cantatas, a large number of scores of film and theatre music, fifteen string quartets, fourteen concertos, four orchestral suites, four symphonies, six chamber symphonies, fourteen sonatas, and a great mass of vocal, and piano music.

After taking his Baccalauréat degree in Latin, Greek, and Philosophy he entered the Paris Conservatoire at the age of eighteen, and two years later a work of his was performed for the first time in public – a *Sonata for Violin and Piano*. Milhaud was only twenty-two when war broke out in 1914, and, after working for a time in Paris for a refugee organization (where he had André Gide as a colleague), he found himself in 1917 attached to the French Legation at Rio de Janeiro when Paul Claudel was the Minister; it was this early contact with Claudel the diplomat that led to his lifelong friendship with Claudel the poet, who was later to be his librettist in many of his major works for the theatre.

'Les Six'

Returning to Paris when the war was over, Milhaud arrived just in time to be enrolled as a member of a group of young composers who were then beginning to be talked about, having been christened first of all (by Erik Satie) 'Les Nouveaux Jeunes' and later (by the critic Henri Collet) 'Les Six' – the name by which they were to be known for many years to come. His companions in this group were Arthur Honegger, Francis Poulenc, Georges Auric, Louis Durey, and Germaine Tailleferre; their musical 'Mentor' was Erik Satie and their literary spokesman Jean Cocteau, who formulated in a brilliant little brochure of aphorisms, called *Le Coq et l'Arlequin*, the aesthetic principles by which the Six were supposed to be inspired. As a matter of fact, however, what united these young musicians was not any special common doctrinal conception as to what the new music in France was to be like; the real bond between them was the simpler one of friendship and artistic camaraderie. For it soon became clear that each member of the group was a distinct personality with a style of his (or her) own and in a few years' time they had begun to drift (musically speaking) apart.

Early Works and Early Influences

Milhaud from the first asserted his individuality, and in all of his works, from the earliest to the latest, one is pretty sure to find those distinctive qualities that have given him the international reputation he holds to-day. First among these come the peculiar almost brutal directness of utterance so characteristic of the composer of *Christophe Colomb* and the somewhat aggressively truculent manner some people find antipathetic. In a sense, indeed, he seems to have progressed, or rather developed, less than the majority of his contemporaries, especially in his actual musical style, which remains in the later works very much what it was at the beginning. For example, his predilection for the rather crude and monotonous effects that polytonal harmony can be made to yield has never left him; it is just as clearly manifested in many of his mature works as it was in the early *Le Bœuf sur le Toit* or the very remarkable incidental music he wrote for Claudel's adaptation from Aeschylus of the *Choephori* and for the same author's satirical drama *Proteus* (1920).

His residence as a young man in South America had, as might be expected, a certain influence upon his music, and it is to his recollections of the sights and sounds of Brazil that we owe such characteristic pages as the piano *Saudades do Brazil* (with titles culled from place-names around Rio de Janeiro) and the cinema-symphony based on

South American tunes and rhythms, to which Milhaud gave the name, seen on an inn or restaurant sign in Rio, of *Le Bœuf sur le Toit*. Its sub-title (in English) was *The Nothing-Doing Bar*, and the music accompanied a sort of pantomime, with masks imagined by Cocteau, in which the celebrated clowns, the Fratellini brothers, played the principal parts. All this was at that time (February 1920) very 'new' and 'futuristic', and the production of *Le Bœuf* marks the beginning of a period of more or less experimental work in the arts, which was to make the twenties famous. Milhaud's score set the fashion for the hard, chromium-plated, streamlined, bustling sort of music, bristling with 'wrong note effects', which became for a time a sort of international musical lingua franca that already pointed the way to the neo-classical cult by which it was succeeded. The whole movement, too, had repercussions in the social world of the snobs; but it is perhaps not generally known that the fashionable Parisian cabaret and night-club, which exists to this day under the name of 'Le Bœuf sur le Toit', owes both its name and its foundation to the collaboration of Cocteau and Milhaud in this history-making production back in 1920.

It was clear from the beginning that Milhaud's gifts were out of the ordinary; already the music he was writing as a young man was forceful and original, and in a work like *Les Choéphores* he showed that he could rise to the heights of Aeschylean tragedy, although some critics may have thought his methods of creating an atmosphere of terror and anguish unnecessarily crude and violent and un-Hellenic. For he introduces whips and hammers into his score and makes his Chorus groan and whistle and shriek; but there is real power here and dramatic force and imagination, which make this one of Milhaud's outstanding creations.

Operas and Ballets

He has written much for the stage (as will be seen from the list of works quoted above) both in the form of opera and ballet. Of the ballets the early *La Création du Monde* is one of his best works, and the music accompanying the mysterious evolutions of the first beings on earth to emerge from the primeval slime is charged with a most compelling melancholy and poetic nostalgia. *Le Train Bleu* (1924), written for Diaghilev, is an amusing but unimportant skit on the fashions of the day and the snob world of the Riviera and makes use of American dance rhythms. *Salade* (1924) is an essay in the style of the Italian *Commedia dell'arte* in the modern idiom; in it some of the characters sing as well as dance. In 1946 a ballet on the theme of E. A. Poe's *The Bells* was produced in Chicago, and during a visit to France in 1948 Milhaud composed for Roland Petit a ballet entitled *'adame Miroir*.

One of his first attempts at opera was *La Brebis Egarée* (1923) on a text by the Catholic poet Francis Jammes, with whom the composer had become friendly some ten years previously. To this production he gave the unusual title of 'a novel in music'. In 1926 he produced two miniature mock-serious operas, *Les Malheurs d'Orphée* and *Le Pauvre Matelot*, both very much of their period, and typical Milhaud – vivid, unconventional, uncompromising. Four years later came the première at the State Opera in Berlin of one of Milhaud's biggest creations, perhaps his masterpiece.

Christophe Colomb

The opera is in two parts and twenty-seven tableaux. Cinematographic projections take the place of scenery, and the action is described and commented on by a narrator who links the various scenes together in a kind of spoken but rhythmic recitative to the accompaniment of a battery of percussion instruments. The unusual *mise-en-scène* is explained as follows by the author of the libretto, M. Paul Claudel: 'The basic idea is that the drama is like a book that one opens, then communicating its contents to the public. The audience, through the medium of the chorus, questions the narrator and the characters in the drama and asks them to explain what is going on. It associates itself with their emotions and feelings and encourages them with its advice and applause. It is like a religious service in which the congregation participates all the time. ... The audience wants to know what is going on in their hearts and minds, and to be initiated into those mysterious premonitions that reach them from outside through the agency of Destiny or Providence. ... This is the reason for the screen at the back of the stage, which takes the place of a back-cloth. It forms a kind of spiritual landscape, instead of the old material one. On this screen are projected ... all sorts of images, now clear, now confused, according as they belong to the present or to the past, to reality or to the world of dreams. In this way the action takes place, in a region mid-way between the spectators and a world of thought made visible, of which the actors are the interpreters.'

The title itself lends itself to a symbolic interpretation – in French at least – for Christophe Colomb(e) means Christ-bearer and Dove, and throughout the text there are many allusions to doves. For example, Christopher is compared to the dove that was dispatched from the Ark to find land, his own mission having been to discover a new continent. Milhaud has treated this theme with all his characteristic vigour and directness of utterance. His polyphony may be harsh, but the effects obtained are massive, and the music is close-knit in texture and moves with a kind of violent intensity. The lyrical element is almost entirely absent. Percussion effects, as is usual in a Milhaud score, abound, the choral numbers are full of a restless energy and the whole work produces an impression of rugged power. It has not been given as an opera in this country or, we believe, in France; but the B.B.C. broadcast it in a concert version from the studio in January 1937. A shortened version, as incidental music to J. L. Barrault's production of Claudel's play, was heard in London in 1956.

Two years after the Berlin production of *Christophe Colomb* in May 1930 another full-length opera by Milhaud was produced – this time at the Paris Opéra. Entitled *Maximilien*, it was based on the story of the unfortunate Emperor of Mexico, but the harshly polytonal idiom in which it is written produces a monotonous effect and militated against its success. His next operatic work, *Médée*, was the last to be produced in Paris before the occupation, having had its première there in 1940. Milhaud then left for the United States to take up the post of Professor of Music at Mills College, Oakland, California.

Instrumental Music – pre- and post-war – and Songs

His pre-war production was very considerable and comprised a quantity of songs and chamber and instrumental music of all kinds, which poured from his pen in profusion. Before 1940, for example, he had already written nine string quartets (there are fifteen to-day) although many of these, it should be said, are on a miniature scale. He experimented, too, with all sorts of combinations of instruments and undertook such *tours de force* as setting to music the words of catalogues of flowers and agricultural implements. (But did not Rameau declare that he would not hesitate, if necessary, to set the *Gazette de Hollande* to music?)

Among his best songs must be counted the fine set of *Poèmes Juifs*, whose inspiration seems to be strongly racial in character – (Milhaud himself comes of Jewish stock); and, in a different category altogether, the satirical *Soirées de Petrograd* in which the composer pokes acid fun at types of Russian *émigrés* who at that time (the early twenties) were beginning to flood into Paris. Here the wit of the words, by M. René Chalupt, is easily matched by the malicious, allusive music, often uncompromisingly discordant, but as pungent as a caricature by Daumier or Forain.

Two other works belonging to the pre-war period deserve mention, because they show another side of Milhaud's versatile art; they are *Scaramouche*, providing light material for badinage between a pair of high-stepping and mettlesome pianos, and the delightful *Suite Provençale*, which makes use of themes from the composer's native Provence. Some of them were used by another Provençal musician, the seventeenth-century operatic composer Campra.

Of Milhaud's post-war production it is not possible to speak in any detail, but it includes an opera, *Bolivar*, four *Symphonies* (the third is choral, a *Te Deum*), two cantatas, *Couronne de Gloire* and *La Naissance de Vénus*, a second and third *Piano Concerto*, a *Concerto for Two Pianos*, one for clarinet, one for violin, and one for cello (the last two being the second of their kind). He has also written a *Suite for Violin and Orchestra*, two *Sonatas for Viola and Piano*, a *Sonata for Violin and Harpsichord*, six *String Quartets* (Nos. 10 to 15), songs and piano music, the suite *Opus Americanum* and the ballet *Man of Midian*, Opus Americanum No. 2 – in all some sixty-four opus numbers between 1940 and 1942. His latest big work is the five-act opera *David*, composed in 1952 and first performed in a concert version in Jerusalem in 1954. The opera has since been staged at La Scala in Milan and in English at Hollywood Bowl in September 1956.

Milhaud was made Chevalier de la Legion d'Honneur in 1933, appointed a member of the Governing Board of the French National Radio in 1934, member of the Consultative Committee of the Opéra Comique in 1936 and member of the Governing Board of the Paris Conservatoire in 1937; in 1943 he became an Honorary Associate of the National Institute of Arts and Letters of New York. He is married and has one son, Daniel, born in 1930.

CARL NIELSEN

1865–1931

NILS L. WALLIN

Descent

Carl Nielsen was born at Sortelung on the island of Funen. The people from this part of Denmark were of old looked upon as superior to their fellow-countrymen coming from other districts. 'It is well known', says the inhabitant of Funen, 'that we are the best people in the whole country. We do not show off our knowledge and ability before other people, but nevertheless everyone knows that we are the most intelligent and distinguished people of Denmark. But the very best thing with us is that, whatever becomes of us, we never cease to be natives of Funen.' Carl Nielsen was a native of Funen. Never did he lose touch with the Danish soil, with the effects and colours over the landscape of Funen – least of all with its songs and melodies. And Carl Nielsen had the opportunity deeply to imbibe the atmosphere of this Danish countryside, for during his childhood he was never permitted to get away from either its toil and drudgery or its natural joyfulness and gaiety. His father was a craftsman, a house-painter, and the financial circumstances of the family often were as bad as could be. There were many children, Carl being the seventh of twelve, and they all had to work hard to help their father and mother keep the wolf from the door.

In this home, however, there was not only poverty. There was also a good deal of fine old peasant culture. His father was a renowned country musician, and he and his village fiddlers were always asked to play when there was a feast in the district. His mother was endowed with a clear voice, which several of her children inherited, and among her relatives we find a blind organist. Carl Nielsen's older brother, Sophus, had a gift for imitating birds by whistling, and often when they were walking together across the fields he would whistle improvisations, which for his younger brother became part of the landscape around them. Some of these impromptus appear in *Spring in Funen*, the idyll inspired by the composer's home district.

The Danish Peasant Boy

Under the influence of the rich musical life of his home, the dormant musical genius in the little boy began by and by to assert itself and crave for expression. Carl Nielsen was not, however, a musical prodigy like Mozart and Mendelssohn. His first instrument was the fiddle, on which as a child of five or six he used to pick out the Danish peasant songs. The greatest musical experience during his early years was, however, his first acquaintance with the piano. About this he himself narrates in his memoirs: 'Yet I had heard music before, heard my father play the violin and the cornet, heard my mother sing and myself tried my ability on the little fiddle. But this was something different. Here the notes were lying as a brilliant row before my eyes, I could not only hear them, I could see them, and I made one great discovery after the other.'

At the age of seven he began to compose small tunes, but since he could not write down the notes, though later on this was taught him by his school teacher, he had to invent a notation of his own. By this time he had made his first appearance – as triangle player in Lumbyes' *Dagmar Polka* – and now he also got acquainted with the art of counterpoint, although in a rather primitive form. Instead of accompanying the principal part of a dance tune by secondary parts, the Danish musicians of this time used to improvise independent and greatly varying parts with a certain melodic value of their own. (This is still customary in the north of Sweden and Norway.) The young musician was fascinated by this way of playing, which, as he states later on, was of great importance in developing his talent for counterpoint.

The Young Man

The years of his boyhood went by in an even rhythm. In the winter he went to school, and in the summer he used to watch geese and cows for the squires in the neighbourhood. In the year 1879, at fourteen years of age, he had to choose a profession and was apprenticed to a grocer just outside the town of Nyborg. Here he had to weigh out salt and soap and manipulate weights that were often too heavy for his delicate frame. He was not suited for this work and longed eagerly for something different. One day he ran across a school book in English, and for a long time he spent his nights studying this language, hoping that linguistic knowledge would make it possible for him to get rid of the detestable work to which he was fettered. If he had a knowledge of English – so he thought – the whole world would lay open before him. He entertained plans of migrating to America. He did not, however, have to carry these plans into effect, for this interlude, which meant a pause in his development as a musician, came to an abrupt end, the grocer being forced to shut up shop.

About this time there was a vacancy in the band of the sixteenth battalion in Odense; Carl Nielsen applied for the situation and got it, in spite of his fourteen years of age. He now came to live in a town, he received regular instruction in music, and – what was not least important – he had opportunities of listening to music of a kind hitherto unknown to him, and to practise quartets as well; also, despite the bad pay, he hired an old piano and began to study classical music. He became acquainted with Mozart's and Beethoven's sonatas, and one day he came across Bach's *Das Wohltemperierte Klavier*. He also made progress as a composer. At regular intervals his fellow-musicians would play compositions for wind instruments by the youngest member of the band. Soon he had also written his first quartet for strings, a rather impersonal work, it is true, but nevertheless astonishingly fresh and vivid to have been written by a youngster who had as yet had very little schooling. It was this work that paved the way for him towards great music. For one day Carl Nielsen took a day off and went to Copenhagen to show his work to Niels W. Gade, the most prominent Danish musician of the time. This visit resulted in his being entered on 1 January 1884 at the conservatoire of music in Copenhagen as a student of violin and composition.

Manhood

It is not necessary to describe in detail his life after this date, for seldom has one outwardly passed so calmly and without dramatic effects as did that of Carl Nielsen. About his life as a creative artist, however, we may indeed say that it was by no means undramatic. As a composer he was to be an object of never-ceasing dispute, beloved and detested. His time as a conservatoire student scarcely gave any hint of what was one day to become of this young musician. He attended to his studies and in due course – in the year 1889 – he was admitted to the Royal Opera orchestra as a violinist. The chief orchestral conductor at the Royal Opera was by this time no less a person than Johan Svendsen, and it is natural that Carl Nielsen should receive from him many stimuli of great importance for his further development as a musician. In 1908 Nielsen succeeded Svendsen as chief orchestral conductor, and in this place he remained until 1914, when he became conductor of Gade's musical society. In 1927 – after forty-three years – he once more took his place at the conservatoire, but this time as its Superintendent, a post he then held until his death in 1931.

The Artist

The importance of Carl Nielsen's music as an inspirer of Scandinavian music in the twentieth century can scarcely be overrated. No other composer's work, except possibly that of Sibelius, has meant so much. All his compositions – from the works of his youth, which were perhaps to a certain degree influenced by Brahms, but were nevertheless of a genuinely Danish character, to the great symphonic and dramatic works and fascinating small songs of his manhood – show a freshness and greatness, attained perhaps by no other European composer during these years of critical re-valuation in the field of music. In the symphonies and chamber music, in the dramatic works and small songs, in the motets and the cantatas – everywhere we encounter a quality that is altogether inexplicable. It strikes us as an anomaly in European music of the twentieth century. Apart from that of Brahms on his first works, it is difficult to find a single trace of outward influence. His music is polyphonic, but it is not chromatic, as is the music of his contemporary Reger. His works are characterized by well-balanced, powerful, and pure melody, melody that makes us think of the Gregorian Choral. There is perhaps no great master whose works are fuller of virile, unsentimental power and depth than are Nielsen's six symphonies. Yet his music, which does not at all conform to contemporary romantic ideals, has many points in common with such modern currents, for example, as we encounter in the music of Hindemith. But with Nielsen the feeling for melody is purer and more conspicuous, and characteristic of him is his own statement that 'a third is a wonder, and a fifth is a gift from God'. We must look upon the great power of Nielsen's music primarily as the expression of his straightforward, frank, and finely humorous personality, early acquainted with a simple hard life in a socially humble environment.

What he attained may be said to possess an objective value, far removed from eccentricity and subjectivity. When we listen to a work by this master, we seem to experience all the wonders of nature. It is, as it were, music with its sources in the Universe itself. Characteristic is the name that the composer gave to his fourth symphony, *The Inextinguishable*. This composition is not meant to have a programme, he tells us, but only a 'suggestive hint of the sphere of music proper'. In this phrase he intends to express his opinion that there is one thing that music alone is capable of fully expressing – the elemental will to life.

SELIM PALMGREN

1878–1951

NILS L. WALLIN

Finland in the Nineteenth Century

Apart from genuine folk-music, Swedish and Finnish music had a strong middle-class and romantic orientation in the nineteenth century. For the most part this musical culture was the concern of dilettanti and connoiseurs. Towards the middle of the century in Uppsala, the university town not far from Stockholm, we find a centre in which this lyrical Leipzig-influenced romantic music found typical expression. In the *salons* there drawing-room ballads, lyrical piano pieces and – not to be overlooked – male voice quartets all flourished. Everywhere in Finland and Sweden men's choirs were formed with a lyrical or patriotic repertoire, an exact analogy to the German *Liedertafel* movement. As chamber music came to need more and more skill from the performers, the piano became the object of love of the educated classes, and every 'finished' young girl in Sweden or Finland was able to play the highly modern upright piano. Soon this development resulted in an academically biased music that little by little acquired certain rigid forms and rules. At the same time this music served the national movements, which in Scandinavia were at first associated with circles among and round the students. Not least in Finland did these signals find a response, and both in the Swedish speaking and in the purely Finnish speaking parts traditions were formed, such as the male quartet, that are still strong as expressions for co-operative patriotic tendencies. But the stylistic fixation of these romantic ideas did not permit the rise of any composer with his own characteristics. Though Sweden, Norway, and not least Denmark produced towards the end of the century a series of original composers, Finland had to await the appearance of Sibelius. Even his teacher, Martin Wegelius, was still an eclectic composer of the academic type, in spite of his ability.

Wegelius was not only responsible for the education of Sibelius, but he also fostered a long series of other eminent Finnish composers. Gradually it could be felt that the traditionalism of the younger composers was being infiltrated by more daring sounds. The source of this development is to be sought in new ideals, perhaps due to Sibelius or perhaps to French impressionism. But even to-day modern Finnish music can be distinguished from Danish and Swedish. It is less experimental, less nervous, and more uniform in its search for new expressions.

Selim Palmgren belongs to the composers who began their careers in the Finnish tradition and who could yet achieve something very valuable in music. Though he has been able to add to Finnish culture less of value than Sibelius, he has handed down the tradition from Wegelius and his contemporaries to his own pupils at the Sibelius Academy in Helsinki.

Training and Influences

Selim Palmgren was born on 16 February 1878, in Björneborg, the son of a merchant, Carl Frederik Palmgren, and his wife, Emma Kristina Jansson. The young musician grew up in a typical middle-class home, which faithfully carried on the middle-class culture of the mid-century. It is easy to count the Scandinavian composers who spring from social groups not belonging to the middle-classes. Nowhere is it possible to find any analogy to the working class poets who have been of considerable cultural influence in these countries. Selim's brother and sisters were musical. His sister was able to teach him to play the piano at the same time as he learned another side of music, song in various forms, from his two sisters and his brother Allan. The latter sang and composed quartets. During his school years at the Finnish classical Lyceum in Björneborg he received even still more important impressions. He sang second bass in the school choir: moreover he was a frequent visitor to the rehearsals of the town orchestra. During these years, when his young sense of music was most impressionable, he was receiving those vocal and instrumental impressions that in his later life were to be useful to him for his own compositions. Especially fruitful was his experience in the choir. Here he trained his sense of harmony and learned to understand conditions in the lyrical men's choir. His own works in this genre during the following years are most satisfying to perform.

After Palmgren had passed his student's examination he, like Sibelius, was enrolled at the Helsingfors Institute of Music where Martin Wegelius was the leading light. Wegelius had succeeded in attaching Ferruccio Busoni to this institution as a teacher of piano, and even after Busoni settled in Germany he continued to work for Scandinavian music, both as an interpreter and as a teacher. Palmgren having finished his studies in Finland developed his piano technique further with Busoni in Berlin, while at the same time he worked at composition with Klatte and Bergel. He finished his years of study in Italy during the years 1906 to 1909.

Great tasks as composer, pianist, and conductor awaited Palmgren when he returned to his home country after these years abroad. In 1909 he was appointed conductor of the Åbo Musical Society Orchestra. This was considered remarkable, for on earlier occasions artists from the rest of Scandinavia or from the continent had been preferred for this post. At the same time as Christian Sinding, in 1921, he became a teacher of composition at the Eastman School of Music, connected with the University of Rochester, New York. He stayed there for five years and was then requested to take over the post of teacher in piano at the Sibelius Academy in Helsingfors; he was made a professor of composition there in 1939. Since 1930 he has also been first musical critic on one of the leading newspapers in Helsingfors, *Huvudstadsbladet*, and chairman of the Finnish Union of Composers. In 1947 he was elected chairman in the Teasto Ry, an association that safeguards the economic and legal rights of composers. He has received among other honours membership of The Royal Swedish Musical Academy and the Knighthood of The Finnish White Rose.

Achievement

Selim Palmgren's production includes five *Piano Concertos*, two *Suites* for orchestra, the opera *Daniel Hjort*, the *Cantata* written for the 700th anniversary of Åbo in 1927, *The Loveliest Land* for chorus and orchestra, songs for solos and chorus, pieces for piano and for violin, and arrangements of folk-songs. Symphonies and chamber music are completely absent from his life of compositions, if we disregard a small sonatina for piano. Although his piano concertos in their structure belong to the large musical forms, their content has an unquestionably lyrical feeling, which brings them nearer to the composer's minor works. This is also to be seen from the associative titles given to three of them – *The Stream* (No. 2, 1913), *Metamorphoses* (No. 3,

1916), *April* (No. 4, 1928). The last *Piano Concerto*, No. 5 in A major, was written as lately as 1940. Just as in the rest of Palmgren's works for piano, the writing of these concertos is brilliant, and from the pianist's point of view they are very well constructed. This is, however, a feature found almost everywhere in his compositions. The solo songs are marked by strong feeling and their declamatory style bears witness to Palmgren's great understanding of the performer's requirements for a satisfactory effect. In this connexion it is also relevant that Palmgren has been married to two outstanding singers, both of whom have helped and inspired him in composing his songs. In 1910 he married the well-known singer, Maikka Järnefelt and, after her death in 1929, Minna Talwik, in 1930; she still frequently sings her husbands' songs.

Next to Sibelius, Palmgren was the Finnish composer best known to the world outside Finland, and in Scandinavia he was among the most famous. Fundamentally the same can be said about his music as about that of Christian Sinding. Although Scandinavian in its tendencies, its style is not specifically Finnish; its impressionistic tendencies link it very easily with the general style of European music, and this has naturally facilitated the expansion of Palmgren's art.

Unlike Sibelius, who completely withdrew himself, Palmgren continued throughout his later years to take an active part in Finland's musical life. His countrymen could hear his much appreciated piano playing when he accompanied his wife; he was 70 years old when he conducted all his five piano concertos, which were given as a single series played by various soloists. He shared his day between his duties as teacher at the Sibelius Academy and his work as a composer, and in the evenings he acted as a severe critic. He continued carefully to cultivate his humanistic education, founded at the University, chiefly through his main hobby, which was the study of history. He died in Helsinki on 13 December 1951.

HANS PFITZNER

1869–1949

DONALD MITCHELL

Background and Early Years

It is not to be denied that Hans Pfitzner, in a life-time almost as expansive as Richard Strauss's, made his mark in music; yet it is strangely difficult to give positive reasons to support this statement, since his attitude towards contemporary musical movements and musicians was always such a negative one. The only solid constructive fact about Pfitzner would appear to be the existence of his own music. He certainly did not lack the ability to create.

Pfitzner's whole life was characterized by what has been said of the novelist, E. M. Forster – 'a deliberate refusal to be heroic'. He did not lead the spectacular, dramatic career of a Mahler: he had no public life worth speaking of. His works were even less played in this country than those of his neglected contemporaries Reger, Mahler, and Busoni. But abroad he stands as one of the great, particularly in Switzerland, where his music is frequently performed. In Germany he is hailed as *Meister*. 'For nationalist reasons,' writes Professor E. J. Dent, 'he has recently come into considerable prominence ... although his intense Germanism is purely poetical and in no sense political.'

Pfitzner was indeed intensely German, and it is thus surprising to learn that he was born in Moscow on 5 May 1869, nine years after Mahler, four years before Reger, and three years after Busoni. His father was a musician who had received his training at Leipzig and played the violin capably in the Moscow Opera House. His mother was an extraordinarily intelligent woman, a brilliant pianist, who came of a family of German extraction living in Russia.

The Pfitzner family eventually returned to Germany, where the father became conductor at the Stadttheater in Frankfurt. Hans attended the Secondary School there and showed remarkable musical gifts, entering the conservatoire in 1886 and remaining until 1890. There he was a pupil of the Russian composer, Ivan Knorr (who had been appointed principal teacher of composition on the recommendation of Brahms), and studied piano playing under James Kwast, later intimately connected with Max Reger. To increase further the variety of national influence she had already met, one of Pfitzner's closest friends at the conservatoire, a German student, James Grun, was born and educated in England. Grun proved to have a not inconsiderable literary talent and was responsible for the libretti of the two operas *Der arme Heinrich* (1891–3) and *Die Rose vom Liebesgarten* (1897–1900).

Some of the works Pfitzner wrote whilst still at the conservatoire were published: the *Cello Sonata* Op. 1, a group of songs Op. 2, and a *Scherzo for Orchestra*.

Coblenz, Mainz, and Berlin

After Pfitzner had left the conservatoire in 1890, he devoted almost all his time to the composition of the opera *Der arme Heinrich*: the score was finished in the summer of 1893. During this period he worked hard as a teacher at the conservatoire in Coblenz and did all he could to bring about a first performance of his opera at Munich, but his efforts met with no success. In 1894 he secured a post as conductor at the Mainz Stadttheater and after much desperate struggling managed to have his opera staged on 2 April 1895. It was a totally inadequate performance, but all who saw and heard the work could not be but impressed and moved by the idealism of its composer.

The next season saw Pfitzner risen to the exalted position of paid second conductor at Mainz, and he was able to include in a programme in November 1895 his incidental music to one of Ibsen's dramas. After the first production of *Der arme Heinrich* in Frankfurt, in January 1897 Pfitzner moved to Berlin, where he taught conducting and composition at Stern's conservatoire and conducted voluntarily at the Theater des Westens. Pfitzner's list of compositions was beginning to grow: amongst other works, there was a large output of songs, a work for alto, women's choir, and orchestra, *Der Blumen Rache*, and, most important of all, the *Piano Trio* Op. 8, which is a key to the rest of Pfitzner's chamber music. But the work that most occupied his attention was the new lyrical opera *Die Rose vom Liebesgarten*. The libretto was again by James Grun, but of a very different, and more attractive, nature than the one he provided for *Der arme Heinrich*. The work was given a first performance at Elberfeld on 9 November 1901, but the subsequent production at

Munich on 21 November 1904 was a much more significant event and has since been treated as the opera's true first performance.

Mahler and Palestrine

The production of *Die Rose* had wide repercussions and did much to add to Pfitzner's stature as a composer: Munich, for instance, developed into the centre of the Pfitzner movement. *Die Rose* was yet again produced in Vienna in April 1905, on this occasion under the direction of Gustav Mahler, which once more brought Pfitzner's name before the public; apart from this, his relations with Mahler give some indication of Pfitzner the man.

Pfitzner had visited Mahler at Crefeld in 1902 and pleaded for a performance of his work, but Mahler, in the words of his wife, 'refused coldly, calmly, tersely'. There the matter rested, until at Basle, in 1903, Pfitzner and Mahler came together at a performance of the latter's gigantic *Second Symphony* in the city's cathedral. Pfitzner, finding Mahler's wife a deal easier to get on with than the mercurial composer, and with a certain amount of justifiable business acumen, asked whether he might send her the MS. of his *String Quartet*, Op. 13. It was dispatched and shown to Mahler, who declared it to be 'the work of a master'. Next, the piano score of *Die Rose vom Liebesgarten* was displayed on the piano rest, and before long, his resistance subtly weakened, Mahler shared his wife's enthusiasm for the work and elected to perform it.

For the first rehearsals of *Die Rose* Pfitzner went to Vienna (alone, it appears, although he had married the daughter of James Kwast in the summer of 1899) and was, according to Mahler's wife, 'frightfully nervous: kept a stern eye on the slightest unpunctuality on the part of the company and was so self-centred that no one could hope for indulgence.'

Pfitzner did not care for Mahler as a man or musician, and much time was spent in unfruitful discussion. 'Each purposely misunderstood the other, and at the end each felt insulted.' Mahler, of course, was hardly the most tolerant and sympathetic of mortals, but, for all the temperamental difficulties that were encountered, he conducted the opera magnificently and said that nothing had been written to touch it since Act I of *Die Walküre*. Pfitzner, as if to make amends for his clumsy behaviour, wrote a conciliatory letter to Mahler in 1908, first naïvely apologizing for not being able to admire him wholeheartedly as a composer and continuing ' ... I must explain that I am cursed with what for me is a disastrous candour, which goes to incredible lengths in my relations with a person like yourself.' The letter closed amicably enough with '... my thanks for your friendship, which is an unqualified happiness to me'.

At this time Pfitzner was living in Strassburg and had completed his *Piano Quintet*, Op. 23. He was teaching composition there and conducting. Whatever qualities he did not possess in common with Mahler, both men expected blind co-operation – more than that, subservience – from their colleagues; both men aroused intense and vindictive opposition in others. On one occasion Pfitzner was conducting *Die Meistersinger* and learnt, just before the curtain rose, that the artist singing the part of Beckmesser was going to default after the first act, intending that his sudden absence should ruin the production. Pfitzner coolly conducted the first act, handed over to his deputy for the second, assumed Beckmesser's costume, shaved off his beard and sang the part 'with incomparable humour and a gusto that carried his audience away, so that the evening which was planned to be his downfall became an evening of triumph.'

World War I saw the first production of Pfitzner's greatest opera *Palestrina* (1912–15) in Munich in 1917, a work on an enormous scale. The libretto was written by Pfitzner himself and is based on the life of the Italian composer and his own experience as an artist. It takes five hours to perform, allowing for intervals, and provides an almost complete spiritual and musical experience. 'It is,' writes Professor Dent, 'dreadfully tedious, but it has much that is wonderfully beautiful and its lofty idealism compels sincere respect.' The year 1918 saw the E minor *Violin Sonata* in print; in its first two movements it mirrors the emotional anxieties of the war years.

Between Two Wars and After

After more teaching at the Munich Academy, Pfitzner retired to Unterschöndorf am Ammersee. Owing to World War II little information of his post-1939 activities is available. It seems that he was obliged to give an account of himself before a de-Nazification court and that he was duly de-Nazified. What brought him into such dubious judicial surroundings it is hard to say, but no doubt his deep-rooted and deep-seated nationalism was suspect until the authorities were assured that it was genuinely patriotic rather than political.

Certainly his 'deviation' – if, indeed, there were one – did not bring him into disfavour with his country's music lovers. His eightieth birthday fell on 5 May 1949, and it was royally celebrated by Pfitzner Concerts throughout Germany and Austria. He died in Salzburg seventeen days later. A *Goethe Cantata* on which he was working was left only partly complete.

Pfitzner's final compositions included the vigorous and sometimes percussive *Piano Concerto*, Op. 31 (1923), the *Violin Concerto*, Op. 34, (1925), the *String Quartet*, Op. 36 (recently rewritten as a symphony), his last opera *Das Herz* (1931 – a variant of the Faust theme), a '*kleine*' *Symphony*, Op. 44 (1939), a *Symphony*, Op. 46 (1940), and a *Phantasy for Orchestra* (composed during World War II and first performed at Nuremberg after the end of hostilities in 1945).

Coda

Pfitzner's critical writings prove that he had a sharp, polemical tongue and justify his reputation for sour temper and deep pessimism about the future of music. His aggressive criticism (which in turn has made Pfitzner himself the subject of bitter controversy) has been misunderstood in this light. For Pfitzner, to do him justice, was no pessimist. In his music we discover an unbending idealist with a deep faith in inner, spiritual vision and inspiration, particularly apparent in the contemplative slow movements that abound in his works. Joined to this profound seriousness of purpose, and to his reverence for Wagner the mystic and the moralist rather than Wagner the sensualist, was Pfitzner's delight in the romantic legacy of Schumann, the fantasy of Marschner and Weber, and the little known exploits of the musical novelist E. T. A. Hoffmann. But Pfitzner's stylistic characteristics extend even further back, to the North German school of contrapuntists, as a glance at the cadenza to the last movement of the *Piano Concerto* or many passages in *Palestrina* shows clearly enough; and he had a rough, somewhat sardonic humour far removed from the *fin-de-siècle* atmosphere of the late nineteenth century.

There are no more autobiographically revealing scenes than those in *Palestrina* where the composer has his music dictated to him by a choir of angels and where Palestrina, careless of the world's tumult, remains content with his music, which is the result of a spiritual union between God and the artist. In those pages of *Palestrina* not only lies some of the best of Pfitzner's music; they also express his whole attitude to his life and art.

WILLEM PIJPER

1894–1947

RALPH W. WOOD

A Career's Composition

The career, from cradle to grave, of Holland's foremost man of music in modern times, which at any rate is how many regard him, had in itself most of the attributes necessary for a fine composition. It had consecutiveness, unity, purpose, tension, and even something corresponding to consistency, and distinction, of style. Perhaps the one thing it might have been said to lack was curve. The purpose, tension, and continuity were too thorough-going for any notable alternation of moods, for any pattern. Far from futile or barren, it lacked, as a career, conclusiveness. And the actual finish was ill-timed.

In a more literal sense than often when the phrase is used, Pijper's life was 'all of a piece'. Rather than triumphantly finding consistency, parallels, manifestations of the one underlying character, in the diverse assortment of interests and activities that usually make up a man's life, in Pijper's we are confronted by a basic, perpetual, dominating feature or two, of which all that he ever did and was seems merely a conjunct, and not at all diverse, series of aspects. From that handful of mental and physical facts that constituted Willem Pijper as a person, as a separate, isolated materialization of – shall we call it? – the Life Force making its appearance on 8 September 1894, and ceasing to exist on 18 March 1947, they almost, the things he did and said, his ambitions and his achievements, appear to be mere offshoots, inevitable but incidental.

The Desire to Know

The lust that possessed Pijper to such an extent that it shaped his whole career, controlled all his activities, and even had a decisive and comprehensive influence on his creations, was the lust after knowledge. Most men have at some time or other in their lives a thirst for information about some particular, congenial subject. Many have a generalized curiosity, which at any rate when culture is already their background, or when education supplies it, can lead to the breadths and depths, above all to the specializations, of scholarship. Few indeed pursue truth with such persistence, with such system, and with so determined an aligning of the factual with the theoretical, so wide-cast a net for parallels and inter-relations and all-governing basic principles, as Pijper did.

Although 'instincts' is no doubt a word to be used charily, something of a light, and not too false a one, can perhaps be thrown on the mystery of Pijper's character (a mystery that is at least as dark as that lurking behind the behaviour and demeanour of most of us) by saying that he combined the instincts of a grand-scale philosopher with those of a musician. Combinations of such a type can indeed be found elsewhere. What makes Pijper's calibre tempt us much closer to the epithet 'unique' is the discipline and system with which he harnessed his curiosity or rather with which it harnessed itself, all through.

If it is true that at the age of five, not yet taught all the notational signs and obliged therefore to invent his own, he was trying to put on paper little tunes out of his head (or, more likely, from his fingers), equally is it true that, as soon as his father, at the same time as teaching him to play by ear, had taught him his letters, he began avidly to read. Apparently he read in many fields, but from the first biology seems to have had for him a twin attraction with that of music. He went to school for the first time only at the age of fourteen, and then (it was a 'gymnasium' – Latin, or classical, grammar-school) he is said to have startled his teachers by the range and comparative profundity of the learning he had already acquired, such were the fruits of his reading at home up to that point under the influence of his natural hunger for knowledge.

Biology and Psychology

All his life he remained a keen student of biology. According to Piet Tiggers: 'In particular he was interested in that part of biology dealing with the habits and the utterances (voices) of animals, including those of human beings. People could often come upon him absorbed in work on this subject, and it was a strange thing to see Pijper sitting surrounded with all the comprehensive papers of that literature. ... He could talk impressively about the movements of unicellular organisms. ... His reasoning came down to this: everything in this world is movement; Art also is movement, first of all music, for the Muses know no rest; no music is imaginable without action and relaxation, without thesis and antithesis, without germ and the process of growing. ...' Whether or not that really represents Pijper's thought, and whether or not one anyway dismisses it as a mixture of mumbo-jumbo and platitude, it is certainly true that much of Pijper's music was composed on a 'germ-cell' principle, which dictated its structure and content, though certainly on the one hand rigged with Pijper's purposeful and, as it were, scientific experimentations in harmony and rhythm, and on the other carried on emotional tides or on programmatic and descriptive courses. ... He was also interested in psychology and psycho-analysis, and the unfinished opera *Merlijn*, upon which he was working on and off for five or six years before his death, gives indications of astrological researches.

He seems never to have come to the end of his appetite for knowledge, his fever of self-education. In all directions he read and ruminated systematically, with purpose. As a composer, too, his methods, his whole career, were such that he may be regarded as 'self-taught' in a sense rather more exact and extreme, to a degree rather greater, than what is anyhow true of a composer of quality.

Early Years

Pijper was born at Zeist, a village near Utrecht, and his formal musical tuition began when, aged about eight, he was put to study under a local pianist, Helena van Lunteren. Before that he had been taught by his father, who seems to have been able to play both violin and harmonium. No deductions (unless indeed we choose to play with the idea of some possible, unknown, remote ancestor) can be made from the fact that 'Pijper' is the word in those parts for the medieval town-musician. Stress tends, on the other hand, to be laid on Pijper's parents, working-class folk, being members of a Calvinist community in the light of whose rigid faith music appeared probably not too reputable. It does seem, however, that their son's indubitable bent for music caused them later on to dream of his perhaps becoming the village's church organist. During, and indeed in advance of, his father's teaching him the notes, Pijper had been engaged in little creative dabblings, but when he went to Vrouw van Lunteren he gave up those struggles and characteristically set himself to obtain a complete mastery of the piano. When he went to the Gymnasium, however, he returned to composing and had then the added stimulus of being able to try over his products with some of the other boys.

Upon leaving that school, at seventeen, he was placed at the Utrecht College of Music, where he worked under the principal, Dr Johan Wagenaar. Wagenaar advised him to concentrate on theoretical subjects, and he did, taking his diploma after three years (which brings us to 1915). It caused him no distress not to become an organist, but he did not allow his piano-playing to lapse, and in fact he was to come before the public on many occasions as a pianist, especially in performances of his own works.

At the College of Music he composed much choral music, as well as songs, piano pieces, and works for violin and piano and cello and piano, and also his first *String Quartet*, dedicated to Wagenaar, a work in which he arrived at a bitonal technique.

Influences

There followed a period of Gallic influence, when he immersed himself in both the music and the literature of France. Verlaine as well as Debussy cast a spell over him. He duly made *Fêtes galantes* settings. Debussy naturally had his share in moulding Pijper's technique and style, but so also did both Stravinsky and Schönberg. Pijper's way always was to observe and study much and to carry out thorough experimentation.

As late as 1917–18 his music was showing (in, say, his *First Symphony*) that he had not missed the something of a Mahler boom that had taken place, particularly in Holland; but not long afterwards he had 'advanced' his technique enough to be dubbed, even if not quite accurately, an 'atonalist'. That first symphony (performed at once by Mengelberg in Amsterdam) was called the *Pan Symphony*, because it is 'actually an elaborate description of nature'. This preoccupation with nature, not to speak of his conception of links and parallels between biological processes and musical ones, never left him, although it became more subtle and more purely technical. Another strand of interest, coming into prominence soon after the French phase, was in the Greek drama. Incidental music for *Antigone* appeared in no fewer than three versions, in 1920, 1922, and 1926. He also wrote music for *The Bacchantes* (1924) and *The Cyclops* (1925). Theatre-music, in fact, occupied him a good deal, and apart from his operas

Halewijn (1933-4) and *Merlijn* (1939-46, unfinished) he produced music in 1930 for *The Tempest* and in 1937 for *Phaeton* (van den Vondel). The earlier opera was founded on an old Dutch ballad, which Pijper himself had set in 1920 (*Heer Halewijn*) for eight-part unaccompanied choir. He was much occupied with his native folk-music throughout his life, making a number of settings for choir and for solo voice as well as some *Old-Dutch Dances* for piano (and also editing several collections). Otherwise his main output was of the three *Symphonies* (1917, 1921, 1926), the *Piano Concerto* (1927), *Six Symphonic Epigrams* (1928), the *Cello Concerto* (1936), the *Violin Concerto* (1938), *Six Adagios for Orchestra* (1940), and the mass of chamber music (among which may be included the *Sonata* and the three *Sonatinas*, for piano).

Composer and Teacher

All through this creative work ran, side by side with the other interests and influences, Pijper's peculiarly scientific and at times mathematical conception of the technique of composing. His schematic approach to form and harmony, to construction *in toto*, was balanced by an insistence not only on the over-riding function of emotion but on the crucial importance of melody. The man who as an infant had laboured to write down snatches of tune before he really knew his notes, made his pupils spend the major part of their time composing tunes and then studying those tunes with the utmost care to see all the possible implications, however far-reaching, that they could be found to carry.

He had many pupils, among them Henk Badings, Henrietta Bosmans, Rudolf Escher, Hans Henkemans, Piet Ketting, Guillaume Landré, Bertus van Lier, Karel Mengelberg, Robert de Roos. He was a teacher to whom have been variously ascribed by those pupils themselves such assets as intense personal magnetism, breadth and profundity of vision, impatience – verging on harshness – in face of shoddiness or falsity, in all other ways great kindliness and receptivity, above all the power to give to others the inspiration of his idealism and knowledge while drawing from them, into free fruition, their own individualities. When teaching, he relied largely on illustrations from his own works and expositions of his own ideas and speculations about not merely musical technique but other subjects and things in general. In his own instinctive conception all those matters were, in fact, clearly allied and inter-dependent, and with the utmost energy and enthusiasm he, as it were, spilt both that conception and his own personality over on to his pupils. He taught harmony at the Amsterdam Conservatoire just after World War I, became principal tutor of composition there 1925-30, and was Director of the Rotterdam Conservatoire from 1930 till his death.

The Critic

As a critic he brought to bear the same qualities and the same convictions. In this sphere, however, he had to commit his ideas to paper and the written word, whereas with cronies and pupils he was wont to put up a vigorous and reasoned attack on letter-writing and to insist that the only valid method of intellectual communication was the give and take of talking. He was music critic to the *Utrechtsch Dagblad* for some years in his late twenties, and then founded – with Paul F. Sanders – the short-lived periodical *De Muziek*. Two volumes of his collected critical writings were later published: *De Quintencirkel* (*The Circle of Fifths*) and *De Stemvork* (*The Tuning-fork*).

Pijper the critic was unconventional, forceful, searching, eager to vanquish the unmusicality of the Holland in which he lived, eager to bring to life instead the musical distinction that he declared had once been Holland's and that he believed, or wanted to believe, was still inherent in his countrymen and only temporarily hidden under the conservatism and philistinism he attacked so bitterly. Among his articles were studies of a good many contemporary composers, including those under whose influence he himself, as a composer, passed.

He was for a time director of the Utrecht Wind Sextet. Against his five *String Quartets*, two *Trios for Piano and Strings*, two *Violin Sonatas with Piano*, two *Cello Sonatas with Piano*, and *Sonata for Violin Solo* are to be set the *Septet* for wind, double-bass, and piano, *Sextet* for wind and piano, *Wind Quintet*, *Wind Trio*, and *Sonata for Flute and Piano*. As well as serving on many government committees and working for the I.S.C.M., he was appointed secretary, after World War II, of a government commission to investigate the question of fostering orchestral and operatic enterprise.

Just as everything else in his life was all of a piece and consistent from start to finish, so was Pijper's physical health. As a child he was so sickly that he could only go to school when he was fourteen. Bad health dogged him all his days, though it was only in fact a brief illness that brought about his death in his fifty-third year. One has only to see photographs of his spare frame, and lean, stern, rather worn features, to be able to imagine how integral a part of his existence ill-health was.

He was much addicted to travel by automobile and has been described, in fact, as 'a passionate motorist'. Even there, however, he looked for connexions with the rest of his inter-related interests, and in *De Auto* (June 1936) he published an anonymous study of 'The Artistic Side of Motoring'!

ILDEBRANDO PIZZETTI

B. 1880

D. MAXWELL WHITE

Drama and Life

In 1932 Ildebrando Pizzetti issued with Respighi a manifesto deploring the 'cerebrality' of modern music: 'In the musical world reigns the biblical confusion of Babel. ... We are against this art that does not have any human content.' For Pizzetti music is the warm, sincere expression of life in all its complexity of human passion and grief. Unlike Casella and Malipiero, he has not been a revolutionary. Though a highly original musician, he has seen no need for a radical break with the nineteenth-century Italian tradition and he values romantic music as highly as he admires the works of Palestrina and Monteverdi. Pizzetti is an austere, contemplative composer, esteemed by academicians and the *avant-garde* alike. His music is of many kinds, vocal, instrumental, choral, and operatic; but there is little for the keyboard. All his work shows a systematic development over the years – the transition from a predominantly lyrical musical language towards the realization of his conviction that all great art is the expression of conflict and its resolution.

Early Influences

Pizzetti was born at Parma in the province of Emilia on 20 September 1880, the son of Teresa Fava and Odoardo Pizzetti, a piano teacher. He went to school at the Reggio nell'Emilia Gymnasium. When he was fifteen he entered the conservatoire of music at Parma. Here he attended Telesforo Righi's school of harmony and counterpoint. He left in 1901 with a diploma in composition. Giovanni Tebaldini, the Director of the conservatoire, wanted Pizzetti to be an organist, but Pizzetti, for whom music was now a consuming passion, was bent on becoming a composer. He was attracted especially by choral music. At harvest-time he liked to go into the Emilian countryside and hear the peasants singing; for in Emilia there was still a tradition of choral improvisation and in these sombre choruses he heard 'the eternal voices of his native land ... glorifying God and Nature.' About this time Pizzetti also visited a Benedictine monastery, where the monks were said to be keeping alive the tradition of Gregorian chant. But Pizzetti felt that their cold interpretation of this fervent monody was inadequate, so, back in Parma, encouraged by Tebaldini, he began a systematic study of primitive liturgical music. He read treatises by Greek and Latin theorists and the early church musicologists; his studies led him to the Greeks, and he gradually came to appreciate the inexhaustible richness and variety of the ancient modes. Pizzetti now began to envisage a new vocal polyphony as a musical medium free from all contrapuntal *clichés* and suitable for conveying every shade of emotional expression.

D'Annunzio and La Nave

In 1905 Gabriele D'Annunzio, a determining force in twentieth-century Italian affairs, was composing the tragedy *La Nave*, a work dedicated to the Adriatic sea and animated by the poet's desire to stir the passions of Italy – to 'Arm the prow and set sail against the world.' Pizzetti noticed a fragment of *La Nave* containing a chorus in a review. He set the chorus to music and sent D'Annunzio the manuscript. He had to write three times, but D'Annunzio finally replied inviting him to compose the choruses and instrumental dances for the play. Pizzetti was delighted. Soon afterwards the two artists met at Padua; D'Annunzio christened him 'Ildebrando da Parma' and from then began a difficult but on the whole cordial collaboration that lasted many years.

Pizzetti's settings of the choruses for *La Nave* affirm the contrapuntal and essentially vocal nature of his music. The melodies, though for the most part original, were inspired by plainsong. After so much profound study he felt in his blood the peculiar ethos ascribed to the various modes by the ancient writers; then, by means of polyphony, he sometimes succeeded in giving his melodies 'a richer and more varied expressive character,' while still preserving their modal characteristics. *La Nave* was performed in its entirety only twice, with triumphal success at the Argentina, Rome, and at Venice. At Florence for the sake of economy the rich polyphonic choruses were reduced to a few voices singing in unison. Critics consider that the first, the predominantly lyrical, period of Pizzetti's development closes with the choruses for *La Nave*. From then on his music becomes increasingly dramatic. This transition can be clearly seen between his setting of D'Annunzio's beautiful lyric *I Pastori* (1908) and *Assunta* (1917), a poem in Neapolitan dialect by Salvatore di Giacomo.

The Dramatic Ideal

After Pizzetti graduated he became an instructor at the Parma Conservatoire and he now found time to develop his interest in opera. He gained considerable practical experience of operatic performance by acting as an assistant-conductor to Cleofonte Campanini at the Opera House, and his early years as a composer are marked by a series of operatic experiments. Disliking the contemporary expressions of veristic art – Mascagni and Puccini's bourgeois treatment of character and situation – he did not turn to Verga or Sardou for his libretti, but to Byron, Pushkin, Shakespeare, and Ovid. While still a student he wrote *Sabina* and *Giulietta e Romeo*, works in a conventional nineteenth-century Italian operatic style. In 1902 he submitted a third opera, the *Cid*, based on Guillen de Castro and Corneille, to a one-act opera competition organized by the publisher Sonzogno. The *Cid*, though composed of 'melodic *fioriture* from start to finish', was a landmark in Pizzetti's development. It did not win a prize; it was incomplete in one scene; but it taught him the difference between the lyric and the dramatic and showed him that lyricism existing solely for its own sake weakens dramatic intensity. This discovery gave him a musical direction. Between 1903 and 1907 he worked on four operas. He laid them all aside in turn – *Aeneas* because of its slight 'human interest' and *Lena*, a drama with a contemporary setting, because of its excessive realism. But each attempt was an important step towards his ideal music drama – the realization of his dramatic vision of life in which not only every word and every episode is essential, where lyricism is an organic part of the drama, but one in which the music goes far beyond the poetic text and reveals the depths of the human soul.

Pizzetti's dramatic theories are intimately bound up with his philosophical outlook. He admires the simple, fundamental passions, men and women of superior moral stature, the strong, good man with the strength to affront an adverse destiny. He sees mankind united in a bond of love, Evil part of the Good that life has to offer and human suffering a means of purification. This outlook is reflected in his music, in which the note of pain is almost invariably resolved into a quiet flow of joy and consolation.

Fedra *and* Deborà e Jaéle

For Pizzetti 1908 was an eventful year. He was appointed instructor of harmony, counterpoint, and fugue at the Musical Institute of Florence – the Institute of which he later became Director (1917) – and in the same year he grew absorbed in the study of Greek tragedy. He was attracted by Euripides and began to write a libretto based on the *Hippolytus*. His friend D'Annunzio was enthusiastic, but asked him to discard what he had written and wait for him to compose a drama on the same theme, which he offered him 'fraternally and generously'. This was *Fedra*, the tragedy of a human wretch, the symbol of sinful passion, overthrown by moral law.

D'Annunzio's *Fedra* appealed to Pizzetti. It was rather wordy, but he audaciously removed unnecessary details and worked for three years (1909–12) composing an opera in which everything contributed, so far as the libretto permitted, to the dramatic effect. He rejected the conventional aria and linked poetry and music – the thorniest problem in the composition of an opera – with a new kind of eloquent melodic declamation. As D'Annunzio has said this 'effectively supports the dramatic content without ever disturbing the rhythmical life of the poetry.' The chorus does not play a large part in *Fedra*, but it is nevertheless very important, especially in the threnody for two choirs *O Giovinezza, piangi* (Act III), in which the people of Trezene lament the fateful death of Ippolito. The chorus in *Fedra*, unlike those in later operas, does not participate directly in the drama itself; it is still a spectator rather than an actor.

The first performance of *Fedra*, in March 1915 under the direction of Gino Marinuzzi at La Scala, Milan, aroused a bitter controversy.

The years immediately before the war were years of struggle for Pizzetti – a period of crisis that found its spiritual autobiography in the pessimistic *Ouverture per una Farsa Tragica*. He worked for a year on another tragedy by D'Annunzio *La Fiaccola sotto il Moggio*, but in 1915 he destroyed all he had written, because he felt that unless he started to compose his own libretti he would never achieve his ideal drama in music. Pizzetti now discovered a fresh source of dramatic inspiration completely in tune with his own sensibility. He renounced Greek tragedy and D'Annunzio and turned to the Bible. 'In it we can find everything ... people of all the world, with our passions, our aspirations ... our hopes and our wretchedness.' He turned to the Book of Judges and in the war between Israel and the Canaanites found a tale that provided the elements of his own music drama, *Deborà e Jaéle*.

In his libretto Pizzetti modified the Old Testament story considerably. He shifted the stress and created a situation in which the three protagonists, Deborah, Sisera, and Jael, together with a new character, the Chorus – the People of Israel – were brought into a dramatic conflict that could only be resolved in death and expiation. Deborah, a prophetess, exhorts the Israelites and interprets for them the will of God:

> Follow my laws. ... And I will bless your lands.

But the people have done 'evil in the sight of the Lord' and are now in servitude to the Canaanites and their heroic leader Sisera. The God of Israel pities his children, however. He will help them to drive out their oppressors, and the people animated by their renewed faith rise up. But who will deceive Sisera and lure him from his stronghold into the plains? Jael, the innocent wife of an Israelite traitor, once beloved by Sisera, piously offers herself to save her people. Deborah accepts her offer. Sisera discovers the trick, but he does not condemn Jael. The Israelites win the battle; and Sisera, in flight, stumbles back to Jael's tent. But she, though a woman in love, is an instrument of Divine Justice and, on the command of Deborah, implacable against her people's enemy, kills her noble lover. After he is dead only one poor soul senses Jael's grief and bends to kiss the hem of her dress.

Deborà e Jaéle is a drama shorn of all accessories. The language is noble, the action rich in contrasts. And in the music Pizzetti has replaced the usual lyricism of Italian opera with a vigorous vocal declamation. It is a work that embodies all the composer's demands for a music drama with an intense inner life, an interplay of living energies. Pizzetti wrote the libretto in 1915 and worked for six years composing the music. The opera was performed in December 1922 at La Scala, Milan, under the direction of Toscanini.

Deborà e Jaéle was the first of three operas comprising a trilogy of the human soul redeemed by love. It was followed by *Lo Straniero* (1925) and then by *Fra Gherardo* (1927). This was the drama of a fanatical medieval flagellant, suggested by the chronicle of the Franciscan friar Salimbene of Parma. More recently Pizzetti has written other operas based on episodes in Italian history. *Orsèolo* (1935) takes place in seventeenth-century Venice and *Vanna Lupa* (1947) in Florence in the turbulent years of the later fourteenth century. *L'Oro* (1942), a work that portrays the corrupting influence of gold in human affairs, has, however, no specific historical setting.

Apart from opera Pizzetti has composed a wealth of incidental music. After completing *Fedra* he set D'Annunzio's *Pisanella* – an exotic work in which the heroine, a regenerated medieval courtesan, is treacherously suffocated by Nubian slaves beneath a mass of blood-red roses. And in 1917 he was asked to compose the music for a morality play by the fifteenth-century Florentine writer Feo Belcari, *La Sacra Rappresentazione di Abramo e d'Isaac*. Composed unwillingly at a time when Pizzetti was thinking 'dramatically' in terms of *Deborà e Jaéle*, this is a serene and unexpectedly lyrical work.

Philosopher and Critic

Pizzetti is a home-loving man. His life is centred on family affection, study, and the cultivation of his art. He experienced a severe blow in 1920 when his wife died. He first gave voice to his grief in a setting for tenor and chorus of Shelley's *Lament*, and then he wrote a *Cello Sonata*. But even this passionately evocative work reveals his acceptance of suffering and death as a means of purgation. In the third movement the note of pain is subdued and gives place to a melody of consolation. War also left its mark on Pizzetti's music. The *Violin Sonata* (1919) reveals his sense of human anguish. The first movement is a 'hurricane of grief', while the third re-affirms his faith in the joyful return of life after pain. The second movement was written in memory of 'all who know not wherefore they have to suffer.' The theme of this is the musical transcription of a prayer and it clearly illustrates a characteristic of all Pizzetti's melodies; they are syllabic and born of an unvoiced accompaniment of words.

Since World War I Pizzetti has held a number of important teaching posts and carried on composing in his full maturity. Among other works he has written a *Messa di Requiem* (1922), a *Cello Concerto* (1934), a *Piano Sonata* (1943), a *Violin Concerto* (1944), and film music for *I Promessi Sposi* (1941) and *Il Mulino del Po* (1948). He has married again and has two sons and one daughter. In 1924 he was appointed Director of the Giuseppe Verdi conservatoire of music at Milan; in

1931 he won the Mussolini prize of the Royal Italian Academy. On the death of Ottorino Respighi (1936) he accepted the chair of advanced composition at the Accademia di Santa Cecilea, Rome, of which he is now Director.

Besides composing and teaching, Pizzetti has been a prolific writer on musical topics. His criticism is intimately bound up with his creation, and by it he has clarified his musical ideals and integrated his musical activity. It is significant that his most active years as a critic correspond to the period in which he was experimenting with the music drama. Pizzetti looks for the measure of humanity in an artist. For him frivolous and insincere music, works without emotion or vibrant humanity, are bad, a point of view that has led him to censure Schönberg's complexity and judge Debussy's art too aristocratic and lacking in fullness of life. In 1914 Pizzetti founded, in collaboration, a short-lived periodical for the purpose of publishing contemporary Italian music called *Dissonanza*; later he became co-director of the *Raccolta Nazionale delle Musiche Italiane*. His critical articles have appeared in several European music journals. Many of them have been collected under the titles *Musicisti contemporanei* (1914), *Intermezzi critici* (1921), *Musica e dramma* (1945), and *La musica italiana dell'Ottocento* (1946).

FRANCIS POULENC

B. 1899

ROLLO H. MYERS

Erik Satie and 'Les Six'

Everyone knows the story of 'Les Six'. From 1917 to 1927 or thereabouts these musicians set a fashion that, like most fashions, started in Paris and was copied everywhere else. As soon as it began to be copied, however, it ceased to be the fashion. After the war of 1914–18 all the old ideas and values were put into the melting pot and emerged completely transformed. The famous reaction against impressionism set in, and attention was focused for a time upon a group of young men (and one young woman) who, thrown together partly by chance, partly by a similarity of tastes, began writing music that to the ears of the older generation sounded new and strange.

The group came into existence before the war was over and gave their first concerts in 1917 in an old studio at the back of a courtyard in the rue Huyghens, not far from the Café de la Rotonde in Montparnasse. Louis Durey, Georges Auric, and Arthur Honegger were the first to get together; they were soon joined by Germaine Tailleferre and Francis Poulenc, and a little later by Darius Milhaud, just back from Brazil where he had been working at the French Embassy in Rio de Janeiro under the Minister Paul Claudel. These young composers at that time enjoyed the advice and protection of Erik Satie, who encouraged them and called their group the 'Nouveax Jeunes.' It was not until 1920 that they were baptised 'Les Six' by the music critic of *Comoedia*, Henri Collet; he was no doubt thinking of the group of Russian Nationalist composers – Balakirev, Borodin, Cui, Musorgsky, and Rimsky-Korsakov – who were always referred to in France as 'Les Cinq.' They were also sponsored by Jean Cocteau who wrote his brilliant little pamphlet *Le Coq et l'Arlequin* to commend to them the example of Erik Satie and to give them an aesthetic and theoretic background. 'Enough of hammocks, garlands, and gondolas; I want someone to build me music I can live in like a house', said

Cocteau; and so began the cult of homely melodies, crude square-cut rhythms, and a musical atmosphere redolent of circus sawdust and village bands, tempered with a dash of jazz, to give it a more exotic flavouring, and a lavish use of polytonal harmonies.

These, then, were the influences that presided over the *débuts* of Francis Poulenc as a composer, though, as we shall see, he was soon to emancipate himself and develop his art and his personality in quite another direction.

Early Influences and Early Works

He was born in Paris on 7 January 1899. His father came from a family long established in the Aveyron Department (South Central France), while his mother, *née* Jenny Royer, was born in the old quarter of the Marais in Paris. Heredity always plays an important part in the formation of an artist; in Poulenc it certainly helps to explain that dual character so apparent in his music, which seems to oscillate from grave to gay and to fall into two distinct categories, one serious, the other light and frivolous. It can be said at once on the best authority that what we may call the ultra-Parisian side of Poulenc's art is directly derived from his mother, while the more serious and religious works, to which the composer himself attaches the greatest importance, reflect the influence of his father. For Poulenc is a Catholic to whom religion is a reality; for example, he goes often in pilgrimage to the shrine of the *Vierge Noire* at Rocamadour (for whom he wrote his *Litanies*), and he went there before composing his Liberation Cantata, *Figure Humaine*.

In his purely musical formation he owes much to Ricardo Viñes, who taught him to play the piano (Poulenc is indeed a first-class pianist), and to Charles Koechlin, with whom he studied composition; while the four composers whose influence he most readily acknowledges are Chabrier, Satie, Stravinsky, and Ravel. Curiously enough he does not like Fauré, but adores Debussy.

Poulenc was only eighteen when he became one of the Six and made his *début* in 1919 at a concert they gave in the Théâtre du Vieux Colombier (to which they had migrated after growing out of the studio in the rue Huyghens) with a composition for string quartet, flute, clarinet, and voices entitled *Rapsodie Nègre*. This was written in 1917; in the following year he produced his still popular *Mouvements Perpétuels* for piano, as well as the *Sonata* for piano duet; in 1919 there came the miniature song-cycle *Le Bestiaire*, a setting for voice, string quartet, flute, clarinet, and bassoon of six zoological poems from Guillaume Apollinaire's *Le Bestiaire ou Cortège d'Orphée*. These exquisite thumbnail sketches remain to this day one of Poulenc's happiest and most characteristic works; the music is sensitively wrought, spiced with humour and ironically lyrical sentiment (*The Carp* is a little masterpiece) and miraculously fitted to Apollinaire's delightful text.

Collaboration with Cocteau and Diaghilev

It was one of the tenets of the Six that composers should seek their inspiration in 'Parisian folk-lore', which really meant that they should listen to street musicians and to music-hall and circus bands; so when Poulenc set Cocteau's *Cocardes* to music he scored the accompaniment for violin, cornet, trombone, bass drum, and triangle, thus imitating very successfully the sounds produced by a street-corner ensemble. To this phase belong also the *Sonatas* for clarinet and bassoon, and for trumpet, horn, and trombone (1922) and some of the early piano pieces, such as the *Impromptus*, the Suite *Napoli* and *Promenades*. In 1921 Poulenc also wrote the music for *La Baigneuse de Trouville* and *Le Discours du Général*, two scenes in Cocteau's scenic fantasy *Les Mariés de la Tour Eiffel*. The spectacle was completed by the famous *Bœuf sur le Toit*, for which Milhaud wrote the music.

About this time the inevitable happened, and Poulenc found himself commissioned by Diaghilev to write a ballet. The result was *Les Biches*, which, costumes and *décor* being by Marie Laurencin, was produced with great success by the Russian Ballet at Monte Carlo in 1923. Poulenc was now launched. *Les Biches* (which was given in London under the misleading and inappropriate title of *The House Party*) delighted London and Paris audiences with its sophisticated, slightly perverse scenario, the effect of which was heightened by the Marie Laurencin setting, Poulenc's sensuous and lively music and the exquisite dancing of Mlles Nijinska and Vera Nemchinova. In the Ragtime scene the composer showed his mastery of the jazz idiom of the period; in the well-known *Adagietto* he struck a note of romantic lyricism that from then on was to become one of the main characteristics of his later music. Poulenc wrote no more for the Ballet until 1929, when he contributed his *Pastourelle*, now better known in the piano arrangement, to a choreographic production called *L'Eventail de*

Jeanne in which ten composers collaborated, the other nine being: Ravel, Roussel, Florent Schmitt, P. O. Ferroud, Ibert, Milhaud, Auric, Delannoy, and Roland-Manuel. His next ballet, *Les Animaux Modèles*, after La Fontaine, and the latest to date, was written during the war and produced at the Paris Opera in 1942.

After *Les Biches* his subsequent works of importance were the *Cinq Poèmes de Ronsard*, for voice and piano, and the *Trio* for oboe, piano, and bassoon. The *Trio* is a wholly successful and delightful essay in the neo-classical style; the Ronsard songs are, on the other hand, much more romantic and show deeper feeling and a freer melodic line than any of his previous works.

The Songs

Poulenc now entered upon a highly productive period, and new works, especially songs, began to pour from his pen. The *Chansons Gaillardes*, on anonymous seventeenth-century texts, showed him in Rabelaisian mood; these were followed in 1928 by the charming *Airs Chantés*, on poems by Moréas. Apollinaire and Max Jacob were the authors he set in 1931 (*Four Poems* and *Five Poems* respectively); in 1934 came the *Huit Chansons Polonaises*, and then for the first time Poulenc turned to the poet Paul Éluard and set five of his poems in 1935. The same year, for the 350th anniversary of the death of Ronsard, he wrote *À sa Guitare*; and then, two years later, came the cycle *Tel Jour Telle Nuit* (Éluard) in which Poulenc, as a song-writer, attained his full maturity. He set Éluard again in his song-cycle *La Fraîcheur et le Feu* (1950).

During the war years, when he played a prominent part in the 'musical resistance' movement, he continued to pour out songs, among which the settings of two poems by Aragon – *C* and *Fêtes Galantes* deserve special mention. To this period also belong *Banalités* (Apollinaire), *Chansons Villageoises* (Fombeure), and *Métamorphoses* (Louis de Vilmorin). The *Fiançailles pour Rire* (Vilmorin) date from 1939. His settings of poems from Apollinaire's *Calligrammes*, heard in London in 1949, show him at the height of his powers.

All the songs mentioned so far are for voice and piano and will be associated in the minds of most listeners with the wonderful interpretations given them by Pierre Bernac partnered by the composer at the piano; but the choral works, many of them *a cappella*, occupy a still more important place in Poulenc's *œuvre*. Chief among these are the

Sept Chansons and the *Litanies à la Vierge Noire de Rocamadour* (1936); the *Mass* (1937); the four Motets (1938–9); and the *Exultate Deo* and *Salve Regina* (1941). The year 1937 also saw the production of the quasi-surrealist Cantata *Sécheresses* (text by Edward James); but Poulenc's finest choral works to date are almost certainly his big cantata for double chorus *a cappella*, *Figure Humaine*, written during the German occupation on a text by Éluard and first produced in England in 1945 by the B.B.C., and the *Stabat Mater* for soprano solo, chorus and orchestra, first performed at the Strasbourg Festival in June 1951.

Instrumental Works, Début at Opéra-Comique

Poulenc's only purely symphonic work for orchestra is the *Sinfonietta* (performed at the Edinburgh Festival in 1950), but his four *Concertos* are all important in different ways. His first essay in this form was the *Concert Champêtre* for harpsichord and orchestra (1927–8) (introduced by Wanda Landowska), which contains some delightful music; then came the *Concerto for Two Pianos* (1932), which is of a more flippant character; and in 1936 he composed his *Organ Concerto*, notable both for the unusual treatment of the solo instrument and for the accompaniment, in which percussion instruments are predominant. The composer assigns to this concerto a high place among his works. The *Piano Concerto* (1949) was first heard in Europe at the Aix-en-Provence Festival in 1950.

If not exactly a concerto, *Aubade* for piano solo and eighteen instruments (1929) must be reckoned one of the composer's most original and deeply-felt works. It has a choreographic scenario, the theme of which is the sadness of Diana, the goddess, who, vowed to chastity and hunting, suffers pangs of grief as each day dawns and she knows that the cold ritual of her life must go on forever unchanging and unchanged. The music depicts the anguish she feels at daybreak in the consciousness of her destiny and has about it an air of grave melancholy that occurs hardly anywhere else in Poulenc's works. *Aubade* was conceived, according to the composer, in the spirit of the Fontainebleau school and has never yet, in his opinion, received an adequate performance.

The works for piano solo, which succeeded each other at fairly frequent intervals between 1918 (*Mouvements Perpétuels*) and 1944 (A Flat *Intermezzo*) Poulenc does not consider really representative, or even the best examples of his pianistic style, which is to be sought for rather in the accompaniments to the songs. In the solo works he admits to having often yielded to the temptations of pure virtuosity, which would account for the relative superficiality of some of the piano pieces.

Poulenc has composed little chamber music, apart from the *Oboe Trio*, the two *Sonatas* for Violin and Piano and Cello and Piano (the latter dedicated to Pierre Fournier, who first performed it in 1949), and the *Sextet* for piano and wind.

In 1946 he made his *début* at the Opéra Comique with the opera-bouffe *Les Mamelles de Tirésias*, based on an extravaganza by Guillaume Apollinaire, which startled the staid *habitués* of that theatre, where it ran for a time side by side, and most incongruously, with well-worn favourites by Massenet and Gounod. Lavishly produced in a style evoking the exuberance of both music-hall and musical comedy, *Les Mamelles* proved an hilarious entertainment – an enormous satirical farce in the composer's ultra-Parisian manner, but full of genuinely musical inspiration. It was not, however, until 1956 that Poulenc completed his first serious opera, likely to prove one of his major works, *Le Dialogue des Carmélites* (G. Bernanos), which had its first performance at La Scala in Milan early in 1957.

An Appraisal

It is clearly too early to foresee exactly the place that posterity will assign to Francis Poulenc in the hierarchy of composers. He has been called 'a minor poet of music'. The epithet may pass. Few moderns possess his powers of melodic invention and of direct, spontaneous, lyrical utterance. In all his music there is melody; he has a very sensitive and individual harmonic style; and the sheer 'musicality' of his writing is so compelling, the tunes tumble over one another with such engaging candour, the rhythms race and trip along so unselfconsciously, the harmonies slip into their places so easily, and the modulations are so spontaneous and unforced, that the hearer is enchanted before he has time to be critical. It is this pleasure-giving quality in his music that links it with French music of the past – with the old Clavecinists, and later with Gounod, Chabrier, and Massenet. Yet Poulenc has a style to which he manages to be consistently faithful. One may discern in his music here and there an influence – here a whiff of Stravinsky, an echo of Mozart or Schumann; there a faint flavour of the sixteenth century or a reminiscence of the nineteenth (Chabrier); but his inspiration remains essentially individual. It is above all French in its clarity and vivaciousness; now *vieille France* in its tenderer moods, evoking a vision of brocades and satin, or a landscape in Touraine; now purely Parisian, reflecting the gaiety and malice of the *boulevards*, the wit and sophistication of *salon* or *café*. In parenthesis it should be stated that Poulenc has no connexion with Touraine apart from possessing there a country house, where he does most of his composing. And the setting somehow seems appropriate. The landscape of the Loire flowing swiftly past the terraced *châteaux* between the sloping vineyards lining its sandy banks has something of that musical quality we have noted as one of the characteristics of Poulenc's music. Grandiose it may not be, but neither is it trivial. Much of it is thoughtful, even grave in character, and often one can discern an undercurrent of a wistful, almost sad tranquillity that is one of its greatest charms. In an age where politics and metaphysics tend to encroach upon the arts, Francis Poulenc offers us the example of a musician with no axes to grind, no theories to propagate, only music to compose.

SERGE SERGEIEVITCH PROKOFIEV

1891–1953

W. R. ANDERSON

Credit and Debit

Some people would declare Prokofiev one of the most fortunate, others one of the least fortunate, of Russian composers. Take the debit side first: he made a reputation as a humorist, a flouter of conventions, a cocker of snooks. In the wild 1920s his ballet *Chout* (about buffoons), his piano *Sarcasms*, and the like devilries (so mild and comprehensible now) made sober folk consider him an *enfant terrible*. On the side of happiness can be placed the fact that whilst so many composers of those Twaddling Twenties sank, never more to rise, Prokofiev worked through that period, found his neo-romantic level, and also – a second source of satisfaction – found himself (unlike Rakhmaninov) able to live in the new Russia, which has never welcomed 'extremism'.

Prokofiev seems to have achieved a balanced musical life, on his own chosen terms. If genius cannot be claimed for him, he has displayed rich, often dazzling, talent and an occasional high power of synthesis, in the ability to employ certain classical styles without running them into the sands.

A Precocious Opera Composer

Serge Sergeievitch Prokofiev was born on 11 April (old style 23 April) 1891, on the estate of Sontovka, in the government of Ekaterinoslav, of which estate his father was manager. His mother was a good pianist, who played Beethoven to him. He was well founded, and it is not surprising that one of the works by which he is best known should be a *Classical Symphony*, showing the way in which the wine of modern harmonic and key freedoms has fermented in the old bottles of 'form'.

Taught to play by his mother, he seems to have taught himself, at five, to compose, and from then until he was thirteen he produced quite a large amount of music, including the beginning of an opera, at nine. Like almost all creative Russians, he loved fantasy: we remember how many of their operas have been upon fairy-tale subjects, or else upon the scarcely less strange, even weird, historical adventures of ancient Russia. Prokofiev early had a taste for the theatre, which is another characteristic trait of his people; the U.S.S.R. has more theatres than has any other comparable area on earth. When the great upthrust of native composition began in the nineteenth century, one of the forms at which Russians immediately aimed was opera, which usually comes late in the efforts of most nation's composers. So it is not surprising that before he began his formal musical education at the St Petersburg conservatoire, Prokofiev had essayed a second opera, *The Giant*. He had also, probably fired by the work of Tchaikovsky, tried his hand at a symphony, for he had the good luck early to get some help from one of Tchaikovsky's friends, Taneev, and also from Glière. *The Giant* was begun at seven, *The Deserted Islands* at nine, and *The Feast* (after Pushkin) at twelve. Of these, the last only was orchestrated. A *Symphony in G* also belongs to these pre-teen years, and at thirteen he wrote and scored *Undina*, in four acts!

So to the conservatoire he took a great bundle of manuscript. His chief teachers there were Rimsky-Korsakov and Liadov. Others who helped him were Glazunov, Nicolas Tcherepnin in conducting, and for piano Madame Essipova. Most of the work he did not find congenial; his temperament was not suited to the then pretty solidly classical outlook of the place. The professors were all leaders in their various realms of composition, but Prokofiev was not an easy youth to lead or manage. Going his own way, with fewer friends than most youths make (one of the closest was the composer of many symphonies, Miaskovsky), he worked at symphonic poems, an opera, *Maddalena* (still in manuscript), two *Piano Concertos*, and the piano pieces entitled *Sarcasms*, which have a sting in them. Besides these he wrote dozens of pieces – one account puts them at a hundred, and names a *Symphony in E minor*, six *Piano Sonatas* (one of which was later revised and published as Op. 1), two *Violin Sonatas*, and some ninety miscellaneous piano pieces. Little of this was ever published. In 1909, besides *Maddalena*, there was a *Sinfonietta*; in 1910, *Dreams* and *Autumn Poem* for orchestra, in 1911 the first *Piano Concerto*, and in 1912 a *Piano Sonata*, a *Toccata*, and a violoncello *Ballade*; in 1913, the second *Piano Concerto*; in 1914 the *Scythian Suite*, four movements about the legendary people of that name, barbarians of the steppes from the Carpathians to the Don. This music, it was felt, expressed a spirit that had not shone in Russian music since Borodin's intense imagination glowed in the *Prince Igor* dances.

The Virtuoso

Naturally, not all this music was well received. A piano concerto procured for the composer the Rubinstein Prize, in 1910, and here we meet Prokofiev as both composer and concert virtuoso – the latter activity one that for a good part of his life brought him fame. The piano concerto form had been much neglected for a generation or two; since Tchaikovsky (d. 1893), Anton Rubinstein (d. 1894), and Brahms (d. 1897) there had been very few such works; one thinks only of those by Saint-Saëns, Grieg, Rimsky-Korsakov, Liapunov, and MacDowell, few of whom wrote more than one or two examples; and as the turn of the century approached the number of such works thinned out noticeably.

Prokofiev's first concerto was milder meat than his second, which was an early sample of the kind of 'modernism' that brought protests from an audience: sounds that were to be renewed, and augmented, when the ballet *Chout* roused some cries of derision from listeners not then so hardened to off-centre harmony or Russian humour as now we are.

Many of Prokofiev's conservatoire contemporaries thought of him chiefly as a concert pianist (he won a prize of a grand piano), but he had learned some important lessons about the composition of a concerto, the main one being that the old purely display work was finished: that type had worked the soil of virtuosity to exhaustion. The newer concerto idea, to be used in many an experimental fashion, and by none more cleverly than by Prokofiev, was to explore new keyboard-orchestral partnerships, of much more nearly equal rights, to delve, too, among key-freedoms and cultivate new whims of harmony.

A Five-Period Output

It was in 1914 that Prokofiev set out to make his way in this world: not the easiest of times for culture. He had already sampled the second of the five periods into which he himself has divided his development – the innovationary spell. Now, in wartime, he continued his work in a land that was rapidly coming to the revolutionary boil.

He felt ripe for an intensification of his style, in a third period, which he named motory: hard, keen rhythms, tough harmonies, clear-cut form, and the element of the grotesque that constitutes yet another of his five leading qualities: the last, and for many the most grateful, is the lyrical, developed later. He found how to exploit what was perhaps always his freshest talent – the whimsical, Puckish, ironic strain that sounded so natural. He himself did not care for the word grotesque, implying as it does something twisted, unnatural; he preferred to consider the trait one of jesting, in a new way, not as Beethoven, with his jolly roughness, looked at humour, but as a man of the twentieth century faced – who knows with what stiffening of fibre? – the oncoming rush of mankind to embrace death instead of life.

None would blame a composer for following a bent for diversion. Not that one imputes to Prokofiev mere frivolity; but he had intense, perhaps even extreme, enjoyment in that never-ending fascination of the artist's setting himself new problems and finding new solutions for old ones. This aspect of any artist's world is often overlooked by those who are not themselves creators. The onlooker cannot always be expected to think the particular problem worth either inventing or solving, but he must allow the artist to choose his own problems, to treat them according to his own talent and humour and to experiment in public with possibly dangerous explosives.

The Gambler *and the* Classical Symphony

In the few years before the ultimate explosion of Bolshevism took place, Prokofiev was working at several such problems. The chief works, apart from sonatas, several of which exhibit interesting variants of classical procedure in a form that had largely lain dormant (as regards the structure) since Beethoven died, are *The Gambler* (1916) and the *Classical Symphony* (1917). The former was an opera (revised in 1928) based on the Dostoievsky tale of the man who learns to gamble from a retired General whose child he tutors. The General, financially in the power of a French so-called '*marquis*', has financial expectations from his aged mother, hopes that are disappointed. The tutor falls in love with the General's stepdaughter, and for her sake he gambles, to try to re-establish the General's fortunes. Though he wins, she regards him as a dangerous, indeed, hopeless gambler, and so his love is lost to him. From this opera, which remains in manuscript,

Four Portraits, plus a *Dénouement*, were extracted, for an orchestral suite, demonstrating much of the excitement of the gaming scenes, with a picture of the fighting old mother, whose youth and background are suggested by the use of folky themes. In employing such native material Prokofiev has been notably more sparing than the majority of his teachers. Probably they appeal less to the sophisticated, possibly rather sardonic artist, such as we may take this composer to be, than to the man of more simple-minded nature. In the *Portraits* we get a powerful depiction of the once-dominating, now weakening old General; the whole forms perhaps as exact an indication of the composer's mind as we have.

In the *Classical Symphony* we find a clearer line of strength in melody, an element with which Prokofiev has not always been sufficiently credited, as he has mildly complained, his humour and whims having, naturally enough, taken the ear of the public (whether or not they always liked the expression of these qualities). In the fresh exploitation of classical simplicity and clarity Prokofiev was something of a pioneer in 1917. One might compare the aim, though of course not the idiom, with that of Ravel. Prokofiev was, then, leading both this neo-classical fashion and that of fantasy and extreme harmony, which seemed to have come to a head in Diaghilev's production of the ballet *Chout* in 1921. It is obvious that in more than one way Prokofiev was feeling his way towards greater interest in a simpler style, strong in melody of a quite individual kind, with fresh piquancy. His melodic lines are among the most easily recognized personal traits. They are not just modern. His music in this period has a frank, unshaded visage, open to sun and air. The thinking is not on a grand scale: themes and patterning matter much, but feeling never goes deep, nor can it be denied that this last remark is almost always true of Prokofiev. Strong emotion is not his forte. The brash jollity of the finale of his symphony has an almost childlike charm; it asks to be met half-way. Melodic sport, bold attacks, easy impulses make a sufficient meed of pleasure and give a good measure of the spirit of Prokofiev in his mid-twenties.

American Adventure

With the Revolution of 1917 he felt unable to cope. He left Russia and lived in the United States of America and other countries, for three years, in Bavaria and in Paris; he toured Japan, he appeared in

London for a time. He was away from his native land until 1933, in a period when the world passed through the war, and music through yet another of its teething-times, that must ever and anon be renewed: the art is always being born again, with all the attendant troubles and joys of youthfulness.

Prokofiev was busy composing works, from opera to concerto, ballet to symphony – a score or so of items. The Chicago Opera commissioned and produced in 1921 *The Love of Three Oranges*, a whimsical, satirical tale after Prokofiev's heart, by the Italian Carlo Gozzi. Here the composer displayed his talent for both fairy-tale fantasy, beloved of the Russians, and the element of farce, which at this time appeared to be paramount in Prokofiev's musical will. Perhaps fancy, rather than keen imagination, has ever been his strong card. The *Oranges*, with a complicated fabular plot about queer Court intrigues, sorcerers, a curse and all manner of machinations, was, on its own ground, a resounding success. Prokofiev was his own librettist and proved himself a true son in the Russian fantasy-succession, not just an expatriate cosmopolitan, as so many others, of various nations, became in the years when Paris was the arty centre of the world and when Diaghilev's ballet was the rage, reached its greatest artistic height and then declined.

With all his delight in modernism, Prokofiev always set his face against jazz, which he detested: detecting, as the finest artists have divined, its inherent sterility.

A Twofold Development

With these two sides of his work, the operatic-fantastic play and the concerto, the composer continued his twofold development. There were works for piano and orchestra (No. 3), and one for violin and orchestra, both begun earlier, in his Russian residence. Here his warmer, more lyrical spirit had full play. The conductor Kussevitzky was always one of Prokofiev's most enthusiastic supporters; it was he who brought out the *Violin Concerto*, in 1923, at a Paris concert. On the ballet side, the sharper idiom prevailed. In 1927 Diaghilev produced his *Pas d'Acier*, steely enough, to be sure, and perhaps not without a suggestion that the composer's thoughts were upon developments in his native land, so largely to be associated with the name of Stalin, the Man of Steel.

In 1929 Brussels heard and saw *The Gambler*, revised, and a third

Symphony was produced at Paris. His fourth was written in compliment to Kussevitzky's Boston Symphony Orchestra, on its fiftieth anniversary (1930).

In Harmony with the U.S.S.R.

Then the pull of the homeland became too strong to resist; after a first tentative return, he settled once more in Russia, where he found himself in harmony with Soviet aspirations, in which he became a fully active co-operator, realizing, as he has said, that one must feel 'the day that is to be' and agreeing with the strong Soviet bent for music rooted in the mind and heart of the people. It is therefore natural that the satirical side of Prokofiev's art should have slipped into the background, though the music for a humorous film, *Lieutenant Kizhe*, provided him with an occasion for deploying again some skittish wit. Kizhe was an imaginary character invented by an officer of the Czar. Once named, the Lieutenant's existence must be continued and accounted for; and thus the comedy fulfils itself, amid clashes and contretemps. The music is most familiar in the form of a *Suite*, Op. 60.

In nearly all the subsequent music old asperities have been softened. Prokofiev had continued to compose freely (his opus numbers are near the nineties), and in veins in which he pursued his own gospel of beauty: as he said, 'I steadfastly believe in aiming at beauty of expression', which includes a clear lyrical impulse. He had pleased the Soviets, delving into the music of the people for such works as *Partisan Zhelezniak*; he then provided, in *Peter and the Wolf*, some children's fairy-tale music of a simpler type than anything in his operas. Here (1936) he is at his most amiable. The score is full of the kind of Lewis Carrollean fun that children love. Prokofiev had, he agreed, renounced complexity.

As a contributor to the Russian revival of the heroic spirit, especially associated with ancient legends of valour, he wrote the music for the Eisenstein-Vasilev film, *Alexander Nevsky*, which is known round the world. The theme is the defeat of Teutonic chivalry in 1242. There is a *Suite* of 'symphonic frescoes' in seven movements, from the film, depicting solitude, battle scenes, with triumphal choruses, making up perhaps his greatest purely native composition. He wrote in 1936 for the new orchestra of the Fine Arts Committee in Moscow an *Overture* on Russian themes; he has a *String Quartet* on

Kabardinian melodies, ballet music for *Cinderella* and *Romeo and Juliet*; two operas, *Semion Kotko* and *Betrothal in the Monastery* (based on Sheridan's *The Duenna*), a *Cantata* dedicated to Stalin, and a symphonic suite from his music to the play *Egyptian Nights*, produced at Moscow's Kamerny Theatre in 1935 and given seventy-five performances that year; it is based on the Cleopatra of Shaw, Pushkin, and Shakespeare.

A Matured Style

So we find Prokofiev settled down, in his fifties, to the apparently full enjoyment of a busy composing life as an honoured citizen of the U.S.S.R. from which he fled at the Revolution. He had found his final form of congenial expression, basically lyrical, melodic, and economical. His talent (it can scarcely be called genius) was most highly suited to the stage. Though economical in matter, he was prolific in output: in the first five years after his return he wrote twenty-seven works, most of them of some extent.

He frequently wrote to his American friends, greeting them on behalf of Soviet composers and telling of their year's work. When Germany invaded Russia in 1941 Prokofiev's first work was a *Symphonic Suite* bearing, as title, that date; then he wrote a cantata, *Ballad of the Unknown Boy*, and, most important, perhaps, of all his wartime work, a five-act opera on Tolstoy's *War and Peace*, which received a concert performance at the end of 1945. More film music followed, for *Kotovsky* (a hero of 1918) and for *Partisans in the Ukrainian Steppe*, about other warriors of the recent struggle. He was also working on a historical film, *Ivan the Terrible*, collaborating again with Eisenstein. He returned in 1944 to the symphonic form, with No. 5; a sixth *Symphony* came in 1945; and the final one, the seventh, not long before his death. To the *Piano Sonatas* he added Nos. 7 and 8. He greeted peace with an *Ode on the End of the War*, concluding in joy, hope, and a finale, which he called 'Ring out, ye bells and cymbals'.

Prokofiev died in Russia on 4 March 1953, three days before Marshal Stalin.

SERGEI RAKHMANINOV

1873–1943

W. R. ANDERSON

The Exile

There is an element of sadness in Rakhmaninov's story. Like Glinka and Prokofiev, he became an exile from his native country, not, like Glinka, willingly shaking off that dust (and even spitting upon it), or like Prokofiev, after long absence returning cordially to make a new life in the new U.S.S.R. Rakhmaninov, finding it impossible to live happily when the revolution began, left Russia and ended his days in California as an American citizen.

We have a large degree of authentic news of his life and development in his own words, for he told his story to Oskar von Riesemann, and it is published in book form as *Rakhmaninov's Recollections*. The story there told goes up to the date of publication, 1934, and there is little to add about the last decade of a life that extended to within a few days of seventy years.

A Comfortable Life

Rakhmaninov was born into much the same kind of life as Glinka, that of comfortable country-house owning people. His father, like Glinka's, had been an Army officer, retiring early to manage the large Northern estate. *His* father had been musical and was for a time a pupil of John Field, the Irishman who wrote Nocturnes from which Chopin drew some stylistic ideas. This grandfather was a keen musical worker to the end – a type of those amateurs from whom sprang the school of Russian music in the mid-century: very few of those whose names are most familiar to us – Rimsky-Korsakov, Musorgsky, Borodin and the rest – were brought up to music as professional men in the first place. It is this development of creative artists from an almost entirely amateur strain that is so remarkable a feature of the Russian musical scene in that century.

Rakhmaninov's father had married the well-dowered daughter of a

General. They had six children, three girls and three boys. Sergei was the middle boy.

The Darker Side of Temperament

Perhaps something in the landscape, as well as in his heritage of temperament, gave a dark tinge to much of Rakhmaninov's art; the sombre element is marked; even his orchestration is darker than that of the composer to whom he has been likened, Tchaikovsky. It is in a certain type of brooding thought that Rakhmaninov excels the older man, a deeper aspect that is not always readily perceptible.

In the very first words that Riesemann quotes from Rakhmaninov's lips, about his childish memories, we find him contrasting the impressions of good and bad, of the sad and the happy, as a boy of four, when his mother gave him his first piano lessons. A very early impression was of playing a tiny piece while his grandfather put in an accompaniment to it and delighted the child with praise of his partnership. Rakhmaninov gives the other side of the picture also – an aspect that life never for long allowed him to lose sight of – the sorrows of childhood. Even his punishments had a musical reference, for instead of being made to stand in the corner, he was put under the piano by his disciplinarian mother; the father being much more indulgent, and even tending to spoil the child. There we find one of those cross-pulls in a family, which may have a good deal to do with the formation of a child's character. Rakhmaninov later considered that there had been much good for him in the clear ordering of his time in youth.

Conflicting Influences

Naturally the father leaned towards the idea of the military profession for one or both of the two sons he then had. Like almost all his class, he scoffed at the idea of music as a profession fit for a gentleman. The more perceptive mother decided that Sergei was to be a musician. The decisive factor was a decline in the fortunes of the family due to the father's carelessness. While the elder brother went into the army, Sergei, thanks to the devotion of the governess who taught him the piano, Mlle Ornazkaya, got a scholarship at the conservatoire at St Petersburg, to a flat in which city the family removed in 1882, not, however, happily: dissensions had caused a rupture, and the father and mother separated for the rest of their lives.

Here was a painful event in the experience of a boy of nine, whose mother's affection towards him was now less warm. Her old discipline relaxed, and Sergei was 'spoiled' by his grandmother. Talented as he was, he found that he could without much exertion keep up with, and go beyond, most of his classmates and make a sufficient impression upon his not very outstanding tutors; so he often played truant.

One of the boy's strongest impressions of the time was the beauty of his sister Helena's singing. Her death at seventeen was a lasting sorrow to him. Another grief was soon to come – the loss in a diphtheria epidemic of his second sister.

Another type of singing gave him pleasure also, that in the city's church choirs. He reproduced on the home piano much of the music he heard in the churches.

Finding that the apparently lazy boy did not progress particularly well, his mother, taking the advice of the pianist Siloti (a favourite pupil of Liszt's), sent him to the Moscow conservatoire to be taught by Siloti's old master Sverev. Before the change, his last months were made happy in a holiday at his grandmother's small country place.

A Fresh Start

At twelve, we find him beginning his studies afresh, this time in earnest: living in Sverev's house with two other pupils, under the eye of the teacher's sister, who was much stricter in discipline than was Sverev himself, of whose severity rumour had given the boy an exaggerated idea. Though irritable, even to violence, with the foolish or lazy, Sverev was, as Rakhmaninov recalled, 'an unusually humane, fine, and noble-thinking man', with a 'vivacious and sparkling intellect', most generous in giving the boy free tuition, board, and clothing (the last a kind of uniform common to all school pupils). The master treated his pupils almost as equals.

Alas, in 1889 Rakhmaninov found Sverev too little regardful of what the youth considered the rights of independence, and they parted, Rakhmaninov going to live with an aunt, Mme Satina. During his time with Sverev he had heard all the best music and plays that were going. That was a strongly formative period, when he acquired social as well as musical graces, was supervised in his reading and put upon the high road of culture, whilst he laboured hard at his music, once having the distinction of playing before Anton Rubinstein and of being present at a dinner that Sverev gave in the great pianist's honour. Rakhmaninov vividly remembered a series of historical recitals that Rubinstein gave, one of the landmarks in the history of the pianoforte recital.

To Rakhmaninov occurred something of the same disappointment as Rubinstein experienced, in that the pianistic virtuosity of each tended to overshadow his composing; each felt that people tended to rank the former as the more important and praiseworthy pursuit. In his later years Rakhmaninov found no lack of enthusiasm for his works, at any rate among amateur music-lovers.

A memorable holiday, after the first year with Sverev, was spent in the Crimea, improving his weak side, theoretical knowledge, and enjoying the summer bathing and picnics. The work he put in enabled him, on his return, to pass into the harmony class of Arensky, never, however, a first-class teacher, though Rakhmaninov got on well enough under him. He was showing the good results of his change from the uneasy home to the discipline and hard work at Sverev's.

A Tchaikovsky Worshipper

He now began to compose and came under the notice of Tchaikovsky, a friend of Sverev's. He gave the master great pleasure by arranging his *Manfred* symphony for two pianos. The jealous rivalry between the school of St Petersburg, which harboured most of the livelier, more liberal and 'modern' composers, and the conservative one at Moscow had its effect upon Rakhmaninov, who was thus brought up to consider Tchaikovsky the greatest of masters and the more progressive band at St Petersburg – Rimsky-Korsakov and his tribe – as an inferior company. Perhaps, in this formative period, Rakhmaninov took on too strong a tincture of the style of Tchaikovsky, the idol of the Moscow school. He never fully threw off that influence, though there is more originality in Rakhmaninov, and more strength in his moods, than many of those realize who enjoy superficially similar moods in Tchaikovsky. The introspective temperament was common to both, the tendency to melancholy sentiment. That is a national trait – most notable of all in literature; but the particular colouring and depth of this aspect of character had not in the two quite so much in common as some have thought.

Rakhmaninov moved on to Taneev's composition class in 1886–7 and went on to Siloti for pianoforte. Taneev, like most of the Moscow professors, was a great believer in the German classics and a disbeliever in the Petersburg crew, under-estimating them as being amateurs.

An injudicious summer bathe at this time brought on an attack of malaria, which affected the young man's powers of concentration for a while.

An Opera in a Month

Siloti left the conservatoire before the four-year course was up, and in 1891 Rakhmaninov took his final examination after three years, proving that he could dispense with the extra year's work. He ended his college course with the composition of an opera, *Aleko*, as an examination test. This he wrote in a month. Sverev, the loyal believer in Rakhmaninov's fine future, added a gold watch to the official prize, the 'Great Gold Medal', which his teacher Taneev had in his day also won. The name of Rakhmaninov was duly cut upon the marble tablet in the hall.

His opera was performed in 1893, and the publisher Gutheil began to take an interest in the young composer's works. He had taken a furnished apartment (its prophetic name was 'America') and now began his concert career, composing freely the while. A tone poem on Lermontov's *The Rock* was one work; another was a choral piece, which a Moscow choir sang in 1893. His conducting life began with his directing his opera, an event darkened by hearing of the death of Tchaikovsky. To the master's memory he dedicated an *Elegiac Trio*. A good deal of his time had to be given to teaching the pianoforte. In 1894 he made a concert tour with a violinist; in 1897 came out his *First Symphony* — in St Petersburg, not the congenial Moscow. It was not then successful. The failure, he said, changed him deeply, weakening his confidence so much that he felt inclined to give up composition. He went back to his aunt's, heavily depressed.

The sun shone again when an invitation to conduct an opera company run by a wealthy amateur allowed him to give up the drudgery of teaching. He conducted Glinka's *Life for the Czar* and other native works, besides some of the operatic classics. Here he first met Shalyapin. But again he felt the inclination to compose and so gave up the post.

Widening Sympathies

In 1898 the Philharmonic Society of London invited him to conduct. The famous *Prelude* in C sharp minor had begun its blended beneficent and baneful work: he was becoming known as a composer. Yet his mental uncertainty continued. In 1900 he had some hypnotic-suggestion treatment from a Dr Dahl, which worked a cure. To the doctor Rakhmaninov dedicated a composition upon which the treatment had allowed him to work – his second *Piano Concerto*.

His marriage took place in 1902 to Natalie Satin. As 'best man' appeared Siloti, who had been very kind in helping him with money to enable him to compose in something like comfort. Part of the honeymoon was spent at the Wagner Festival at Bayreuth, when Rakhmaninov was deeply impressed by the power of *The Ring*. His sympathies widened: soon, he came to admire Rimsky-Korsakov of the Petersburg clique. His own success in the rival city of Moscow was now ripe and rewarding. In 1905 he became conductor at the Imperial Grand Theatre, where he again had Shalyapin as principal bass.

After the war in which the Japanese were successful there was much unrest in Russia. Rakhmaninov never found himself in sympathy with revolutionary movements, such as came to a climax in 1917.

His career was now well under way. His operas *Francesca da Rimini* and *The Miserly Knight* were produced in 1906. But he had far too much work to do in Moscow to be able to find enough time for composition, so he went away to Dresden, where he lived at first very quietly indeed, among a few friends. One of them was Nikolai von Struve, who, becoming manager of Kussevitzky's publishing firm, brought in Rakhmaninov as one of the advisers upon compositions to be published for the benefit of the writers, not the publisher.

In Dresden he wrote his tone-poem after Böcklin's *Isle of the Dead* and his *Second Symphony*, as well as an unfinished opera on the subject of *Monna Vanna*.

A Triple Reputation

Having now two daughters, he felt the need of a greater income and so began to take more concert work. It is in this way – as composer, conductor, and pianist – that Rakhmaninov made a triple reputation; but in so doing he never seemed to satisfy himself about his true destiny.

He took part in Diaghilev's first season of Russian ballet in Paris (1906) and bowed to the demand for his appearance upon platforms by leaving Dresden in 1908. For a short time he enjoyed life as a gentleman farmer on the estate of the Satins and became fond of motoring in the early days of that sport.

In 1909 he paid his first visit to the United States, where he was to end his days. His third *Piano Concerto* was written for that occasion. He made a tour as pianist with the Boston Symphony Orchestra and also conducted his *Second Symphony* in several large cities. He was offered the post of conductor of the orchestra, in succession to Max Fiedler, but declined, as again he did when the offer was renewed nine years later.

On his return to Russia he was elected vice-president of the Imperial Russian Musical Society, controlling much of the official musical life of the chief cities. From 1910 to 1914 he made many tours, conducting a good deal and towards the end of his Russian days playing less than formerly.

Skryabin was a challenging new force, and there were Skryabin-Rakhmaninov feuds by devotees, in which Rakhmaninov took no part. His temperament was vastly different from Skryabin's, but he saw no use in such squabbles. He was now writing little and wishing that he could find solitude, which he always craved, for composition.

The End of Life in Russia

In 1914 he was in England again. During World War I he gave many concerts for charity, but was of course much restricted in touring. When the Russian Revolution came to pass, he conceived it 'mishandled'. In 1917 he had made, with the ready permission of the Bolsheviks, a tour in Scandinavia; thereafter he took for a time a small house near Copenhagen, leaving nearly everything behind in Russia. He had to earn money and so took up again his career as pianist. Offers came from the United States, and he took a great decision: to settle there. From his arrival in November 1918 his common plan of work was to appear in Europe from October to December and spend the rest of the season in the States. He thus had little time or congenial conditions for composition.

A letter that he and two others wrote to the *New York Times* in 1931 resulted in a boycott of his works in the U.S.S.R. Ten years later he gave the proceeds of a New York recital, more than 3,600 dollars, to war sufferers in his native land. He became a member of the American Federation of Musicians in 1941 and was admitted to American citizenship in the year in which he died, shortly after he had bought a home at Beverly Hills, California. His death resulted from complications after pneumonia and pleurisy. He left a widow and two married daughters, Irene Wolkonsky and Tatiana Conus.

In 1944 a Rakhmaninov Fund was organized in his memory, to give opportunities to young American artists in the three aspects of the musical career that he so distinguishedly pursued, those of composer, pianist, and conductor, and to foster exchanges of young artists between Russia and the U.S.A. The composer's widow was made Honorary President of the organization, the pianist, Horowitz, President, and the conductor, Kussevitzky, Chairman of its artists' advisory committee. Its regional and national biennial competitions for pianists were first held in 1946 and 1947, those for composers (annual ones) in 1947 and 1948. Their broad aim is the discovery and fostering of new native talent.

MAURICE RAVEL

1875–1937

MARTIN COOPER

Early Years

Maurice Ravel was born at Ciboure, near Saint Jean-de-Luz in the department of the Basses Pyrénées. He was the elder of the two sons of a Swiss engineer married to a Basque wife and, although the family moved to Paris the very year in which Ravel was born, he was always aware and proud of his Basque blood. In 1878 his brother Édouard was born and a comradeship began that was to last all Ravel's life. At the age of twelve he was already having lessons in theory and pianoforte, and in 1889 he entered the Conservatoire. Two years later he made one of the friendships that also was to last all his life, when he graduated from Anthiome's preparatory pianoforte class into that of de Bériot and met Ricardo Viñes, the brilliant Spanish pianist, who was to do so much for the propagating of modern French pianoforte music, including that of Ravel. Viñes was exactly the same age as Ravel and shared his musical tastes. The music of the Russian Nationalists was new to Paris in the nineties and created a great impression on Ravel, especially Balakirev's *Tamara*, which seemed to reveal an entirely new musical world, full of poetic beauty and significance and yet free from the abstract philosophical or symbolic tendencies in fashion among the pupils of Franck and the followers of Wagner. Of French musicians Chabrier alone instinctively attracted both Ravel and Viñes, and there is a nice story of the two sixteen-year-old boys visiting the composer and playing his *Valses Romantiques* for two pianos. Erik Satie, whose *Sarabandes* and *Gymnopédies* had appeared in 1887 and 1888 and *Gnossiennes* in 1890, exercised an influence not entirely musical. His works suggested more than they actually stated – a mental attitude hostile to all pretentiousness and a severe, original style combined with a deliberately mystifying quality, which appealed to the fastidious and dandified side of Ravel's character.

The Prix de Rome Withheld

Ravel seems to have begun his musical career with a quite distinct musical character, which developed but never really changed during his whole life. His first known compositions – *Menuet Antique* and *Sites Auriculaires* (1895) and the *Deux Epigrammes de Clément Marot* (1896) – showed an unmistakable individuality. When in 1897 he entered Fauré's composition class, his concern – and fortunately Fauré's also – was to perfect and mature his power of self-expression rather than to form a musical personality. The first public performances of his music got him a bad name with the critics and with the officials of the Conservatoire. The title *Sites Auriculaires* suggested the influence of Satie and the possibility of deliberate mystification; but the appearance of his pianoforte piece *Jeux d'Eau* in 1901 and the *String Quartet*, dedicated to Fauré, in 1904 made it quite impossible not to take him seriously as a composer. He had been placed second in the competition for the Prix de Rome in 1901 and competed again in 1902 and 1903, but failed on each occasion to win the prize. He was certainly not conciliatory in his attitude, and it speaks highly for the acumen and insight of the elderly, and immensely successful, Massenet that he should have argued in favour of Ravel's introduction into his prize cantata of a slow valse obviously modelled on the style of contemporary operetta. Finally in 1905 Ravel was disqualified in the preliminary competition and not even allowed to sit for the final test. This overt act of injustice could not be allowed to pass. Romain Rolland wrote an open letter of protest and for a short time the musical world was torn by the pros and cons of the *affaire Ravel*. However, he never won the *Prix de Rome*, and his treatment by the officials of the musical world on this occasion bred in Ravel an increased spirit of independence and a deliberate discounting of all criticism.

Piano and Ballet Music

He had been a great dandy from his early years at the Conservatoire – exquisite waistcoats, immaculate shirts and a very, very carefully trimmed black beard, varying in cut from hidalgo to Assyrian. He had the dandy's temperament – disdain of popularity, passion for perfection, and aloof, almost secretive manner; but that the manner and the beard masked a sensitive, even affectionate, character is plain from his music and the loyal friends whom he collected round him. He lived with his family, to whom he was devoted, and they in their turn appreciated him and his music. Love seems to have played little or no part in Ravel's life, and much later, when he was famous and no longer young, he half explained, half excused this apparent fundamental deficiency in his character. 'I prefer a beautiful engine to a beautiful woman. Music is really my only mistress.'

His friends were half protective, half in awe of him, and he expected a good deal of them. They were at this time mostly artists of the younger generation, as avid for new artistic experiences and as intolerant of official routine as he was himself. A group of them – which included Ricardo Viñes, Léon Fargue, Édouard Benedictus, and Maurice Calvocoressi – nicknamed themselves *les Apaches*, and they would foregather after concerts and then sit up most of the night discussing and playing music. It was for them that Ravel wrote the set of pianoforte pieces entitled *Miroirs* (1905), and these were followed three years later by *Gaspard de la Nuit*. Ravel's writing for the pianoforte owed a great deal to his study of Liszt, a composer who was then largely discounted by both critics and public. Ravel was always fascinated by technical achievement, whether in music or engineering or the construction of mechanical toys: it was the technique of pianoforte writing rather than the emotional atmosphere of Liszt's music that attracted him. Other friends beside *les Apaches* were admitted to his intimacy. The Godebskis and their two children provided him with almost a second home. To them he dedicated his *Sonatine* for pianoforte (1903), and for their children he wrote *Ma Mère l'Oye* (first as a pianoforte duet with one very easy part, in 1908, and arranged as a ballet and orchestrated in 1912). It was on their yacht that he wrote the *Rapsodie Espagnole*, one of the very few of his works to appear first in orchestral form, for although Ravel was a born orchestrator, a large number of his orchestral works appeared first as pianoforte music. Even so there is no hint of the transcription about them, so perfectly did he possess the technique of both mediums.

It was perhaps the coming of Diaghilev and the Russian Ballet to Paris that gave him the greatest stimulus to orchestral writing. Diaghilev, with his unfailing flair for new talent, soon commissioned a work from Ravel, and during 1910 *Daphnis et Chloé* was written at the Godebski's house in the country. Even then he did not neglect the pianoforte, and in 1911 his *Valses Nobles et Sentimentales*, played on the first occasion without publication of the composer's name, caused a sensation among musicians and led to some amusing and revealing wrong attributions of authorship. Diaghilev, realizing the possibilities of the music on the stage, asked him to orchestrate the *Valses* for him, with the result that the year 1912 saw three ballets of Ravel performed by the Russians – *Daphnis et Chloé* and two transcriptions, *Ma Mère l'Oye* and *Adelaïde ou le Langage des Fleurs*, adapted from the *Valses Nobles et Sentimentales*. The year 1911 also saw the performance of Ravel's only full-dress opera, *L'Heure Espagnole*, one of the most brilliantly successful of his achievements in the lighter vein. Franc-Nohain's story caused a certain amount of scandal and has earned the work a good many hard names, from the 'miniature pornographie-vaudeville' to the chestnut of 'The Immoral Hour'. It was certainly not the amorous intrigues of the plot that attracted Ravel. For him the attraction probably lay in the neatness and piquancy of Pepita's solutions of her many problems, in the Spanish background and, perhaps most of all, in the multiplicity of clocks in the clockshop, which tick and whizz and whirr their way through the score. Ravel never showed greater orchestral skill or greater musical power in general than in the composition of these years. If *Daphnis et Chloé* is his masterpiece, *L'Heure Espagnole* is not far below it in musicianship.

The War, Stravinsky, a New World

Ravel was nearly forty when war was declared between France and Germany in 1914. The Russian Ballet had brought him fame, and his friendship with Stravinsky had opened up new musical prospects. Each work was to Ravel the solution of a problem, partly technical and partly expressive, and this accounts for the superficial variety of styles in his works. His personality was marked but Protean. Whether he was setting Greek folk-songs or evoking Spain, inspired by fairy tales, early nineteenth-century dance-forms, or Alexandrine romance, his music is unmistakable. His sense of style in the abstract expressed itself in the different styles he adopted and there was no question of pastiche in the narrow sense of the term. Stravinsky, after the composition of *Le Sacre du Printemps*, was interested in just the same sort of problems as Ravel, and each composer influenced the other in his development after 1912. The summer of 1913 they spent together in Switzerland, working on the orchestration of Musorgsky's *Khovansh-*

china. In his memoirs Stravinsky tells how he played Ravel his new Japanese poems and how Ravel, 'who had a taste for instrumental filigree-work and subtleties of style', was immediately enthusiastic and decided to do something of the same sort.

This was the origin of the *Trois Poèmes de Mallarmé*, the work in which he approached most nearly to the atonality of Schönberg. Stravinsky had just heard *Pierrot Lunaire* and had been impressed by the novelty and subtlety of Schönberg's instrumentation, though he absolutely rejected what he felt to be 'a return to the aesthetic world of Beardsley' in the poems and general atmosphere of the music. In choosing texts of Mallarmé, Ravel showed a literary taste that did not in real life always distinguish his judgements. He had very little literary training and was to the end of his life apt to mistake a superficial paradox for a new and original truth, a novelty of the *salons* for a genuine discovery.

The declaration of war found Ravel at Biarritz. Every summer he liked to return to his native Basque country and to spend his holidays in the atmosphere that he somehow felt to be that of his own race. His father had died some years earlier, but his mother was alive and Ravel still lived with her when he was in Paris. It was her death in 1917 that brought his war service to an end. He had tried to enlist in 1914, but been refused and forced to content himself with helping to care for the wounded evacuated to Biarritz. During 1916 he did reach the front as a lorry-driver, and his experiences there, added to the death of his mother the next year, caused a breakdown and started the insomnia from which he suffered for the rest of his life. In 1916 his refusal to join a 'National League for the Defence of French Music', which aimed at boycotting the music of German composers in France, made him unpopular in certain Chauvinistic quarters, while it told in favour of his integrity and breadth of vision as an artist.

The works that issued from the years of the war were the *Piano Trio* (1915) and the *Tombeau de Couperin* (1919) for pianoforte. Into this last work Ravel put, besides all his admiration for the French clavecinists of the eighteenth century, some of the feelings stirred by the horrors of the war, and by the death of his mother and many of his friends. On the surface there is little but elegance, charm, and a feeling for the atmosphere of a period; but compared with the earlier works for pianoforte the *Tombeau de Couperin* shows evidence of more human feeling, more warmth, and less exterior decoration and effect.

It was the pathetic requiem of a man without faith, the tiny human monument constructed over against the death that he believed ended everything. In the *Trio* Ravel was experimenting again. He had always upheld the music of Saint-Saëns against its numerous detractors, and in the *Trio* and, five years later, in the orchestral poem, *La Valse* (1920), his music bears the traces of Saint-Saëns's influence – the aiming at a purely exterior, plastic effect in a kind of neo-classicism, which at the same time did not reject modern and exotic elements, as in the jazz rhythms and the Pantoum of the *Trio*.

Travels Abroad

Hitherto he had travelled very little outside France, but in the years after 1920 a kind of wanderlust seized him. He visited Holland, Italy, Spain, England, Poland, Belgium, Hungary, Rumania, Switzerland and, in 1928, the United States. Many causes probably contributed to this change in his habits. The death of his mother had broken up his home, although his brother Édouard gave him a flat in his house and made up in every way possible for the blank left in Ravel's life. More important still, a new generation had come to the fore with different artistic ideals and revolutionary theories: Ravel was not *vieux jeu* but he was equally no longer *avant-garde* in the musical world. Added to all this was the profoundly disintegrating effect of insomnia, which breaks up the whole natural rhythm of existence and acts as a permanent irritation on the nervous system of any man, let alone a sensitive, highly-strung organism such as Ravel's.

Many of the journeys were undertaken in connexion with performances of his works, for he was now a European figure. Yet his character was singularly unchanged. The old dandyism still persisted and he arrived for a few weeks in the United States with twenty pairs of pyjamas, dozens of shirts, and fifty-seven white ties. The beard had disappeared long before, but the face revealed beneath was none the less a mask. The smallness, neatness, and extreme elegance of Ravel's exterior appearance seemed in many ways an expression of just the personality suggested by his music, but it gave no hint of the more emotional and sensitive side of his nature. His appearance was rather a deliberate warning off of those who sought to invade the unbroken solitude of his inner life. One critic has expressed this emotional reserve of Ravel's music very well, comparing it with that of Albert Roussel. 'In Roussel's music', he writes, 'the soul is hidden once and for all: whereas in Ravel's, she hides her face afresh in each work'. It is not that Ravel's music is exactly coquettish, but it often seems that he is on the verge of an avowal, that an emotional confidence is hovering on his lips, when he suddenly thinks better of it and resumes the mask of an impersonal artist.

One side of his character found entirely new expression in 1922, when he bought himself a house at Montfort l'Amaury, about thirty miles from Paris. He spent endless care on the decoration and prided himself on the perfection of each room. Sham Greek and sham Chinese jostled each other, mechanical toys and period pieces. The result was the height of artificiality, but then, as Ravel protested when critics called his music artificial – 'Does it never occur to them that I am artificial by nature?' And so in a sense he was. 'Ravel instals himself in front of a Mozart sonata or a Saint-Saëns concerto just as a painter instals himself in front of a group of trees.' He found his inspiration in art rather than in nature, and in that sense he was an artificial composer; but there was no question of insincerity or pose. His mask, which many people mistook for pose or conceit, was not consciously assumed defence, but as natural as a shell on a snail's back. And it was this extreme sensitiveness that determined the developments of his last years.

Ravel found it difficult to grow old as a musician. His whole life had been independent and spent in, as it were, passive resistance against the authorities of the musical world. Now he saw himself becoming a classic, no longer a leader of the musical world in France; each new work he wrote was not eagerly awaited and furiously discussed, but rather accepted, with varying enthusiasm but unvarying and, to a man of Ravel's nature, irksome respect. His reaction was very much that of the poet Yeats, who found himself at the end of his life in the same position, and it may be summed up in the one word – of unhappy memory – appeasement. Both Yeats and Ravel were pathetically anxious to stand well with *les jeunes*, and in order to do so both were ready to make some modifications in their latest works. Their fundamental characteristics were, of course, quite unchanged, but they made concessions on the surface, gestures of friendship towards the dictators of musical fashion. It was not a very dignified attitude, but very understandable.

Last Works, Tragic End

Ravel had written nothing for the theatre since *L'Heure Espagnole* when he collaborated with Colette in *L'Enfant et les Sortilèges*, which was first given at Monte Carlo in 1925. This was another nursery story; it was like *Ma Mère l'Oye*, only more fantastic and on a larger musical scale. In it Ravel found an outlet for two apparently conflicting tastes – his feeling for children and for the grotesque. The naughty child who runs amok, and is then haunted by various animals, pieces of furniture and crockery that he has hurt or broken, appealed to the shy, sensitive child in Ravel and to the artist who nearly twenty years before had found a voice and expression for the animals of the *Histoires Naturelles*. *Bolero*, on the other hand, was a technical experiment rather in the manner of Alban Berg's more pretentiously named *Invention über eine gleichmässige Achtelbewegung* (Invention on a regular quaver figure) in Act 3 of *Wozzeck*. Its astonishing success surprised the composer himself and his surprise gave way to amusement when an enterprising American film company asked for the filming rights under the impression that *Bolero* was an opera. To him it was a technical experiment and nothing more, whereas the *Pianoforte Concerto for the Left Hand*, written for the one-armed Austrian pianist Wittgenstein, meant a good deal more, in spite of its superficial resemblance to a technical *tour de force*.

The Last Years

This and the *Pianoforte Concerto* of the following year were Ravel's two last works. In 1932 he had a motor accident from which he apparently made a complete recovery, but it was not long afterwards that he began to complain of inability to concentrate, mental tiredness, and various failures of the reflex nervous system, which all pointed only too clearly to some kind of affection of the brain. Ravel never became insane or anything approaching insane. For the last six years of his life he sank into an increasing mental torpor, but he never lost his reason; he might have been happier if he had. He was aware of his affliction and pathetically conscious of the desire to compose, which he was quite unable to satisfy. He would spend long days on the veranda of his house at Montfort l'Amaury gazing at the sky, waiting. '*Que faites-vous?*' a friend asked him one day. '*J'attends*,' he answered. It was then that the emptiness of his life apart from his music must have weighed most heavily on him. Finally in December 1937 he decided to risk the only possible operation that might save him. He entered a Paris nursing-home and survived an operation on the brain, but it was no use; he had a relapse and died three days after Christmas. His malady was officially described as shrinkage of the brain, an ironic death for a composer whose music was the very embodiment of that specifically French form of intelligence – instinctive, intuitive grasp of a musical problem and, simultaneously, of its solution.

Music and Character

Ravel had hardly any pupils. The only composer who worked for a time with him and confesses a great debt to his help is Vaughan Williams, who spent some months with him in Paris in 1909. Otherwise Ravel is as solitary a musician as he was in his personal life. The intense reserve of his nature has been traced to his Basque mother, whom he idolized. Her portrait hung over the piano at Montfort l'Amaury – a quiet, dignified-looking woman, not beautiful, but with the same close-set piercing eyes as her son and an oddly unworldly look, which he too preserved in spite of his worldly success. Looking back, it seems odd that anyone could have accused Ravel of imitating Debussy; their characters were completely different. The sensuous element in Debussy's music, so evident from the beginning, though far from absent in Ravel, is of secondary importance in his music, which appeals to the linear, architectural sense rather than directly to the physical senses. Debussy worked by repetition and variation, fundamentally in the same way as the Russian composers, whereas Ravel's structure derives from the classics. The whole-tone scale and chords of the ninth, dominant features of Debussy's music, are nearly absent from Ravel's music, and the sense of colour, which makes Debussy's music a kind of development parallel to the work of contemporary French painters, is virtually absent in Ravel. The power of evocation is strong in both, certainly, perhaps stronger in Ravel than Debussy, who painted from nature rather than from other works of art as Ravel did. Ravel was the less original but the more perfect artist. His music lacks the profoundly creative quality of Debussy's: it is more consciously made, more *voulu* as the French say, and more concerned with surface beauty. He manipulates, dissects, reorganizes sounds like a surgeon (or like his engineer father?). Stravinsky's *mot – le plus parfait des horlogers suisses* – leaves something out of account, for

Ravel's creations have a more personal, living quality than any mechanical constructions, however deliberate and, in a sense, mechanical their origin. Ravel would, I think, have been fascinated by modern plastic surgery. The reformation of living tissue, the creation of beauty from disaster, would have appealed to the artist and the technician in him, and the consummate skill involved would have won his whole-hearted admiration.

There could be no more fitting close to any short study of Ravel's life than the words in which one of his friends and his few pupils, Roland Manuel, summed up his character. 'He had more frankness than elegance, more courtesy than cordiality: more sociability and humour than ease of manner : more devotion to friendship than indulgence in camaraderie: and more ingenuousness than anything else. He never suspected evil or treachery. In twenty-six years I never heard him speak against anyone nor ever knew him ask for anything for himself, except permission to serve his country.' Few men could ask for a better epitaph.

MAX REGER

1873–1916

DONALD MITCHELL

Brand and Weiden

Reger was born in Brand, a small village in the Bavarian Fichtelgebirge, on 19 March 1873. His father, Joseph Reger, was a village schoolmaster, a man, it appears, of considerable musical ability. His mother, Philomena, was a sensitive, intelligent woman, fine-looking, with deep-set eyes, a broad, high forehead, and a wide, curiously pessimistic mouth. A comparison of photographs shows Reger to be very much the son of his mother.

Reger's childhood, spent in an environment of Bavarian meadows and forests, was restricted but on the whole happy, and this in spite of the fact that his father gave way to prolonged drinking bouts and that three younger brothers died in their early years. One sister, Emma, grew up with Max.

The nearest town to Brand was Weiden, and there Reger's father was employed as a teacher in 1874. Max was at the Kindergarten from 1878 to 1882 and at the secondary school from 1882 to 1886; he entered the school that was to prepare him for the university in 1886. The only lessons in which he lacked talent were drawing and physical training.

Throughout his schooling, mixed up with the work and the games, were the music-lessons given him by his parents. His mother taught him the piano at the age of five, and his father later contributed the violin and rudimentary instruction in harmony. Reger showed some skill, but nothing outstanding: in any event it had been decided that he should keep to the family tradition and be a teacher also.

But in 1884 an important event occurred. The young Reger's musical education was taken over by Adalbert Lindner, the organist at the Weiden church. He was an accomplished musician, a stern follower of Hans von Bülow, but a kind and sympathetic man. At once he perceived the latent possibilities of his pupil, and the first completed composition – an *Overture in B minor* for flute, clarinet, string quartet, and piano – was secretly dispatched to the famous Hugo Riemann, who replied in encouraging terms and enclosed a copy of one of his own text-books. Through Lindner, Reger was introduced to the Mozart and Beethoven piano sonatas, Chopin, and Schumann, and on Sunday afternoons there was regular music making. As Reger's musical horizon steadily widened, it began to occupy almost all his attention, hopes, and desires.

In 1888, when a youth of fifteen, he went to Bayreuth, where he heard *Parsifal*: it is reported that this event finally determined him to become a musician. A flood of compositions followed in the winter of 1888 to 1889 – songs, a *Largo* for violin and piano, a *Scherzo* for strings and flute, and a three-movement *String Quartet*. In the summer of 1885 his father had cunningly constructed a *Hausorgel* and Reger had begun organ studies, besides playing at the local (Catholic) church services.

However his parents still had the firm notion that he was to be a teacher, and when it came to the point of his making a profession of music their attitude was one of caution and anxious resistance. Riemann, on the strength of the *String Quartet*, which showed amazing technical facility and resource, offered to take Reger as his pupil at Sondershausen conservatoire, but it was only after much pleading that a compromise was made with his parents and their consent obtained.

On 8 April 1890 he left his home to go to Sondershausen, his family uncertain about his future, he concerned only to fulfil what he knew was within himself.

Sondershausen and Wiesbaden

Riemann's relations with his new pupil were of the friendliest, and the Riemann family were Reger's chief support during the years he spent at Sondershausen and Wiesbaden. He worked hard at counterpoint and already was obsessed with fugue. It was not altogether surprising that he swiftly became Riemann's favourite.

Bach, Beethoven, and Brahms were his gods, and Wagner dominated him less and less, although he never lost a genuine affection for the creator of *Parsifal*. Apart from the knowledge he acquired, Reger, the plain, simple, devout Catholic youth from Weiden, found himself forced to rub shoulders with a crowd of students who, says Guido

Bagier, must have seemed to him 'like apparitions from another world'.

In the autumn of 1890 Riemann and his family left Sondershausen for the conservatoire at Wiesbaden and Reger decided to accompany them. The period at Wiesbaden was much more important than that at Sondershausen. Wiesbaden itself was a well-known town, the people more sophisticated, more consciously cultured.

Reger, through the good offices of Riemann, himself taught the piano and organ at the conservatoire, and he was kept busy with private lessons, perfecting his own remarkable piano technique and slaving away at canon and fugue and the final stages of counterpoint. He also began giving public concerts with other students of the conservatoire and pressed on with his composition. His letters paint a clear picture of the immensely active existence he led: yet he was not without his troubles. Again Reger did not succeed in compromising, this time with the tastes of the music-lovers of Wiesbaden – he was too outspoken and his explosive humour was misunderstood – and his *Piano Trio*, Op. 2, found no favour with Frau Dr Riemann, who remarked sourly after its first performance: 'Yes, yes – if one *must* go one better than Brahms or Beethoven'.

First Publications and Marriage

But there were advantages gained through being in the Riemann circle. He met Elsa von Bagenski, whom he afterwards married, and the English publisher Augener. Augener accepted Riemann's recommendation and made a seven year contract with the delighted Reger. He published from 1891 onwards, the two *Violin Sonatas*, Op. 1 and Op. 3, the *Piano Trio*, Op. 2, the organ works, Op. 7 and Op. 16, several collections of songs, a book of piano pieces, Op. 17, and, significantly, two books of canons that go through all the major and minor keys. The publications enjoyed no great success, but were at least some proof to his parents that his ability had won a measure of recognition.

In 1893 he was 'quite retired' (twenty years old!) and cooking for himself. He lived in rooms and was happy if he had sufficient to smoke. In a letter to Lindner he confided that '... they tell me I have become very bitter. I don't know how right that is, but I don't want to change my circumstances except for the better – more money is always useful'.

The first Reger concert took place in 1894 at the Singakademie, Berlin, and Reger was busy at a *Symphony in B minor*, dedicated to Brahms. The work was never finished, but Brahms sent him an inscribed photograph, which was rapturously received. In 1895 Riemann left Wiesbaden, and Reger took charge of his theory class, something of an achievement for a man of his age.

His career was rudely interrupted in 1896, as he had to carry out his period of military service. On account of being a student-teacher at the conservatoire he was obliged to do only a year's cadet training with the 80th Infantry Regiment of Wiesbaden. Throughout 1886 and 1887 he was still able to study a certain amount and appeared to find an energetic army life not at all to his distaste.

One of the brighter events of 1897 was the Berlin performance in March of his *Organ Suite*, Op. 16, by Karl Straube, the great organist who became Reger's lifelong friend and who was responsible for the first performances of most of his organ works. But in many other ways life was not running so easily. He had come more and more into open conflict with the Wiesbaden music-lovers, and it seems that his military companions were a hard-drinking, reckless crowd of fellows, whose company and habits did Reger physical harm and left their mark on him in later years.

He had to leave the Infantry Regiment after nine months, suffering from bad feet and a severe throat infection, but continued his work at the conservatoire and completed a big *Piano Quintet* in C minor (published posthumously). Some emotional crisis must have been reached in March 1898 just before he fell seriously ill. His mother, still anxious and doubting, wrote to Heinrich Geist: 'I am Max Reger's mother and you will know what love and worry prompts me to write ... with what high hopes did Max go from us eight years ago and what has the world turned him into? His landlady has telegraphed that someone will have to come. She wants to turn Max out, but he won't go and frightens her with his behaviour. ...' Whether Geist influenced Reger we do not know, but in June 1898 he returned home to Weiden and for three years was engaged in an unbroken spell of composition.

Weiden

Until his departure for Munich in 1901, Reger lived again at Weiden; the years he spent there were almost exclusively devoted to composition, and he heard little besides what music he made on his own new Blüthner grand piano. He read much, enthused wildly over Ibsen's plays, wrote to Wilhelm Gottschalg: 'I can work hard providing I am careful over alcohol' and appeared to avoid those excesses in which he had been led to indulge at Wiesbaden. Work was his one occupation, and he applied himself to his task with a fanatical single-mindedness. His opus numbers rose during the Weiden period from 19 to 62. This enormous output ranges from the *Hymne an der Gesang* for male choir and orchestra, Op. 21, to the three great *Choral Fantasias* for organ, Op. 52, which were written in ten days: it includes the third *Violin and Piano Sonata*, Op. 41, the magnificent *B-A-C-H Fantasia and Fugue* for organ, Op. 46, the two *Romances* for violin and small orchestra, Op. 50, two *String Quartets*, Op. 54, the C minor *Piano Quintet*, Op. 64, songs, piano pieces, *Sonatas* for violin alone, and compositions for the organ too numerous to mention. In 1898 a new publisher was found, Joseph Aibl of Munich, and, with Straube publicizing the organ works at Wesel, slowly Reger's name began to be better known.

But Weiden could not hold Reger for ever: in 1901 he felt the need to break fresh ground and decided to move to Munich. There his publisher was, he had managed to establish himself as a composer, even if his status was a hotly-debated one, and he was confident of his own powers. In any event it would be pleasant to have a flat of his own. He left on 31 August 1901.

Munich

At Munich Reger plunged into a hectic existence, of which the chief aim was to earn enough money to support himself in comparative comfort. There was still the same incredible opposition he had encountered at Weiden and earlier at Wiesbaden: but now he had as many staunch friends and admirers as enemies, and even his detractors had to take his music seriously.

Composition was again well to the fore. The notorious C major *Violin and Piano Sonata*, Op. 72, which aroused the most noisy discussion in the Press, dates from this period: as does the fine D minor *String Quartet*, Op. 74, the first three books of the charming *Schlichte Weisen*, Op. 76, and the giant *Variations and Fugue* on a theme of Bach for piano, Op. 81, besides two large-scale works for two pianos, Op. 86 and Op. 96.

Nevertheless, Reger was able to attend all the concerts of note, crammed in private music-lessons, wrote musical criticism for those journals that allowed him a hearing and found time on 27 October 1902, to marry Elsa von Bagenski and move to a new flat in the same street.

Virtuoso or Composer

Riemann's insistence on his pupil's perfecting his piano technique now began to have results, and for the next few years Reger had concert engagements over all Germany and sometimes outside it. He was a virtuoso pianist: and, of course, one way of getting his chamber music performed was to play it himself. Munich still treated him as a Kandidatus Giesinghaus (Giesing being the local asylum), but he had a 'crazy success' in Vienna in 1904, and Switzerland received him hospitably.

One of Reger's ideas in moving to Munich was to secure a position in the Munich Academy, and at the end of 1904 the unbelievable occurred and he was appointed to the staff. Thus it appeared on the surface that at last some of the striving for recognition was over. But it was not to be. He made bitter enemies of other members of the Academy and in July 1906 was forced to request permission to resign his post: it was granted, but only after he had offered it twice. The first time it was withdrawn for what Reger non-committally termed 'political' reasons.

Two of Reger's mature orchestral works date from the Munich period, and one non-political reason for his resignation from the Academy was that he wanted more leisure for composition. There were the *Sinfonietta*, Op. 90, and the G major *Serenade*, Op. 95, and both works were immediately successful with the public. Nikisch conducted the *Serenade* in Berlin, and Reger conducted it himself in St Petersburg to which he travelled with his wife in December 1906. He followed with a concert tour, visiting Holland and returning to Germany again. Whilst in the midst of this activity, he received a telegram: 'Reger nominated as successor of Zöllner to the Conservatoire and University of Leipzig. Congratulations.'

He had no hesitation in exchanging the bickering and squabbling at Munich for Leipzig with a better salary attached to it, and he departed for his new home on 22 March 1907. There were no regrets at leaving Munich; indeed, one of his opponents – a Dr Louis who had made impossible comments on the *Sinfonietta* in the Press – had been serenaded with a cats' concert by Reger's irate pupils. So there was at least one cheering memory to take away with him, although he pretended to disapprove of the whole affair.

Leipzig

Reger went to Leipzig with high hopes and Leipzig proved to be the summit of his career. He was at the height of his powers as a man and musician, his works were being played over all Europe, and he was celebrated both as a composer and theorist. In Leipzig, his circle of friends embraced Joseph Haas, Max Klinger (the sculptor), Paul and Julius Klengel, Edgar Wollgandt, Dr Reinhold Anschütz, the faithful Karl Straube and the poets Martin Boelitz, Dehmel, and Liliencron. He received honours from foreign academies, the University of Jena conferred upon him the degree of Dr Phil. honoris causa and Berlin the degree of Honorary Doctor of Medicine.

It could hardly be said that Reger suffered from lack of recognition and yet, marring the triumphs, were a malicious plan to run him out of Leipzig and the usual grotesque attacks in the Press. His stay had an adverse beginning, with his wife ill and he himself none too content with his conductorship of the Paulus Choir. It was part of his duties as Director of Music at the University to conduct this student choir, but his association with it was not a successful one.

In July 1908 he refused to accept the position of Professor in Composition at the Vienna conservatoire, as Leipzig was celebrating its Jubilee in 1909. But eventually the Paulus Choir got so completely out of hand (Reger found himself being blatantly insulted at rehearsals) that he handed in his resignation as Director of Music, declining to take responsibility for the conduct of the choir at this function.

The winter of 1908 was one of furious concert touring – thirty days with twenty-six concerts: and he was working hard besides at his *Violin Concerto*, Op. 101, the *Piano Trio*, Op. 102, and the *Symphonic Prologue*, Op. 108. At home in 1907 he and his wife had adopted a small girl, Christa, and now in 1908 they adopted a second child, Lotti. Even this action of Reger's was perverted by his detractors, who could not believe that some sordid double motive did not exist: the simple fact that Reger loved children was not to be taken seriously.

And so the wretched series of misunderstandings continued. It seemed as if this immense man, with his extravagant cloak and wide-brimmed hat, was a misfit. Perhaps it was because he stood last in the great tradition of German music and his pointed, biting humour resulted from his distress at the crumbling world that was mirrored daily in the 'incapability and inability' of his pupils.

In 1909 Reger was intent on completing his gigantic setting of the *100th Psalm* for choir, orchestra, and organ, Op. 106, the *Clarinet Sonata*, Op. 107, and the wonderful E flat major *String Quartet*, Op. 109. He journeyed in May to London, where he gave successful recitals at the Bechstein Hall and was warmly entertained at the Royal Academy of Music.

When 1909 had passed into 1910, *Die Nonnen* for choir and orchestra, Op. 112, the D minor *String Quartet*, Op. 113, and the monumental F minor *Piano Concerto*, Op. 114, were in print. March saw preparations afoot for the first great Regerfest in Dortmund, Osnabrück following suit in 1911.

Meiningen

With *Die Nonnen* struck off the list of Gewandhaus concerts, and no explanation being given, 1911 began badly and once again the Press was 'shouting' against him. But in March he was offered the conductorship of the famous Meiningen Orchestra; glad to escape from Leipzig – as he had been to escape from Munich and Wiesbaden – Reger accepted the post, nevertheless deciding to continue his lessons at the conservatoire and remain house-pianist at the Gewandhaus. He wrote to a friend: 'They are very annoyed in Leipzig that I am launching out as a conductor – the pig composes, plays the piano, now he even trys to conduct!'

But for an interval in June when his mother died, what was left of 1911 was spent in concert tours and in making the necessary arrangements for the move to Meiningen. On 1 November the new flat was occupied and Reger was at once admitted into the select Meiningen Court circles.

For the next two years, he was entirely absorbed in directing his orchestra, which encouraged him to compose a group of big orchestral works: the *Concerto in Olden Style*, Op. 123, the *Romantic Suite*, Op. 125, and the D major *Ballet Suite*, Op. 130. He was an expert, if not brilliant, conductor, being indeed hampered by his vast size, but his programmes were enterprising, and the three festivals he organized in 1913 failed neither artistically nor financially. He grew ever more intimate with the Duke of Meiningen, who made him *Generalmusikdirektor* and increased the orchestral salaries.

In many ways the years with the Meiningen Orchestra were the most placid of Reger's life, in spite of all the work and the difficulties to which he had to reconcile himself, along with a sophisticated Court and the obstructions of a proud Prime Minister. But he was, as he said of himself, 'pursued by misfortune', and in March 1914 after a tour with the orchestra, had a total nervous collapse and was obliged to cancel indefinitely his engagements. The Duke wrote a sympathetic letter to his wife.

Reger entered a Sanatorium at Meran, in the southern Tyrol, and there he rested and regained his strength; but his doctors found it imperative that he should give up Meiningen if his health were to be preserved, and his withdrawal was reluctantly accepted by the Duke in April 1914. Reger did not leave Meran until June, already determined to move to Jena to be nearer to the conservatoire at Leipzig.

The year 1914 saw the composition of *Variations and Fugue* on a theme by Mozart, Op. 132 (dedicated to the Meiningen Orchestra), the second *Piano Quartet*, Op. 133, and the *Telemann Variations and Fugue* for piano, Op. 134. There is no doubt that Reger was extremely tired. His last compositions show much of the old exuberance and a new clarity both of thought and expression: but there is a sense of inner weariness and fatigue, and a serenity not far off resignation.

Jena and the End

Reger returned to Meiningen, completed the purchase of his house at Jena – appropriately situated at Beethovenstrasse 2 – and planned to move there in March 1915: but August 1914 brought War with it, a catastrophe that blotted out and made insignificant all that had gone before. Reger found himself working in an office for the military staff at Meiningen and was called-up in the Landsturm on 18 August, but rejected as unfit for any form of military service. The war could not stop his creative ability and he worked at the *Hymnus der Liebe*, Op. 136, for solo voice and orchestra and *Eine Vaterländische Ouvertüre*, Op. 140. This *Ouvertüre*, closing with a chain of German hymns, was the one patriotic musical gesture he made: there was a rather ironical incident with the Directors of the Leipzig Gewandhaus, who declined to play the *Ouvertüre* as it was thought premature to play *Nun danket alle Gott* when the outcome of the struggle was as yet so uncertain.

In Meiningen, Duke George II having died, the new Duke had dismissed the musicians of the orchestra in a panic, and Reger was expected to support them, although his contract had already ceased. To his honour he did everything possible to assist those members and their families who were in need of financial aid.

In 1915 he wrote the *Requiem (For the Fallen)*, Op. 144b, for solo voice, choir, orchestra, and organ, and his mood had changed from that of the bombastic *Vaterländische Ouvertüre* to one of disgust and despair with the war and the Government that was controlling it. But he moved to Jena into his villa and settled down with his wife, two children, and Walde the dachshund. He continued with his lessons and concerts at the conservatoire, invited his friends to inspect the house, and composed. The gentle *Träume am Kamin* for piano, Op. 143, and the *Clarinet Quintet*, Op. 146 – his last chamber work – were written amongst other things, and Op. 86 and Op. 93 were orchestrated.

On 10 May 1916 Reger left Jena for Leipzig. He had arranged to meet Straube (now in the Field Artillery) at the house of a mutual friend and afterwards to proceed to Bitterfeld, where his wife awaited him, for a concert. In the evening, whilst with Anschütz and Straube he had a sudden stroke and was escorted to his hotel. In the morning he was discovered dead in his bed. A light in the room was still burning, a paper he had been reading still grasped in his hand. His spectacles remained perched on his nose. Thus did Reger, who was wholly a musician, a music-maker whose inspired contrapuntal thought was condemned as sterile academicism or imitation Bach, who had struggled so hard during his life, slip calmly into death. With Teutonic solemnity, a laurel wreath was placed about his head.

Reger was cremated, but an *Ehrengrab* was erected in the Friedhof at Weimar. Apart from his name the gravestone bears no inscription. If he had chosen one himself, possibly he would have used the words with which he half-humorously, half-ironically, closed a letter to Marie Klinger: 'Max Reger, Director of Music at the University, Teacher at the Royal Conservatoire, Member of the Association of German Piano Tuners, the Pedagogic Music Union, Honorary Member of the Skat Club "Grün" in Essen à Ruhr, composer, pianist, conductor, brain-owner, and German subject'.

OTTORINO RESPIGHI

1879–1936

D. MAXWELL WHITE

Education and Travels

Ottorino Respighi occupies an equivocal place in the history of contemporary music. Though his works have always been extremely popular both in Europe and America, critics have not agreed on their real artistic worth. Some critics have heralded Respighi as a major composer in the twentieth century rebirth of Italian instrumental music, but for others he is, though undoubtedly a master of orchestral colour, a 'dilettante of subtle sensations'.

Respighi was born at Bologna in Italy on 9 July 1879. His family was musical. His father was a good pianist and his grandfather had been an organist and choirmaster. Respighi began his musical education with his father, but when he was twelve he entered the Bologna Liceo Musicale, the musical Lyceum of his home-town, and began to learn the violin in the class of Federico Sarti. Respighi stayed for eight years at the Liceo. In 1898 he studied composition, first with Luigi Torchi and then with the instrumental composer and conductor, Giuseppe Martucci. Martucci had an important influence on Respighi, as on Casella. He put him on his guard against the current vogue of veristic opera and awakened in him a lasting interest in instrumental music.

Respighi left the Bologna Liceo with diplomas in composition and violin playing. He then decided to study for a time abroad. He went to Russia (1900) and became the first viola in the orchestra of the Opera Theatre at St Petersburg, and in the following year he took some lessons in composition from Rimsky-Korsakov. For Respighi, fresh from the staid Liceo in Bologna, the impact of Rimsky-Korsakov's subtle blending of instrumental colours was an overwhelming experience. He studied at St Petersburg for only a few months, but these were sufficient to leave him with a phenomenal facility in weaving richly coloured orchestral tapestries.

The year 1902 found Respighi in Berlin taking a course with Max Bruch: then between 1903 and 1908 he became a concert artist. He returned to Italy to play the viola in the Mugellini Quintet, and during these years he composed the works that first made a name for him as a composer. In 1905 he wrote a *Notturno* for orchestra, and three years later he composed his first opera, *Rè Enzo*, a comic work for a benefit performance of students at Bologna. The following year Respighi returned to Berlin for a short time and earned his living as a pianist in a singing school. It was not until 1913 that he was accorded academic recognition. In that year he was appointed Professor of Composition at the Royal Liceo di Santa Cecilia in Rome.

As a composer Respighi, while remaining essentially Italian, benefited from his general European musical culture. Prunières, the French musicologist, has described his music as 'an able compromise between the counterpoint of Strauss, the harmony of Debussy, and the orchestration of Rimsky-Korsakov – the whole tinted with a little Italian melody'. But Respighi's compositions viewed as a whole are most varied. All have a solid architectural construction. Sometimes the music is impressionistic and rich in refined harmonic effects, at other times it is archaic and boney. Some works savour of the ancient modes, whereas others overflow with baroque grandiloquence.

The Roman Symphonic Poems

Respighi is best known as a composer of symphonic poems. He had a natural inclination for creating picturesque and colourful scenes, and between 1916 and 1928 he wrote three orchestral works expressing the dignity and ancient grandeur of Rome. The first of these, the *Fountains of Rome*, was a set of musical impressions portraying with great sensitivity the feelings that four of the most beautiful fountains of the baroque period inspired in the composer. The moods are well contrasted. Each fountain is caught at an hour when it seems to be immersed 'in its own true light'. The *Fountain of Valle Giulia* at dawn, the first, opens with a sweet oboe tune and paints a pastoral landscape, while the *Fountain of Trevi* at midday, brilliant with pealing brass, depicts the chariot of Neptune drawn in procession by sea-horses followed by a train of tritons. The *Fountains of Rome* was first performed at the Augusteo in Rome, in March 1917 and conducted by Antonio Guarnieri.

The second of Respighi's symphonic poems, the *Pines of Rome*, appeared in 1924. According to the composer, whereas in the *Fountains of Rome* he had attempted to give a musical 'impression of nature', in the *Pines of Rome* he uses nature merely as a starting point 'in order to recall memories and visions'. In it the age-old pines so typical of the Roman landscape become 'testimony for the principal events in Roman life'. The work is characterized by the most lavish instrumentation. Harp, organ, celesta, bells, piano, and even six *buccine* or Roman bugles contribute to the riot of colour. The music begins by portraying children at play in the pine-groves of the Villa Borghese. Suddenly the scene changes and we see 'the shades of the pine-trees fringing the entrance to a catacomb. From the depths rises the sound of a mournful psalm-singing, floating through the air like a solemn hymn'. In the third picture, the *Pines of the Janiculum*, Respighi introduces into the score a gramophone record of a nightingale singing. The final movement portrays the solitary *Pine-trees of the Appian Way*. And here, the score tells us, the composer has a fantastic vision of bygone glories: 'trumpets sound and, in the brilliance of the newly-risen sun, a consular army bursts forth towards the Sacred Way, mounting in triumph to the Capitol'.

Respighi's third symphonic poem evoking Roman life was the *Feste Romane* (1928). In it, rhapsodically and with ever larger orchestral resources, he portrayed the Roman mob swarming in the Circus Maximus and the strident joy that accompanied the feast of *Epiphany*.

Transcriptions, La Boutique Fantastique

Respighi made use of the traditional symphony orchestra for rendering original and picturesque musical impressions. He also used it for his arrangements of old music. On his return from Russia, under the influence of his former master Luigi Torchi he began a series of musical transcriptions. For better or for worse, as Guido Gatti the distinguished Italian critic writes, 'he desired to readjust the old masters to the taste of his time' – to the opulent, bourgeois, cultivated taste of pre-1914 Italy. In 1908 he 'modernized' the exquisite and highly charged *Lamento* from Monteverdi's opera *Arianna*. But later on he arranged two sets of old lute airs with more restraint. Respighi's most successful adaptation, however, was his arrangement of the music for the ballet *La Boutique Fantastique*.

Diaghilev, the Russian impresario, looking for suitable ballet material, discovered an album of music written by Rossini in his old age. The set contained pieces with such entertaining titles as *Abortive Polka* and *Castor Oil*. Diaghilev asked Respighi to orchestrate these for a ballet in one act. *La Boutique Fantastique* is a work on the ever popular theme of animated toys in revolt. The scene is a quaint little toy-shop in the 1860s on a quayside overlooking a Mediterranean bay. And the whole is an exuberant and mischievous satire, with a touch of burlesque, on the rich tourist shoppers who go there. Respighi orchestrated Rossini's music most wittily; Derain designed the costumes and Massine was the choreographer. *La Boutique Fantastique* was a great success; first produced at the Alhambra Theatre, London, in 1919, it has remained a favourite ballet ever since.

Respighi composed a number of other ballets, including *Scherzo Veneziano* and the biblical *Belkis: Regina di Saba*. *Gli Uccelli*, a suite of arrangements of music by Pasquini and other early composers, was used in 1942 by Robert Helpmann for his light-hearted ballet, *The Birds*.

Chamber Music and Songs

From 1913 onwards Respighi taught composition at the Liceo di Santa Cecilia, Rome. Six years later he married the singer and composer Elsa Olivieri-Sangiacomo, one of his pupils. And then in 1923, in succession to Enrico Bossi, he was elected by Government Commission to be Director of the Liceo. Respighi did not remain long in this office. He kept his finishing course in composition, but he was becoming increasingly popular as a composer since Toscanini was performing his works, and in 1925 he resigned his office so that he could devote himself to composition and go on tour. He visited America in 1926 and six years later he went there again on a concert tour. In the same year (1932) he was nominated an Academician of Italy beside Mascagni.

Respighi's delight in composing colourful music with a pictorial content resulted at times in a certain superficiality. The *Feste Romane* is banal in comparison with the *Fountains of Rome*. But there is another side to Respighi's talent, and it has been said that the more he restricted his instrumental forces the better he was as a composer. Some critics consider that Respighi's best music was written in his songs and chamber music. He himself thought he was above all a writer of songs. He composed some fifty-two in all. In tune with the archaising part of his nature he set with great beauty and simplicity a number of old texts, but one of his best songs is certainly *Il Tramonto*, the setting for mezzosoprano and string quartet of a poem by Shelley.

In the field of chamber music Respighi shows the same admirable restraint as in the songs – a restraint so often lacking in the large orchestral works. He makes use of plain chant and the ancient modes, though not with the spiritual conviction of a Pizzetti; here too the discipline of his classical training with Sarti at Bologna shows to good effect. These disciplines can be heard in the *Quartet in the Dorian Mode* and in the suite *Vetrate di Chiesa*, a work coloured by pedals and written to convey the rich, changing atmosphere of a medieval church.

Opera

Respighi also wrote a number of operas. In *Semirama* (1910) he owes much to the cosmopolitanism of Richard Strauss, but this was only a passing phase. In his later work he tries to return to Verdi's *Falstaff*. But most of Respighi's operas are disappointing. They are not fully conceived in dramatic terms, and they illustrate what has been called his paradox: Respighi is theatrical in his symphonic works and symphonic in his operas. Guido Gatti complains that in *Belfagor* (1923) – a work based on 'the fable telling of the devil who comes to earth to experiment with matrimony and is cheated even by the most simple people' – the balance is continually destroyed by the orchestra, which is 'like a wall between the public and the action'. Respighi's final opera – except for the posthumous *Lucrezia*, which was completed by his widow – was *La Fiamma* (1934). This is a vital, well-wrought work based on a Norwegian play by G. Wiers Jenssen with a new setting in seventh-century Ravenna. Here the colourful mosaics in the Byzantine churches gave Respighi a remarkably good opportunity for realizing his music in glowing orchestral terms.

Respighi was ill at ease as a composer of opera. This led him towards the kind of drama in which the dramatic elements are reduced to the minimum. *Maria Egiziaca* (1931) is a mystery triptych for the concert-room in three episodes. It has also been performed with stage scenery. It brings to mind Pizzetti's *Sacra Rappresentazione di Abramo e d'Isaac*. The style is austere and has model affinities, but the work lacks the contrapuntal tension and the spiritual participation on the part of the composer that makes Pizzetti's music so satisfying. Nevertheless, parts of *Maria Egiziaca* with its clarity and calm show Respighi's music at its best.

Respighi is frequently named with Casella, Malipiero, and Pizzetti as a prime mover of the twentieth century Renaissance of Italian music. His effective, solidly constructed symphonic works have certainly been of great importance in the present revival of Italian instrumental music. Yet the instrumental music of this Renaissance has really followed entirely other paths than those set by Respighi. The true revival has been due to the re-establishment of contact in the years after World War I with Italian music of an earlier age. Respighi's music on the other hand, though composed for the most part in the post-war years, is in a pre-1914 and largely Germanic instrumental idiom.

Respighi died in his villa at Rome on 18 April 1936 at the age of fifty-six, after a long illness. In the following year his remains were taken to Bologna, his native city, and buried amongst the illustrious dead.

ALBERT ROUSSEL

1869–1937

ROLLO H. MYERS

A Limited Appeal

When Roussel died in August 1937 France mourned the loss of one of her most eminent composers. Outside France (and possibly Belgium) his death meant little to the ordinary musical man in the street, because his music had never really penetrated abroad beyond a small and restricted circle of connoisseurs. Even to-day it is difficult to say whether the appreciation index for Roussel's music has gone up or down, especially as there have been few opportunities, in this country at least, of hearing any of his major works. Those who look upon Roussel as a really important figure in contemporary music find it hard to understand why his work has been, on the whole, so strangely neglected. One reason may be that, since his music is admittedly 'intellectual', its appeal must *ipso facto* be limited. It may also be that, as is often alleged of Fauré, for example, or our own Elgar, the Roussel vintage is not for export. I do not find this argument convincing. If good wine needs no bush, still less does good music need a passport. The frontiers involved here are not national but intellectual or, if you prefer, spiritual. The truth is that there will always be a kind of art appealing mainly to a minority (who probably like to think of themselves as an *élite*), and the music of Roussel, for the time being at any rate, must apparently be included in this category.

Yet no one could maintain that Roussel has ever been made the object of a cult. The very idea of such a thing would have been abhorrent to him. Detesting publicity of any kind to an almost morbid degree, he always held himself aloof from the cliques and clans that have long been a feature of the musical world in Paris, and both in his life and in his works he was a shining example of that rarest of qualities to-day – integrity.

Sailor and Musician

Albert Roussel was born on 5 April 1869, at Tourcoing, an industrial town in French Flanders. Losing his parents while still a child, he was brought up by his grandfather, the Mayor of the town. He showed a strong musical bent as a boy, but it had been decided to make a sailor of him, and he was sent to the Collège Stanislas in Paris, where he made a special study of mathematics in preparation for the Naval School, and at the age of eighteen joined a training ship at Brest. He remained in the Navy until he was about twenty-five and then resigned his commission in order to take up music seriously. During his seven years afloat, Roussel had already tried his hand at composition, and it was on the advice of the Director of the Roubaix Conservatoire, to whom he had shown some of his work, that he decided to give up the Navy and devote himself to composition. Thus, like Rimsky-Korsakov, he came to music from the sea. This circumstance is not without its bearing on the evolution of Roussel the musician; it was the Navy that gave him the love of travel and the exotic, which remained with him all his life, and his love of the sea, which impelled him to choose as his country retreat at Varengeville on the Normandy coast the quiet house whose windows looked out across the English Channel. In the words of a French critic: 'He kept the adventurous spirit of the sailor, and for him each new work was a fresh port of call.'

Tradition and Emancipation

This suggests the right approach to Roussel and his music. For, although his training at the Schola Cantorum, where he was a pupil of Vincent d'Indy, gave him solidity and that essential seriousness of outlook to be found in all musicians nurtured in the Franck-d'Indy tradition, his personality and temperament were anything but conservative. In fact, his style and harmonic idiom became freer, and increasingly emancipated and individual, the older he grew. More than almost any other contemporary French composer Roussel somehow managed to combine the wisdom and traditions of the past with all that is most vital in present-day musical tendencies and technique. Harmonically, for example, some of his later music contains passages as daring as anything you will find in Stravinsky or Bartók; yet Roussel's music is never unbridled or sensational – you feel all the time that a keen intellect and a fine sensibility are working hand in hand. He was a good friend to young rising composers, and the interest he took in the latest and most advanced tendencies in music is shown by the fact that he was for a time President of the French section of the International Society for Contemporary Music. Yet he never attached himself to any 'school', or dabbled in any kind of 'ism'; although he had forged for himself a very individual idiom, which he wielded in a masterly way, he never strove to be original – still less to *épater le bourgeois*; that would have seemed to him an utterly senseless waste of time.

Voyage to India, Padmâvati, *World War I*

His life, after his retirement from the Navy, was not an eventful one. He studied for six years at the Schola and then joined its teaching staff in 1902. One of his earliest published compositions – the *Piano Trio*, Op. 2 – dates from this year, and two years later he began to write his first symphony – *Le Poème de la Forêt* –, which was not, however, produced in its complete form until 1908, in Brussels. The following year Roussel went on a journey that was to prove one of the great fertilizing influences of his life and a source of inspiration for some of his finest works. For this journey took him once again to Cochin China (which he had seen for the first time some twenty years earlier while serving with the Fleet) and also to India; it was from impressions gained while visiting these centres of Eastern civilization that Roussel was impelled to write the three Symphonic Poems, *Évocations*, and the Opera-Ballet, *Padmâvati* (Paris Opéra, 1923), which may be considered one of his finest and most representative works. This was begun in the fatal year 1914, but was not completed until the war was over and the composer back in civil life again, after serving in the army (Red Cross and Motor Transport) and surviving the battles of the Marne and Somme and the siege of Verdun. He left the army with his health seriously impaired and from then onwards lived a more or less secluded life, dividing his time, always working and in the company of his devoted wife, between his Paris flat and his house by the sea in Normandy.

Stage Works

The work by which Roussel is probably best known outside France, *Le Festin de l'Araignée*, was also his first work for the stage. It was in the form of a ballet on a scenario by Gilbert de Voisins, inspired by the writings of the great entomologist Henri Fabre, and was commissioned by the Director of the Théâtre des Arts, where it was produced in 1913. Ten years later it entered the repertory of the Opéra Comique, where it is still often given. The delicately descriptive music that Roussel wrote for this little tragedy of insect life reveals him as a sensitive and poetic musician, but cannot be considered really representative of the composer of *Padmâvati*, *Psalm 80*, the *Piano Concerto*, the *Suite* in F, or the *Third Symphony*.

In his next work for the stage, the one-act opera *La Naissance de la Lyre*, which followed *Padmâvati* at the Opéra in 1925, Roussel turned from the Orient to Greece and took as his subject the legend of the origin of Apollo's lyre. His librettist was the celebrated Hellenic scholar Théodore Reinach, a personal friend of the composer; the production of this work at the Opéra seemed particularly appropriate, since Garnier's masterpiece is surmounted by the effigy of Apollo holding in his outstretched arms his triumphant lyre.

Bacchus and Ariadne, another ballet on a Greek subject, this time with libretto by Abel Hermant, was given at the Opéra in 1931, and four years later Roussel was invited to write a ballet with chorus on an episode from Virgil's *Aeneid*, entitled simply *Aeneas*, which was produced by Hermann Scherchen in Brussels. It is unlikely that posterity will consider the music inspired by these themes from Greek and Roman mythology, although of a consistently high quality, to be on a level with those earlier works written under the stimulus of his sympathetic knowledge of, and temperamental affinity with, Hindu literature and folk-lore. But it is characteristic of Roussel the artist that he could make himself almost equally at home on the Mediterranean, in the shade of an Indian temple and under the colder skies of the Atlantic and his own native Flanders. And so, towards the end of his life, he penned that *Rapsodie Flamande* in which the Flemish strain in him, of which he was fully conscious, expressed itself in music, vigorous and square-cut, that in the words of a Belgian critic, 'conjures up a vision of our Flemish peasants struggling against the wind with heads thrust forward, firmly planted between their wide shoulders, with clenched jaws and fists, as described by Verhaeren in his poems or by de Coster in his *Thyl Nylenspiegel*.'

Then again we have that other Roussel, the Roussel of the great setting for chorus and orchestra of the Eightieth Psalm, a most effective and impressive piece of choral writing, which ought to be heard more often.

Symphonic and Instrumental Music

Of the purely orchestral works *Pour une Fête de Printemps* (1920) is one of the most characteristically Roussellian. It also heralded his 'new manner', a break-away from whatever vestiges remained of the influence of either Debussy or the Franckists, and its rather acid harmonies were frowned upon in certain quarters. But there is a lyrical fervour about it that gives it warmth and life, and its harmonic acerbities are as stimulating as dry champagne.

There are four symphonies, of which the *Third Symphony* in G minor is the strongest, with a memorably fine slow movement; the *Fourth Symphony* in A major is concise and pithy and remarkable for the clarity of its design and texture. Remarkable, too, are the famous *Suite in F* and the *Sinfonietta* for strings, which seem to contain the quintessence of Roussel's fine and completely unsentimental musical thinking.

He did not write a great deal for the piano – the *Suite*, Op. 14, and the *Sonatina*, Op. 16, are the outstanding works for piano alone – but the *Concerto*, Op. 36, is in a class apart and must be considered one of Roussel's major works. So little prominence, from a virtuoso's point of view, is given to the solo instrument that it is understandable why the work has not proved popular with pianists, but from a purely musical standpoint the *Concerto* is an astonishingly original and powerful achievement and deserves to be better known. The only other work in this form is the *Concertino* for cello and orchestra, Op. 57, a late work written for the principal cellist of the Amsterdam Concertgebouw Orchestra.

Of the chamber music the works that merit attention are the early *Piano Trio*, which shows the influence of the Franck-d'Indy principles of cyclic construction, the *Violin and Piano Sonata*, and the late *Trio* (Op. 58), for violin, viola, and cello. At the time of his death Roussel was working on a *Trio* for oboe, clarinet, and bassoon, which was left unfinished and will never be published.

The Songs

As a song-writer Roussel will be remembered for some finely chiselled and subtly elusive settings of contemporary French verse and translations from the Chinese; of the latter *La Réponse d'une Épouse Sage* is one of the best known. Not conspicuous for their purely melodic interest (Roussel was not a melodist) and totally devoid of sentimentality, these songs demand from the singer a fine sense of style and an ability to convey every shade of irony, humour, melancholy, levity, or tenderness, however discreetly suggested; this is music in which nothing is underlined and from which all emphasis is barred. Among the best known songs are *Le Bachelier de Salamanque*, *Le Jardin Mouillé*, *Jazz dans la Nuit*, *Le Jeune Gentilhomme*, *Cœur en Péril*, and *Sarabande*.

The Aristocratic Approach to Music

It was with reference to the songs that the late Claire Croiza, who was one of their finest interpreters, evoked the saying of Debussy: '*Le génie musical de la France c'est quelque chose comme la fantaisie dans la sensibilité*', which does seem to sum up the particular quality that is the key to an understanding of Roussel's music. He never pretended that he wrote to please and, unlike the apostles of a creed enjoying a certain vogue in some countries to-day, was not afraid to say that 'it is not necessary for a symphony or a drama to be as popular as a ditty by Mayol'. Indeed he declared that 'music is the most hermetic and least accessible of all the arts' and that 'the musician, even more than the poet, is completely isolated in the world, alone with his more or less incomprehensible language. With the exception of one or two fine works that might be written for the people ... all the rest, taking into account the relations existing at present between music and the masses, must be destined for the ears of only a very small number'. About his own music, in any event, this would appear to be a true saying. For it was like himself – reserved, fastidious, aristocratically aloof. Roussel the man, in fact, was in some ways as 'hermetic' as he thought good music must be. He had, according to those who knew him well, an extraordinary faculty of withdrawal; at such times he seemed to live internally, having but slight contact with the external world. Yet he was simple and entirely unassuming, generous and considerate to all around him, absolutely disinterested, and always ready to encourage without thought of self-interest any young musician in whom he discerned talent.

Summing Up

The time has probably not come yet for a final assessment of Roussel's place in European music. To some his work may seem to suffer from an excessive preoccupation with 'pattern-making', harmonic innovations for their own sake, and experiments in construction and design, and to be somehow lacking in fire and warmth and human emotions. But this music, although completely unsentimental, is never frigid. The art of Roussel is characteristically French in its avoidance of sensationalism and over-emphasis; the balance between sentiment and intellect is perfectly preserved; and, to sum up, we feel it to be the product of a fine and fastidious mind nurtured in the best traditions of the humanism that is the basis of our Western civilization. In paying a last tribute to Roussel, Charles Koechlin, who had been his friend and colleague, found words that could not be bettered and might well serve as his epitaph: – *'C'était un artiste complet – un musicien, un penseur, un homme'*.

ARNOLD SCHÖNBERG

1874–1951

RALPH W. WOOD

Beginnings

Arnold Schönberg was born on 13 September 1874, in Vienna, of Jewish parents. When he was eight he was sent to the Realschule, where by the time he was sixteen he had reached the sixth class. In his early education music was included to the extent that he was taught the violin, and it is interesting to know that he composed little pieces for two violins to be used in his lessons. Subsequently he found a place in a group of youngsters, schoolfellows of his, who would play chamber-music together and for whom he wrote several trios. Later he taught himself to play the cello and composed a string quartet. As to theory, also, he was self-taught.

There was not at that time any idea of his making music his life work. Nor even does there seem to have been when, having left the Realschule upon the death of his father, he went on for several years working at music by himself without any supervision. His father had been a merchant, but managed when he died to leave Schönberg unprovided for. Schönberg became a bank clerk. His friends, like himself, were far from affluent. Old schoolfellows, they would be, and new acquaintances picked up in whichever coffee-house happened to be the one that they were for the moment using, in true Viennese tradition, as their meeting place. The young musical bloods into whose company he gravitated were all on fire about Wagner, in particular the Wagner of *Tristan*, which would be the starting point for technical and aesthetic discussions of great earnestness. It was a schoolfellow's poem that Schönberg set in composing his first song, in 1893, for the occasion of a charity show at Kierling-by-Wien. He wrote several songs. He was himself, Wagner or no Wagner, an enthusiast for the music of Brahms. Indeed for those two, and for Mahler, he preserved a lifelong admiration. When a movement of his string quartet was played to the blind pianist and organist, Labor, the latter declared that he ought to become a musician. He objected that he was only self-taught and that he couldn't even play the piano, but Labor waved that aside. On the other hand, when his boss went bankrupt Schönberg was nothing but happy at the loss of his job and swore to his friends, who were prepared to be aghast, that never again would he enter that kind of situation.

Meanwhile, advice upon which Schönberg did act (he was twenty at the time) was that he should show some of his work to Alexander von Zemlinsky. Zemlinsky was interested. He offered to give Schönberg some lessons in counterpoint, an offer that was accepted. The short course that ensued was the only such instruction that Schönberg, later to enjoy so much renown as a contrapuntist, ever received. Zemlinsky and Schönberg had quickly become close friends. Zemlinsky was the conductor of an orchestral society, Polyhymnia, which Schönberg joined as a cellist. The summer of 1897 found Schönberg at work on the piano arrangement of Zemlinsky's opera *Sarema*. At the same time he was writing a *String Quartet*, which, after it had been drastically revised in deference to Zemlinsky's criticisms, was performed. The première was in the 1897–8 season at the hands of a quartet specially got together by the Wiener Tonkünstlerverein. The following season it was done by the Fitzner Quartet. With unusual emphasis it has to be recorded that this, the first work by Schönberg to be offered to the general musical public, was received by them with great favour. All that need be added is that it was music entirely conventional in style and that it has since been lost.

The Scandal Starts

Schönberg and the public wasted little time, however, in getting on to what was to become their traditional footing. The quartet was followed by an unfinished symphonic poem and then he turned again to song writing. Two settings of poems by Karl von Lentzow that were to form Op. 1, and the No. 6 of Op. 3, *Freihold* (dedicated to Zemlinsky), were sung for the first time at a recital by the Viennese singing-teacher Gärtner, with Zemlinsky at the piano. The accompaniments were unusually complex, the general style was showing distinct signs of differentness, and the upshot was a 'mild "scene"' in the concert-hall. 'And from that time', Schönberg in later years remarked to Egon Wellesz, 'the scandal has never ceased'. Meanwhile, spending the late summer of 1899 at Payerbach with Zemlinsky,

Schönberg had composed within three weeks, during the September, a string sextet, based on a poem by Richard Dehmel and named *Verklärte Nacht*. Of this Wellesz records that it 'staggered the musical circles in Vienna in 1899'.

Another early friend of Schönberg was Josef Scheu, the pioneer of musical education for the masses in Austria and initiator of working-men's choral societies. He got Schönberg into the position of choirmaster of the metal-workers' *Sängerbund* in Stockerau (near Vienna), a small body of singers with whom Schönberg gave, for instance, successful performances of Brahms's part-songs. At the time when, in 1901, he married Mathilde von Zemlinsky, his friend's sister, he was conducting not only the Stockerau working-men's choir but similar organizations in the Meidling district of Vienna and in the neighbouring town of Mödling. His resolve never again to be a bank clerk had been kept; rapidly but insensibly it had got itself established that music was to be his career; and, needless to say, he was in a bad way financially. His next composition had been the *Gurrelieder* (for soli, chorus, and orchestra, with text by the Danish poet, J. P. Jacobsen), which he had begun in March 1900, and of which before summer first and second parts were finished and a beginning made on the third. But the necessity of earning some money caused an interruption, during which he was scoring other men's operettas, and he only resumed in March 1901. His actual composing was habitually done at a lightning pace.

Vienna Left

After their marriage Schönberg went with his wife to Berlin, in the hope of more lucrative employment. For a short time there he was conductor at Wolzogen's Buntes Theater, a 'sort of artistic cabaret'. He tried his own hand at writing the *Überbrettllieder* that he conducted. It must be recognized as characteristic that he turned out a specimen with a trumpet obbligato of such intolerable difficulty that the piece's first performance was its last.

It is evident that his poverty was only relative; for when, having in April 1901 finished the composition of the *Gurrelieder*, he turned to the orchestration, he ordered from Messrs Waldheim and Eberle some special 48-stave manuscript paper for the purpose. (The orchestra employed is of fantastic hugeness.) The paper was supplied to him in August 1901 and he plunged into the task. After some interruption he was again orchestrating the *Gurrelieder* in Berlin about the middle of 1902. He had to put it aside in favour of scoring operettas. He tried again to finish it in 1903, when he spent the summer in Payerbach again. He got no further than the middle of Part II. But Richard Strauss had been shown Part I in 1902 and forthwith procured the Liszt Stipendium (of substantial value) and a teaching post for Schönberg – aged twenty-eight and himself virtually self-taught – at the Stern Conservatoire, in Berlin. Another happening in Berlin, 1902, was the composition of part of his symphonic poem *Pelleas und Melisande*, after Maeterlinck's play. It is not without point to mention that this score contains the first example of a trombone glissando.

What material Schönberg provided after his twenty-ninth year for the biographer's, as distinct from the musicologist's, pen can be disposed of briefly. Thenceforward his career, about equally divided between composing and teaching, was that of a completely established, however much a pilloried, musician.

Vienna Revisited

He returned in 1903 to Vienna, where he lived under the same roof as Zemlinsky and began teaching harmony and counterpoint at the school of the well-known progressive educationist, Eugenie Schwarzwald. Among the first students to attend his courses there were Alban Berg, Egon Wellesz, Anton von Webern, Erwin Stein, and Heinrich Jalowetz. He was a great success. His pupils were many of them working at the Institute of Musical History in Vienna University. The director of the Institute was Professor Guido Adler, who, though not perhaps ready to go all the way with Schönberg, gave him recognition and encouragement. Adler was a friend of Mahler, and introduced both Schönberg and his pupils into the orbit of that great man. The whole atmosphere was one of enthusiastic revolt against the dead academicism of the conservatoire. Mahler, at the time director of the Court Opera-house, became a strong supporter of Schönberg (even though, like Adler, he had his reservations). In 1904 the Vereinigung Schaffender Tonkünstler was formed to promote, in face of Vienna's generally conservative spirit, 'free creative art'; Alexander von Zemlinsky, Oskar Rosa, Robert Gounod, Erich Wolff, and Joseph von Woess were members, and Schönberg was president. It only lived for one adventurous winter season.

It was in 1907 that Schönberg began his activities as a painter. He produced a large number of portraits, nature-studies, and 'colour-visions'. The phase led up to an exhibition of his paintings in the autumn of 1910 and then gradually subsided into a complete relinquishment of this form of self-expression. It is perhaps worth noting here that in his opera *The Lucky Hand* (completed 18 November 1913) he makes use of 'colour dynamics' – a crescendo in the orchestra is accompanied by, on a screen, a 'crescendo' of colours (e.g. red – brown – green – dark blue – purple), and so on.

War, Revolution, Exile

From Vienna Schönberg went in the summer of 1911 to Munich and then back to Berlin. He was there still when called up for military service in December 1915. A man turned forty, he was under arms for two spells of garrison duty in Vienna, December 1915 to September 1916, and July to October 1917. In 1918 he settled down in Mödling, where – apart from a number of visits to foreign countries – he remained for some six years. From 1925 he was in Berlin again. Dismissed by the Nazis in 1933 from the eminent pedagogic position he held there, he went to Paris and thence to the U.S.A., where he spent the rest of his life.

By his first wife, who died in 1923, Schönberg had two children. Milhaud has given an interesting account of a visit paid to the Mödling home in 1921 by Poulenc, Marya Freund, and himself. The walls were covered with Schönberg's paintings – 'Faces and eyes, eyes, everywhere.' The composer himself was in process of studying the French horn and could be heard in the garden practising. Twelve years later Milhaud was to meet Schönberg again, in Paris, a refugee, with a second wife and a little girl, *en route*, as it turned out, for America. The second marriage, during the Berlin period just ended, had been to the sister of Rudolf Kolisch, the well-known violinist and quartet leader.

In 1921 Schönberg abandoned the Jewish faith. In a Paris synagogue, on 24 July 1933, just seven weeks after his dismissal by the Nazis, he formally re-embraced that religion. Formalism on one side, he seems in fact at no time, as Wellesz points out, to have lost his intensely Jewish religious feeling. Though military service, teaching and perhaps subtler influences had combined to render him comparatively barren as a composer between 1915 and 1920, he had been engaged desultorily on a big sacred work. Originally conceived (in

1910) as a large oratorio in three parts, of which the first was to be on a text by Dehmel, with Schönberg to write the other two poems himself, the thing was never completed. He did write the poem for the second part, *The Death-dance of the Principles*, and both the poem and some of the music for the third, *Jacob's Ladder*. The three-parts plan was in any case abandoned, and *Jacob's Ladder* was to be a single, independent oratorio. During a similar period of little musical productivity, 1930 to 1936, he wrote the libretto for his biblical opera, *Moses and Aaron*. And there is also his play, *The Biblical Way* (1927). All these writings, so far from being, say, stylized, pseudo-classical structures, have every appearance of being, as indeed acquaintance with any of Schönberg's music might lead us to expect, complex and almost desperate efforts to express the conflicts and crises of a tortured spirit, an at once widely and intricately searching intellect.

The Man and the Composer

The truth is that Schönberg was a musician whose whole life had a cohesion, an interdependence of parts, rarely found, or at any rate rarely so evident, among composers. And really that is confirmed, rather than obscured, by the fact that his actual composing, though following one fairly coherent, all-through curve of development, was chaotic – crammed with unfinished tasks and unfulfilled projects, with false starts and shelvings and postponements – often a matter of simultaneous work on different conceptions and of a tumultuous flow of unregulated and sometimes almost unregulatable ideas – and mostly achieved in rather widely separated spurts of intense creation.

That there were disturbances at many performances of his works, from the *First Quartet* and *Chamber Symphony* (Vienna, 1907) right through to the *Variations* for orchestra (Berlin, 1928), is probably well known, though their serious character may need emphasizing; a concert at Vienna in 1913, for instance, where works by Webern, Zemlinsky, and Berg shared in the opprobrium, culminated even in blows, policemen, and business for the law-courts. On the other side of the picture were: the heroic promotion of performances of his works in the early Vienna days, from 1903 onwards, by the Rosé Quartet, the Ansorge Verein, the Wiener Tonkünstlerverein, certain vocalists and instrumentalists from the Opera (not to speak of Mahler himself); later, the devotion of such men as Eduard Steuermann and Otto Klemperer; the special Schönberg number of the Viennese musical magazine *Der Merker* (in which the text, by the composer, for *The Lucky Hand* was printed), 1911; the Viennese recognitions of his fiftieth birthday – a special number of the *Anbruch*, the opening of the Arnold Schönberg Bibliothek für Moderne Musik, and a celebration at the Town Hall, including an address by the *Bürgermeister* and a performance by the chorus of the State Opera of his *Peace upon Earth*, which had hitherto been considered practically unsingable; his being made an honorary member of the Academy of St Cecilia in Rome, 1925; festival concerts in the U.S.A. to greet his arrival there in 1933; in 1937 the appearance in a Japanese musical periodical of a special Schönberg number.... And between those extremes may be placed certain extraordinary measures that Schönberg was from time to time led to take. After the disturbances at the premières of the *D minor Quartet* and the *Chamber Symphony*, in 1907, he had a note printed on the tickets for a further concert of his music that same spring to the effect that they entitled purchasers to quiet listening only and not to expressions of opinion, whether applause or the reverse. The following year similar causes led to a repeat performance of the *F sharp minor Quartet* to an audience of 'specially invited guests'. In 1909 he wrote a special preface on the programme for a performance of the *Three Piano Pieces*, Op. 11, part I of the *Gurrelieder* (with piano accompaniment), and the *Fifteen Songs* from Stefan George's *Book of the Hanging Gardens*, to 'make the connexion between the successive compositions more intelligible'. In November 1918 he founded in Vienna a Society for Private Musical Performances, designed to give knowledge of modern music to artists and music-lovers 'free from the corrupting influence of publicity, with newspaper critics barred from attending, applause and hissing forbidden, and the members pledged to give no public report of the proceedings'. Very shortly after that he had his *Chamber Symphony* studied in public rehearsals, without any actual performance, 'so that people could get acquainted with the artistic construction of the work'.

The Teacher and the Man

Apart from those already mentioned, Schönberg's writings include the *Manual of Harmony* (1911 – new and revised edition, 1922), a book on *The Fundamentals of Musical Composition* (written in America), a booklet prepared for use at a Californian summer-course – *Models for Beginners in Composition*, an essay *Problems of the Teaching of Art*

(1911), and *Style and Idea* (1950). His prestige as a teacher was tremendous, and his actual record of appointments, beginning after the Schwarzwald days, is impressive in itself: 1910, teacher of composition at Imperial Academy of Music (Vienna); 1911, ten lectures on composition at the Stern Conservatoire (Berlin); during the war, between periods of military service, conducted a 'seminary for composition' at Vienna; 1918 to 1920, held the seminary at Mödling; 1920 to 1921, lectured on theory at Amsterdam by instigation of Mengelberg; 1925 to 1933, successor of Busoni as Professor of master-class at Prussian Academy of Arts (Berlin); 1933 to 1934, teaching in New York and in Malkin Conservatoire, Boston, U.S.A. (had to give up owing to ill-health); 1935 to 1944 (age limit dictated his retirement), Professor of Music, first at University of Southern California and then at University of California, Los Angeles, where he died on 13 July 1951.

In his early thirties, in Vienna, Schönberg's composing was practically all done in the small hours of the night, so busy did teaching keep him: in his sixties, in California, he was still teaching assiduously, though also turning out a succession of major compositions. It would be easy to assume that this lifetime of teaching was caused above all by the necessity of earning a living. Or it would be almost as easy, perhaps, to imagine that it was due to an eagerness to proselytize, to gain and train disciples in the new kind of composing inaugurated by Schönberg himself. Both notions, however, would be considerably wide of the mark. 'Schönberg', says Wellesz, 'is known to be a passionate teacher; he was so from the beginnings of his career. ...' But it was not for any indoctrination with his own methods of composition that he was impassioned. 'Nothing is farther from Schönberg's ideas' (Roger Sessions) 'than instruction in the twelve-tone system or in the modern idiom'. His two consuming preoccupations were an exhaustive grounding in harmony and counterpoint (on traditional lines) and the development of whatever was in the individual pupil. His teaching was 'almost fanatically rigorous in its ceaseless striving after mastery of resource ... as free as teaching can be from any essential dogmatic bias'.

About Schönberg the composer it is important to recall a saying of his cited by Milhaud: 'If a composer does not write from the heart he simply cannot produce good music.' Perhaps the best thing to remember of Schönberg the teacher is the opening of the preface to the *Manual of Harmony*: 'This book I have learnt from my pupils'.

WILLIAM HOWARD SCHUMAN

B. 1910

W. R. ANDERSON

Self-Help

Schuman, like Aaron Copland, is a New Yorker who developed fairly late musically. He is probably the most nearly self-taught of the present generation of American composers. Most of his learning was attacked through his sense of necessity; for example, he has told how, feeling a strong desire to play a Beethoven piece in his school orchestra, he took to the violin at the age of eleven, persuading his business-like father to buy him a beginner's instrument, which cost twelve dollars.

Moving on to High School, he got into the swing of jazz; the precociousness of American children is well known to us, as is the hold that dance music has over them. Young Schuman organized his own jazz band, not only playing the fiddle and double bass, but also appearing as vocal soloist. He had been stung into true musical life by hearing his first symphony at the late age of eighteen, but for a living he had largely to work in the lines wherein he had shown early skill, among the Tin Pan Alleys of 'popular' music. Few serious composers could have survived so long an apprenticeship to, and some degree of mastery in, the lower regions of the art.

An Unusual Upbringing

Schuman had written music for some of the camp shows organized while he was a Counsellor or young people's superintendent at one of the hundreds of summer camps so popular in the States; this one, Camp Cobbossee, was in the wooded state of Maine. Finding a facility in the production of ditties such as the adolescents liked – and their passion for which forms a major problem for American music teachers – Schuman rooted out a writer of lyrics and with him turned out a quantity of items for music hall and night club performers. One such title was *In Love with the Memory of You*.

Here was a queer outlook for the future serious composer, galvanized into real musical life at eighteen on hearing a symphony orchestra. True, he has said that for the next five years he 'ate and slept' music, which he pursued as a listener in New York's concert halls.

There used to be attributed to the dear old lady of legend that happy if muddled belief that George Mozart, the well-known music-hall performer, was 'a comedian by night, a composer of symphonies by day'. Something like this state of things seemed likely to become the fate of the would-be composer William Schuman, but one letter distant, in name, from a famous forebear. But his symphonic days were not yet; at first (as he told Ross Parmenter in a *New York Times* interview) he was busy enough, writing melodies for his partner's lyrics. The harmonizing and scoring had to be done, as very often happens in such matters, by experts. But the musician in Schuman was alive and could not be satisfied with the harmonies turned out by the worthy but slick hacks who operated upon his tunes. The obvious thing was to set to and learn the job himself, to study harmony and the art of writing for the piano and then of scoring for the orchestra.

New Vistas

He therefore tackled harmony, first with Max Persin and then with Charles Haubiel. The vistas thus opened up led him to the bold step of deserting business for music: for he had at first no other prospect than of having to earn his living in some mercantile pursuit. He had enrolled at New York University with the object of developing the particular skills required in the business of advertising. Realizing in good time that he needed a higher type of education if he were to take advantage of the most obvious opportunities for the trained musician – among them, that of teaching – he decided to develop the general culture that is even yet not invariably found among professional musicians.

At Columbia University, then, he worked for his B.S. and proceeded to the M.A. One of those Foundations that have proved so valuable to aspiring young American artists, the Guggenheim, provided him with a Fellowship, enabling him to pursue his studies (as it had similarly helped Aaron Copland) freed from the immediate necessity of attempting extra-musical work or of returning to those financially profitable but spiritually destructive music hall and night club shades from which his strong will had withdrawn him.

Symphonic Inspiration

A scholarship took him to the Mozarteum at Salzburg in 1935, and there his ambition flowered with his powers. His compositions had hitherto been very short pieces; he would now begin a symphony. This he wrote amid the inspiring surroundings of the city and woods that had known Mozart, the city with its twelfth and thirteenth century basilicas, its seventeenth-century cathedral modelled upon St Peter's at Rome, with its castle of the prince-bishops crowning the Mönchsberg, its museums and palaces, its lovely landscape and all its past associations of glory, magnificence, and romance, as well as the forebodings of the future.

That was a memorable summer, perhaps the most enlightening of Schuman's life. In the next year he was happy in coming into friendly association with Roy Harris, a composer twelve years his senior and by then well established in American favour. Harris gave him helpful criticism, advice, and encouragement.

Composition on a large scale was now pursued vigorously. A second symphony appeared in 1937. Serge Kussevitzky, conductor of the Boston Symphony Orchestra, and one of the best friends American composers ever had, brought it to a hearing.

The Professor

Meanwhile, Schuman had become a professor at Sarah Lawrence College, living in the country at Larchmont: he prefers the country to city life. He went on the board of the League of Composers and won one of the many competitions that have been sponsored in the United States by various bodies, official and otherwise, some by business men and others by combinations of musically-interested people. Schuman's *Choral Étude* took the first place in a contest for an American composition, jointly sponsored by the government's Federal Music Project, the Columbia Broadcasting Company, and a music publishing firm. This piece is sung to wordless syllables, unaccompanied, and is thus an unusual study in choral tone and harmonic colour effects.

Man of the People

The *American Festival Overture* is one of the comparatively few works of this composer's to have been so far performed at London concerts. It is another of the pieces first made known by the Boston Orchestra and its conductor, having been written in 1939 for a series of concerts of native music by this orchestra. There is a touch of home-town familiar happy reference in the fact that the first three notes, a 'motto', F, D, F, are a play call of New York schoolboys. 'In the city', said the composer, 'it is yelled on the syllables "Wee-auk-ee" to get the gang together for a game or festive occasion of some sort. This naturally suggested itself for a piece of music composed for a very festive occasion'. But the piece is not programmatic. The idea came to mind before the origin of the theme was recalled. It is a brilliantly scored piece, notable, however, for economy that yet suggests fullness; of the 359 bars, only the last five are scored for full orchestra.

A few of Schuman's works have been recorded in the United States for the gramophone, notably the two named above, the *Choral Étude* and the *American Festival Overture*, as well as an unusual work, a *Quartettino* for bassoons. There is a secular cantata, *This is Our Time*, which was given during the famous New York City series of outdoor summer concerts at the Lewisohn Stadium in 1940. A *Third Symphony* and a *Fourth Symphony* were produced by Kussevitzky and Ormandy (with the Philharmonic Orchestra), respectively. This last-enumerated work won an award, somewhat oddly instituted by the music critics of New York for the most noteworthy new American composition of the season. (It might be thought a little invidious for an association of critics to crown a work thus, but it is certainly a courageous act, and America is a great country for awards, citations, diplomas, 'Oscars', and the like.)

'*I Write by Singing*'

Of this *Fourth Symphony*, which won the 1942 award, the composer said that, having a passacaglia melody in mind long before he began the work, he derived from this the theme of a chorale and then used it as the subject of a fugue, the form thus arising not in any conventional shape, but as the logical conclusion of what he described as 'a song from beginning to end' – one to which a respected American critic pinned his faith as 'a work of great power, elemental grandeur, and inevitability of structural and emotional content. I know,' he added, 'of no American symphony that is its peer'.

In regard to the singing quality the composer has remarked, of his method of composition in general, that 'I write by singing, not by sitting at the piano'.

As to Schuman's appearance at the age of thirty-two, the interviewer described him as having dark brown, almost black eyes, thinning, close-cropped black hair, a fresh complexion, and a ready smile. 'Far from suggesting the bohemian, he looks as if he had stepped from the page of a fashionable man's magazine'.

During the war he offered his services to the government, but as they were 'courteously declined', Schuman remained at his desk, where the composer's struggles have to be waged. 'His battle,' he says, 'is the battle of the empty music-page'. Schuman has put his strength also into the arduous yet happy round of the teacher. One thinks of Holst in England, similarly divided in labours, though never in musical aims.

When asked for notes on his works, Schuman has remarked that he has given up the practice, as he thinks 'very little is accomplished beyond confusing the innocent listener'. By 1946 he had written, besides the four symphonies (one – powerful, austere music with exciting rhythms – was heard at the International Society for Contemporary Music festival in London in that year), three *String Quartets*. Among music written during the war years are works large and small. Remembering his New York school days, he wrote a *Holiday Song* for a field-day celebration by some of the city's elementary schools. Then there was *A Prayer in Time of War*, a *Pianoforte Concerto* in 1942, and in 1944 some music, including songs and a Coronation *Te Deum*, for the proposed production by Margaret Webster and Billy Rose of Shakespeare's *Henry VIII*. For the latter impresario's *Seven Lively Arts* he wrote a sketch. His sympathy with popular diversions was also shown in some music for military bands and, most notably, in an opera, *The Mighty Casey* (the exploits of 'Casey at the bat' being famous in American baseball folklore). Another familiar native figure, William Billings, the patriotic tanner-composer of sacred music, was commemorated, two centuries after his birth, in an overture bearing his name. Then there have been two more symphonies (one for strings), another string quartet and several ballets: *Undertow*, *Night Journey*, and *Judith*; with a revision of the violin concerto. One of the most recent works is an orchestral *Credendum*, commissioned by the U.S.A. division of UNESCO: an article of faith, shaped in three movements, *Declaration*, *Chorale*, *Finale*.

College President

Schuman's works already exceed the number of his years. Honours and distinctions continue to be bestowed upon him – the composition award of the American Academy of Arts and Letters (of which he is a Fellow), the degree of Mus.D. from Chicago Musical College, and so forth. He is now President of the Juilliard School of Music, a remarkable New York Institution comprising a Graduate School, an Institute of Musical Art, and a Summer School. The establishment was set up under the foundation provided in 1920 by the munificence of A. D. Juilliard. Besides helping towards the publication of native music, the Foundation's Graduate School awards scholarships to gifted North American students. The addition in 1926 of the Institute of Musical Art provided an undergraduate section offering complete musical education. From 1931 the Summer School operated to give intensive short-period study. An Opera School, part of the Graduate scheme over which Schuman presides, produces several works yearly. It is to be hoped that the now solidly established composer will not be swallowed up in Schuman the administrator. The United States deeply needs creative artists of his calibre, but Schuman does not appear to have been moved to produce many large-scale works of recent years. *Judith*, a choreographic poem, was played by the Louisville Orchestra, which undertook an ambitious programme, seeking to make known more native music than most orchestras, necessarily guided largely by box-office considerations, ever can. It was recently remarked that the three largest orchestras in the States had played eleven native works in one year, this being regarded as a very good record. The Kentucky orchestra is in a more fortunate – indeed, in an almost unique – position; through the energy of some Louisville citizens in 1948, the new-works policy was inaugurated, and the Rockefeller Foundation later made a grant of $400,000 for 'a project to stimulate, encourage and foster the creation, performance and recording of new musical works by living composers'. The records were issued, from 1955, by subscription, among the native composers in the first series being Creston, Cowell, Riegger, Peggy Glanville Hicks, Sanders, Ward, and Bacon. All nationalities are eligible, and there is a subsidiary scheme for student composers, ten of whom are annually chosen for $500 prizes. Every work commissioned was to be performed four times in the annual Louisville Orchestra series of forty-six concerts.

YURI SHAPORIN

B. 1889

M. MONTAGU-NATHAN

Lawyer into Musician

Yuri Shaporin, who appears to be one of the most serious composers in the Soviet group, has acquired a reputation for being an inveterate 'polisher'. An extremely 'nice' attitude towards the fitness of a given work for publication is presumably responsible for the somewhat slender dimensions of this composer's published output. Curiously enough, Nature seems to have taken an unusually long time to decide whether he would shine more as a legal luminary than as a musician, and he did not receive a clear 'call' to adopt a musical vocation until close on twenty-four years of age.

As the author of a thoughtfully considered and well-expressed thesis on the subject of operatic dramaturgy, in which he insists that a fully reciprocal understanding between librettist and composer is essential to the achievement of a combined musical and dramatic verity, one would expect him to have made up his mind at least about the kind of dramatic music required of himself. Yet his only opera, which was begun in 1925, had apparently not yet been finished at the moment (1940) when the above-mentioned literary essay was published. His only symphony, on the composition of which he embarked soon after beginning the opera, was not completed until six years later.

Political Permutation

At first blush it does not seem to matter a great deal to an audience how long the composer of a work has delayed its issue. Similarly, when reading Walter Pater, another polisher, who is notorious for his fastidiousness in the choice of a word or phrase, we do not wonder how long it took him to decide upon the expression 'a hard, gemlike flame' in his oft-quoted definition of success, nor do we speculate as to the number of alternatives he discarded before reaching a decision.

But for more than one reason a composer is differently placed. If he is a pioneer with a modernistic outlook, any considerable delay will render what seemed, say ten years before, somewhat daring, several degrees less novel to those who eventually hear such music. Moreover, the peculiar circumstances attending the work of composers who are pledged to convey, however vaguely, a political message, constitute a danger of a kind that has not hitherto confronted creative artists outside Russia. This difficulty is the more acute for those who create slowly, since an ever-changing political background cannot fail to affect the transmission of their message.

Parts of Shaporin's unpublished opera, *The Decembrists*, have been made available for, and have actually received, performance on the concert-platform. There is evidence that, in this instance, the music proved too modernistic for the subject on which it attempts to comment, for one Slavonic critic has referred to the Russian political crisis that inspired the opera as having occurred in the twentieth, instead of the nineteenth, century! This class of discrepancy has hitherto been the unchallenged prerogative of Hollywood.

Shaporin, having been born in 1889 (at Glukhov – once a very active Ukrainian musical centre) has not been so long in the creative field as that date would suggest. Its deceptiveness in this respect is, of course, to be accounted for by the unusual time-lag between his birth and the beginning of his serious musical studies, and his somewhat deliberate creative process has also to be taken into consideration. Intended for the law, he studied at St Petersburg University until 1913, when he appears to have become for the first time convinced that music was his real *métier* and enrolled himself as a student at the conservatoire. During the four years spent in that institution he studied with three highly-esteemed teachers, namely, Sokolov, Cherepnin, and Steinberg, all of whom were pupils of Rimsky-Korsakov – the last-named being, in addition, that composer's son-in-law. The influence transmitted from the parent source has, however, been confined so far to the region of general orchestral technique; as to other aspects of Shaporin's creative output, it is the general opinion that certain derivative characteristics may be traced to such varied influences as Borodin, Musorgsky, and, strange as it may seem, Rakhmaninov.

Man of the Theatre and Cinema

In common with other Soviet composers, and with Shostakovich in particular, Shaporin associated himself for a time principally with music for the theatre. For such a region of musical activity he was peculiarly well suited, having a very decided flair for the dramatic art. During the civil war that followed the Brest-Litovsk treaty he was helping to organize the affairs of a theatre devoted to serious drama at Petrozavodsk. A little later he was concerned in the founding of the Leningrad Bolshoi Theatre, a project in which he was joined by Maxim Gorky, Lunacharsky, and the poet Blok.

He eventually became Director of Music in this institution and was responsible for a considerable amount of incidental music for the plays there produced. Among these were Labiche's *Un Chapeau de Paille d'Italie*, Schiller's *The Robbers*, *King Lear*, *Tartuffe*, *Boris Godunov*, and *The Storming of Perecop*. The music to Leskov's *The Flea* (adapted for the stage by Zaminsky), which contains plentiful allusions to Russian folk-song and lore and employs such national instruments as the balalaika and the domra, was eventually arranged as an orchestral work. For the Labiche play he adopted the style associated with nineteenth-century vaudeville.

Proceeding from the theatre to the cinema Shaporin has furnished music for some important film productions – two of them having a military and war-time interest. The first was in honour of the great general, Suvorov, and the second, *Minin and Pozharsky*, celebrates the founding, in 1611, during the Time of Trouble, of a kind of Home Guard in defence against the Polish invader.

Apart from these works, and a number of contributions for the voice, to texts from Pushkin, Tyuchev, and Blok, in which Shaporin shows a distinct appreciation both of vocalistic utterance and of the expression of sentiment in terms of musical accompaniment, the composer's reputation rests, at all events outside Russia, upon two completed works – *The Decembrists* not yet being available for comprehensive and detailed appraisement. The *Symphony*, which is for orchestra and chorus, consists of four movements. The first bears the Russian caption 'Byl', which may be roughly translated as 'In Bygone Days'. Following this comes the sections entitled respectively Dance, Lullaby, and Into Battle. In this final movement the orchestra is itself enlarged and is amplified by a brass band. To those familiar with the propagandist methods prevailing in the Soviet Union it will be no surprise to learn that the inspiration of this work is said to have emanated from a contemplation of 'the love of the Russian People for their Fatherland'.

The narrative first movement – a revolutionary song, *Yablochko* ('The Little Apple') – contains folk-material, its second theme, with variations, being one already familiar (as was *Dubinushka*) in the days of the 1905 abortive rising; it has since been used by Glière in his ballet *The Red Poppy*. The Dance is not, as one might expect, in complete contrast with the first movement, its mood having something in common with the spirit of the preceding section. The Lullaby serves as a lyrical slow movement, culminating in a bridge to the militant finale. Here the brass band links up with the orchestra as a special medium for the introduction of really martial music, such as the popular *Budenny's March*. The symphony concludes with a 'mass song' distinctly of folk character. Judging by its themes alone, the *First Symphony* may safely be reckoned as a deliberate appeal to the proletariat, which conformed to the purpose imposed upon such creations as far back as Tolstoy's notorious essay, *What is Art?*, now apparently a principal aim of those composers who have pledged allegiance to the Soviet dispensation. It was first performed in 1933 at Moscow under the direction of Albert Coates and reached this country two years later.

Anachronistic Music

The work by which Shaporin is best known in Western Europe is, of course, the monumental Cantata entitled *On the Field of Kulikovo* – commemorating the great battle of 1380 in which Dmitri Donskoy inflicted a crushing defeat over the Tatar hordes. Its score bears an inscription alluding to the decisive character of the conflict and conveys a hint – accidentally appropriate to a later period – that such a victory could justly be claimed as having rendered a signal service not merely to Russia but to the entire continent of Europe. It should be pointed out that this work as a whole consists of a 'nice derangement' of epical material. It was inspired by the poem written by Alexander Blok in 1908, whose text must then have been regarded as possessing principally an archaeological interest. For at that time the prospect of even one world war in which Russia would be involved must have seemed remote in the extreme.

When Shaporin began, about 1920, to sketch the cantata, that conflict was already history, and the likelihood of a repetition on a much larger scale can hardly have been prominent in the composer's mind. By the time of the completion of *On the Field of Kulikovo*, however, the stormclouds were already again wearing a menacing appearance, and at its first performance in Moscow in 1939 (the composer had now been appointed professor at the new capital's conservatoire) there must have been few who were not convinced that a gigantic outbreak was certain to supervene. And when the Cantata was performed, through the medium of broadcasting, before an English audience, in November 1945, both its text and its music had assumed a significance that neither Blok, the poet, nor Lozinsky, who after Blok's death emendated and amplified the text, nor Shaporin the composer could ever have anticipated. It is for this reason, no doubt, that some who then listened to the work felt that the musical expression was insufficiently intense. Music describing an air raid of 1917 vintage could hardly be expected to do justice as a description of the havoc wrought when whole towns were to be virtually destroyed in one air-battle. Shaporin's music thus seemed just a little old-fashioned and created the impression of an under-statement about events whose terrors could hardly be exaggerated.

The dramatic action, in brief, begins with a description of the Don Valley and its vast expanse of steppe. The *dramatis personae* of the conflict are portrayed – Dmitri, his warriors, the People, who are made prominent protagonists in the spirit of Musorgsky's treatment, and the heroic womanhood of the nation are all dealt with in turn. There is a particularly significant chorus of knights – in the third movement – giving a vocal account of the nocturnal descent of Mamai and his Tatar horde. The fifth episode emphasizes the imminence of battle and is punctuated by trumpet calls, which eventually announce the beginning of the bloody conflict. This ends in the heroic death of Dmitri and a large number of his followers – a loss referred to in the final episodes in music that both commemorates the fallen and celebrates the victory. An epilogue is devoted to a warning that future attempts at invasion must be met in the heroic fashion displayed on Kulikovo's Field.

There has been a hint that Shaporin has found it necessary to compose further music to the same effect, but containing a still more vehement and insistent exhortation to the address of his compatriots.

A work composed subsequently to the above-described cantata, entitled *A Saga of the Defence of the Fatherland*, was produced in Moscow in 1944. It may be anticipated that when an opportunity is afforded us of hearing this composition it will prove to contain the spirit of the time revealed in higher relief than in its forerunner.

DMITRI SHOSTAKOVICH

B. 1906

M. MONTAGU-NATHAN

Subversive Symphonism

Forming an estimate of the value of Shostakovich's creative output would not, in normal circumstances, present undue difficulties; the composer has provided an abundance of material, beginning with the *First Symphony* (Op. 10) and concluding (at the moment of writing) with the second *String Quartet* (Op. 69), composed when approaching his fortieth year. But in scanning the list of his works we observe that eight items preceding the symphony have been suppressed on the ground of their having been inspired by a 'misguided ideology'. This somewhat nebulous term, when translated into the current jargon of the Soviet administration, appears to signify that the works in question contain in an insufficient degree a quality that has never hitherto been sought by the musicologists of the world. It is known, in the circles in which Shostakovich moves, as 'Socialist realism'.

A combination of circumstances must be held responsible for a suspicion that whilst he is a highly capable composer he is prevented by certain influences from revealing his true individuality and is actually forced to disguise it with utterances whose substance, one charitably assumes, is 'inspired'. 'The classic composers,' he has stated, 'either consciously or unconsciously ... bolstered up the rule of the upper classes. Music is no longer an end in itself.' Such dicta might easily suggest that Beethoven was a stubborn opponent of social reform, or that Brahms's Cambridge symphony was, consciously or unconsciously, a glorification of the wealthy undergraduates of the pale-blue persuasion. In scrutinizing Shostakovich's output as a whole, and considering it simply as music, one is reminded that every composer 'not excluding even the greatest of the classics', has displayed in his creative work what is termed a 'visiting-card'. Now Shostakovich's *carte-de-visite* is adorned with musical quips and cranks that may evoke wreathéd smiles from those whose acquaintance with his output happens to be slender. If, for instance, such people are inclined to learn something about 'this new Russian fellah', and they decide to listen, or listen-in, to the Polka from the satirical ballet, *The Golden Age* (Op. 22), the resultant impression will probably be that the composer, when so disposed, is capable of clowning like any Grock. But on turning, say, to the *Piano Concerto* (Op. 35) our investigator will discover that the clowning threatens to assume the function of a visiting-card, and as the 'little piece of paste-board' is decorated with emblems that, although appropriate to the earlier occasion, are quite out of place in a work of this kind, he will quite likely fail to be amused.

We can, in fact, hardly blame the enquirer for coming to the conclusion that Shostakovich's gift is somewhat marred by intrusions – conscious or unconscious – of that xylophone in his bonnet. Those who are better versed in the conditions obtaining in the composer's immediate environment may be pardoned for suspecting that the intrusive instrument may be operating as part of the paraphernalia designed for the propitiation of the proletariat, which is one of the declared aims of the Soviet musical dispensation.

And the conclusion reached by those who have been able to examine chapter and verse of Shostakovich's creative material is that, owing to circumstances not altogether within his control, he has been induced to become a sort of musical Jekyll and Hyde. He appears to be a composer who, if left alone, would probably devote himself to bold and earnest experiment, ultimately attaining the enviable condition of a successful and highly dignified pioneer. Writing, however, as he seems to do, under the shadow of a hammer and sickle, suspended by a horse-hair that has already once been severed by the displeasure of a bureaucratic Dionysius, our musical Damocles is apparently obliged to garnish his experimental compositions with condiments that will render them palatable to the million.

Early Studies and First Works

Dmitri Shostakovich was born on 25 September 1906 in St Petersburg. His father is described as being very musical; a talent for piano-playing in addition to the possession of a pleasant tenor voice seems tolerably good evidence of the accuracy of such description. Sophia Kokovlina, his mother, herself a pupil of the St Petersburg conservatoire, was the boy's first teacher. To such a parental influence is no doubt due the fact that at nine years of age he had already composed a *Theme with Variations*. Two years later, after the Revolution, he celebrated a politico-musical novitiate with the composition of a *Hymn to Liberty*. Having exhausted his mother's tutorial resources he entered the Glasser School, duly passing on (in 1919) to the conservatoire; there his piano teacher was Nikolaev, whilst Steinberg (Rimsky-Korsakov's son-in-law) took charge of his studies in composition. He graduated from that institution in 1925.

A considerable proportion of his subsequent creative work was devoted to music for a variety of films and plays. This deviation is probably to be traced to his having been obliged for some time to contribute material assistance to his parents by presiding at the piano in cinema houses. His first serious composition, the *Symphony* (Op. 10) in F minor, written when he was nineteen years of age, was performed, under Malko's conductorship, at the conservatoire on 12 May 1926, and met with so striking a success that its composer, despite his brilliant talent as a pianist, resolved at once to devote himself to a creative career. After a *Piano Sonata* (Op. 12) and the *Ten Pieces for Piano* came the *Second Symphony* (Op. 14), a *pièce d'occasion* celebrating the tenth anniversary of the October Revolution. It is in one movement and has a choral ending, to a text by Bezimensky. This poet is described by Mr Gleb Struve as the 'recognized bard' – at that date – of the Communist Party. It is significant that, according to this distinguished authority, Bezimensky's extremely successful career as a poet was interrupted by the change in policy that occurred in 1932. The obvious inference to be drawn from this information is that what may happen to a political poet may quite likely be the fate of a Party-minded composer.

The Proletariat Dictates

Vladimir Protopopov, in an article in *Sovietskaya Muzika* on Rimsky-Korsakov's operatic forms, expresses the opinion that *The Golden Cockerel* may be regarded as the structural fount and origin of subsequent Russian operatic music and mentions Stravinsky, Prokofiev, and Shostakovich as Rimsky-Korsakov's foremost lineal descendants. If Shostakovich's first operatic essay, *The Nose*, written in 1927–8 and produced in Leningrad on 13 January 1930 does not closely resemble the much-discussed Diagilev version of Rimsky-Korsakov's fifteenth opera as produced in Paris and London in 1914, the choice of Gogol's remarkable fantasy as text established a sort of affinity with the composer of *A Night in May* and *Christmas Eve Revels*. It is clear that the incidence of the dictatorship of the proletariat was already operating in musical matters. Shostakovich, evidently feeling the pulse of the people, considered it necessary to explain in a programme-note that a satirical treatment was 'indicated' by contemporary political considerations, and, as supplement to the programme book, there was a referendum calling upon the audience to record votes in respect of the opera generally, the clarity of the music, the quality of the production, and the vocal demeanour of the singers. This method of introducing an opera would appear to render the hitherto respected labours of the accredited music critic completely supererogatory.

Shostakovich's next work – ignoring a somewhat unexpected *Tahiti-Trot*, the manuscript of which, we are informed, was lost, and the incidental music to Mayakovsky's insect play *The Bedbug* – was a *Third Symphony*, in one movement, written to emphasize the political significance of the First of May, a day sacred to the Labour organizations of the world. This work, again, was provided with a choral conclusion, which delivers a message with a Trotskist flavour appealing for a universal uprising. Another composition of important dimensions was the ballet, in three acts, entitled *The Golden Age*, produced in October 1930 which must have preceded Jooss's production of *The Green Table*. The whole ballet reeks of socio-political satire. The end served by such a work has now become somewhat *démodé*, and the title of the comic Polka, *Once upon a time in Geneva*, has a detrimentally reminiscent flavour that dates it as significantly as its once somewhat startling discords. Meanwhile he was still occupied with compositions of an ancillary order, such, for instance, as the incidental music for Piotrovsky's play, *Rule Britannia*. This remains unpublished, and we can only conjecture as to the treatment of that inspiring ditty.

At this point we are confronted with the most dramatic episode, and the least comprehensible, in the composer's career. From 1930 to 1932 he was occupied in writing an opera based upon Leskov's *Lady Macbeth of Mtsensk*. The essential feature of its plot is a domestic triangle formed by a woman, Katerina Izmailova, her lover, and their victim, her husband. From a mass of critical and quasi-political polemic provoked by the work one gathers that the composer had found it necessary to explain that in his view a lampooning of the old régime in revolutionary terms had become overdue. But the really puzzling circumstance is that, when first produced, on 22 January 1934, this opera was received with immense enthusiasm by the general public, and one would therefore imagine it to have thus fulfilled the official condition of being designed for and acceptable to the million. The conductor himself wrote an introductory note in the programme proclaiming the work to be the product of genius – concluding with the boast that any attempt upon the part of foreign operatic composers living and working in capitalist communities to rival this masterpiece must inevitably prove vain. The opera remained successful for two whole years.

Then, in 1936, came a most astonishing outburst. *Pravda* had made the discovery that the opera was 'all wrong'. It failed to fulfil the condition that music must be confined to the expression of 'Socialist realism'. As a result of this extraordinary *dénouement* – the stranger in virtue of the opinion of those competent to judge that some of the music of this opera is equal to that of the *First Symphony* – Shostakovich resolved that a period of fasting and prayer might be salutary. During these exorcisations he received consolation from an extra-musical source. Soon after completion of the opera he had married, and the union was proving fruitful. His *Piano Concerto* (Op. 35) – first performed in October 1933, with the composer as soloist – was apparently judged suitable for the proletarian ear, but Shostakovich began to outline a further symphony that would be acceptable to those who regarded music as a plank in the political platform. This, however, his fourth work in that form, having been rehearsed by the Leningrad Philharmonic Orchestra in December 1936, was withdrawn by its composer. That step was taken on the urgent advice of the orchestra, but there was also adverse criticism from others present at the rehearsal. To a three-act ballet, entitled *The Limpid Brook* (Op. 39), composed in 1934 and produced during the following year, the critics had been equally hostile. *Pravda* even went the length of complaining that parts of its score had previously been used in an abandoned work and spoke scornfully of music that could serve to express two different meanings. It is stimulating to imagine what defence of such a practice would have been advanced by Musorgsky and some of his confrères.

SHOSTAKOVICH

Trying again

Our composer, nothing daunted, determined to have another shot. The *Fifth Symphony* (Op. 47) had a personal programmatic basis and purported to be a musical record of his own life experience and a philosophical commentary thereon. Shostakovich described it as 'The Reply of a Soviet Artist to Merited Criticism.' This time he had made sure. We are only able to consider this symphony as music. Comment on the information that the work is descriptive of the development of its creator's personality 'within the revolutionary events of our time' would be out of place. The symphony, first performed in Moscow in January 1938, is in four movements and is scored for a largish orchestra, including the apparently inevitable xylophone, glockenspiel, and a celesta; a piano is treated as an orchestral unit. A novel feature of the Largo is the division of the violins into three sections. Generally speaking the instrumental part-writing is superior to the orchestration. The salient feature of the work is the impression it gives that the composer is being subjected to occasional reminders that the million must be mollified, and one assumes that certain conspicuous intrusions are due to such elbow nudging.

The *Fifth Symphony* was greeted with a positive welter of panegyric, to which an eminent poet and a celebrated airman contributed their flights. A leading Moscow music critic's quota took the form of congratulations to the composer on having successfully overcome a former tendency (exhibited, it was alleged, in the *Macbeth* opera) to write music in which a leftward bias was displayed. The significance of this political term in such a context has puzzled more than one commentator.

The character of the now familiar *Piano Concerto* (Op. 35) may possibly be influenced by the succession of film compositions that preceded it. It is unlikely that any other work in that form has ever been the vehicle for so hearty an exhibition of high jinks. For, with the exception of some dignified sections of the second and third movements, the concerto seems more appropriate to the circus than to the concert room.

Since this outstanding success Shostakovich has composed four more symphonies. The *Seventh Symphony*, as all the world knows, was written during the siege of Leningrad and first performed at Kuibishev in 1941 after no less than forty rehearsals. In the opinion of many its aesthetic value is not equal to that of the youthful *First Symphony*.

A *Ninth Symphony* has been performed by the Leningrad Philharmonic Orchestra under the conductorship of Kravinsky. In the composition of this work, which, although it contains five movements, occupies only twenty minutes in performance, Shostakovich appears to have been again assailed by musico-philosophic doubts. Originally intended as a work in celebration of victory, it was eventually offered as a bridge between the previous symphonies and a promised tenth in which the prowess of the Red Army was to be suitably acclaimed.

Shostakovich has now completed his *Tenth Symphony*, a work begun as far back as 1947, one year before the famous, or perhaps infamous, decree promulgated by the notorious statesman, Andre Zhdanov, who, a little before his death, fell into governmental disfavour. The published programme of this decree may be briefly stated. The 'formalist' tendency in music was pronounced to be 'anti-People'. The Soviet Art Committee was given power to 'improve' the state of affairs in Soviet music and to 'liquidate' its faults. Soviet composers were urged to develop a consciousness of their duties to the proletariat. This last clause was obviously inspired by the theories of Tolstoi's *What is Art?* The People were to be the judges of what was meritorious in music and what was not. But it soon became evident that the taste of the proletariat coincided more or ess with that of high-level personages in the Kremlin. We have in this country a number of professional authorities on all forms of music and that is why we have no need to rely upon the judgement of the humblest addict of the Light Programme or of members of the Cabinet about the merits or demerits of a new opera or symphony. It has particularly to be borne in mind that Zhdanov conceived a personal dislike of Shostakovich and that the latter was therefore obliged on occasion to pander to this highly placed individual. That is why in the *Tenth Symphony* we observe such an odd mixture of styles as those of Brahms and of a movement at times somewhat more appropriate to the circus than to the concert room.

The 100,000 Rubl Quintet

The second *String Quartet* (Op. 69) – one of the composer's most recent published works – is a curious example of that genre. The thematic material of its first movement, or 'overture', is arid; it is not grateful to the listener and must inevitably become tedious to the players. After this the first violin embarks upon a lengthy recitative, alternating with a 'romance' in which his fellow-instrumentalists are privileged to share. Despite some comparatively passionate outbursts, in which the leading violin does most of the love making, the part writing for the other instruments adheres so closely to the melodic horizontal as to create a decided feeling of monotony. Real charm is approached in the *Valse*, but when the solo is ceded to the second violin the leading part consists of 114 repetitions of one note – apparently a characteristic device. The final movement, a theme with variations, is a skilful and spirited development of fragmentary material.

It seems likely that Shostakovich may in the future devote himself more closely to chamber music. The *Quintet* (Op. 57), first performed at the Moscow Festival of Soviet Music, was not only hailed as a masterpiece containing features hitherto undiscoverable in chamber music, but won for its composer the Stalin Prize of 100,000 roubles – a sum whose dimensions would have given the late W. W. Cobbett financially to think!

In 1942 the association of three artists known as the Kukriniksi issued a caricature of Shostakovich bearing the accoutrements of a one-man-band together with a bayoneted rifle to which are attached some presumably lethal crotchets. His seven-fingered hands are busy with a piano keyboard. This is surely a comprehensive portrait of a musician whose activities have ranged between the composition of a suite for jazz-band and the preparation of a new version of *Boris Godunov* in which the orchestration is revised with the intention of heightening the political significance of that long suffering work. If the munificent awards such as that earned by his *Quintet* continue, the resultant immunity from material cares may enable Shostakovich to forsake music in which such features as xylophones (and steam-whistles) are conspicuous and to devote himself to that region of the musical art that has always been reserved by the great masters of the past for the expression of their most aristocratic, and entirely non-political, utterances.

JEAN SIBELIUS

B. 1865

CHRISTOPHER GRIER

The Man and the Country

Although Finland has not had such an unhappy history as Poland, it can look back on centuries of domination, first by Sweden and then by Russia. Tucked away in the North-east corner of Europe, with a population of three million, it cannot hope to play a decisive part in world history. What it can do, and has done, is to attain a remarkably high standard of living, to defend its rights, and to make an important contribution to the western way of life. For its size, it has produced an astonishing number of writers and artists. To mention but a few, Aleksis Kivi, Runeberg, Alvar Aalto, and Wäinö Aaltonen have all exerted an influence on European and American civilization, but it is of a composer, Jean Sibelius, that men think first when Finland is mentioned. Basically he is a professional musician, but on the foundation of his art he has built up a reputation of nation-wide importance. The aura of greatness is even reflected on those who are privileged to visit him at Järvenpää: they return in much the same spirit as did the Hebrew prophets after communing with Jehovah.

It is in no sense derogatory to Sibelius to say that his fame has come about not only through his own endeavours, but also because of the period in Finnish history through which he has lived. He grew up in the uneasy times of the last years of Czarist rule and became associated in the national consciousness with those who were in artistic and political revolt against the alien authorities. Such works as *Kullervo* and *Finlandia* were recognized as important calls to freedom and to a rebirth of Finnish culture. At the same time his compatriots realized that he was gradually making a world-wide reputation with his symphonies. He became an ambassador not only of Finnish music but also of Finnish independence. Thus as well as love and appreciation of Sibelius the composer, there is in his country also pride in Sibelius the man. His story is that of a highly intelligent and determined national composer who has fought his way into the ranks of the world's great symphonists. Constant Lambert's summary of his progress is characteristically apt. 'When we look at Sibelius's *Finlandia* and then at his *Seventh Symphony*, we may well agree with George Moore that art must be parochial in the beginning to become cosmopolitan in the end.'

Early Years

Jean Sibelius was born on 8 December 1865 at Hämeenlinna. His father, Dr Christian Gustav Sibelius, was medical officer to the Territorial battalion stationed in that small thriving town. He himself came from a long line of professional men and government officials, who were nearly all of pure Finnish origin, but who had taken to Swedish customs and speech on settling in the southern coastal district of Finland. Dr Sibelius's wife, Maria Carlotta Borg, came from the same social background, but was of more mixed Finnish and Swedish blood. (It should perhaps be pointed out that Swedish was, and to a much less extent still is, the language of the professional classes in Finland.) Thus Jean Sibelius is of mixed origins, and though he grew up in a Swedish-Finnish household, he has never allowed the question of nationality to bother him in the slightest. That problem he has left to the agitations of 'Swinnish' last-ditchers and Finnish nationalists. His life has been an admirable synthesis of the best of the Swedish cultural elements and of the purely Finnish traditions.

His father died when Jean was two and a half, and he was thenceforward brought up by his mother and grandmother, who also allowed him frequent visits to his father's brother in Åbo. He grew up in cultivated surroundings, for his family were keen amateur musicians, and his mother refused to allow the death of her husband to cast an unnatural gloom over the household.

In the last century, Hämeenlinna was an enterprising and artistic minded township. There was a busy social and musical life, in which the officers of the Russian garrison played an important part. One of its main educational features was the famous Hämeen Lyseo, which, as Karl Ekman says 'represented one of the first conquests of the victorious advance of Finnish culture – the fruit of self-sacrificing idealism and determined labour'. Sibelius entered the school in 1876 and was to profit immensely from the high quality of its teaching. His taste for mathematics and literature, expecially the Swedish-writing poets, went hand in hand with *joie de vivre* and enthusiasm for everything he undertook. His contemporaries have spoken of him as a dreamer or as a visionary, but also as a practical and alert youth, who could harness his ideas into practical form. Perhaps the most noticeable feature in his temperament was his love of nature in all its variety. This absorption in natural surroundings is a quality that has remained with him all his life and is one part of the key to understanding his compositions.

As a youth he showed artistic talent, but no more. He studied the piano, but it was not until he was fifteen that the irresistible lure of music came upon him. He took up the violin and made such rapid progress that he was soon able to play in a trio in his home circle. This had two results: he was introduced to the chamber music of the classical period, and it stimulated him to composition. Furthermore, in 1881, he came upon a copy of Marx's *Musiklehre*. He profited so much from the teaching of this book that his knowledge of Form was adequate to tide him over the later period of instruction at the Helsinki conservatoire.

The Music Student

In 1885 he matriculated from school. Music was his passion, but as a member of the professional classes he realized that his relations would not encourage his taking it up as a career. Thus in the autumn of that year he was enrolled at Helsinki University in the faculty of law, which was the proper study on which to base an official career. At the same time, however, he became a special student at the Music Academy, taking lessons in violin playing and theory. This uneasy double allegiance lasted for a year, by which time it became clear that his enthusiasm and developing talents should be concentrated on music alone. With the consent of his relations in September 1886 he became a full-time music student. The first obstacle had been overcome.

The three years that he spent at the Academy in Helsinki were invaluable. The director was a remarkable teacher, Martin Wegelius, strict and with strong convictions, but possessing the gift of gauging the needs of his pupils. On looking through some of Sibelius's early compositions he saw that they contained more than mere talent, but were as yet held back through lack of technique. He prescribed a severe course of study, which Sibelius, to his credit, realized was what he needed. At the same time he carried on a creative life of his own, which was appreciated in his own small circle. There was a conflict of interests between pupil and teacher in that respect, for Wegelius was a convinced Wagnerian (to the exclusion of Brahms from the Academy's curriculum), whereas Sibelius was repelled by Wagner and leaned more towards Grieg and Tchaikovsky.

In those days Helsinki, in its capacity as a provincial capital, was a small cheerful town, untroubled by political problems. Sibelius spent most of his time with his musical contemporaries, but he himself has left accounts of his meeting with Topelius, the poet, and Edelfelt, the painter. Far more significant was his meeting with Busoni, who was at that time teaching in Wegelius's conservatoire. Although further on in his remarkable career than Sibelius, and coming from a widely different and cosmopolitan background, he was about the same age. He was drawn to Sibelius not only by their common musical interests, but also because he recognized that in Sibelius's work lay potentialities far beyond those of the average student. In after years Busoni's help was to be invaluable.

If this friendship with Busoni had a musical significance, his growing acquaintance with the Järnefelt family had a social and nationalist significance. This family represented a type with whom Sibelius had not so far come into contact. Aristocratic, and highly cultivated, the Järnefelts believed in the fusion of art and the military-official life. General Järnefelt himself was a Finn with a deep love for his own country, who had made a distinguished military career in the Russian Empire. His three sons all took up artistic careers; his daughter Aino was to become Sibelius's wife.

Berlin and Vienna

In 1889 his course was completed; his A minor *Quartet* was the last work to be written at the Academy. By the age of twenty-four he had already made his mark; the next step was further study abroad, which in those days meant Germany, and for Sibelius was to be Berlin. In the autumn of that year he made his first trip overseas, armed with a letter of recommendation to Albert Becker, a highly respected composer and theoretician.

Sibelius's year in Berlin was not fruitful for composition, but it had other, and at this time more important, compensations. Becker put him through an extremely arduous course of study in the classical models; this was a thorough groundwork on which Sibelius was to build later. Further, he was now able for the first time to hear masterly playing (Joachim and von Bülow were in their prime) as often as he wished. Contemporary music was, however, a sore subject, for the Brahms-Wagner feud was at its height, while the most popular composer of the time was Bungert. Work was not easy amid the many distractions of a great capital city, but Sibelius kept stimulating company, particularly among fellow Scandinavians. Besides developing his literary tastes, he was finding his way to an appreciation of what his own country had to offer. His meeting in Berlin with Robert Kajanus, the conductor of the Helsinki orchestra, and the hearing of Kajanus's *Kalevala Symphony* were important. Ringbom quotes Sibelius as saying that this work was not the decisive event that led him into a study of the national epic, the *Kalevala*, but rather the encouragement of an interest he was developing for himself.

In the summer of 1890 he returned to Finland to prepare for his final period of study abroad, and to the great satisfaction of his own relations and of the Järnefelts became engaged to their youngest daughter, Aino. Later in that year he set off for Vienna.

Here he spent some very profitable months. Hans Richter, to whom Wegelius had given him a letter of introduction, sent him to Robert Fuchs for study in orchestration. At the same time he became a pupil of Goldmark, who was able to correct Sibelius's tendency to conceive orchestral music in terms of his first enthusiasm, chamber music. Neither man appears fully to have appreciated the characteristic style of Sibelius's compositions, but they were able to teach him the niceties of orchestral technique.

This was probably one of the happiest periods of Sibelius's career. The life of a student in the atmosphere of Vienna, so much more liberal than Berlin, was attractive. He moved freely in artistic circles, without becoming a mere musical courtier; he was aware of his growing ability, and he could enjoy the civilized amenities of such a city. Sibelius has often admitted that his lifelong devotion to Strauss waltzes dates from this period. But by the summer of 1891 his course was over, and he had now to return to Finland to apply his knowledge.

Return to Finland

He came back to find his country in a ferment. As a counterblast to the Russian attempt in 1890 to destroy Finnish laws and rights, a patriotic revival was under way. This was summed up by a journal *Päivälehti*, to which all the young Finnish intellectuals and artists subscribed. The same enthusiasm was displayed by the Swedish-Finnish literateurs, although they had slightly different aims. Sibelius belonged to both groups and became closely associated with Gallén-Kallela, the Finnish painter, and Tavastjerna, the Swedish-Finnish poet. During the first year of his return, Sibelius lived mainly at his grandmother's house at Lovisa, working on a large-scale symphonic poem, which was to be the musical manifesto of the recreation of Finnish mythology. The triumphal première of *Kullervo* early in 1892 brought him immediate fame.

For the next five years, Sibelius became a teacher, both at the Academy and at the Philharmonic Society, and also played second violin in the Academy quartet. This kept him busy enough, but he found time to compose extensively during this period. Songs, choral works, piano solos, and several well-known orchestral pieces date from these years. He did, however, enjoy a great advantage from having an orchestra on which to try out his compositions, a benefit he owed to the imaginative support of Robert Kajanus, the conductor of the Philharmonic Society Orchestra. *En Saga* (1893) was Sibelius's answer to Kajanus's request for a popular work for the repertoire. A little later the *Karelian Suite* came into being as incidental music for a pageant arranged in Vipori (the capital of Karelia) in November of that year.

The warmth, colour, and artistic traditions of the south have inevitably possessed an enormous attraction to those living in a northern climate. Sibelius has always emphasized the importance of going abroad and of combining the best of cosmopolitanism with inherited national traits. His travels in 1894 to Italy, Bayreuth, and Munich were the first of many similar expeditions. Meanwhile in Helsinki he became a member of the Symposium, a gathering consisting of Kajanus, Gallén-Kallela, and any other forward-looking artists of nationalist leanings. A permanent record of one of these meetings can be seen in Kallela's famous picture, now hanging in the Helsinki Athenaeum. Legendary as was the alcoholic endurance of the symposium members, it was an admirable clearing house of ideas.

The Kalevala *and Nationalist Strivings*

Throughout those years of ferment, Sibelius was digesting the *Kalevala*. This epic of Finnish mythology is a collection of ballads assembled by a mid-nineteenth century physician and scholar, Elias Lönnrot. To the enthusiasts of 1890 it was a treasure trove, on which a modern Finnish-speaking culture could be based. Lönnrot's expectations were fulfilled musically by Sibelius in his tone poems and pictorially by Axel Gallén-Kallela.

The Nationalist revival at this period can be measured by Sibelius's first group of songs, settings of Finnish rather than Swedish verse, and, more significantly, by the first version of the Lemminkäinen cycle, *Lemminkäinen and the Maidens*, *Lemminkäinen in Tuonela*, *The Swan of Tuonela*, and *The Return of Lemminkäinen*. These had their premières in 1896.

Shortly afterwards an important change was affected in Sibelius's fortunes, when the Senate granted him a small annual pension of 2,000 Finmarks. This far-sighted move was the answer to a press campaign to allow Sibelius more leisure for composition.

For the next few years Sibelius was busy. His suite *King Christian II* was performed in February 1898, and later in the same year he was off again to Germany, mainly in order to place his compositions with Breitkopf and Härtel in Berlin. His success in that venture was the preliminary move towards European recognition. On his return he completed his *First Symphony*, in E minor. It is easy to claim that it is derivative, with many side-glances at Tchaikovsky and Borodin, and lacking in the more subtle characteristics of his later compositions. Nevertheless, its power, its depth of emotion and heart-searchings, made a deep impression.

Its appearance coincided with a new wave of Russian oppression. A strict censorship was clamped down upon the press. It was a testing time for all Finnish artists. Sibelius's answer was the Finale to a set of Music Tableaux, which after various changes of title became known as *Finlandia*. Its effect was prodigious. Abroad it became widely popular as an effective piece of music; at home it had primarily a political significance. Its note of defiance was such that it was for years suppressed in Finland and only allowed to be played in other parts of the Russian Empire under an assumed name. The events of the last fifty years have done nothing to lessen its significance. To the Finns, it has the importance of a national anthem.

Then followed two years of extensive travel abroad. The European tour of the Helsinki Philharmonic Society under Kajanus, with Sibelius as supernumerary conductor, meant that he himself had the opportunity of meeting musicians throughout northern Europe and that his works, as represented by *Finlandia*, two Kalevala legends, and the *King Christian Suite*, received international hearing. Later he returned to Berlin, where he wrote the bulk of his *Second Symphony*.

From 1902–4 Sibelius was living in Helsinki, and from this period date some songs, and two compositions that have acquired different reputations, *Valse Triste* and the *Violin Concerto* (1903). But he found it increasingly difficult to work satisfactorily in the capital – there were too many distractions – and in 1904 he decided to build a house in the country at Järvenpää, some miles out of Helsinki. Here he has stayed ever since.

Visits Abroad

The year 1905 was important for Sibelius. His works were played in Berlin at Busoni's *Moderne Musik* series, in England under the direction of Granville Bantock, and in Milan by Toscanini. Finally he was able to make his first visit to England, in order to conduct his *Second Symphony* in Liverpool. During his stay he met a large number of musicians, including Sir Henry Wood, who was to do much for his music in this country.

The next few years were occupied by constant travel and composition. He visited England frequently, often staying with Granville Bantock or Rosa Newmarch. At home, however, he was beset by financial problems and worried by an infection of the throat that forced him to give up many of the pleasanter indulgences. It was a time of stress, but there is little sign of it in his *Third Symphony*, the *Belshazzar Suite*, and the tone poem *Pohjola's Daughter*, which all received their premières in September 1907. But it showed in his *String Quartet, Voces Intimae*, which he was composing in 1908 and 1909. All the doubts and uncertainties that assail an artist in the bleak middle years of his career can be felt in this composition, the first piece of chamber music he had written since his youth.

Meanwhile in America his music was having a great success, even if in Europe it still had many detractors. Undeterred he carried on, leading up to the work that was to cost him the most sublime labour, his *Fourth Symphony*. On its first appearance in April 1911 the audience was nonplussed. Its introspective and spiritual character, from which all emotion and sensuousness had been banished, was not one to be absorbed at first hearing. Next year it was received with hoots in Gothenburg, when Sibelius's influential Swedish champion, Wilhelm

Stenhammar, introduced it. In this country it was sympathetically received and neglected thereafter. Like so many of the greatest artistic creations, it demands that the listener should play an active, intelligent role rather than one of passive absorption. Rosa Newmarch quotes a saying of Delius of about this time. He was overheard to drawl after a Sibelius performance, 'Damn it, this is not conventional music'. It did not shock, as did some modern music; it had a more original and indefinable appeal.

Proof of Sibelius's European fame came in 1912, when he was offered a Professorship at the Vienna conservatoire. He declined the honour, which would have involved leaving Finland, but he listened instead to a proposal that he should pay a visit to the United States. Carl Stoeckel, his American host, required of Sibelius both his presence and a new work for the Norfolk Music Festival, an institution of the highest musical value. The composer arrived with *Oceanides* in his pocket, and returned to Finland in July 1914, stunned by the welcome, inspired by the performances, encouraged by the critics' praise, and decorated with an honorary D.Mus. of Yale University.

World War I

For the first three years of World War I, Finland was not directly affected by the struggle. But for Sibelius it brought trials of the body and the spirit. He was at first cut off from his publishers, Breitkopf and Härtel, until he made an arrangement with the powerful neutral publishing house of Wilhelm Hansen in Copenhagen. Financially he was in a weak position and was reduced to writing large numbers of small-scale light works, which were in effect pot-boilers. The difficulties of travelling, except through Scandinavia, were peculiarly irksome to one like Sibelius, who found stimulus in foreign lands. He felt cut off and forgotten. Nor was he unaware of the larger issues. The unrelenting slaughter was an appalling answer to his belief in the importance and strength of European civilization. But he refused to lose confidence in mankind. His words to Bengt von Törne are typical of his faith. 'Civilization is strength and not weakness. . . . Look at the great nations of Europe and what they have endured! No savage could have stood the things that they have gone through. It is civilization that has given them such moral strength and courage.' His musical challenge to the times is to be found in the *Fifth Symphony*, which received its première on his fiftieth birthday in 1915. The confidence and optimism of the great striding theme of the last movement proclaims his belief in the future. Even his decision to continue writing symphonies was not an easy one, for as a form it was losing favour in Europe. He could have stepped aside into easier, more popular paths, but he realized that what was best in him could only be expressed in symphonic form.

In January, 1917 Civil War, taking its cue from Russia, broke out in Finland. It was a bad time. For some months Sibelius continued to live at Järvenpää, in the power of Red Guards who neither knew of nor cared about his national and international importance. In considerable danger of his life, he attempted to carry on with his work. At last, his brother, Professor Christian Sibelius, Eero Järnefelt, his brother-in-law, and Robert Kajanus induced him to seek the comparative safety of Helsinki. On 12 April the crisis was over, and the German army entered the city, freeing southern Finland from the Bolsheviks.

Final Works

The end of the war led to a new burst of creative activity. Besides replanning his *Fifth Symphony*, he was at work on his *Sixth Symphony* and even sketching out a *Seventh Symphony*. At the same time he wrote two cantatas, piano pieces, and some short orchestral compositions. Foreign tours were resumed, with a visit to London in 1921, where he shared a concert with Busoni, and a tour of Norway and Sweden in 1923. That year he completed his *Sixth Symphony*, and in 1924 he finished his greatest and most mature work, *Fantasia Sinfonica*, now known as the *Seventh Symphony*.

The nation-wide celebrations on his sixtieth birthday, 8 December 1925, were on an even larger scale than those held in the discouraging days of 1915. Finland itself was now free and looking forward to years of prosperity. Honours were heaped on Finland's most distinguished citizen, and the President himself was present at the official celebrations. Abroad Sibelius's position was firmly established. Henceforth discouragement would spring only from his own high standards of self criticism. But the list of his published compositions was nearly complete. Only three more considerable works were to come to light. The first was the tone-poem *Tapiola*, which was commissioned by the New York Symphony Society and first conducted by Walter Damrosch in 1925. Astonishing as a study in orchestral technique its emotional effect is overwhelming. The first two lines of the introductory quatrain give us the clue.

> Wide-spread they stand, the Northland's dusky forests
> Ancient, mysterious, brooding, savage dreams.

The Song of Väino for chorus and orchestra was a last return to the *Kalevala*, while his incidental music to *The Tempest* was a commission from the Copenhagen Royal Theatre. A few short works followed, but with his Opus 116, three compositions for violin and piano, he called a halt. From 1929 until this day he has not published a note of music.

Retirement

Since then Sibelius has lived quietly in retirement at Järvenpäa. His seventieth, eightieth and ninetieth birthdays have been celebrated *maxima cum laude*, but otherwise he has made no stir abroad. He was pleased by the invitation of the Edinburgh Festival to be guest of honour in 1947, but such an expedition would have been out of the question. With increasing age he has been reluctant to have his privacy invaded, especially by the press. He has, however, always been ready to welcome musicians, particularly those from this country and America.

What has he composed since 1929 and why is it withheld from publication? The secrecy around the first question has led to a bundle of contradictory rumours, but there are many possible solutions to the second. With *Tapiola* and the *Seventh Symphony* he seems to have reached a climax of orchestral virtuosity and creative endeavour. They sum up his whole career. If, as appears likely, he has indeed written an eighth and even a ninth symphony, he may fear that they would be misunderstood. His experiences with music critics have not been happy at any time, and it is understandable that he should wish to avoid with a last work any imputation of anticlimax. In any event we do well to respect his privacy. Everyone must feel a natural curiosity, but Sibelius has given so much to the world already that no useful purpose is served by prying into his motives.

The Complete Man

In his youth, Sibelius was famous for his high spirits and his enthusiasm. Later portraits and sculptures show us a man of iron, bleak and forbidding, and have led to some misunderstanding. They show the reticence and aristocratic nobility of his mind, but they underplay the epicure, the witty philosopher, and the cosmopolitan lover of all that life has to offer. He represents the musician of all round intellectual interests; by conviction, and by the lonely path he has followed, he is an unashamed individualist. His training and his development have not enabled him to sympathize with many of the musical trends of recent years, and his comment on Arnold Bax is significant. 'Thank God he can write a melody, and is not ashamed to do so.' In the same way that he regards Mozart and Mendelssohn as the two greatest geniuses of the orchestra, his own predilections have become increasingly classical. In his music, as in his life, the workmanship is always assured, but he achieves greatness with the grander orchestral structures. As Constant Lambert rightly said, 'He is a citizen both of Finland and the world. His symphonies are not Finnish Symphonies but symphonies by a Finn'.

ALEXANDER NIKOLAEVICH SKRYABIN

1872–1915

MARTIN COOPER

A Difficult Problem

There is no composer more difficult to assess than Skryabin. Opinions of his music range from ecstatic enthusiasm, though that is rare now, to something very like contempt, as expressed by M. D. Calvocoressi in his *Survey of Russian Music*. The truth, as usual, lies somewhere between these two extremes. Skryabin's music is intensely subjective – that is to say, the listener's reaction to it will always depend to a large extent on other, not directly musical, traits of his own psychological make-up. Skryabin himself was fully aware of this and welcomed it as a sign that his creations were not 'just music', but something that seemed to him far deeper and more important. In telling the story of his life I shall try to be as objective as I can and to give as reasonable an account as possible for my judgements, favourable and unfavourable. No man can do more and many writers on Skryabin have done a great deal less.

Alexander Nikolaevich Skryabin was born in 1872 (25 December 1871, old style) in Moscow. On his father's side he came of a family of soldiers, though his father Nicholas studied Law and spent most of his life in the Russian consular service. His mother, Lyubov Petrovna Shchetinin, was a brilliant pianist, a pupil of Leschetizky and winner of the Gold Medal at the St Petersburg conservatoire. He was their only child; hardly a year after his birth his mother died of tuberculosis. His father entered a career that kept him for the rest of his life abroad, and the child was brought up at his grandmother's house in Moscow, where a maiden aunt acted as a second mother to him. He was extremely spoiled by the two women, and his father is not likely to have introduced any note of austerity in the child's life on his annual visits to Moscow from Constantinople, Erzerum, or wherever he held his successive posts.

At eleven he entered the Military Cadets' School and, though he showed not the slightest aptitude for soldiering, he remained a member of the Cadet Corps for the next nine years. He lived at the house of an uncle who was also a tutor at the Cadets' School and so avoided the rougher life and sterner discipline of a boarder. He was plainly and unquestionably talented from the beginning, not only as a pianist, but as an intensely imaginative and individual personality. His first pianoforte lessons were begun in 1883 with G. A. Conus of the Moscow conservatoire. A year later he left Conus for Zverev, and in 1886 he started his theoretical studies with Taneev, though he did not enter the conservatoire until January 1888. Taneev had succeeded Hubert as principal of the conservatoire in 1885, and under him Moscow developed more and more as the centre of the 'non-nationalist' school of Russian music. The central problem for Taneev, in the words of M. D. Calvocoressi, was 'to keep to Western usage in all its purity, and steer clear of everything that might smack of vernacular innovations and all innovations on unconventional lines'. He was a magnificent contrapuntist, a sincere and single-minded artist, and a great teacher. Skryabin was to develop along very different lines from his master, but he never forgot the debt he owed him in all matters of musical workmanship and technique.

Moscow Conservatoire and After

At the conservatoire Skryabin did not occupy any very outstanding position; but his contemporaries included both Rakhmaninov and Medtner and the standard was therefore high. The decisive influence in his development as a pianist was entrance into the pianoforte class of Safonov, who succeeded Taneev as principal in 1889, but he could not get on with Arensky, with whom he studied composition for a short time. When he left the conservatoire in 1891, Skryabin had already composed a considerable number of pianoforte works, some of the earliest dating back as far as 1885. His great enthusiasm in these early years was for Chopin, but, though the style is obviously strongly influenced by Chopin, the character of the most of his works is distinct and individual. The years from 1893 to 1897 were spent in concert tours, in holiday travels and in composition – three *Sonatas*, twelve *Études*, a *Concerto*, and no less than fifty-one *Preludes*, all for the pianoforte. In 1898 he accepted the post of professor of pianoforte at the Moscow conservatoire, and for the next six years he was rather unhappily engaged in his professorial duties, and composition was comparatively neglected.

He had married in 1897 a brilliant young pianist, Vera Ivanovna Isakovich, and in 1904 he set out with her on a long tour of Western Europe, which kept him out of Russia for the next five years. Oddly enough the only compositions that date from the years of his professorship at the conservatoire were orchestral – a *Rêverie* (Op. 28) and two *Symphonies* written between 1900 and 1902. Safonov was already an enthusiastic admirer of his work, and in Belyaev Skryabin had found a patron, a publisher, and a second father. There were already signs, however, that Skryabin's path was not to continue so completely free of obstacles, and a growing section of the Moscow public and critics adopted a hostile tone towards his music.

Travelling in Italy, France, Switzerland, and Belgium, supported by an allowance from Belyaev and another from a rich and admiring pupil, Skryabin could devote himself entirely to composition and to the elaboration of what in the last few years had become even more important to him than composition itself – namely, a religious synthesis in which the arts, and chief of them music, should play a wholly new and leading role. Up to the time of the composition of the third *Piano Sonata* (composed in Moscow during the year 1897) Skryabin had been content to be a musician, primarily a composer and secondarily a pianist, though his pianoforte playing was of the very highest order. During the years at the conservatoire his interest in non-musical subjects was aroused, and especially in the various forms of esoteric mysticism that had their vogue in the intellectual world of the day. Skryabin was never a thorough-going theosophist, it is true; but he found later in the writings of Blavatsky and in the conversation of theosophical adepts a form of inspiration that he had perhaps been unconsciously seeking since he was a boy.

Before his marriage his life had been stormy; he drank a great deal at one time and confessed later that as a young man he had found alcoholic and sexual excitement an almost necessary stimulus to musical creation. The characteristics that distinguish his early composition from those of Chopin, with whom the superficial resemblance is so striking, are just what this admission would lead one to expect – a certain atmosphere of tension and suppressed excitement alternating with moments of sensuous ecstasy, in which already sensation seems to predominate over emotion. In his first symphony Skryabin already attempted to express, in the final chorus, his gradually growing ideal of art as the principle of social, religious, and philosophical unity, and during his first year abroad his whole mystical point of view was developed and crystallized in the music of the *Third Symphony* (*Poème Divin*). Music was now definitely a Way of Knowledge or Illumination to Skryabin, and he lost all interest in its other aspects and eventually in all music but his own. As his greatest works were written after this change in his whole mentality, it is essential that some explanation should be given of these mystical beliefs.

Occultism

Skryabin's mysticism was not theocentric; indeed, it was hardly theistic. The first principle of the universe he spoke of as Creator, God, Death, or New Life indifferently; the fundamental idea was that of creative spirituality. Good and Evil he considered merely as two complementary exhibitions of energy and the two polarities were rather the principle of Activity and Passivity, the one creative and the other receptive, the one centripetal the other centrifugal, Male and Female. In the first process of creation those two poles were mystically united and they separate only in order to create the world and then unite again. This first phase of creation was called by Skryabin the 'creative agony' or the 'lust for life', and it was duly to be followed by the second, complementary phase – the process of dematerialization. 'This world glitters with the imprint of the Creator Spirit's beauty, but at the same time it moves further and further away from the Creator, diffusing itself in protean phenomena without number. ... The tortured universe awaits a miracle, awaits the last great Act of Fulfilment, the act of union between the male Creator-Spirit and the Woman-World.' This union could be prepared and eventually accomplished, he believed, by means of art, or rather a synthesis of all the arts, in the hands of a messiah; and he was convinced that he himself was that messiah. 'I am nothing: I am only that which I create. The fate of the universe is decided. I will to live. I love life. I am God. I am nothing. I wish to be everything. I have engendered that which is opposite to me – time, space, and number. I myself am that which is opposite to me, because I am only that which I engender. ... I will to be God. ... The world seeks after God, I seek after myself. The world is an impulse towards God, I am an impulse towards myself. I am the world, I am the search for God, because I am only that which I seek. ...'

Now nothing is easier than to make fun of such a system and the outpourings it occasions, to write off their author as mad and his theories as ordinary hallucinations. If we consider all the later works of Skryabin, though, written not simply at a time when he held these beliefs but under their direct inspiration, it is just not possible to accept so simple a solution. One of Skryabin's own closest friends, the critic Leonid Sabaneev, was a conscious 'positivist', who denied the objective truth of all mystical beliefs; yet even he was forced to confess that Skryabin's personality had some hidden power, his imagination was possessed by some overwhelming vision, which he was unable to express in words but could only translate directly into music. Clearly any art conceived as a means of religious initiation can have two aspects. As a rite of evocation its magic may be either black or white, cathartic and theurgic or ecstatic and satanistic, and Skryabin himself came to divide his works into those two categories, at least for a time. Since he was a performer as well as a composer, he came to look on the performance as well as the creation of a work as a rite, whose object is the attainment of a new degree of spiritual illumination, a deeper initiation into the life of the spirit. His ideas met with very little sympathy among musicians, but his close circle of friends, with whom he shared all his plans and his hopes for the future, included a number of poets – Vyacheslav-Ivanov, Baltrushaitis, and Balmont among them.

During the second year of their travels Skryabin's relations with his wife deteriorated. It seems fairly certain that she, a very capable pianist, had married what she thought was another musician and that, as Skryabin developed an ever deepening, and quite soon an almost exclusive, interest in his mystical beliefs, she found herself living with an entirely new person with whom she was largely out of sympathy. During 1905 they parted, and for the rest of his life Skryabin lived with Tatiana Feodorovna Schloezer, a sister of the critic Boris Feodorovich Schloezer and originally a pupil of Skryabin. They were unable to marry, as his first wife refused to grant him a divorce, and this caused much bitterness and unhappiness in a *ménage* that was in every other respect extremely happy.

The New Style

With the fifth *Pianoforte Sonata* and the *Poème de l'Extase* (both written between 1905 and 1907 in Switzerland and Paris) Skryabin achieved a new step forward in his purely musical development. His style was now wholly original, because it was the vehicle of a wholly original personality. The intellectual content of his faith was perhaps the least important, and the most ill-defined, thing about it. What was unquestionable and constant was the inspiration it represented to the composer. This esoteric spirituality, which took such fantastic forms on paper or in conversation, did inform and mould a genuinely 'new' music quite out of accord with the general tendency of the period. The opening years of the present century were overshadowed by the 'Wagner epigones', with their vast and magnificent technical accomplishments, their rich and luscious orchestration, and their fundamental spiritual poverty and unoriginality. Into this world Skryabin introduced an entirely different element, half sensuous and half spiritual – an element of magic and the supernatural. Each of his works was conceived as a solemn religious rite culminating in a dance of spiritual intoxication for which the very music of the spheres would hardly be too ethereal or too magnificent. His intimate friend Sabaneev was convinced that the psychological basis of Skryabin's whole character, of his music and of his mysticism, was a profound and all-pervading eroticism. In his life the erotic element was canalized, and after he had settled down with Tatiana Fedorovna Schloezer there seemed to have been no further emotional disturbances. Perhaps for this very reason his music becomes more and more sensuous and the movements that in earlier works were marked *caresse ailée*, *accarezzevole*, *con delizia*, *molto languido*, *con una ebbrezza fantastica* gradually extend their specific erotic colouring over whole works. The words that recur most frequently in his own discussions of his works reveal the set of Skryabin's mentality – fire, light, soaring, vertiginous, caressing, imperious, intoxicated, venomous, lightning-like – and Sabaneev's description of his playing completes the picture. He played 'as though he were all the time caressing some imaginary substance, which came to life under his caresses, assuming different forms with Protean variability'. He was frankly contemptuous of his own earlier lyrical compositions, and his search was never for new emotions, but for new *sensations*, not for their own sake, like a mere sensationalist, but for their richer initiative power, their further revelation of spirituality.

The death of Belyaev in 1903 left Skryabin without an editor and severely complicated his financial position. After various abortive attempts to recoup himself he finally embarked on an American tour in November 1906. Safonov was in America and conducted his orchestral works, but he was a strong partisan of Skryabin's wife and, when Tatiana Feodorovna joined Skryabin in January 1907, their relationship nearly caused a public scandal. Engagements were cancelled, contracts broken, and they left America with hardly enough money for their journey, arriving in Paris with thirty francs between them. They were finally rescued by Kussevitsky, who had just founded the new Russian Music Edition in Berlin and now offered Skryabin an allowance of 5,000 roubles a year in return for the exclusive rights of publishing all his works. This offer was gratefully accepted, and the last half of 1907 and the whole of 1908 were spent abroad, partly in Switzerland, but latterly settled in Brussels. Finally, in January 1909, after an absence of nearly five years, Skryabin returned to Moscow, making his home there for the rest of his life.

The 'Mystery'

He was just thirty-seven and at the height of his fame. No one could have guessed that he had only six more years to live and the knowledge would have shattered all his fondest hopes and revolutionized his whole conception of his mission. All his forces were now bent on the preparation of 'the Mystery', the final Act of Fulfilment that he believed was to herald the end of the world, the consummation of all human history in which 'mankind was to achieve divinity and the godhead humanity'. He was not alone in his apocalyptic beliefs. Alexander Blok was writing in much the same vein as Skryabin in the first poem of his volume *Yambi*

> Oh! I would live madly!
> Eternalize all that exists,
> Humanize the impersonal,
> Embody the failing and weak!

Although the majority, perhaps, of the official musical world was hostile or suspicious in its attitude towards Skryabin and his music, he was the centre of an adoring circle of friends, enthusiastic admirers of his music, some of them sympathetic with his mysticism.

His public appearances in performances of his own works were the occasions of wild enthusiasm on the part of the public, and a tour of the Volga towns, organized by Kussevitsky in the spring of 1910, resembled a triumphal procession rather than a series of concerts. In March 1911 Kussevitsky gave the first performance of what was actually to be Skryabin's last orchestral composition, *Prometheus* or *The Poem of Fire*. It was in this work that Skryabin first made systematic use of a 'new' chord, a 'Promethean' harmony, which was to dominate, in slightly varying forms, all his last works (from Op. 60 to Op. 74). On his own account he seems to have arrived by empirical methods at this rather arbitrary structure of superimposed fourths, but he was delighted when he discovered that it could be related scientifically to the use of the upper partials of the ordinary harmonic series, hitherto not employed in the conventional or classical harmonic idiom. Much contempt has been poured on Skryabin's would-be innovations, and those who are out of sympathy with his music in general have emphasized the fundamentally artificial and sterile nature of his harmonic experiments. Here again, theory is a poor guide. Skryabin's 'promethean harmony' is a dead end, in the sense that he soon exploited all its possibilities, just as Debussy exploited all the possibilities of the whole-tone scale; neither represents a genuine revolution in harmonic practice. Skryabin was not, however, concerned with musical revolutions but with the ushering in of a new era of world history, with the end of this world as we know it, the world of Matter and Multiplicity, and the creation of a new world of Spirit and Unity. His harmonic experiments were merely means to that end and if they enabled him, as they did, to create a new atmosphere in his music, that was sufficient justification in his eyes.

After *Prometheus*, every composition of Skryabin was a conscious preparation for 'the Mystery' and in the last five pianoforte sonatas (Ops. 62, 64, 66, 68 and 70) and the last eight pianoforte pieces (*Vers la Flamme, Guirlandes, Flammes Sombres*, and the five *Preludes*) we have the nearest approximation to the music that he conceived to be the culmination not only of his own development as a composer, but of the whole history of music. The synthesis of the arts that was to be the vehicle of the Mystery puzzled Skryabin. Already in *Prometheus* he had experimented with a light-keyboard, which was to provide a symphony of colour simultaneous with the symphony of sound; but that was not enough. He wanted movements, scents, even sensations of touch, not merely to accompany his music, but to be used, in his own words, 'contrapuntally', so that a phrase beginning as music appealing to the ear might end as a colour or scent appealing to the eye or nose. As time went on and the complexities of their problem became clearer to Skryabin, he did not give up hope, but he planned and started work on a *Preliminary Act*, which was designed as an introduction to the Mystery itself. He took great trouble to master, as he hoped, the technique of poetry in order to write the text, and each of the last pianoforte sonatas is a kind of approximation to the music of the *Preliminary Act*, which he was already meditating, though none of it was committed to paper.

England and the End

Soon after the performance of *Prometheus* Skryabin quarrelled with Kussevitsky, who had certainly become rather possessive and domineering – and, Skryabin maintained, mean – in his attitude towards one whom he seemed to consider his protégé. This rupture once again complicated Skryabin's financial situation, but he was by now so famous, both in Russia and abroad, that he was able to make a considerable amount of money from his compositions and concerts. Henry Wood was interested in his orchestral works and *Prometheus* was given during the 1912–13 season in London with considerable success. England interested Skryabin particularly for several reasons. In the first place London was the centre of the theosophical movement, and some, at least, of the success of his works in England he attributed to theosophical sympathy and interest. England also was the key to India, and a journey to India was one of the dearest of Skryabin's wishes. The Mystery, he believed, was to take place in an Indian temple, and he had even gone so far as to make enquiries about the conditions of buying land and building the necessary shrine. Finally, England was the foremost representative in the modern world of that hierarchical structure of society in which he saw the only hope of the world's future. Russia and England, he believed, could and should dominate the whole world between them, and he was a passionate advocate of every kind of cultural and political bond between the two countries. In February 1914 he visited London and *Prometheus* was given in his presence. He did not achieve an interview with Annie Besant, as he had hoped, but was pathetically pleased to have been received by her secretary.

The outbreak of the war was hailed by Skryabin as the beginning of the cycle of cataclysms that was to herald the end of the present world order and to culminate in the performance of the Mystery. He never lost faith in his own messiahship, but in these last years he began to believe that he was perhaps one of several messiahs whose task it was to prepare humanity for the great consummation. At the beginning of April 1915 he returned to Moscow from St Petersburg, where he had been giving a concert and, feeling ill, took to his bed a few days later. A carbuncle appeared on his upper lip, as once before while he was in London. But this time the infection soon spread to his whole face, succeeded by general blood-poisoning and finally pleurisy. On 14 April he was dead. No note of his music for the *Preliminary Act* was written, the Mystery had not even been touched, the messiah was gone – the whole fantastic structure of Skryabin's imagination collapsed like a house of cards. No sooner was he dead than his music began to suffer an eclipse. Enthusiasts, who had been won by his personality and the indefinable quality of genius that all who knew him admitted, lost interest when his personality was no longer there to inspire them. The majority of critics and historians now write contemptuously of his music, let alone of the man; seldom has a great reputation broken down so suddenly and apparently so finally. And yet – the last word has not perhaps been spoken on Skryabin. His influence has been great from the purely pianistic point of view, for he carried the nineteenth-century pianoforte technique, which originated with Chopin, to its utmost conclusion and beyond. The quality of his music is unmistakable, and its power, nervous to the verge of hysteria and a strange blend of eroticism and spiritual imagination, is yet undeniable. His music can never be negligible; the passionate hostility it arouses is a witness to that. But those of us who never knew Skryabin, never heard him play his own music or felt the apparently irresistible fascination of his musical imagination, will probably never appreciate his music at its full worth. His whole existence and the whole corpus of his composition provide a permanent witness to the power of the ideal and the supernatural in human life – however misinterpreted and oddly expressed. In a prosaic and materialistic age he shone like a flame of spirituality, and though such fires may sink so low that they may seem extinguished quite, they never wholly die.

RICHARD GEORG STRAUSS

1864–1949

COLIN MASON

Strauss, the Prodigy

We are apt to consider Richard Strauss a modern composer. Yet he was born a year earlier than Glazunov and made his mark equally young. He was ever a prodigy, and like most prodigies he ran through an entire career in a few years, soon to fall victim to a premature part-oblivion. He was certainly an infant and juvenile prodigy and even more certainly an adolescent one; at twenty his name was known, if not famous, through the world. At thirty he was world famous and at forty almost the leading spirit in the whole of European and American music. At fifty he had passed the climax of his fame, and after the first world war, in spite of the respect he received for many of his qualities as an artist, his reputation gradually declined and his fame became somewhat obscured under the weight of later developments. An additional contributory cause of this obscurity was his residence in Germany after the accession of Hitler to power in 1933. Results or news of his activities hardly crept abroad during those twelve years. But suddenly, after the war, there was a resurgence of interest in him, a burst of activity from him, and during the last five years of his life he enjoyed another phase of world popularity and attention.

Musical Background

Richard Strauss was lucky enough to pick the right parents. His father, Franz Strauss, was a horn player of the Munich Court Orchestra, a fine musician and one of the most famous exponents of horn playing in his day. His mother was a wealthy brewer's daughter. Thus the household lacked neither the material comforts nor the congenial musical atmosphere to make life agreeable and quick progress easy. At the age of four Richard had begun to learn the piano from his mother and to take regular lessons from the harpist of the Court

Orchestra. At six he wrote a little *Schneiderpolka* for piano and also a Christmas song. He then went to an elementary school at Munich for general education, continuing his piano lessons and taking the violin under Benno Walter, leader of the Court Orchestra. In 1874 he entered the Gymnasium for eight years, still mixing a severe musical training with his ordinary school subjects. Soon after entering the Gymnasium he began to study harmony, counterpoint, and orchestration with F. W. Meyer, the Court music director, and in 1880 he embarked on a public career as a composer when Frau Meysenheim, one of the singers at the Opera, gave three of his songs their first public performance. Before he was seventeen, the quartet of which his violin master was leader had played in public his *String Quartet* in A, and Hermann Levi had conducted his *First Symphony* in D minor.

The Young Traditionalist

Strauss's education until this time had been entirely classical. Franz Strauss's sympathies were not extended to the modern music of Wagner and Liszt, and he took care that his son should be sheltered from their horrid din. It is therefore natural that in these early compositions there is no hint of the style of the later Strauss; nor was there to be for some years yet. In 1882 he went from the Gymnasium to the University of Munich to attend a year's lectures on philosophy and aesthetics. During this period he composed numerous large-scale classical instrumental works, including two *Sonatas* and two *Concertos*, nearly all of which were immediately performed in Munich.

For fresh conquests Strauss decided to visit Berlin in the following winter (1883–4). His success was considerable, and several of his works were performed there. He also completed another *Symphony*, in F minor, during his stay in Berlin, which carried his name across the Atlantic to New York. There Theodore Thomas gave the *Symphony* its world première in December 1884. Thus at twenty Strauss was known as a composer in two continents (though only three cities) by adolescent works now long forgotten.

These successes, however, were of less importance to Strauss's career than Hans von Bülow's interest in him at Berlin. Von Bülow first played Strauss's *Serenade*, Op. 7, with the Meiningen Orchestra, then invited Strauss early in 1885 to conduct a work himself with the Meiningen Orchestra at Munich. The results must have impressed him, for in the same autumn Strauss was appointed von Bülow's assistant at Meiningen. During these years he had passed from Mozart and Beethoven to Mendelssohn, Schumann, and Brahms, whose influence became apparent in his works at that period. At Meiningen he added to his stock Berlioz, Liszt, and Wagner, who, at least temporarily, superseded rather than supplemented all former influences on him. The man who is said by Strauss to have effected his change of outlook from classical to romantic was Alexander Ritter, a contemporary of von Bülow and a champion of Liszt and Wagner. That such a comparatively unknown person as Ritter could have had this influence on Strauss, and von Bülow apparently none, has been doubted by some biographers, but it should be remembered that after a month of initiating Strauss into the art of conducting von Bülow left Meiningen for Strauss to succeed him as chief music director. Whoever was responsible, from 1885 Strauss began to assume the mantle of Wagner and Liszt, as he would doubtless have done, though perhaps a few years later, even without the acquaintance of either Ritter or von Bülow.

The Revolutionary Awakes

He did not retain his position at Meiningen long. In April 1886 he relinquished it to make a trip to Italy, which inspired him to write his first work in his new style, the symphonic fantasia *Aus Italien*, really his transitional work from the classical to the expressionist manner. On returning to Germany he took up a new appointment, as third *Kapellmeister* of the Munich opera. In this capacity he gave the first performance of *Aus Italien* in Munich the next year, and in the three years of his stay there emerged as the Strauss we know, with the three works by two of which he is still most often represented in the English concert hall, the symphonic poems *Macbeth*, *Don Juan*, and *Tod und Verklärung*.

Around these works arose great controversies, and in the general clamour of approval on the one hand, and of abuse on the other, Richard Strauss the first was trampled underfoot in order that Richard Strauss the second might succeed to his dominions and conquer many others. Meanwhile in 1889, his appointment at Munich being at an end, the composer took up another, this time for five years, as assistant *Kapellmeister* at Weimar. It did not fall to his lot there to conduct the most important works, and his activities were anyhow interrupted by a long illness apparently caused through overwork. In the spring of 1892 he contracted an inflammation of the lungs, which necessitated a holiday and convalescence trip to Egypt and Sicily, occupying over a year in all. Fortunately Strauss was not too ill to compose, and managed during the year to write his first music drama, in Wagnerian style, *Guntram*. He wrote his own libretto, considering at that time that Wagner's procedure of writing his own drama, libretto, and music was now the only possible one for intelligent operatic composition. The music-drama was begun at Cairo in December 1892 and completed at Strauss's country home at Marquardtstein in September 1893. On his return to Weimar for the following season, it was put into production and given its first performance under the composer's direction at Weimar on 12 May 1894. The success was only moderate, possibly because of the Wagnerian tendencies of both music and drama. Its immediate effect upon Strauss was to put him rather at a loss and to discourage him from operatic composition for another six years.

A Premier Conductor

Later that summer came an invitation that marked the beginning of a career for Strauss as one of the world's leading conductors, when Frau Wagner asked him to direct the first Bayreuth performance of *Tannhäuser*. The singer who played Elizabeth in this, and had already sung Freihild in his own *Guntram*, was Pauline de Ahna, whom Strauss married later that year, on 10 September.

Autumn 1894 brought another change of appointment. Strauss returned once more to Munich, no longer as third *Kapellmeister* but now as first. His duties must have devolved largely upon his assistants, for in the next few years he covered nearly the whole of Europe as a composer and conductor. First in 1894–5 he was asked to conduct the Berlin Philharmonic Concerts after von Bülow's death. Then each year until 1898 he visited Hungary, Italy, Spain, Russia, Belgium, Holland, Switzerland, France, and England (1897), besides many large towns in Germany and Austria. His energy was incredible, for despite all this rushing about the world, he found time to compose *Till Eulenspiegel* and *Also Sprach Zarathustra* (both 1894 to 1895), some forty songs, *Don Quixote* (1897), and *Ein Heldenleben* (1898), all of which received early performances.

This frantic period came to an end in 1898, when Strauss was appointed conductor of the Berlin Royal Opera House in succession to Weingartner. He then settled down for a year or two to the composition of his second opera, the one-act *Feuersnot*. In this he gave vent to some of his bitterness at his comparative lack of recognition in Munich, his native town, where Wagner too had made little headway before him. Strauss obviously now regarded himself as Richard the Second, spiritually and musically the direct descendant of Wagner, and found it not beneath his dignity to let it be known. *Feuersnot* was first produced at Dresden in November 1907 without attracting as much attention as his instrumental works.

English Associations

Strauss was then thirty-seven and probably the most discussed composer in Europe, or even in the world. His own constant touring had never ceased – sometimes he preceded, sometimes followed his fame, but he was always travelling. From 1902 began his closer association with England, when at a Düsseldorf festival he proposed a toast to Elgar, 'the first English progressivist', a comment that did not please all Englishmen. Later the same year he came to England to give some of his own works, including *Enoch Arden*, the *Violin Sonata*, and several of the symphonic poems. But it was in the next year, 1903, that Strauss first became generally accepted in England, when he came with Mengelberg in June to conduct the Amsterdam Orchestra in a Strauss festival. Many of his important orchestral works were performed, some for the first time in England.

In 1904 Strauss visited America, taking with him the brand new *Domestic Symphony*, which he had been composing the previous year. This he presented to America, conducting the first world performance in New York on 21 March 1904. Like nearly every work of his in the previous ten years, the *Domestic Symphony* raised a great noise in the world wherever it was performed. But the outcry and controversy that had so far arisen round his work paled into insignificance before that caused by his third opera, *Salomé*. The opera was first performed, like *Feuersnot*, at Dresden, in December 1905. The production left the musical conservatives horrified, the moral prudes scandalized, the religious even more so; but *Salomé* has held the stage in Germany and with some alteration even crept into England and America.

Meeting with Hofmannsthal

Here at forty Strauss was at the height of his fame, the world's foremost composer. In his everyday life he was now settling into something of a routine, interrupted only by travel abroad, and that less frequently than before. In the summer he worked at his country house, in winter he came to Berlin to conduct the Opera. His life became comparatively uneventful except for the productions of his operas as they appeared, and these no longer aroused the clamour throughout the world that his third one had done.

In 1907 Strauss became interested in Hugo von Hofmannsthal, ten years his junior, but already regarded as one of Austria's great dramatic poets. Strauss first decided to set Hofmannsthal's Sophoclean tragedy *Elektra*, and thereafter ensued a collaboration as productive as that between Mozart and da Ponte. Their beneficial effects upon each other were undoubtedly great. From it Hofmannsthal gained a wide reputation beyond Germany that, if it was not entirely what he deserved, was probably more than he would otherwise have achieved yet. Strauss too benefited from the contact with a brilliant dramatist possessing a very keen musical sense, whose influence was undoubtedly part of the cause of Strauss's change of operatic style after *Elektra*.

By this time academic honours and appointments were no longer of any material importance to Strauss, but in 1908 he accepted the post of General Music Director at Berlin. In 1910 he relinquished his conductorship of the Berlin Opera and in that year also was elected to the Akademie der Künste. The chief event of 1909 was the production of *Elektra* at Dresden on 25 January.

The collaboration with Hofmannsthal was constant. They first made together some considerable attempts at *Semiramis*, but soon abandoned it to take up *Der Rosenkavalier*, in which signs of Strauss's love of Mozart began to show themselves. He had always retained a fervent admiration for Mozart's art, though his own was as unlike it as could be; his advice to students who came to show him their new symphonic poems was always to study the classics. But his respect for Mozart's ideals and love of his music had not previously been reflected in his own work. Now, however, having explored what seemed to be the whole range of musical expressionism and realism, he began to return to classical artificiality.

Strauss completed *Der Rosenkavalier* on 26 September 1919 at his new country house at Garmisch, and it was first produced, at Dresden once more, in January 1911. In the meantime he had made yet another trip to London to conduct *Elektra*, which had entered England on the heels of *Salomé*, once she had broken down the barriers of English morality. From this time Strauss devoted himself almost exclusively to the composition of stage works. He and Hofmannsthal decided to write a pocket opera *Ariadne auf Naxos*, to be combined with Molière's *Le Bourgeois Gentilhomme*. Its first production took place in a festival of Strauss's works at Stuttgart, to celebrate the opening of the new Hoftheater. Subsequently Strauss realized that his design was too extravagant to secure many productions, and he made two more versions, of which the second is the definitive one. In this, Molière's drama is condensed and paraphrased into a fully Hofmannsthalian prelude, and *Ariadne auf Naxos* becomes a complete independent opera.

Past the Climax of Fame

The only other important work Strauss completed before World War I was his first attempt at ballet, the *Josephslegende*, composed for Diaghilev and produced in Paris and London under the composer's direction shortly before the outbreak of war. From that time Strauss's fame began to decline; for political and social rather than musical reasons he fell into comparative obscurity during the war, and when it ended he had to some degree been forgotten in the world outside Germany. His production between 1914 and 1919 consisted mainly of the *Alpine Symphony* and *Die Frau ohne Schatten*, another Hofmannsthal opera; one tragedy of the war led to another work, the *Parergon zur Symphonia Domestica*, which was written for piano (left hand alone) and orchestra, for the repertoire of Paul Wittgenstein, a talented pianist who had lost his right arm on active service.

During the war Strauss was created director of composition at the Royal High School for Music, but in 1919 he resigned his Berlin appointments to go to Vienna, where he had been invited to take up a post as co-director of the Vienna State Opera. Here he lived, when he was not busy travelling, in a mansion built on land presented to him by the State as a token of regard for his services to art. His new opera received its first performance there a year after the war.

Much of his time in the first post-war years was spent in travelling again, after the enforced confinement to his own country. He visited America in 1922 and England in 1923, but also managed to compose a ballet pantomime, *Schlagobers*, and an opera, *Intermezzo*. His association with Hofmannsthal had temporarily ceased, so the text of *Intermezzo* was his own. Both these works were produced in 1924, the ballet at Vienna, the opera at Dresden.

Quieter Years

Having reached the age of sixty, Strauss gave up his Vienna post in that year and virtually retired from active musical life, devoting himself and his decreasing energies more to composition. A man so used to a mobile life in three continents could not, however, give this up at one stroke, and almost until the outbreak of World War II, when he was seventy-five, he continued to make periodical trips abroad.

In 1926 he renewed his collaboration with Hofmannsthal in another opera, *Die Aegyptische Helena*, and later still in *Arabella* (not completed until after the poet's death). Both these were first produced in Dresden, now once more the normal city of Strauss opera christenings, in 1928 and 1933 respectively. The latter year marked the accession to power of Hitler and Strauss's return to Berlin as a result of his election as President of the Reichs Musikkammer. By his eminence he was spared any unpleasant attentions from the Nazi purifiers, though he fell into general disfavour when at Dresden in 1935 he produced *Die Schweigsame Frau*, an opera to a libretto by the Jewish Stefan Zweig, who had already been forced to flee from Germany. In June, the month of its première, he relinquished his official position and retired almost permanently to Bavaria.

Work with Zweig was of course impossible now, so a suitable librettist was found for Strauss in the officially approved Dr Joseph Gregor, who was responsible for the texts of Strauss's next three operas, work on which carried him to 1939. A further period of obscurity inevitably followed when war broke out, and he was virtually captive in his own country. But he was far from inactive, and from the war years date the last operas, *Die Liebe der Danae*, which was to have been produced in 1944 but was cancelled owing to the attempt to assassinate Hitler, and *Capriccio*, first produced in Vienna. Besides these there were *Concertos* for oboe and horn, a *Serenade* for various solo instruments, and *Metamorphosen*, an abstract symphonic poem for twenty-three solo strings, written for the Collegium Musicum, Zurich. None of these works shows the slightest sign of any falling off in creative power or mastery, and they have a rare serenity that few composers achieve.

Last Years

Conditions could hardly have been encouraging for work, and no better proof than these compositions is required of Strauss's mental vigour and flexibility in old age. At eighty he was as active and alert as a man of sixty and keen as ever in his constant search for new things to say. He passed his last years in conditions as reasonable as his country could afford at the time, and his eminence was too great for disfavour to be carried far. Vienna made an effort to pay him due tribute with a festival on his eightieth birthday, and after the war he even took up travelling again, coming to London in autumn 1947 for the Strauss Festival. In 1949 his eighty-fifth birthday was widely celebrated, but shortly afterwards he began to experience severe heart attacks, and, after about two weeks' illness, he died at his house in Garmisch on 8 September 1949.

IGOR STRAVINSKY

B. 1882

W. R. ANDERSON

A World-Shaker

For a long time little was printed about the early career of the most discussed, most exciting composer of our time. With the *Chronicle of My Life* (Gollancz, 1936) we have his own story: not a complete biography, he says, but a budget of major and minor facts. To this anyone who writes about Stravinsky naturally turns with gratitude and cordial acknowledgement of his main source of information. So few composers ever write on unruled paper. This one comes near, in his *Life* and his art, to an objective standpoint; perhaps that is ideal for autobiography, but what about creative art? This composer's has largely by-passed the old kinds of emotion. Some would propose psychological (even psychiatric) investigation of so extreme a modernist; but his actual life, though passed amid many artistic storms, on the whole appears to have been, inwardly, reasonably happy. He has enjoyed to a rare degree that pleasure of the artist's (often overlooked by laymen) – positing and solving new problems. Few men have crowded into a few years more stirring novelty or have exercised greater influence on their day and generation.

His Background

Igor Stravinsky was born at Oranienbaum, near St Petersburg, on 5 June (old style, 18 June) 1882. His father, a fine dramatic singer, was the chief bass in the capital's Imperial Opera. In the winter they lived in the city, and during the summer young Igor, in the country, heard folk-music, one of his keenest pleasures then and a striking influence in much of his writing, perhaps most happily crystallized and creatively coloured in *Les Noces*.

It was not until he was nine that he had serious piano lessons. He was fond of improvising and has always enjoyed that exercise: the 'direct contact with the physical medium of sound' has been more inspiring than an attempt merely to imagine music in the mind, without any mechanism. This need for objectivity is often emphasized.

By reading his father's opera scores he gained great facility; on his first visit to the opera he heard Glinka's *Life for the Czar*, a vivid work that remained delightful to him. The influence of Glinka is felt in some of Stravinsky's best work. When he went to hear his father sing in Glinka's second opera, *Russlan*, he had the thrill of seeing Tchaikovsky, for the first and only time in his life. This was but a few days before the older composer's death.

Stravinsky retained great respect and affection for Tchaikovsky's music and took the trouble many years later (in 1921) to write a letter, meant for the press, to Diaghilev, when the *Sleeping Beauty* ballet was in preparation. He wrote of 'our great and beloved Tchaikovsky' and of the happy memories then recalled of his life in St Petersburg, praising the older man's simplicity and spontaneity, his power of melody, to be able to create which, said Stravinsky, is a rare and precious gift. He referred also to Glinka's possessing it and took the opportunity to get in a hit at German music.

He felt the 'profoundly Russian' appeal of Tchaikovsky's art, which 'drew unconsciously from the true, popular sources of our race'. He noted also that Tchaikovsky worshipped Mozart, Couperin, Glinka, Bizet, which left 'no doubt of the quality of his taste'.

It is not surprising that surely, amid many strange devices and revolutionary harmonies, Russian folk-music fermented in Stravinsky during at any rate the first part of his career. When he became Parisian, cosmopolitan, many found a change, but in early years he was a thorough Russian of his time. Not yet, however, was he to find himself in art. He was happy in neither school nor friendships. Probably there was in him, besides a temperamental loneliness, something of national melancholy.

As may be found with Glinka and other Russians, there was often a genial uncle of the land-owning or professional class, more or less 'liberal' in opinion, who had artistic tastes. Stravinsky's uncle was of the free-thinking type, to whose nationalistic enthusiasms (often, in those days, directed against the government) the simple peasant arts were congenial; yet there was not lacking in Stravinsky's circle a liking for symphonic music, whether of Tchaikovsky or Brahms. The German influence was still strong.

A Fresh Field Needed

Young Stravinsky, then, had a sound upbringing in concert-going, falling under the spell of the composers, such as Rimsky-Korsakov and Glazunov, who had developed from the older pioneers. He was to become a pupil of the latter, but before that he explored contemporary French music, which widened his ideas. Debussy and Chabrier appealed most to him. But his parents thought of the law as a safer career than art; yet they went so far as to let him study harmony, as well as the piano. In this new work he found little joy: he had no taste for the labour of absorbing others' rules. He puts down much of his aversion to a weak memory, and laziness, but it was probably an instinctive attempt to avoid methods that, for his spirit, would have been weakening. Stravinsky needed a clear fresh field for what he had to do.

Harmony on established grounds bored him, but, like all creators, he enjoyed discovery, and solving personal problems, which he wanted to set himself. He found, however, some piquant pleasure in counterpoint, that weaving of melodies and rhythms in which he was to produce such a work as *The Rite of Spring*. Yet in any wide sense Stravinsky is not a great contrapuntist. His study of this aspect of music was entered relatively late – at eighteen. At the University he had met Rimsky-Korsakov's son, and during a summer holiday in Germany in 1902 he consulted his friend's father about his music. There was, however, the study of law, which must for the present continue; and at twenty he was old for entering conservatoire life. Rimsky-Korsakov, a professor at this institution, advised Stravinsky to work hard at fundamentals and come to him again later.

At Loose Ends

This was easier said than done. Stravinsky did not see where to find the right teachers. The capital was full of all manner of artistic and literary societies, some of them reactionary, some advanced. The young man had the good sense to realize his need of discipline, while yet he could not accept the prevailing aesthetics of the more academic school. He was never of the type that takes up any other person's creative habit or track: as he says, discipline is vital for the student, 'but only as a means of obtaining freedom, and strengthening himself in his own method of expression'.

In 1903 he had a few weeks with Rimsky-Korsakov, orchestrating some pages of the piano score of the master's work, which they would then together compare with the master's own scoring: Stravinsky's task was to think out why the other had scored as he did. It was a capital means of education and proved congenial. Resuming in the autumn, Stravinsky stayed about three years with his master, orchestrating the classics and later composing a *Symphony*, which was largely influenced by Glazunov's style.

In 1905 he could leave the University, his law course ended. This same year he became engaged, and he was married in 1906, still continuing his pupilage with Rimsky-Korsakov and writing a little music, including a suite, *Faune et Bergère*, for which his friend's influence procured a performance by the Court orchestra.

Launched

He now sailed off on creative seas, with his *Scherzo Fantastique* and the opera *The Nightingale*, based on the Hans Andersen story of the bird that sang to the emperor and finally conquered death by its song. Some years passed before the work was finished, and the composer later re-modelled part of the music as a symphonic poem, which was afterwards used by Diaghilev as the basis of a ballet for which Matisse designed scenery and costumes.

Some songs were also written whilst he worked with Rimsky-Korsakov, a happy connexion severed in 1908 by the latter's death. Stravinsky had sent him *Fireworks*, but it arrived only when the master was dead. In his honour Stravinsky wrote a *Funeral Song*, which was played at a commemorative concert.

It was then that Stravinsky fell in with Diaghilev, with whom he was to be associated for the rest of the somewhat stormy life of that great entrepreneur. Stravinsky began by orchestrating part of the Chopin music used for *Les Sylphides*, but his first great success came when he was invited to compose music for *The Firebird* for the Russian season of 1910 in Paris. The stimulus of being associated with artists like Fokine, Pavlova, Nijinsky, Karsavina, and of seeing works such as the *Prince Igor* ballet, set Stravinsky's energy afire, and he began the aspect of his career that many will always consider the finest. With Golovin's 'magnificent setting' and the splendid conducting of Pierné, *The Firebird* was a landmark. Then came *Petroushka* (1911), which Stravinsky first thought of as a piece for piano and orchestra, the piano to be a wilful puppet who fights the orchestra and loses. Before long the idea turned to its perfect means of expression in ballet: the tragedy of the dolls, of Petroushka and his soul-less wiles, 'the immortal and unhappy hero of every fair in all countries'. Perhaps there is a bit of Petroushka in Stravinsky.

At various places – Clarens, Beaulieu, St Petersburg, Monte Carlo, Rome – the work was shaped, with a gap during an illness caused by nicotine poisoning. Rome gave him some special pleasures of antiquity and art, before *Petroushka* was produced, under Monteux, in Paris, with Nijinsky as the puppet-hero.

The Appeal of Paganism

While he was finishing the earlier *Firebird* he had an idea for *The Rite of Spring* (*Le Sacre du Printemps*) – an unexpected vision of a pagan ceremony, in which a maiden danced to death to propitiate the Spring god. A painter friend, Roerich, joined Stravinsky in developing the idea. At the family estate at Oustiloug he went to work, spending some time also at Clarens, which he found a kindly place for creation. At this time he heard more Debussy and Ravel (finding in the former always a good, understanding friend) and, at Bayreuth, *Parsifal*. 'Art as religion and the theatre as a temple' had no attraction for Stravinsky. Wagner passed over his head – or under his feet.

He tells of his struggles to teach Nijinsky the rudiments of musical notation. Herein Stravinsky seems to have had unexpected patience, travelling to the various places in which the ballet company was appearing and putting up with Nijinsky's overweening ways.

While working on *Le Sacre* he collaborated with Ravel, to a small degree, in making some additions to, and partial orchestration of, Musorgsky's *Khovantchina*, which had been left unfinished at the composer's death.

After 120 rehearsals *Le Sacre* was produced in 1913. There was noisy opposition, which the composer did not stay to hear. Devotees and denigrators made open war, whilst the ballet went on unheard (says Carl van Vechten) 'except occasionally, when a slight lull occurred. The figures on the stage danced in time to music that they had to imagine they heard.' A young man behind him was so stirred that he stood up and began to beat rhythmically on van Vechten's head with his fists.

Half a dozen performances exhausted Parisian patience. In London applause outmatched hissing, and in Paris, the year after, the work, in concert performance, had solid success.

Stravinsky put down some of the ill-luck to Nijinsky's incomprehension. Physical distress followed, in typhoid fever, during which his French composer friends were very kind. Back home at Oustiloug, Stravinsky felt unfit for large-scale work and wrote a few small pieces, songs, and the like, until a new Moscow theatre asked for *The Nightingale*. But the enterprise failed, and Diaghilev took up the opera.

Wartime Divagations

When World War I began, Stravinsky was exempted from military service and lived in Switzerland, writing *Les Noces*, that powerful picture of a Russian wedding, with some other choral and solo music. He had made friends with Ernest Ansermet, since widely known as one of the finest interpreters of Stravinsky's music, and with others in an artistic circle, including Ramuz, the Cingria and the Mora brothers, Chavennes, and others.

Sending his mother back to Russia, he made various foreign journeys, having difficulty in maintaining a wife and four children, largely because he could not obtain from Russia money due to him there. He had hard work to keep warm in winter. There was a hope of visiting America, but that, for the time, faded.

A visit to Spain much impressed him, though he did not get much inspiration from its folk-music. Another illness, intercostal neuralgia, attacked him in the winter of 1916–17, after which he took up again *The Nightingale* for Diaghilev.

Just after the Russian revolution of 1917 he sat up all night in Rome, orchestrating the *Volga Boat Song* so that it could be played instead of the now impossible *God Save the Czar*. When he was crossing the Italian frontier with Picasso's portrait of him, the guards confiscated the picture, which, they insisted, was no portrait, but a military plan. In the war he lost a beloved brother, who was in the Russian army, and also one of the oldest of the family's retainers. With a few friends, all like him short of money, he planned a small travelling theatre and orchestra, for which he wrote *L'Histoire du Soldat*, another folk-tale, about the deserting conscript who becomes the prey of the Devil. This was produced in September 1918 at Lausanne, with an orchestra of seven, playing as soloists. Influenza prevented the hoped-for tour.

Transition Time

The period from 1917 (*Renard*) to about 1923 (*Les Noces*) may be regarded as one of transition between Stravinsky's romantic days and his 'neo-classicism', which we find in *Pulcinella*, a ballet arranged from some of Pergolesi's unpublished works (Paris, 1920).

It was now possible to settle in France and to come to London for various performances, among which was an unfortunate one of the *Symphonies for Wind Instruments*, dedicated to Debussy's memory. He orchestrated parts of Tchaikovsky's *Sleeping Beauty* and worked at *Mavra*, an opera based on a Pushkin story. For three years he lived at Biarritz. In playing his *Concerto* and other works he developed a reputation as an executant, in Europe and the U.S.A., but always suffered from stage fright, which he believes is chiefly due to the fear of forgetting the music. He found new pleasure in playing Beethoven's works, purely as sound-structures.

On his first visit to America, in 1925, he found 'a weakness for the freakish and sensational, but also a real taste'. There he settled, making the land his home. The Library of Congress in 1927 commissioned the ballet *Apollo Musagetes*, and to the Boston Symphony Orchestra he dedicated the *Symphony of Psalms* in 1930. In 1934 he had become naturalized as a French citizen, but the United States now claim him. He has continued to compose and has had the satisfaction of having one of his sons (the other is a painter) play a second piano in his concerto for two unaccompanied instruments.

The Rake's Progress, produced when Stravinsky was nearly seventy, is an operatic setting of Hogarthean scenes. The composer's passion for pasticcio has not abated: he borrows from many past styles, but always in his own wry, often biting way. He touches a new tenderness and disdains not the prima donna's soaring flights. Despite an unconvincing libretto and plot (by Auden and Kallman), Stravinsky and Hogarth are surely well met.

His 'classical' moods produced their highest art in the ballet *Orpheus*, which some consider to parallel more aptly than any other modern work the clarity and grace of Gluck. Sympathy with what might be described as a contemporary tragedy led him to write a vocal *Elegy* for the poet Dylan Thomas, in which he employs (as he has elsewhere done in fuller form) one of the basic 'tone-row' principles of Schönbergian type, now so fashionable. A critic noted the effectiveness of the vocal writing in this piece, 'enclosed within the ritualistic antiphonal canons for quartets of trombones'. There are some Shakespeare songs and a *Cantata* for female choir-soloists and a small chamber-combination, on fifteenth- and sixteenth-century lyrics; a *Septet* for piano and wind, full of his still exciting rhythmic devices; and, in a renewal of his liking for ritual, some more sacred music: a *Mass*, and a *Canticum Sacrum* inspired by St Mark's, Venice, in five parts, to suggest cathedral's five domes.

The Philosophic Realist

He is a realist. 'Most people,' he thinks, 'want from music a drug—dope'. He thinks music teaching almost wholly bad, failing to get at music's 'essence and substance'. For him, 'composition is a daily function, which I feel compelled to discharge. I compose because I am made for that and cannot do otherwise.' He does not deny the possibility of 'inspiration', but will not wait upon it. The public has not been faithful, but he does not complain; he is honest with himself, calm, detached. He thinks he was, in earlier days, a little spoiled. He doubts whether many ever really understood him. He insists on the necessity of the public's self-activity; many, he thinks, lose their relish through passivity and laziness. Though patient, he complains that conductors pull his music about to fit their own ideas of interpretation.

Somewhat bleakly cheerful, then, he goes his way, strong, indifferent to the world's kicks or applause, yet not himself harsh: he put up wonderfully well (according to his *Chronicle*) with the tantrums of the ballet crowd. He seems to have patience and dour good humour. He has made hosts of friends in his perhaps rather narrow circles, but there is always about him the sense of expatriation. He did not think fit to seek, like Prokofiev, a fresh moulding of life in the U.S.S.R. Rakhmaninov, we remember, gave the same impression of a rather lonely spirit. We may be glad that generous America has cherished Stravinsky and given unfailing, if not uncritical, appreciation. Indeed, he was exceptionally honoured in being invited to fill for a period the Charles Eliot Norton Chair of Poetry at Harvard University, this being the first occasion in history, as far as one knows, when a musician has thus appeared as professor of another art: one, however, so closely allied to his own. His lectures have been published under the title *Musical Poetics*.

JOSEF SUK

1874–1935

RICHARD GORER

At the Second Desk

Among all the great string quartets of the past the reputation of the Bohemian String Quartet still remains pre-eminent, not only for the fire and consummate technique with which they played, but also for their sureness of interpretation. The latter quality was due to, of all people, the player of the second violin, who was not only a skilled executant but also a distinguished composer and could therefore indicate subtleties that an executant pure and simple, however intelligent, might overlook. The name of the second violinist was Josef Suk.

Youth to Marriage

He was born in 1874 in the village of Křečovice, the third son of a schoolmaster who, early recognizing his son's talent, decided, when he was only eight years old, that he should be trained as a musician. The little Suk's musical education was intensive, but he had a happy childhood. 'I was the darling of my parents,' he wrote, and he says of his father that he was kindness itself, but of strong character and very religious. On one occasion little Josef was so entranced by the playing of a cellist visiting Křečovice that he followed the musician to the next place he was visiting and then was unable to find his way home.

Besides being of strong character Anton Suk must have had a certain mechanical ingenuity, for, finding that his son's legs were too short to reach the pedals of the organ, he constructed a second pedal board that the little legs could reach. When he was eleven years old Suk came to Prague and entered the conservatoire. His principal teachers at the outset were the violinist Benevic and Josef Foerster.*
He completed his course in 1891, but stayed on for a further year studying chamber music and playing with the cellist Hanuš Wihan,

---

* Not J. B. Foerster (1859–1951), the contemporary Czech composer.

for whom Dvořák wrote his cello concerto and who subsequently became the cellist of the Bohemian Quartet. Suk also graduated to Dvořák's master class of composition. From this class came many of the Czech composers of the next generation, the most significant exception being Ostrčil; but among Dvořák's pupils may be mentioned Novak, Karel, and, in lighter vein, Oskar Nedbal, who was the first viola player in the Quartet, though later he left it and turned to conducting and to composing operettas.

The tradition is held that Suk was Dvořák's favourite pupil, though there does not seem to be much substantial evidence for this. It is true that Dvořák held that the more gifted a student was, the more severely his work should be criticized, and he seems to have treated Suk with as much harshness as so good-natured a man was capable of. On the other hand there is no doubt of Suk's devotion to Dvořák, but, even before he left the conservatoire, he had come to look at the older master not only as a teacher but also as a prospective father-in-law. This feeling was certainly not reciprocated: Dvořák did not want a musician for a son-in-law.

It is true that the only complaints he could bring against Suk were a lack of accuracy in noting down the numbers of the railway engines that passed through Prague and an extravagance in music paper due to his habit of writing very large notes. Neither of these objections could be regarded as fatal, and his daughter Ottilie seemed to show no likelihood of marrying anyone else, so that Dvořák eventually consented to the marriage, which took place in 1898. As far as is known the union was idyllically happy. At the time of his courtship Suk, in common with such composers as Ostrčil and Janáček, had been very impressed by the work of the romantic and mystical poet Julius Zeyer: one of his best-known works, *The Fairy Tale Suite*, was originally written as incidental music to Zeyer's play *Radůz and Mahůlena*, and later he provided music for the play *Under the Apple Trees*, which is little more than a eulogy of a happy marriage.

Early Compositions

While still a student Suk had begun his career as a composer. His Opus 1, a *Piano Quartet* in A minor, was completed in 1891, and from then until 1906 his compositions appeared at regular intervals. It is significant of the change which was to overtake the composer that during the fifteen years 1891 to 1906 his opus numbers rose to twenty-

which, however, it antedates by four years. He followed this up with something utterly different, a two-act ballet entitled *Harnasie*, based on legends of the brigands of the Tatras: it is a sensational work, overflowing with wild and dramatic rhythms and colours. He was fully aware of the complete change that had come over him: 'I have developed,' he wrote, 'into a national composer, not only subconsciously but with a thorough conviction, using the melodic treasures of the Polish folk.' A visit to the Kurpie province in the north, and acquaintance with the local folk-music there, beautiful but quite unlike the music he had heard in Zakopane, led to the publication of *Twelve Kurpian Songs* for solo voice and six for chorus; they do for Polish folk-music something of what Bartók did for Hungarian and increased his already great reputation.

Decline and Collapse

In 1929 he again fell ill. He was obliged to resign from the conservatoire and to spend nearly a year at Davos, from which he returned so greatly improved that, although he continued to live most of the time in the health-giving air of Zakopane, he accepted the post of Rector to a new Academy of Music in Warsaw: he resigned, however, a year later, owing to a change in policy. During this period he wrote his *Second Violin Concerto* and a *Symphonie Concertante* (both in Polish nationalist style), designing the latter for himself to play the solo piano part, as well as a carefully-reasoned treatise on *The Educational Role of Music in the Social Order*. Again his health broke down: he suffered from throat troubles and his voice became weak. In 1935 he went to France and felt a little better in the flowery perfumed country round Grasse; but the following year in Paris, where he was greatly cheered by the success of his *Harnasie* at the Opéra, he was so weak that he was forced to rest in bed all day in order to conserve his strength for the evenings. A further summer was spent in Warsaw and a winter in Grasse, in an increasingly hopeless struggle against tuberculosis: finally he was taken to a sanatorium at Lausanne, where he was so far from realizing his true condition that he ordered quantities of music paper to work on. A few days later, on Easter Sunday 1937, he died in the presence of his beloved sister Stanisława. His body was taken back to his native land and buried in the vault for distinguished Poles in the Skałka church, Cracow.

JOAQUIN TURINA

1882–1949

HENRY RAYNOR

Childhood and Youth

Joaquin Turina, the son of a painter, born in Seville in December 1882, is perhaps the outstanding example of the nationalist composers whose works are almost unexportable in spite of great popularity in their native land. From an output that includes four operas, several orchestral works, a large amount of piano music of varying dimensions, and a quantity of chamber music, only a handful of pieces are known in this country.

Turina was a born musician; as a small child, he accompanied the songs of his school-fellows on an accordian, and piano lessons gave him so intense an interest in serious music that he was sent for lessons in harmony and counterpoint under the organist of Seville Cathedral, who also taught him the rudiments of composition, for Turina was already busily engaged in composing. His main interests, as a boy, were religious music and Italian Opera, and these two interests meet in his first recorded composition, *Las Coplas de la Pasión*. Though his parents had intended that he should study medicine, Turina's overriding interest and swift progress in music made obvious the choice of the art as his career.

His first appearance in public was at the age of fifteen, when he played Thalberg's *Fantasia* on Rossini's *Moïse*. The notice he received from the Press showed him that, although his aim was composition, an alternative career as a pianist was open to him, and the claims of performance and creation became rivals that he had to reconcile for the sake of his own future progress. Seville had no more to teach him, but by the time he went to Madrid in 1902 he had completed his first opera, the unpublished *Sulamita*, based on *The Song of Solomon*. Madrid offered the twenty-year-old pianist-composer a wider acquaintance with music than had been possible in Seville. Trago, the most eminent Spanish pianist of the day, gave him piano lessons:

Sulamita made a profound impression on the musicians of the capital, including Chapelnikow, the conductor of the Sociedad de Conciertos. A meeting with Manuel de Falla, six years Turina's senior, and the impact of the works of Albeniz changed the direction of his mind; so far, his models had been drawn from Italian *verismo*, but the existence of an essentially Spanish style moved him towards nationalism, and performances of works by Dvořák, Tchaikovsky, and Rimsky-Korsakov showed him the possibility of a fusion of the symphonic tradition and Nationalist themes. The change in his attitude is noticeable in the music he wrote for *Fea y con gracia*, a farce by the Quintero Brothers, shortly before he left Madrid.

The 'Paris Andalusian'

After three years of rapid development, both in mastery of technique and ideas, Turina left Madrid for Paris in 1905, enrolling as a student at the Schola Cantorum under Vincent d'Indy, whilst continuing his piano studies under Moskovski, whose reactionary outlook and devotion to salon music he found shocking. Turina was able to carry on his friendship with Falla in spite of the fact that Falla was a Debussyite at a time when all the big guns of the Schola were trained on 'Debussyisme'. Besides Falla and his compatriots, whose influence on him had already been profound, Turina came into contact with Stravinsky, Ravel, Dukas, and Florent Schmidt and, as a pianist, collaborated with the Parent String Quartet, whose leader was responsible for the first performance of most of the music Turina wrote for violin during his stay in Paris. The influence of d'Indy and the training of the Schola remained with him for the rest of his life, but he was able, after a time, to reconcile the formal notions he acquired in this way with a real sympathy for and understanding of the works of Debussy.

His second concert appearance, in 1907, when he played Franck's *Prelude, Chorale, and Fugue* and Albeniz's *Iberia* and joined the Parent Quartet in a performance of his own Op. 1, the *Quintet* for piano and strings, led to his meeting with Albeniz, whose personal influence upon the young composer was as marked as the influence of his compositions had been. After meeting Albeniz, Turina wrote that he defined his artistic creed as 'Spanish music, with an outlook towards Europe.'

The *Piano Quintet*, cyclic in style, has been reckoned by some authorities as Turina's finest piece of chamber music. The teaching he was receiving, and his part in studying the quintets of Brahms and Franck with the Parent players, had left his nationalism in temporary abeyance and deepened the complexity of his work, but the quality of the *Quintet* only gained recognition when the exotic nationalism of some of his succeeding works had won popularity for his music. In the same year, perhaps partly owing to the presence of willing collaborators, came the *Sonata Española* for violin and piano, which remains unpublished, and his Op. 2, the piano suite, *Sevilla*.

For the remainder of his time in Paris, Turina was busy as an accompanist and concert pianist, giving concerts of his own music and that of Falla, Franck, and the contemporary French composers. The Paris correspondent of *La Correspondencia de España* classed him with d'Indy, Debussy, Schmidt and Ravel among the masters of the day, and his position in France was secured. His course at the Schola ended in 1907; though for the next ten years his work was to show some diffidence in choosing between the popularly-national and the scholarly, he had by this time evolved the idea of a personal style from the diverse influences to which he had been receptive. In the note he wrote for the first performance of his *Sonata Romántica*, Op. 3, written in memory of Albeniz in 1909, he declared, 'This sonata aims to reconcile romanticism, modernist harmony, Debussy's tonality, and the forms of d'Indy whilst expressing the emotions of the Spanish race.' Two years later came the *String Quartet*, Op. 4, which won a more immediate success than the earlier *Quintet*.

Return to Spain

Turina's brief visit to Madrid, in 1912, for a performance of some of his own music and works by Falla, had won them both the nickname 'the Paris Andalusians'. The new work given on this occasion was the *Escena Andalusia*, for violin, piano, and string quartet, a piece so imbued with popular national feeling that its right to be considered chamber music has been denied. In the notice of the concert in the Madrid *La Epocha*, however, the critic not only wrote highly of Turina's abilities as a pianist, but hailed him as the true successor of Albeniz and praised the *Escena Andalusia* for its simplicity, nobility, poetic descriptive power, and intensity of colour.

Turina's final departure from Paris came in 1914, after the presentation of a highly laudatory address from the Schola Cantorum, signed by d'Indy. Madrid became the scene of his most prolific years. *La Procesio del Rocio* had received its first performance there in 1913 and had gained an immediate success; at its first Parisian performance, shortly before the composer's return to Spain, its popular descriptive tendencies caused some comment, but it is a work that demonstrates Turina's attempt to strike a stylistic balance between poetically descriptive ideas and the semi-popular national materials he used to express them.

The Madrid of 1914 was highly conscious of music; Spanish audiences had developed a passion for Wagnerian music-drama, Italian opera was as popular as ever, and Diaghilev was introducing the Russian ballet to the city. Turina had never lost his early desire to work in the theatre and became conductor to Diaghilev's orchestra. His own first opera, *Margot*, was produced in 1914, his second, a musical miracle-play, *Natividad*, in 1916, and his third, *La Adultera Penitente*, in 1917; these three works are to librettos by Martinez Sierra. *Natividad* prompted the composition of the 'poem for orchestra,' *Evangelio de Natividad*, Op. 12, in 1915.

Turina had by this time written a considerable amount of criticism for *La Tribuna*, of Madrid, and *Revista Musicale*, as well as programme notes for many of the novelties performed at his concerts: in 1917 his *Enciclopedia Abbreviada de Musica* was published. Dedicated to d'Indy, this book is the fruit of Turina's training at the Schola, and Sopeña, his biographer, describes it as the finest study of music in the Spanish language to date. After a discussion of the musical situation at the time of writing, Turina continued with a history of music that dealt chronologically with all developments up to that of Schönberg and ended the book with a study of the technique of composition. As the standard work on music in the Spanish language, this *Enciclopedia* has had a profound effect on musical thought amongst younger musicians in Spain.

The nineteen-twenties were a time of immense activity for Turina, in concert giving and criticism as well as composition. The *Sinfonia Sevilla*, of 1920, won him a national prize and extended his prestige. It was followed in 1923 by a fourth opera, his last complete work in this form, *Jardin de Oriente*. A fifth opera, *Pregon de Flores*, after a play by the Quintero Brothers, was never completed. In 1925, the year of *La Oración del Torero*, his best-known chamber work, originally written for four guitars and re-arranged for string quartet, Turina visited London to conduct the first English performance of the *Sinfonia Sevilla* under the auspices of the B.B.C. In 1929, as a result of the success of his *Enciclopedia*, he was invited to deliver in Havana a series of lectures on the evolution of music. The lectures have not been published, but the tour led to a further extension of his prestige amongst Spanish-speaking peoples and was accompanied by a large number of concerts of his own and contemporary Spanish and French music.

Later Years

The nineteen-thirties, for Turina as for the rest of Spain, were a dark age, and marked some slackening of his output. The *Sonata*, Op. 61, for guitar, the second *String Quartet*, and the *Rhapsodia Sinfonica*, the first of his works for piano and orchestra, date from 1931. In 1932 his wife died, but his popularity and the demands of concert giving left him little leisure, despite the darkening of his horizon. The *Piano Concerto* of 1935, first performed a few months before the Civil War, was his last extended work. On his election to the Academy of Fine Arts in Madrid at about the same time he addressed the academy on one of the subjects closest to his mind – the relation between music and the plastic arts – an obvious choice for the composer son of a painter.

Throughout the Civil War, Turina was in Madrid, suffering a loss of popularity and some distrust for his right-wing views, but with the 'liberation' of the capital by Franco's troops, his position was augmented with official honours, and in 1941 he was created National Music Adviser in the Commisaria General de Musica of the Ministry of Education. From the end of the Civil War he contributed a weekly critical article to *El Debat*, but Turina's criticism was an exercise of wit rather than a contribution to musical thought. His biographer finds it a paradox that an accredited leader of the musical life of Spain should have been able to reconcile his position as a composer with the writing of a weekly article more valuable as humour than as criticism. Many of these weekly essays are included in *Colleción de Artículos y Criticisma*. As the nineteen-forties progressed, the slackening of his creative efforts became more marked, and the last few years of his life gave us little that might add to his reputation as a composer. He died on 28 January 1949.

Estimate

Turina's work has not so far won beyond Spain popularity proportionate to the regard it enjoys at home; possibly that failure is due to the extent to which his music is rooted in picturesque nationalism. Sopeña defines his quality as Àndalusian Universatility, and there can be no doubt of the elegance and refinement of his best work. Under pressure from a variety of contradictory musical influences, he set himself the high aim of reconciling the world of d'Indy with those of the modernists and of Spanish folk-song, but his works show little power of organic growth and development, and his most successful music depends less on the formal qualities to which he aspired than on an enjoyable succession of charming ideas.

RALPH VAUGHAN WILLIAMS

B. 1872

A. E. F. DICKINSON

English Saga

Englishmen never know when they are beaten. That was roughly the ominous situation in English music 100 years ago. It was accepted that the music to be heard should consist chiefly of Italian and other foreign operas, and Handel or Handelian oratorio, from Mendelssohn downwards. There was almost a dislike of any positive relation between music and the vernacular, which survives to-day in an opposition to opera in English that has no parallel abroad. When that relation sprang to fresh life in the productions of Gilbert and Sullivan, it was in patter and parody and sentimental expression, not far from pantomime.

It was all, at best, magnificent but unpromising, the counterpart of the hired palms and starched shirts, which also strove for attention on every possible and impossible occasion. There is a place for the music so strongly national that it passes most frontiers, or (like *The Messiah*) so urgent that it will always fulfil a need; but when such foreign or pristine art begins to dominate the national scene, creative talent rises in permanent eclipse. A little later, the Crystal Palace concerts developed under Manns and Grove. Here the German tradition was no less definitely the prime concern.

The Pioneers

It was the peculiarly rich virtue of Parry and Stanford that between them they realized the immeasurable force of German music, but also its verbal contacts and its broad base, in the shape of a responsive public of performers and listeners. Parry revived oratorio, cantata, and song with the native freshness of *Job*, *Prometheus Unbound*, and the *English Lyrics* volumes for solo singer. Stanford, more versatile, ranged from *Te Deum* and *Stabat Mater* to the exquisite *The Fairy Lough* and *The Blue Bird* and three or four characteristic operas. But these key-men of a period of transition, for which renascence seems now the right term, were also educationists in the full sense; not only at Oxford, Cambridge, and the Royal College of Music, where they both were directing influences, but also, for example, at the Leeds Festival.

Encouraged by Sullivan's unprecedented and incredible all-English orchestra at Leeds, Stanford trained English orchestral students for a place in the nation's orchestras and trained them in all styles, including the latest from Room 49 (opportunities usually denied to students on the continent). He was also continually pressing on the Leeds committee their responsibility for well-arranged and enterprising programmes: negatively, freedom from the *Messiah-Elijah* rut; positively, acceptance of *The Dream of Gerontius* as an unquestionable priority, whatever private reactions. Stanford was largely instrumental in bringing Richter and Joachim into our musical life, vital and indispensable influences on performing standards. (Imagine this happening in Germany.) Parry stood for the incredible Wagner and a great many other disturbing individualities. One look at an Elgar score that Jaeger, the Novello reader, had brought round, and Parry was in a hansom on the way to urge performance of the new *Variations* on Richter. That was on a romantically stormy night in 1899.

These men lived and worked with a loyalty to music that remains historical. With their very different personalities, they were often voices in the desert, crying, 'In this muddled, cosmopolitan, Anglophobe musical society prepare – home-made music for truly English listeners.'

Art and Life

Such was the critical period, of scattered outposts rather than an established front, in which Vaughan Williams grew up. It was indeed a time of enigma and dream, though few read the signs. For an observant and patriotic music-maker the temptation, by which Parry was often to be beguiled, was strong: to divert creative energy in a lifetime of parochial, ethically idealist music, on one side, and on another side in organizational, perhaps institutional, effort. There might also be such inroads on a craftsman's time as examining and lecturing, and the increasing lure of folk-song 'collecting', besides all the tiresome demands of committees, social parasites, and good causes. (In a typical period not long ago I saw Vaughan Williams at the première of an opera of questionable merit, and later heard on the radio (1950) his speech for the presentation of the R.P.S. Gold Medal – two personally unprofitable evenings that could easily become 200). It must be stated, then, once and for all that, though Vaughan Williams has performed signal services to local and national music in the Folk-Song Society, hymnody, Leith Hill Festival (Dorking), Royal College of Music, university examination boards, and many more occasional contacts, he has never forgotten that his main vocation is composition – hard, work-by-work composition, not symphonies in sixes or songs by the score – and a friendly gruff manner has not concealed from his friends where his heart lies. This understood, his comings and goings, and the wayward chronology of his varied output, find their true and modest place in this short account of his life.

Of the composer's non-detachment, it may be sufficient to quote (in confirmation of all the available personal impressions of private companionship and public spirit) a typical sentence from an article on 'The Composer in War Time' reviewing sundry reactions. 'Whatever this war is, it is not boring.' This criticism of escapists could be easily paralleled in peace-time utterances and verified in the trend of his actual or implied texts, no less idealist than Parry's and usually more trenchant at that. As often as not, Vaughan Williams's music is no more detachable from his outlook on the world or his centre of reference than was the art of his fondest muse, J. S. Bach. Like Bach, too, he has been too much concerned with listening to the inner voices to claim serious attention for himself.

Let the reader think of the rising composer whose head is crammed with nothing but *entrées* and openings – and certainly no one now makes it his business to keep an English composer alive – or again of the Wagner type, which cannot divorce personal advance from the spread of Me Societies and from the promotion of a positively hostile group-attitude to those who fail to admire the one and only living Master. If it then be considered how little encouragement Vaughan Williams received before he was fifty, and how meagre an allowance of current performance since then, the evidence for the makings of a disappointed, unsettled composer is striking and humiliating. That, in fact, Vaughan Williams has consistently avoided both the meanness of the egotist and the steady push of a common type of church or college dignitary, that he leaves no trail of clique or institution about his movements, is an earnest of the serene spirit within.

Contemporary Significance

Vaughan Williams's career can thus be followed with the confidence that in the main it has been supremely worth while; worth living through and worth living with. Because of the latter claim, this life commands the special interest of the present generation. We who have lived in his mild and magnificent eye, and more, cannot but regard as in some measure ours his progress from a correspondence course in harmony to the position of most-sought president of every musical society in the kingdom. However intensely and lastingly satisfied with the various experiences denoted by the titles of works, we cannot restrain, in the long run, a curiosity to know what kind of environment and special propulsions made possible so unpredictable a course of musical effort and expression, and what were the successive stages of this inner growth.

Coming from a family in which names of judges have significantly recurred, Vaughan Williams was born into favourable circumstances. His father was rector of Down Ampney in Gloucestershire. Home and private lessons in harmony, piano, and violin continued at a preparatory school. A Bach Album (Berthold Tours) came to hand and might be regarded as the thin end of a permanent wedge. Piano-duet arrangements (at that time the chief home contact with the bigger things of music) included Handel choruses and Haydn symphonies. Handel was then the accepted great composer, Bach an interesting figure. The piano album revealed that here was something more than a variation of the Handel type.

School Days and College Influences

Vaughan Williams went to Charterhouse School at the age of fifteen and stayed three years. He began in Saunderites, the Headmaster's House, and then moved as a monitor into Robinites. The latter was chiefly a waiting house of small boys, but the Housemaster, Mr Robinson, was music master and provided permanent access to a piano. A Robinite House photograph in the possession of a contemporary 'shows him looking very much as he is now – firm mouth, eyes looking out into the distance, hands firmly planted on his knees, and the whole indicating a "master of the event".' Some compositions were performed in the school hall and were admired by a power in the land, a piece of encouragement the composer seldom received again. It was something that the Headmaster permitted the use of the hall for such frivolity. Of other things one can only guess; but somewhere or other Vaughan Williams picked up that first-things-first and generally direct, unaffected, and disinterested way of living, of which mention has been made. The abundance of college students conspicuously lacking in these foundations of character inclines me to believe that whatever the inevitable hardships, philistine influences, and general lack of a musically cultivated school life, the impress of the Charterhouse groove was not unhappy.

There seems to have been no doubt about the career to be followed up. Vaughan Williams went straight to the Royal College of Music, then on to Cambridge, and after that (1895) back to the Royal College. He thus encountered in turn, as composition teachers, Parry, Charles Wood, and Stanford, and the trenchant Walter Parratt for the organ. In Parry he found a sympathetic and informative tutor, whose serious and English music he admired, and whose inherent nobility of character none could forget. Wood taught many useful technical tricks for Mus.Bac., Stanford provided stimulating barriers. 'Damnably ugly, my boy' was the usual method. Stanford was a very shrewd craftsman and a lovable mentor, even when he was palpably reactionary, and his ability to probe a weak spot (without modern anaesthetics) was uncanny. Perhaps he had now met his match for the first time. Fifteen years later he was championing his former pupil at the orchestral rehearsal of *A Sea Symphony* for the Leeds première (1910). With no more than a vocal score, Stanford picked out mistakes in the manuscript parts and in performance, with a superb acuity of ear. Such a teacher was a magnificently dangerous person on whom to try experiments.

Shortly after leaving the Royal College, Vaughan Williams studied for a while at Berlin with Max Bruch, whom he found congenial in some odd way, and very much later (in 1908) he went to Ravel, who taught him chiefly new values in orchestration and the stimulus of the pianoforte. Previously lessons with Elgar had been sought, refused, and therefore taken *in absentia* – in an examination of the scores of the *Variations* and *Gerontius*.

Hugh Allen and Gustav Holst

Meanwhile other enduring contacts had been made. Choral-society conducting (an activity in which this country can claim European distinction) began at Cambridge; the thin end of another wedge of realistic and far-reaching experience. Here, too, Vaughan Williams struck up an acquaintance with a rather older undergraduate, H. P. Allen, organ scholar at Christ's and fearless doyen of the University Musical Club. This led to heroic performances of *A Sea Symphony* in Oxford and London. It was my own good fortune to sing in the Oxford performance in 1919, when except to the deprived, the unemployed, and other forgotten persons idealism seemed both conceivable and singable as never before or since. For many Oxonians this was the first glimpse of Vaughan Williams's range and power of expression. It came to the last rehearsal, with the composer present, recently out of the R.G.A. and looking very unlike a swimmer in time and space. The following gallery-to-conductor's-desk conversation was heard. 'Dr Allen, would you mind trying from M again?' 'Did you say M or N?' 'Letter Emma' (loud cheers). It was a simple but characteristically direct appeal to the common experience of the moment before serious exploration. I have attended the composer on more workaday occasions of self-introduction at a school. There was still the same auspicious common touch at the foot of Mount Parnassus. (C. B. Rees once voted Vaughan Williams's mischievous frustration of the celebrity-hunter at a lecture on Holst, in a constant but unfulfilled promise to illustrate points later on the beautiful piano in the corner of the room.) The same confidence in the R. V. W. sanity and refreshing comment led Allen, as soon as he was director, to issue an invitation to come to the Royal College of Music, in effect, 'Come up to R.C.M. and be yourself one day a week' – or so Allen described it to me in the last conversation I had with him.

Then there was Holst, most critical of companions. The acquaintance began in 1895 and ripened not only into the finest friendship but also into a particularly grilling custom – of submitting compositions to the other's frank and generous comment. This lasted nearly forty years. Vaughan Williams found in Holst a terrifying integrity. He could not always face it (so he declares). To Holst *Job*, for example, seemed at first not nearly bare enough in texture. On the other side, Holst's *Choral Symphony* aroused in his opposite number a 'cold enthusiasm' more annihilating than almost anything could be. It must have been a perilous and testing association, but in Holst, it seems, the Stanford 'loyalty to music' spoke as eloquently as any second mind can speak to a creator at work. It would be interesting to know if Bartók and Kodály fared as well by each other.

Folk-Song

Of the music heard at this period, two major items must be mentioned. The first hearing of *Die Walküre* at Munich aroused deep feelings of 'recollection'; not an uncommon reaction (A. H. Sidgwick makes the same judgement in *The Promenade Ticket*), but of unusual interest in this instance. It shows that Vaughan Williams could recognize a kindred fancy beneath an alien texture and culture. A similar encounter with English folk-song, beginning with Bramley and Stainer's *Christmas Carols New and Old* and going on to *English County Songs*, is less surprising, but it opened a rich vein of melodic experience, besides summoning much collecting and sorting effort, in the scholarly steps of Lucy Broadwood and Baring Gould and the rest, accompanied later by Cecil Sharp and Holst. It was no light work, picking out the genuine folk-tunes from national airs and 'Vauxhall' tunes. Vaughan Williams joined the Folk-Song Society in 1904 and has always been on its committee or on that of the English Folk Dance and Song Society, in which the F.S.S. became embodied in 1931. He edited and contributed songs for the *Folk Song Journal No. 8* (1905) and read a paper on folk-song composition in 1908. Such delving for hidden treasure must have brought home the often compelling force of words that spring from life. Originally there had been much and understandable professional opposition to the 'new-fangled craze for folk-song', in *The Musical Times* for instance (1895). Perhaps the glee-maker felt a challenge to his livelihood.

The many sociable arrangements, in which the closed-lips accompaniment is a noticeable feature, came later. As late as 1907 Vaughan Williams joined Cecil Sharp and Lucy Broadwood in resisting W. H. Hadow and Arthur Somervell, who as Board of Education men were triumphantly determined to spread folk-song in the national schools. In this matter Vaughan Williams has been a purist (and why not?): he accepted Miss Broadwood's treasuring of folk-song in solitude as nearer the countryman's view than 'the wholesale popularity which we advocate nowadays' (1948). Yet if the sophisticated saga of the

Nibelung myth had showed its peculiar, evocative humanity, much more did the unvarnished tales and plain durable strophes of English country song seem an irresistible cult, to one who realized the rare and indeed ambitious quality of this celebration of common things in the most direct and insistent style conceivable. Folk-song was also, as Parry remarked in his inaugural and prophetic address to the F.S.S. (1899), a sign that 'at bottom our puzzling friend Democracy has permanent qualities which may yet challenge the sordid vulgarity of our great city-populations'. In later years Vaughan Williams has often spoken of folk-song as a vital meeting-point of all musical classes.

It was not easy going. The incredibly persuasive *A Shropshire Lad* (1896) had vindicated the plain style in cultivated circles and proved a musical rallying point to Vaughan Williams and many other composers. Meanwhile, the intimacy and sheer vigour of many folk-songs (*Bushes and Briars, Dives and Lazarus*) made a startling impression, which remained for good. What folk-song has been to Vaughan Williams can be read with permanent enjoyment in his *National Music*, the substance of lectures given at Bryn Mawr College, Pennsylvania, in 1932; a briefer account appeared in *The Radio Times* (22 June 1945). How folk-song has impressed Vaughan Williams the composer can be heard in the intermittent but never quite quenched stream of works that stretch from the *Norfolk Rhapsodies* and *Christmas Carol Fantasia* to the plainer settings of the Ballet *On Christmas Night* and the more recent *The Four Seasons*, for united Women's Institute choirs, in which a famous weather forecast finds a rich and exalted context, from spring-time mating to Christmas benediction.

Hymns and Songs

Doubtless his new folk-song standards stood Vaughan Williams in good stead when he came to edit the music for *The English Hymnal* (1906; enlarged, 1933). It was not easy to determine the latent musical capabilities of our puzzling friend Democracy at worship, so far powerfully directed but also confused by *Hymns Ancient and Modern* and by the various nonconformist hymnaries. *The English Hymnal* proved a historical collection, musically the turning-point for all English hymnaries worthy the name, and it introduced, anonymously, unforgettable tunes, for *For all the Saints* and other hymns, from the musical editor's pen. For a composer the sorting work was a wide and stimulating experience, involving not only choice of the best melodic version and harmony for a tune, but also the finding of suitable tunes for each of 665 hymns, old and new. Speaking to the Hymn Society at the jubilee of the *Hymnal*, Vaughan Williams outlined his original aims: tunes must be authentic, adventurous in range, and of an uncompromising standard. It would be hard to over-estimate the influence of this pioneer collection in its enrichment of congregational life with tunes from Geneva, Rouen, Cologne, Wales, but also from Monksgate and Down Ampney.

Such a prolonged search for and browsing amongst fundamentals, to which Bach's early development offers some parallel, should not be taken for granted. It shows a singularly critical faculty in one who had taken his doctorate by examination at Cambridge in 1901 and might therefore have considered himself completely equipped for any voyage his fancy might suggest. However, during this period, whatever may have been scrapped or withheld, a good many songs appeared, including a D. G. Rossetti cycle, *The House of Life*, the Stevenson *Songs of Travel*, and *Linden Lea* (Barnes). Some of these have since become popular enough to be perennial. In their time they were almost pioneer work, in the track of Parry and Stanford, by their complete avoidance of the royalty ballad in spirit, by their unlikeness to the popular song-cycles of fanciful Asiatic origin, and by their cultivation of the articulate English word in its true dignity and richness of utterance, as Schubert had cultivated German speech. A new musical power justified, too, the esoteric quality of the poetry. Somewhat later, the *On Wenlock Edge* cycle (1909) followed in a more characteristic style, spurred to a greater concentration by Housman's restrained but lifelike portraits of resolution and independence. After that, songs came intermittently and at long intervals and were overshadowed by the larger works in a way that Schubert avoided to the end. But the piano became too definite and limited for Vaughan Williams's later excursions into words and fell into disuse.

Dorking Music

The Leith Hill competition festival, produced in the main by local choirs, began at Dorking in 1905 as a village institution under Vaughan Williams's musical direction, and there it has remained, growing in stature, but perpetually saved from pretentiousness by the director's horror of sophistication. The tale of choral-orchestral output is a striking one, for on each day competition is crowned by combined performance with full orchestra. *Benedicite* and other short works were written for the festival. A performance there, over twenty years ago, of *Blest Pair of Sirens* and *A Stronghold Sure* (not to mention *Jerusalem*) is still among my own strongest memories; and Bach's *St Matthew Passion* has received a special attention, questionable in interpretative detail but not in earnestness of delivery. In 1955, as president, Vaughan Williams had the pleasure of congratulating the choirs on the soundness of their fifty-year foundation, in a witty and heartening speech, reinforced by a song he had written for the festival, with words by Mrs Vaughan Williams.

The importance of Vaughan Williams's firm direction will be appreciated by anyone who has experienced the awkward obstinacy of a certain type of slightly learned and very opinionated committee-member, fearful of changes and too easily put off a work he does not 'care about', as Stanford realized elsewhere. Perhaps Vaughan Williams was fortunate in his committee and his choir conductors; but in a term of years a director obtains the colleagues he deserves, and loyalty to the living needs of native music is at once infectious and antiseptic.

Symphonies and Stage Works

It was at Leeds, however, that the composer's name became established; first with *Toward the Unknown Region* (1907) and then with *A Sea Symphony* (begun 1903, performed 1910 under the composer, revised twice after 1918). The contact with Whitman had its difficulties; there can be rant and verbosity in the cultivation of simple phrases. But on the whole poetic idealism found here a stirring and new release in choral declamation and symphonic development, such as Parry had never been able to achieve in *War and Peace* and its successors. The shaky Leeds performance of the symphony (a typically English, hazardous event) was enough to arouse the interest of H. P. Allen of Oxford, and of many others through him, so that gradually the work became at every musical centre a standing challenge to any choral society with ambitions. Successive or contemporary works included the following: the music for *The Wasps* at Cambridge (1909), with the *Old King Cole* ballet as encore fourteen years later; the *Fantasia on a Theme of Tallis* (the Queen's Hall, 1909); *The Lark Ascending* (violin and orchestra); and, complete with boxing match, the opera *Hugh, the Drover*. The last-named had to wait till 1924 for its first production and *The Lark Ascending* till 1921. *A London Symphony* appeared in March 1914. Considerably revised at the end of the ensuing war, it remained the composer's greatest musical effort for twenty years.

In its overt references to London sounds and songs the symphony showed contacts with the raw material of English life, such as the composer had earnestly pleaded for, in the name of a more distinctive and cogent art, in a wayside article in *The R.C.M. Magazine*. But these were scarcely more than identity labels in a rich tribute to the capital city. When, thirty years later, the chimes of Big Ben had acquired overtones of European (radio) service, which reverberated unspeakably in men's minds in numberless scattered outposts of human liberty, observant listeners realized with a start that, with all its deceptively casual and elusive incidents, the symphony contained a true and coherent sublimation of the national life that carries on in a manner baffling to its most powerful critics and bystanders. The point to be made now is that 'London' suites and overtures are easily produced, and so is fierce or misty music. The bringing together of all these in one orbit was a stroke of more than musical genius. No other concourse of men had been thus celebrated. As titled music *A London Symphony* was sufficiently penetrating, as thematic panorama and as texture, soon to become monumental – it formed the chief native work at the first annual congress of the British Music Society – and later prophetic. It was a Herculean and resourceful effort to match with balanced and coherent music the deep calm, Roman virtue and more wayward, lyrical strains of the Londoner of 1914 (and 1918).

By some such route, vocal and humanitarian in approach, Vaughan Williams found his way in these ten years to the mastery of pure symphony and of the symphony orchestra. After that, he was freer to continue, or at least the nature of a symphonic proposition was clearer, if intimations of a fresh work began to accrue. But for obvious reasons the next symphony, the *Pastoral*, did not appear till 1922, and *Symphony No. 4* in F minor (1935) required an even longer interval for its completion from an earlier start. *Symphony No. 5* in D made a modest appearance in 1943, and *Symphony No. 6* followed, closer than before, in 1948. In so far as the post-war revision of *A London Symphony* was in the direction of a more scorching intensity, the by-product of war experiences, the *Pastoral* appears as a reaction against feverish music. The devastating *Fourth Symphony* cannot be dissociated from the rise of violence in Europe, the *Fifth Symphony* is almost as certainly a study in other-worldliness at a time of general anguish, and the disturbed, ominous *Sixth Symphony* is a warning, mainly of shattering emphasis but ultimately of philosophic quietude.

Sinfonia Antarctica travels from Prometheus to the 'silent cataracts' before Oates and Scott, a tribute to Englishmen who do not know when they are beaten. An utter contrast, the *Eighth Symphony* (1956), is steadily companionable with hilarious wind, meditative strings and vibraphone obligato.

Voices and Orchestra. More Operas

With the Pastoral Symphony may be placed the 'tune for Tertis', the *Flos Campi* suite for viola, small orchestra, and wordless chorus; on the verge of the *Fourth Symphony*, the *Concerto* for one piano, altered later to two pianos, and orchestra. The remaining major works have been more occasional and self-explanatory. Positively religious works, some didactic in season, have included the *Mass* in G minor for voices only, *Sancta Civitas* (1926), *Benedicite*, *Dona nobis pacem* (1936), the short but inspired *Thanksgiving for Victory*, and the long pondered rare, Morality, *The Pilgrim's Progress* (1951); the masque *Job* (1930) presents the apotheosis of the disciplined will, in man or mankind; the Christmas cantata, *This Day* (1954), dedicates that will afresh to truth and justice, in brief ecstatic recollection of a peaceful night that none forget, but also in stern regard for the pioneer sages who go on until they find their true and guiding star. Humanism or the craftsman's pride, rather than the lure of the stage, accounts for the opera *Sir John in Love*, the extravaganza *The Poisoned Kiss*, and the musical setting of *Riders to the Sea* for the stage; and the Norwich Festival for *Five Tudor Portraits* (1936) for the concert-hall. Slighter occasional pieces have been *Pilgrim Pavement* (voices and organ), *Nothing is here for Tears* (a tribute to King George V), *Flourish for a Coronation* (1937), *Six Choral Songs* ('to be sung in time of war' but no less suitable in restless interludes), and the *Te Deum* in G. Film music has included that for *Forty-ninth Parallel* (1941) and *Scott of the Antarctic* (1949). An article in *The R.C.M. Magazine* makes it clear that Vaughan Williams found the wayward demands of film producers thoroughly diverting, while contemplating the more serious possibilities of film music. In confirmation the Scott music proved its wider provenance in the unusual heroic symphony of 1953.

The nearly coincident appearance of *Dona nobis pacem* and *Five Tudor Portraits* may be regarded as a somewhat characteristic pursuit in parallel of the world's need and of local festival demand. When a seriously documentary or religious work has been called for, the composer has brought to the occasion the ripe experience of a habitual musical concern for things that matter, without Parry's weak reliance on ethical declamation. So far the maturity that declared itself after 1918 has revealed a recurrent pattern of timely music, along with casual productions.

War and Peace

In the war of 1914–18 Vaughan Williams served in the R.A.M.C. (Macedonia) and in 1918 as an officer in the R.G.A. in France. He shared the common hazards and deprivations of the front-line soldier and equally shouldered the full responsibility of resorting to the 'terrible arbitrament of force'. He thus brought to his subsequent artistic development, whose significant contacts with war have been indicated, such experience of modern warfare as enabled him to handle the subject, artistically, without the often thin-skinned righteousness of those who have never fought, or the crushed, tortured spirit of those who had broken down under the strain of killing or being attacked. He knew the brutality of war, and that no effort must be spared to prevent its ever happening again; but he was not obsessed with it. He could thus pursue 'pastoral' moods and imagery, or the visionary impact of *Sancta Civitas*, with complete freedom.

In *Job* the tremendous exposure of the violence that threatens to overcome the soul in whom conscience has resigned seems to remember actual war, as the *Dance of the Song of the Morning* reflects the subdued serenity of reconciliation, not the easy optimism of *Then we burst forth* at the climax of *Toward the Unknown Region*. That renewal of violence proved to be the first step in a new direction; it led to the most forcible of symphonies, No. 4 in F minor, out-classing Walton and Stravinsky (*Le Sacre*) alike in its superlative concentration of overwhelming sensations and ruthless inner logic. It is no mere war-symphony, like the Leningrad, but as an echo of Europe in the thirties it has the authentic note of surveying advancing legions that with all their discipline have snapped out of control. Fate was knocking at the door with both fists. It was here, doubtless, that the composer observed of an appallingly frank discord, 'It looks wrong and sounds wrong, but it is perfectly right'; for where naked force is the apparent subject, utter defiance of the established Covenant holds the deeper truth.

In World War II Vaughan Williams kept going what music could reasonably be maintained as total war flourished, and there is plenty of evidence available to show that in all things he earned the title of Uncle Ralph, not only to local hard cases but to genuinely unfortunate musicians, including refugees. For the wider public he wrote *Household Music*, as later a concerto for Rural Schools (1950). When it came to a *Symphony* (No. 5), there were no heroics or didactics, but just music. There is suspense, restlessness, and vagueness, but the prevailing tone is serene and confident, yet not the calm of 'never doubted right would triumph' (in 1942–43). But *Thanksgiving for Victory*, commissioned in time for a broadcast performance in 1945, contrived to convey, at a very difficult moment, a timeless, unquenchable message of Christian faith and national dedication in spite of everything, Hiroshima included. The *Sixth Symphony* is manifestly the work of one too deeply concerned with the world's divisions to find matter for anything more exultant than a philosophic, enigmatic calm. The temptation to write a paean (surely a considerable one, in a Western society reluctant to think and somewhat cowed by the most acute apprehensions) found no response in the depths of consciousness.

This probing of certain works in relation to contemporary events and issues may strain the attention not only of those who found the last war 'so boring', but also of those who consider wars as deplorable but best forgotten in favour of the developed social life that has somehow gone on in spite of their occurrence or imminence. The answer to this is that, quite apart from their rare artistic value, the works discussed show centres of interest that must be regarded as essential and characteristic, unlike the composer's social contacts, hobbies, and tastes in dress and food and flowers. With all his presidential and advisory activities, Vaughan Williams has in fact not allowed his finer perceptions and compelling concerns to be sidetracked by social inducements. The epithet 'ascetic' suggests itself. This would be misleading, except in its root sense of 'keeping in training' for whatever purpose life may reveal to a consecrated humanity.

The Inner Circle

We may now turn to some of the social round of the artistic life that informs the rest. (To do justice to the composer's habits of doing good, at Dorking and elsewhere, would make almost a book in itself. But I shall restrict myself here to Vaughan Williams the musician. Accordingly, my silence on the composer's home life will not be misinterpreted. It may be recorded, however, that his first wife was Adeline Fisher, who died in 1951, and that in 1953 he married Ursula Wood, who had been his first wife's friend and his own amanuensis.) Mention has been made of Stanford. In his life of Stanford, Plunket Greene says that he championed his former pupil throughout. This is not altogether true: Stanford used to speak of the 'decline' after *A Sea Symphony* (i.e. up to the *Pastoral*). He remained a warm-hearted mentor rather than a friend.

Parry was a breezier influence, usually to be recalled with enjoyment at some timely quip. Yet he also was too conservative in taste to be really in tune with the renascence for which he had done so much to prepare. The friendship of Vaughan Williams's Cambridge contemporary, H. P. Allen, developed, perhaps, in connexion with the performances of *A Sea Symphony* with the Oxford Bach Choir and the Bach Choir (London). Relations were not confined to mutual admiration. Vaughan Williams thought Allen took some of the symphony too boisterously; and, though paying the warmest tribute to other things, he summarized Allen's conducting as 'a triumph of the spirit over the letter. His actual beat was deplorable ... and yet he made choirs and orchestras sing and play as they had never done before ... the professional players had neither the time nor the inclination to look behind his technical vagaries and to discover what lay beyond.' This did not prevent Allen from asking Vaughan Williams to join the R.C.M. staff; and the composer informed me that on the Sunday in 1930 on which the *Tahiti* was known to be sinking, with Allen on board, 'we were all hanging on to the wireless', as indeed we were, until news of rescue came through.

Conductors, Critics, Publishers, and Choirs

On the orchestral side, and not seldom on the choral, Sir Adrian Boult has been the composer's most constant protagonist. He sponsored *A London Symphony* (revised version) from January 1918 onwards, and he has been in charge of the first and later performances of the next four symphonies and much other music. To bring these works to the constant attention of orchestras and audiences, in the early days, must often have seemed like promoting an Antarctic expedition, in the prevailing cosy, mild, and dangerously parochial atmosphere of the English musical climate, not to mention the classic-loving audiences on the continent. Here, again, such devotion might have had its disadvantages of alien interpretation. But having been present at several mid-rehearsal discussions, I can testify that Boult has been as ready to fall in with the composer's impulses (on tempi especially) as Vaughan Williams has been consistent in adjuring conductors to play his music as they feel it.

Boult's influence has borne fruit in the work of his pupils. It was supported and in part preceded by Henry Wood in London and elsewhere and by Dan Godfrey at Bournemouth. On the literary side, as music critic of *The Times* H. C. Colles gave the composer's post-war maturity valuable support, at the most critical time of the English renascence. Indeed, I have heard surprised comment at Colles's 'fanaticism' on the subject. Fox Strangways (who found Vaughan Williams rather overawing at times) committed himself in an early article in *Music and Letters* (April 1920), confirmed in later notices of first performances in *The Observer*. Three complementary studies in miniature appeared in book form, beginning in 1928. It may be said that Vaughan Williams has not known serious obstacles to printed publication for the greater part of his productive career; and, incidentally, the moderate cost of most of his music has made it accessible to all classes. But apart from *A Sea Symphony* (a recent accession) no major choral work seems to have been recorded, and no opera.

In 1920 he succeeded Allen as conductor of the Bach Choir and stayed there six years. His superlative aural alertness, critical understanding of music, artistic integrity, and general directness commanded the choir's respect, but, as a conductor, oddly enough, he did not inspire confidence in critical passages. The sincerity of his reading of the Bach *St Matthew Passion* was striking in its somewhat blunt style; and he gave a fine performance of *Sancta Civitas*.

Folk-Song Committees and Honours

As an early, active and prominent member of the Folk-Song Society, where he succeeded Lucy Broadwood as President in 1929, Vaughan Williams has made many friends. His uncompromising attitude to popularization has been mentioned earlier, but, like Sharp, he favoured a more active policy than was generally accepted.

Recently, he has tended to go the other way and support the work of scholarly preservation.

He was an equally sturdy influence in the English Folk Dance Society, where after Sharp's death he became a member of the 'Board of Artistic Control' with Maud Karpeles and Douglas Kennedy and was official adviser on music. He was the decisive factor in the amalgamation of the two societies in 1931 and became President of the E.F.D.S. in 1946. A former chairman of committee recalls a dry opening remark, 'You see I've turned up this afternoon, so there'll be trouble' – a common enough reaction of active and decided minds towards cautious committees – but my informant adds revealingly, 'He is both shrewd and idealistic. He is an example of that very English figure, the natural nonconformist opposition, who is deeply conservative where the traditions are concerned.' Of how many music societies Vaughan Williams is the president or vice-president it would take too long to tell.

He accepted an honorary doctorate of music at Oxford in 1919. In 1935 he received the Order of Merit from King George V, in company with Frederick Gowland Hopkins and John Masefield, distinction enough for a 'nice, unparticular person' who, like Holst, has not wished to be set above his fellows in any official way. It was something like poetic justice to be recognized along with the investigator of vitamins; for what composer in the century has been so deliberately and fundamentally sustaining for all occasions, from a simple gathering for All Saints' Day to the trials of Job, in fable and in fact?

Relative age has made Vaughan Williams without dispute the grand old man of English music. No one before him has arrived at this point and earned so universally the goodwill of fellow-artists, performers, listeners, and organizers. He can look back to a lifetime that has seen the return of English music to the map of Europe, not least through his own struggles for national and local music. It is a matter of deep impersonal pride to his fellow-countrymen that under the quickening influences of English education, English folk-song, and English idealism, as well as of unalterable convictions, again and again the time-spirit, and the spirit that blows, have found him looking out into the distance, firm of purpose, master of the event. Such affirmations cannot be too jealously treasured, by English audiences or any others. They awaken a rare sense of truth in a barbarous world.

HEITOR VILLA-LOBOS

B. 1881

HENRY RAYNOR

Introduction and Early Years

Although Villa-Lobos is one of those composers who seek to fuse the musical traditions of their lands into 'the mainstream of music', and who have thus provided a source of enrichment for the central tradition itself, little of his accomplishment, either as composer of more than 1,300 works or as an educationalist of great influence in South America, is known in this country.

The musical atmosphere of Brazil in his youth was largely European, though tempered by the rhythmic and melodic habits of African music and by the indigenous Indian strain that is still a living force in the interior of the country. The study of Brazilian folk-music began in the second half of the nineteenth century, and Villa-Lobos's immediate predecessors, Alberto Nepomuceno (1864–1920) and Francesco Braga (b. 1868), under whom Villa-Lobos later studied, were European by training and outlook, seeking to transform folk-music into the raw material of a conscious art. The primitive Indian music of Brazil uses a fragmentary pentatonic scale and is less developed than the music of African extraction, though African music is less sophisticated in Brazil than in Cuba or North America. From the foundation of the Escola Nacional Musica, in 1841, interest in European music spread, and Brazil produced its Italianate 'classical' composer in Antonio Carlos Gomes (1836–96). Braga, who studied under Massenet, succeeded him, producing works that show the influence of Wagner, Massenet, and Italian *verismo*. Braga became the first director of the Sociedade des Concertos Sinfonicos, founded in 1908.

Heitor Villa-Lobos was born in Rio de Janiero in 1881, though certain works of reference offer 1882, 1884, 1886, and 1891 as his date of birth. His father, a lawyer, writer, and amateur cellist, gave him his first musical instruction; by the time of his father's death, in 1892, Heitor had begun to teach himself several of the wind instruments in addition to the cello. This independence of mind, which later showed itself to be that of a man capable of learning more from his own mistakes than from the most efficient teaching, was increased by the poverty that followed his father's death. Although his parents had noticed his first attempts at improvisation before he was ten years old, circumstances prohibited any ambitious musical education and the boy set about earning his living by playing in theatre and café orchestras and, after leaving school, by going into business. For a time he was employed in a match factory. It was not until 1901 that he was able to continue his training with lessons at the Brazilian Institute of Music.

First Works

Villa-Lobos's first published composition, a *Salon Waltz*, appeared in 1908 and gave no indication of his future direction, but the first adumbration of his mature style came in 1910, with the *Canticos Sertanejos* (Country Songs), which, though not founded on specific folk melodies, employed local types of tune and rhythmic organization. The composer has since explained that he objects to the quotation of any existing music, but that his themes often 'have the aspect' of folk-tunes. The growth of an overwhelming interest in folk-lore, primarily but not exclusively musical, led him to join a scientific expedition up the Amazon and its tributaries between 1913 and 1915, to study Indian music at first hand. He brought back with him not only a wealth of primitive music that, despite his objection to 'quotation', was to influence his own works, but also a stock of native myths on which many of the works that poured from him in the next few years were to be based. In 1915, the year in which he gave the first concert of his own music in Rio de Janiero, came a *Suite of Dances of the Indian Mestizos*, three pieces of an Afro-Indian type with the explanatory sub-titles that became typical of him: – the *Golden Age*, the *Crystal Age*, and the *Bronze Age*. This was followed, in the next two years, by ten symphonic poems based on Indian mythology; several of these have never reached performance and most are still in manuscript, though *Amazonas* (1917) created a sensation when performed in Paris in 1929. This work deals with a story by the composer's father about the erotic experiences of an Indian girl beset by the gods and monsters of the jungle. The strings are made to play glissandi of the whole harmonic series and are at times bowed above

the Brazilian Pavilion of the New York World's Fair in 1940, owes its theme to a reproduction of the skyline on graph paper, each square indicating a pitch vertically and a time value horizontally. The work is sub-titled *A Symphonic Millemetrization*, and the composer claims to be able to produce countless similar themes from pictures or photographs. One – the author, his wife, and son at breakfast – is reproduced in Nicholas Slonimsky's *The Road to Music*, but it is not notable for melodic quality.

Villa-Lobos's most recent large-scale work, *Magdalena*, an opera first performed in 1946, includes in its orchestration the sound of a cracked pianola and a Ford rhythmically cranked up, devices that come from the world of the off-tune street piano of *Il Tabarro*.

Estimate

The difficulty of evaluating Villa-Lobos's work is complicated by the fact that much of his work is still in manuscript and even more unavailable in Europe. The catalogues are already confused by his habit of transferring movements from one work to another – *Magdalena* uses the *Chorale* of the fourth *Bachianas Brasilieras*: thus future bibliographers will be faced with an almost impossible task in dealing with his music. But, though the power and technical mastery of works like the *Choros* cannot fail to impress, Villa-Lobos is less happy with the music, like his educational works, springing from his sense of duty. The best of his music is programmatic, and of that on a large scale only the early *Cello Concerto* (1917) escapes explanatory subtitles.

The root of his music is picturesque, not because he can achieve no more than the fake-picturesque of the half-timbered public house, but because he thinks about picturesque subjects colourfully. Brilliance of effect, vitality of mind, and this quality of thought have combined in his finest work to produce music that transcends these characteristics, which are not, it seems, in themselves sufficient for greatness. It is easy to believe that he has opened up a mine from which others beside himself will extract valuable ore.

WILLIAM TURNER WALTON

B. 1902

DYNELEY HUSSEY

Oxford in 1914

Forty years ago, before the two World Wars, there were still heads of Oxford Colleges who cultivated, outside their scholastic and administrative duties, a wide and civilized existence, which also comprehended a lively appreciation and even a practice of music. There was, for example, Dr Thomas Case, the President of Corpus – a redoubtable personality who styled himself in politics a Palmerstonian Liberal and who seriously held the opinion that music went to the dogs after the *Eroica Symphony*. Tommy Case, who was the son-in-law of Sterndale Bennett, and so made an exception in favour of Mendelssohn in his condemnation of all post-Beethoven music, was, none the less, a fine musician who tested the quality of young undergraduates by their reactions to Mozart and good vintage port. And there was Dr Thomas Strong, Dean of Christ Church and later Bishop of Oxford. More liberal, in the accepted sense, than his colleague at Corpus, he could be seen at concerts of contemporary music as well as heard playing the classics.

Dr Strong was, therefore, greatly interested when his organist, Henry Ley, drew his attention to the musical precocity of one of his choir boys who spent much of his spare time on the composition of music. The Dean was sufficiently impressed by these untutored efforts to engage the interest of Dr H. P. Allen, then Professor of Music at Oxford and always a willing helper of deserving youth. From him William Walton, born on 29 March 1902, the son of a singing teacher at Oldham, received his only professional training. From the age of sixteen he has been self-taught, apart from such discussions upon problems of composition as he has had with older musicians, Busoni among them, whose advice he sought.

Dr Strong further befriended the boy by securing his entry into Christ Church, as an undergraduate below the normal age, when his voice broke and he had to leave the choir. This was toward the end of World War I, when the comparative emptiness of the colleges made such a relaxation of the rules easier to obtain. During his residence at Oxford, Walton continued to compose, and among the works of this period is the first *String Quartet*, which was to bring his name to the notice of an international audience at the first Festival of Contemporary Music at Salzburg in 1923.

The Sitwells and Façade

Among Walton's contemporaries at Oxford was Sacheverell Sitwell, who came to know him and introduced him to his elder brother, Osbert. From this time Walton became an intimate associate of the Sitwells and their sister, Edith, all poets of unusual, though at that time unrecognized, stature.

In his autobiography Sir Osbert Sitwell has drawn a portrait of the young composer as he was in 1919. He had been invited with his brother to take tea with Walton in his rooms at Christ Church. 'Our host,' he writes, 'not quite seventeen years of age, we found to be a rather tall, slight figure, of typically northern colouring, with pale skin, straight, fair hair, like that of a young Norwegian or Dane. The refinement of his rather long, narrow, delicately shaped head, and of his bird-like profile showing so plainly above the brow the so-called bar or mound of Michelangelo that phrenologists claim to be the distinguishing mark of the artist – especially the musician – even his prominent, well-cut nose, scarcely gave a true impression of his robust mental qualities or of the strength of his physique. Sensitiveness rather than toughness was the quality at first most apparent in him.' And so it has remained, in my experience, though the toughness must be there; for without it such works as *Belshazzar's Feast* and the *Symphony* could hardly have been created. As to the physical strength of that deceptively delicate frame, Sir Osbert records that somehow Walton managed unaided, and without any special tackle, to conjure a large grand piano up a narrow staircase to his room after the removals men had abandoned it on the floor below. This incident, as recorded in *Laughter in the Next Room*, gives an impression of a physical strength worthy of Hercules coupled with the mechanical ingenuity of Leonardo. All he would vouchsafe in explanation of this feat was 'I did it with a bit of string'.

The friendship with the Sitwells soon ripened into an intimate association, so that he became the inseparable companion of the two brothers and sister, their 'adopted or elected brother', as Sir Osbert puts it. The chief musical outcome of this association during its first years was *Façade*. This was a novel kind of entertainment, consisting of the reading, or rather rhythmical declamation, of a series of poems by Edith Sitwell to the accompaniment of music composed by Walton for a small chamber orchestra. The orchestra was hidden behind a painted curtain designed by Frank Dobson, on which there was a huge face with open mouth, through which the poetess spoke. The first performance was given privately in the drawing-room of the Sitwell's house in Chelsea in January 1922. It was repeated in public later in the year at the Aeolian Hall, when its novelty provoked a good deal of ill-informed discussion in the daily Press.

There were eighteen poems in the original programme. Walton provided for them a fanfare-prelude, accompaniments based rhythmically upon the metre of the various poems and an interlude. The music was often allusive, referring by quotation to some of the ideas mentioned in the poems, sometimes used idioms from the popular music of the day or of the Victorian music-hall and was always consistently witty and brilliant. It was, indeed a highly original and accomplished composition for a young man of twenty to produce. The mastery of instrumental effect was remarkable even in an age when orchestration seemed to be an open book to every student.

Some five years later Walton arranged five numbers of the *Façade* music – *Polka, Valse, Swiss Yodelling Song, Tango-Passodoblé,* and *Tarantella Sevillana* – for a larger orchestra, and this *Suite* was played as an interlude during one of the Diaghilev Company's performances at the Lyceum Theatre in the summer of 1927. The *Suite* rapidly gained a wide popularity, and it was actually made into a ballet in Germany two years before Frederick Ashton's production during the Camargo Society's season of 1931.

A Successful Ballet

The success achieved by *Façade* as a ballet brought Walton's name to the notice of a larger public than the devotees of Contemporary Music Festivals. He was no longer one of the unintelligible sect of advanced composers. But if one misconception of his character as a musician was displaced, another was established in its stead. *Façade* and the overture, *Portsmouth Point*, composed in 1925 and based upon a drawing by Thomas Rowlandson, seemed to mark Walton out as the English counterpart of the Parisian playboys of the 1920s. But when the comparison is examined, it is evident at once that there is a greater substance and solidity even in the most frivolous of the Sitwell-Walton pieces than there is in anything that came from the school of Cocteau and 'Les Six'. Consider, for example, *Les Biches* with its decadent atmosphere and its music as thin in substance as the colours of Marie Laurençin who painted the *décor*. There is, certainly, nothing decadent about *Façade*. It might, in its original form, have seemed extravagant, even outrageous in its unexpectedness, but it could never be justly charged with triviality.

Nevertheless, these works – *Façade* and *Portsmouth Point* – are not fully representative of their composer, as we now know him. They were products of the effect upon him of that particular period, the 'post-armistice period', when the relaxation of strain produced a reaction against serious-mindedness. The fashion was for caps over windmills, and Walton threw his with the rest. But there was so much real musicianship underlying what he wrote that his music transcended the mood of the moment and has taken its place among the light classics of our time. There was in it, too, a touch of bitterness, reflecting the mood of Dr Sitwell's satire, that gave *Façade* a palatable astringency.

Whether at this early stage Walton was already master of his craft in all its aspects may, perhaps, be doubted in the light of an anecdote told by Osbert Sitwell. When *Façade* was in rehearsal for its first private performance, the clarinettist enquired whether the composer had ever received some injury from a clarinet-player, as he appeared to bear a grudge against the whole tribe! I am, of course, unable to say whether the particular passage only seemed difficult to play on account of its novelty, as may often happen in the music of an original composer, or whether it was technically impracticable for the instrument, which is more than possible in a composer of Walton's inexperience. In the latter event the offending passage was presumably amended in the light of expert criticism. Much later in his career Walton acknowledged his indebtedness to Jascha Heifetz for the technical revision of the solo part in his *Violin Concerto*. Ever since Mendelssohn's day it has been common form for composers to take specialist advice on such matters. When composing his concerto Mendelssohn corresponded with the violinist David at great length on every point in the solo; Brahms submitted his concerto to Joachim for comment, and Kreisler revised the solo-part in Elgar's. There is, indeed, nothing but common sense in the arrangement.

Two Concertos *and* Belshazzar's Feast

In the meantime, before *Façade* made its appearance as a ballet, Walton had given evidence of his stature as a composer in a *Sinfonia Concertante* for pianoforte and orchestra produced at one of the Royal Philharmonic Society's concerts in 1928 under the direction of Ernest Ansermet. Even in this work, which is in three movements, each headed with a dedication to one of the three Sitwells, there was a certain air of defiant brightness that at first blinded the eye to the more solid qualities of the composition. That criticism on this score was not wholly unjust has been recognized by the composer, who revised the work in 1943, curbing some of the more wilful extravagances and angularities of the original. In particular the beauty of the slow movement, dedicated to Edith Sitwell, has been greatly enhanced by the revision, which here has amounted to a radical refashioning of the fabric of the music.

In 1929, at one of the Promenade Concerts, another work was produced which marked its composer's arrival at mature mastery. No one could say that the *Viola Concerto*, which remains Walton's most beautiful poetic utterance, was either frivolous or trivial. Unlike the pianist in the *Sinfonia Concertante*, whose part (as the title suggests) is treated as 'the first among equals', the violist is given the prominence of the romantic concerto soloist. I well remember that first performance of this lovely work. It was directed by Walton himself, whose conducting had in those days a kind of nervous reticence that did not, perhaps, produce a perfect performance. The soloist was Paul Hindemith, then distinguished as much for his viola-playing as for his compositions. The work made a deep impression, and we in the audience were not to know of the hectic preliminaries behind the scenes, which Bernard Shore, leading violist in Henry Wood's orchestra at that time, has described. The artist's room full of copyists up to the last minute, Walton anxiously supervising the corrections, Hindemith complaining of insufficient rehearsal, and Wood himself grumbling about the invasion of his sanctum by this agitated throng! Perhaps the performance was not impeccable, but the work made its effect and was chosen for inclusion at the International Contemporary

Music Society's Festival at Liège in the following year. On that occasion it was played by Lionel Tertis, who has since been closely associated with the concerto.

Perhaps it was the *Viola Concerto*, rather than the *Façade* suite, which was played at the Leeds Festival in 1928, that suggested to the Festival Committee the idea of commissioning Walton to write an oratorio for the Festival of 1931. Even so the Committee can hardly have reckoned that they would receive a work so powerfully dramatic and original as *Belshazzar's Feast*. In the composition of this work Walton had the collaboration of Osbert Sitwell, who, after the method, though not after the manner, of Charles Jennens, constructed a libretto from various passages in the Book of Daniel and the Psalms. The result was, indeed, so far unlike in spirit to Jennens's libretto for *Messiah* that the Committee of the Three Choirs' Festival decided in the following year that the work was unsuitable for performance in a Cathedral. Sitwell has treated the downfall of Belshazzar with the utmost dramatic forcefulness, and Walton fitted the text with music of extraordinary nervous power. The final chorus of Jews exulting over the downfall of their enemies has a savage ferocity that matches the malignant rejoicing of the Hebrew poet at the destruction of Babylon. Yet finer than the sensational pagan choruses in praise of the Chaldean gods and that triumphant last chorus, and finer, too, than the eerie music accompanying the Writing on the Wall, is the beautiful setting of the penitential psalm, 'By the Waters of Babylon, there we sat down and wept.' This deeply moving music, which is on the technical side the fruit of Walton's experience in the Christ Church Cathedral choir, has a dignity and passion that match the psalmist's words. *Belshazzar's Feast* marks the culmination of the first phase of Walton's development. Those who experienced the tremendous impact of its first performance had full justification for feeling that a great composer had arisen in our land, a composer to whose potentialities it was impossible to set any limits.

Symphony *and* Violin Concerto

The success of *Belshazzar's Feast* placed its composer at the top of his generation in the musical world. Even abroad, where his fame had hitherto been confined to the somewhat restricted circle of the Contemporary Music Society, a wider public began to be acquainted with his music. It was obvious that only one thing was now needed to confirm his position – the production of a symphony. And a *Symphony* was produced, not without difficulty, during the years 1932–35. Walton has never been, despite his great powers of invention and his sure command of technique, a facile composer; everything he writes is hammered out with much mental labour. Latterly his larger compositions have been widely spaced in time. So the first performance of the *Symphony* was delayed beyond the date originally announced, and when it was eventually given, under Sir Hamilton Harty's direction in December 1934, the finale was still unwritten. The first complete performance took place just eleven months later. The strenuous mood and nervous energy that were evident in *Belshazzar's Feast* persist in the *Symphony*, which shows no signs of being laboured, despite the toll it evidently exacted from the composer's resources.

Since Hamilton Harty's death Walton has been the finest interpreter of his own symphony. He is not a great conductor in the virtuoso sense and never conducts any music but his own, but he is capable of communicating his wishes to the players efficiently, and of charging them with the intense electric energy that so surprisingly emanates from his apparently shy and self-effacing personality.

From about the date of the *Symphony* Walton lived mostly in the country and less than ever was seen of him in London musical life, into which he had never entered fully like his contemporary, Constant Lambert. This was a period of rest after the great effort of the symphony. Coronation year, 1937, was marked by the composition of the *Crown Imperial* march, which proved that Walton was capable of wearing Elgar's laureate's cloak, and a new cantata for Leeds, *In Honour of the City of London*, which has never won the success of *Belshazzar's Feast* – perhaps because its merits are of a less dramatic kind. Nevertheless, it too reflects the festive mood of that time.

Next came a commission to write a *Violin Concerto* for Jascha Heifetz, and in the spring of 1939 Walton visited America to discuss the details of the solo part with the violinist. The score was completed in June and the composer returned home, and so was prevented by the outbreak of war from attending the first performance at Cleveland, Ohio, in the autumn. It was first played in England two years later by Mr Henry Holst and proved to be a work in the great virtuoso tradition. The influence of Elgar is noticeable again in some of the writing for the solo, which is of the utmost brilliance and sometimes seems to strain virtuosity almost too far.

War-time Films

The war years were occupied mainly in the composition of music for films. He had already in 1935 written music for the production of *Escape Me Never*. The war-time films, *The First of the Few*, *Next of Kin*, and Olivier's production of *Henry V* evoked some excellent incidental music, much of which has been preserved beyond the ephemeral life of the films in concert suites. The only purely orchestral work of the war years is the *Scapino* overture of 1940, which harks back to the style of *Portsmouth Point*, composed fifteen years earlier. Both these comedy overtures are based upon pictures, the one a drawing by Rowlandson, the other by Jacques Callot of one of the characters in the *commedia dell' arte* – a rascally valet, whom we know better under the names of Leporello and Figaro. Walton succeeded better with this Latin personality than with Rowlandson's rumbustious sailors and their wenches.

Ballet and Chamber Music

The most important product of this period, however, is the ballet, *The Quest*, produced by the Sadler's Wells Company at the New Theatre in 1943. Three years before he had orchestrated the music by J. S. Bach used in Ashton's *The Wise Virgins*. Now for the first time he composed music expressly for a ballet, *Façade* having been adapted from the music of the Sitwellian 'entertainment'. The ballet was derived from Spenser's *Faery Queen* and had choreography by Ashton and *décor* by John Piper. The high purpose of St George's quest and the religious atmosphere of the ballet chimed with the serious time at which it was produced. Owing to war-time difficulties – Ashton had to arrange the dances while serving in the R.A.F. – some of the choreography, notably the dances of the Seven Deadly Sins, was ineffective. But the ballet certainly ought to be revived in a revised edition, for Walton's music is too good to lose and the idea of the ballet is admirable. Only its original translation into terms of spectacle and dance was not, owing largely to the conditions under which it was produced, entirely successful.

Since the war Walton has produced a major work in the *String Quartet* in A minor, his first chamber music since his early days, and one of his finest compositions. To this he added a *Violin Sonata*, which was given its first performance by Yehudi Menuhin and Louis

Kentner in January 1950, while in 1953 he contributed another march, *Orb and Sceptre*, and a magnificent setting on a large scale of the *Te Deum* for the Coronation music of Queen Elizabeth II. In the meantime the composer had received the honour of knighthood in the New Year's Honours List of 1951.

Among his recent larger works the opera *Troilus and Cressida*, with an excellent libretto by Christopher Karsall based on Chaucer's poem, is outstanding. Produced at Covent Garden in December 1954, it was found to be a romantic grand opera, full of fine vocal melody and exhibiting a sure understanding of dramatic composition. The part of Pandarus afforded opportunities for characteristic touches of satire, and the main theme of the opera – the betrayal of fine ideals by human frailty – provided the composer with a subject that he has handled with mastery.

The opera was later given in America and at the Scala Theatre, Milan. In 1956 Walton was commissioned to compose an occasional overture for the Johannesberg Festival at which it was performed in the autumn of that year. Most recent of all is the *Cello Concerto*, written for Piatigorsky; the first performance in Boston, at the end of January 1957, just preceded the first British performance, also by Piatigorsky, early in February 1957.

APPENDIX

A Chronological Index of the Births and Deaths of the Music Masters (Vols. I to IV) and a Few Others

The figure in brackets indicates the age of the composer at his death

c. 1525	B.	Palestrina
c. 1531	B.	Lassus
c. 1537	B.	Vittoria
1543	B.	Byrd
c. 1557	B.	Morley
1562	B.	Sweelinck
1563	B.	Dowland
1567	B.	Monteverdi
c. 1575	B.	Weelkes
1583	B.	Gibbons
1594	D.	Lassus (c. 63)
	D.	Palestrina (c. 69)
1603	D.	Morley (c. 46)
1611	D.	Vittoria (c. 74)
1621	D.	Sweelinck (59)
1623	D.	Byrd (80)
	D.	Weelkes (c. 48)
1625	D.	Gibbons (42)
1626	D.	Dowland (63)
1632	B.	Lully
1637	B.	Buxtehude
1643	D.	Monteverdi (76)
1653	B.	Corelli
1658	B.	Purcell
1659	B.	Scarlatti, A.
1668	B.	Couperin
c. 1675	B.	Vivaldi
1681	B.	Telemann
1683	B.	Rameau
1685	B.	Bach, J. S.
	B.	Scarlatti, D.
	B.	Handel
1687	D.	Lully (55)
1692	B.	Tartini
1695	D.	Purcell (37)
1706	B.	Martini
1707	D.	Buxtehude (70)
1710	B.	Arne
	B.	Pergolesi
1713	D.	Corelli (60)
1714	B.	Bach, C. P. E.
	B.	Gluck
1725	D.	Scarlatti, A. (66)
1732	B.	Haydn
1733	D.	Couperin (65)
1734	B.	Gossec
1735	B.	Bach, J. C.
1736	D.	Pergolesi (26)
1739	B.	Dittersdorf
1741	B.	Grétry
	D.	Vivaldi (c. 66)
1743	B.	Boccherini
1749	B.	Cimarosa
1750	D.	Bach, J. S. (65)
1752	B.	Clementi
1756	B.	Mozart
1757	D.	Scarlatti, D. (72)
1759	D.	Handel (74)
1760	B.	Cherubini
1761	B.	Dussek
1763	B.	Méhul
1764	D.	Rameau (81)
1767	D.	Telemann (86)
1770	B.	Beethoven
	D.	Tartini (78)
1778	B.	Hummel
	D.	Arne (68)
1782	B.	Auber
	B.	Field
	B.	Paganini
	D.	Bach, J. C. (47)
1784	B.	Spohr
	D.	Martini (78)
1786	B.	Weber
1787	D.	Gluck (73)
1788	D.	Bach, C. P. E. (74)

CHRONOLOGICAL INDEX

1791	B. Czerny	1832	D. Clementi (80)
	B. Meyerbeer	1833	B. Brahms
	D. Mozart (35)	1834	B. Borodin
1792	B. Rossini	1835	B. Cui
1796	B. Loewe		B. Musorgsky
1797	B. Donizetti		B. Saint-Saëns
	B. Schubert		B. Strauss, Eduard
1799	D. Dittersdorf (60)		B. Wieniawski
			D. Bellini (34)
		1836	B. Balakirev
1801	B. Bellini		B. Delibes
	B. Lortzing	1837	D. Field (55)
	D. Cimarosa (52)		D. Hummel (59)
1803	B. Berlioz	1838	B. Bizet
1804	B. Glinka		B. Bruch
	B. Strauss, Johann	1840	B. Svendsen
1805	D. Boccherini (62)		B. Tchaikovsky
1809	B. Mendelssohn		D. Paganini (58)
	D. Haydn (77)	1841	B. Chabrier
1810	B. Chopin		B. Dvořák
	B. Nicolai	1842	B. Massenet
	B. Schumann		B. Sullivan
1811	B. Liszt		D. Cherubini (82)
	B. Thomas	1843	B. Grieg
1812	B. Flotow	1844	B. Rimsky-Korsakov
	D. Dussek (51)	1845	B. Fauré
1813	B. Wagner	1847	D. Mendelssohn (38)
	B. Verdi	1848	B. Duparc
	D. Grétry (72)		B. Parry
1815	B. Franz		D. Donizetti (51)
1816	B. Sterndale Bennett	1849	D. Chopin (39)
1817	B. Gade		D. Nicolai (39)
	D. Méhul (54)		D. Strauss, Johann I (45)
1818	B. Gounod	1851	B. d'Indy
1819	B. Offenbach		D. Lortzing (50)
1820	B. Vieuxtemps	1852	B. Stanford
1822	B. Franck	1854	B. Catalini
1823	B. Lalo		B. Humperdinck
1824	B. Bruckner		B. Janáček
	B. Cornelius	1855	B. Chausson
	B. Smetana		B. Lyadov
1825	B. Strauss, Johann II		B. Puccini
1826	D. Weber (40)	1856	B. Sinding
1827	B. Strauss, Josef		D. Schumann (46)
1828	D. Schubert (31)	1857	B. Elgar
1829	D. Gossec (95)	1857	D. Czerny (66)
1830	B. Goldmark		D. Glinka (53)
	B. Rubinstein	1858	B. Leoncavallo

CHRONOLOGICAL INDEX

1859	D. Spohr (75)		1879	B. Respighi
1860	B. Albeniz		1880	B. Bloch
	B. Charpentier			B. Pizzetti
	B. Mahler			D. Offenbach (61)
	B. Wolf			D. Wieniawski (45)
1861	B. Arensky		1881	B. Bartók
	B. Macdowell			B. Villa-Lobos
1862	B. Debussy			D. Musorgsky (46)
	B. German			D. Vieuxtemps (61)
1863	B. Delius		1882	B. Kodály
	B. Mascagni			B. Malipiero
1864	B. Grechaninov			B. Stravinsky
	B. Strauss, Richard			B. Turina
	D. Meyerbeer (73)		1883	B. Bax
1865	B. Dukas			B. Casella
	B. Glazunov			B. Szymanowski
	B. Nielsen			B. Webern
1866	B. Busoni			D. Flotow (71)
1867	B. Granados			D. Wagner (70)
1868	D. Rossini (76)		1884	D. Smetana (60)
1869	B. Järnefelt		1886	D. Liszt (75)
	B. Pfitzner		1887	D. Borodin (53)
	B. Roussel		1888	B. Berg
	D. Berlioz (66)		1889	B. Shaporin
	D. Loewe (73)		1890	B. Ibert
1870	B. Lekeu			B. Martinů
	B. Schmitt			D. Franck (68)
	D. Strauss, Josef (43)			D. Gade (73)
1871	D. Auber (89)		1891	B. Prokofiev
1872	B. Skryabin			D. Delibes (51)
	B. Vaughan Williams		1892	B. Honegger
1873	B. Rakhmaninov			B. Milhaud
	B. Reger			B. Walton
1874	B. Hahn			D. Franz (77)
	B. Holst			D. Lalo (69)
	B. Schönberg		1893	D. Catalini (39)
	B. Suk			D. Gounod (75)
	D. Cornelius (50)			D. Tchaikowsky (53)
1875	B. Coleridge-Taylor		1894	B. Pijper
	B. Ravel			D. Chabrier (53)
	B. Tcherepnin, N. N.			D. Lekeu (24)
	D. Bizet (37)			D. Rubinstein (64)
	D. Sterndale Bennett		1895	B. Castelnuovo-Tedesco
1876	B. Falla			B. Hindemith
1877	B. Dohnányi		1896	D. Bruckner (72)
1878	B. Palmgren		1896	D. Thomas (85)
1879	B. Ireland		1897	D. Brahms (64)
	B. Medtner		1898	B. Harris

CHRONOLOGICAL INDEX

1899	B. Poulenc	1921	D. Humperdinck (67)
	B. Tcherepnin, A. N.		D. Saint-Saëns (86)
	D. Chausson (44)	1924	D. Busoni (58)
	D. Strauss, Johann II (74)		D. Fauré (79)
			D. Puccini (69)
1900	B. Copland		D. Stanford (72)
	B. Krenek	1928	D. Janáček (74)
	D. Sullivan (58)	1931	D. d'Indy (80)
1901	B. Rubbra		D. Nielsen (66)
	D. Verdi (88)	1933	D. Dukas (68)
1903	D. Wolf (43)		D. Duparc (85)
1904	B. Khachaturyan	1934	D. Delius (71)
1906	B. Shostakovich		D. Elgar (77)
	D. Arensky (45)		D. Holst (60)
1907	D. Grieg (64)	1935	D. Berg (47)
1908	D. Macdowell (47)		D. Suk (61)
	D. Rimsky-Korsakov (64)	1936	D. German (74)
1909	D. Albeniz (49)		D. Glazunov (71)
1910	B. Barber		D. Respighi (57)
	B. Schuman	1937	D. Ravel (62)
	D. Balakirev (74)		D. Roussel (68)
1911	D. Mahler (51)	1941	D. Sinding (85)
	D. Svendsen (71)	1943	D. Rakhmaninov (70)
1912	D. Coleridge-Taylor (37)	1945	D. Mascagni (82)
	D. Massenet (70)		D. Tcherepnin (70)
1913	B. Britten		D. Webern (62)
1914	D. Dvořák (73)	1946	D. Falla (70)
	D. Lyadov (59)	1947	D. Casella (64)
1915	D. Goldmark (85)		D. Pijper (53)
	D. Skryabin (43)	1948	D. Bartók (67)
1916	D. Granados (49)	1949	D. Strauss, Richard (85)
	D. Reger (43)		D. Turina (67)
	D. Strauss, Eduard (81)	1951	D. Medtner (72)
1918	D. Cui (83)		D. Schönberg (77)
	D. Debussy (56)		D. Palmgren (73)
1918	D. Parry (70)	1953	D. Bax (69)
1919	D. Leoncavallo (61)		D. Prokofiev (62)
1920	D. Bruch (82)	1956	D. Grechaninov (92)